# A GRASSROOTS LEADERSHIP & ARTS FOR SOCIAL CHANGE PRIMER

## FOR EDUCATORS, ORGANIZERS, ACTIVISTS & RABBLE-ROUSERS

SUSAN J. ERENRICH

DEBRA DERUYVER

International Leadership Association

# PRAISE FOR A GRASSROOTS LEADERSHIP & ARTS FOR SOCIAL CHANGE PRIMER

A much-needed guide to nourish the grassroots by someone who's been doing this for quite a long time. Susie Erenrich has given us a gift that will help build the next generation of leaders and activists. She understands that we must begin with art and culture if we want to stand a chance at changing hearts and minds. — *Andy Shallal, CEO and Founder Busboys and Poets*

As a longtime artist and activist, I'm delighted to welcome this more than timely book that puts it all together. There's a lifetime of wisdom in its pages. — *John McCutcheon, Folk Musician, Activist, and Author*

Whether you're involved in community theatre, socially conscious music, cultural organizing, grassroots leadership development, community building, direct action organizing, politics, resistance movements, or any of the many ways in which we use the arts to work towards a gentler, kinder, more just world, this book will be a valued lifetime friend. — *Si Kahn , Singer-Songwriter, Founder of Grassroots Leadership, and Cofounder of folkVote*

A fearless exploration into what it means to be a leader of social change through the arts. Passionate and unapologetic – exactly the way art should be! — *Professor Jenna Ward, Coventry University*

If anyone thinks the arts – or culture, broadly defined – are peripheral to social activism and change, this collection of essays is the antidote. The emphasis is on leadership and direct action, aimed at working artists, activists, and educators. The focus is grassroots because all politics, including the politics of struggle, is local. The sensibility is rabble rousing, as today it should be. A combination of Saul Alinsky meets Paulo Freire, this book is timely and essential. — *Kevin Avruch, Henry Hart Rice Professor of Conflict Resolution Emeritus, Jimmy and*

*Rosalynn Carter School for Peace and Conflict Resolution, George Mason University*

What Susie Erenrich and Debra DeRuyver have done in creating this anthology is give the world a most precious gift. For those of us who have and who continue to fight the good fight towards a more just and humane world, they offer us a dance, a song, a visual journey down memory lane inclusive of all its joy and heartache for all the successes and setbacks. They offer new and emerging organizers and rabble rousers a guide to what has come before so that they may learn what has worked and what some of the pitfalls are to avoid. This anthology reminds us to never forget to sing our song, dance our love, paint our struggles and dreams, and write and play our story. — *Susan McKevitt, PhD, Author of* What Keeps Them Going: Factors that Sustain US Women's Life-Long Peace and Social Justice Activism

For grassroots organizers, this book is a collection of the works of masters, works to turn to and learn from so that people can go out and lead social change, show us a different world, and help us enact that different world. — *Steven S. Taylor, Playwright and Professor of Leadership and Creativity, Worcester Polytechnic Institute Business School*

A pathfinder and profound work of great heart and hope, paving the way in social change. — *Carolyn Hester, 60s Folksinger Songwriter*

I am thrilled by the range of contributors to this volume, both those whose work I know and those who I have yet to meet. Hailing from theater, song, visual arts, poetry, and other mediums, from across the globe, they are important sources for all of us who embrace both art and social justice. — *Jan Cohen-Cruz, Freelance Writer/Researcher and Faculty Member, Performance Creation MA, Touchstone Theater/Moravian University*

As a life-long educator, organizer, activist, and rabble-rouser, I was delighted to see this guide to the work we do appear in an era where these tasks are more imperative than ever before. It's an inspiring and heartening read, just the thing to sum up long years of hard work and propel new activists along their own paths of action and reflection. — *Ken Hammond, New Mexico State University; Answer Coalition*

Cover art by Laura Symanski, Natsuko Graphic Design.

Kindle: 979-8-9864929-0-2

Paperback: 979-8-9864929-1-9

ILAGlobalNetwork.org

International Leadership Association

# TABLE OF CONTENTS

# FOREWORD

## SI KAHN

### Standing at the Crossroads, Trying to Flag a Ride

*In 1949, my father came to Liverpool*

*Seeking full employment on the Mersey docks*

*The war just four years over and no work for him in Ireland*

*All he asked from England was a steady job*

*It's true that there were jobs, but it was only daily labor*

*Some mornings he was hired for the working crew*

*Sometimes a week went by with hands deep in empty pockets*

*Adversity and poverty were all he knew*

*So, my father and his comrades set out to march to London*

*To ask the King for justice for the working class*

*To tell him those who'd fought the war*

*Had died for more than England*

*And with the peace should come a steady job at last*

*The day they started marching I stood beside my father*

*I thought he was the bravest man I'd ever seen*

*He knelt down unexpectedly and set me on his shoulder*

*And we marched off together to confront the King*

*I do not know how far it is from Liverpool to London*

*I don't pretend that I recall each day and night*

*But when I close my eyes, I can feel his face against me*

*As I rode into London on my father's pride*

*These days when oh so many look for work on every corner*

*When justice seems so distant and the way so fraught*

*I recall us marching and from high up on his shoulder*

*I see the better world for which my father fought*

*We are carried on the shoulders of those who came before us*

*Such an over-used cliché, such a tired, empty phrase*

*But my own father carried me from Liverpool to London*

*On whose shoulders are we carried in these troubling days*

*On whose shoulders are we carried in these days*

As a civil rights/union/community organizer and musician since 1965, I have often found myself making the case that if you are working and fighting for social change that is truly transformative, then grassroots leadership, direct action organizing, and cultural work are all absolutely necessary, but none alone are sufficient. All three have to be complementary, intertwined, simultaneous, working together as part of a unified strategy to make life and work better for all.

While some organizers, cultural workers, and grassroots leaders — including those who came out of and had been shaped by the Southern Civil Rights Movement and *El Movimiento*, the Chicano Movement — felt this argument was only common sense, others were skeptical. So, I was deeply pleased when the book *Grassroots Leadership and the Arts for Social Change* was published in 2017 as part of the International Leadership Association's Building Leadership Bridges series. In a brief review, I wrote:

*As someone who has simultaneously been both an organizer and an artist for over 50 years, it's a deep pleasure to welcome a book that honors the critical but rarely understood relationship between social justice and cultural work. Because organizing helps everyday people build power, it's absolutely necessary if we are ever even to approach establishing justice and equity in this battered world we share.*

*But power alone, however necessary, is never sufficient. It does not necessarily help us become better people, more understanding, kinder, more welcoming and supportive of those we see as different from ourselves.*

*That's exactly what, coupled with strategic social justice organizing, the arts can help individuals and communities do, questioning our assumptions, our prejudices so that we become willing and able to take the radical risk of transforming ourselves even as we work together to challenge and change the world around us.* Grassroots Leadership and the Arts for Social Change *is a contemporary* Guide for the Perplexed *for those who dream of and work for a 'Bread and Roses' future for us all.*

Now, five years later, comes the next iteration in this work supported by the International Leadership Association, coedited by Susan J. Erenrich and Debra DeRuyver, titled *A Grassroots Leadership & Arts for Social Change Primer for Educators, Organizers, Activists & Rabble-Rousers.*

With contributions from 28 different artists plus the editors, one of the book's great strengths is the wide net it casts. Its very breadth creates a dynamic in which a diverse range of artists and activists will find a welcoming home. Whether you're involved in community theatre, socially conscious music, cultural work, grassroots leadership development, community building, direct action organizing, political mobilization, resistance movements, any of the many ways in which we work individually and collectively towards a gentler, kinder, more just world, this book will be a valued lifetime friend.

In it you'll meet and learn from over two dozen wonderful people who are deeply rooted in their communities and at the same time working with a profoundly international consciousness. You'll find yourself confirmed in some of your own beliefs and techniques, challenged in others. You will not only be inspired, you will recognize how inspiring your own work is and has been to others.

To put it another way, *A Grassroots Leadership & Arts for Social Change Primer* is not just a book. It is, in and of itself, an organizing campaign, a work of art, a political guide, an affirmation of possibility, a vision of the beloved community of which Dr. King and many others spoke so eloquently, so passionately. As Dr. Bernice Johnson Reagon, the founder of the African American women's *a cappella* group Sweet Honey In The Rock (among many extraordinary achievements) wrote in "Ella's Song," "We who believe in freedom cannot rest until it comes."

But while we do this righteous work, we can celebrate, we can sing, we can hold out our hands and hearts to each other. We can use our crafts, our arts, our hearts not just to change unjust conditions, but to help sustain each other in this work and in this world which can, at times, be so wearying, so discouraging, so frustrating. And as we do our best, as we are hopeful, discouraged, excited, proud, questioning, determined, this book can serve as a steadfast guide.

The answer to "On whose shoulders are we carried in these days?" is: Each other's.

# REFLECTIONS FROM A LIFETIME OF ORGANIZING

## Strengthening Our Stories

Sometimes when I talk about how — as grassroots leaders, organizers, educators, community builders, activists, rabble-rousers — we need to make sure that art and culture are a central part of everything we do, what I get back is, "That's easy for you to say. You're a professional musician. What about those of us who were told in high school choir just to move our lips and never sing a note? What if we can't even draw water out of a well?"

They often quote Emma Goldman: "If I can't dance, I don't want to be part of your revolution." (She didn't say this, but everyone believes she did.) "But," they continue, "she must have been a good dancer or she'd never have said it. What if you're a grassroots leader/organizer/educator/community builder/activist/rabble-rouser with two left feet (or, I guess, for fairness, two right feet)? Where does that leave you except sitting in the cultural-political wallflower seats at the back of the high school gym?"

They've got a point. But they've also got a problem. If people are going to become grassroots leaders, organize themselves and others, take risks, confront power, they need to feel at least potentially effective. One of the best ways cultural workers can support grassroots leaders, organizers, and the communities in which we work, as we all struggle to build up our skills and self-confidence, is by helping us *strengthen our stories.*

The stories we tell ourselves and each other about where we came from, the work our families did, their values, what they believed, stood, fought for — these also shape our own sense of who we are, what we can and should do. Woven together, strand across different strand, they become part of the fabric that holds and supports grassroots leaders, organizers, campaigns, and organizations in place.

One of the most effective ways to create this community fabric is through the strategic use of culture in its many modes: music, art, poetry, theatre, the multiple methods human beings use to tell stories.

Knowing how to do this is an essential skill for both grassroots leaders and organizers.

You're right. That's easy for me to say.

So, here's a suggestion. If you really are profoundly convinced that you have absolutely no artistic talent, try applying a different approach to the problem. Think about it as an organizational instead of a personal issue, and work to develop a collective rather than an individual strategy to resolve it.

That's what we tried to do at Grassroots Leadership, the organization I founded in 1980 and worked at for the next thirty years.

### Grassroots Leadership — The Organization

Let me use our experience at Grassroots Leadership as a practical case study in how to make cultural work central to grassroots leadership and organizing. To start with, here is an old-fashioned visual:

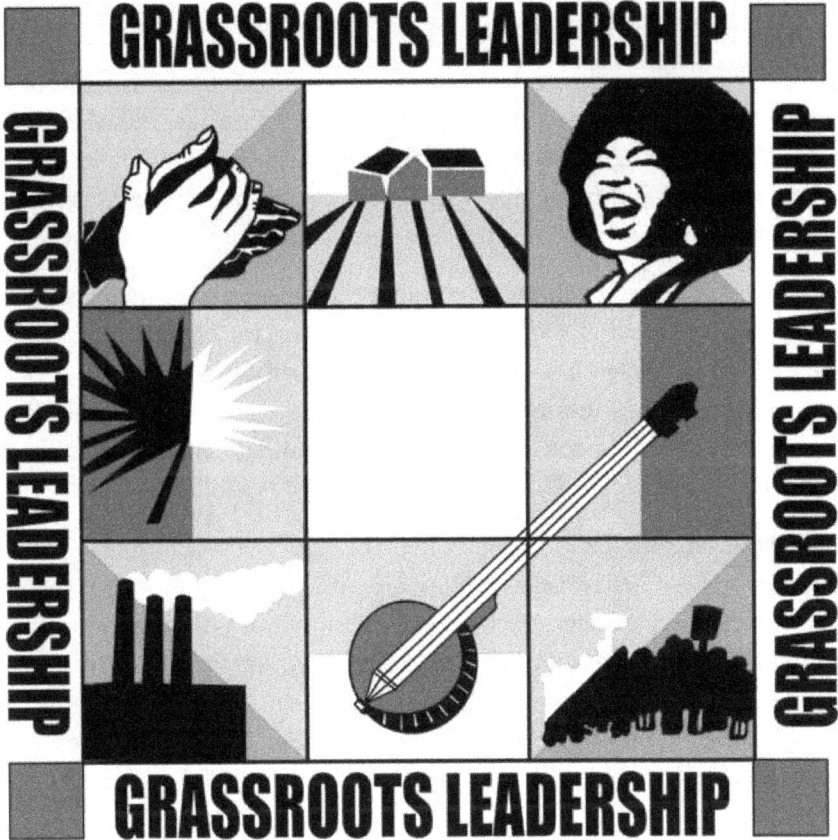

*Foreword Image 1.* Grassroots Leadership Logo, used with permission from Si Kahn

We used this logo at Grassroots Leadership for many years — seven images set inside a traditional Southern quilt pattern. Start with images of the economic reality that poor and working people face: a factory with three smokestacks pouring out smoke, perhaps with toxic chemicals that will endanger the health of those for miles around, perhaps about to close forever.

Go to the farm in distanced perspective, receding from view, much as family farms are disappearing all over the world. Stare at the picture that depicts organizing for power, dark-skinned and light-skinned people together on a picket line. Observe the symbols of hope, of the future: a darker hand and a lighter hand clasped or clapping; a stylized black and white palmetto, the state tree of South Carolina... or is it a rising sun?

Next notice the symbols of song and story. Folksinger/activist Pete Seeger's five-string banjo stretches its long neck diagonally across the square. Gospel and freedom singer Jane Sapp, at that time a Grassroots Leadership board member, sings and shouts in the upper-right corner.

Go back to the hands. If clapping rather than clasped, are they keeping time with the rhythm of what Jane Sapp is singing? Is she one of the people on the picket line, leading the song or the chant, shouting out the demands? Are the hands those of the people on the picket line, keeping time to the song, the chant, the sound of their feet as they march?

These seven images, along with the quilt itself, embody the intersection of grassroots leadership development, direct action organizing, community and organization building, education, and cultural work that has always been central to Grassroots Leadership's mission. They are also a fitting symbol of the way that, as a professional organizer and musician, I've tried to work for the past fifty-six years.

On the one hand, as a civil rights, union, and community organizer, my goal has been to help people who are marginalized, disenfranchised, dispossessed build power for themselves and those both like and unlike them, so they can collectively achieve justice and equity for themselves and others.

On the other hand, I believe power alone is not enough to win a just, equitable world. The experience of oppression does not necessarily make an individual, a community, or a nation wiser or more inherently democratic. When those who have been without power gain it, there is no guarantee they will exercise it more democratically than those who have had it before, or that their values related to race, gender, class, or sexual orientation, to take just these four examples among many, will be more enlightened, humane, or just.

### The Power of Culture: Breaking Through to the Human Heart

Grassroots leadership, community building, educating, and organizing alone, however creative, are rarely enough to change deeply held values and beliefs. To do that, we also need to use the cultural tools that throughout history have proved themselves able to break through to the human heart.

As cultural workers, as grassroots leaders, and as organizers, we need to locate ourselves at that crossroads where activism and culture intersect, so that our work is rooted in both action and reflection. The dynamic tension between these varied ways of thinking and working will only give additional creativity and force to the work we do.

Grassroots leadership and organizing, in other words, must change more than power alone. They must also transform the relationship that oppressed, exploited people have to power. By integrating cultural work with traditional and non-traditional strategies, tactics, and techniques, we can transform the equation. Through a process of celebration and community-building based in culture, art, and craft, we can help people change both their relationship to power, and how they think about and relate to themselves and to "the other."

People and their organizations may win on their issues. But that doesn't necessarily mean they develop new understandings of how and why they won, of power and how it's exercised, of difference and how it's exploited. They may experience the power of numbers, but not necessarily the concurrent power of knowledge, of understanding. Some of the conditions of their lives may change, but they will not necessarily transform their relationship to others, particularly their relationships to others different from themselves, to the "other."

These transformations lie within the realm and are the responsibility of political education. Yet traditional modes of change by themselves aren't enough to create a transformative process that challenges antisemitism, racism, sexism, homophobia, all the other barriers that divide people. Breaking through such rigid, resistant barriers requires velocity, momentum, torque, acceleration of the spirit as well as of the mind. It is a visceral and emotional as well as intellectual process.

Poems, songs, paintings, murals, chants, sermons, quilts, stories, rhythms, fabrics, pottery, dances can literally lift us out of ourselves, sometimes even into the life and consciousness of someone quite different from us.

The power of culture can be an antidote to people's prejudices, our inability to see beyond our own eyes. If people can transform power, culture can transform consciousness and can perform the acts of political education that, when combined with action, make social change transformative rather than merely instrumental.

Yet within the world of traditional instruments for social change, culture is too often a matter of "add music and stir," to paraphrase Charlotte Bunch's famous quotation about women and history. Cultural workers and cultural work itself are often treated as minor adjuncts to the process: a quilt at an auction, a song at a rally, a chant on a picket line. Creative, effective, winning campaigns need to draw on and incorporate the full power that culture can provide, the rich variety of traditional and nontraditional forms available to us: oral poetry, storytelling, *midrash* (interpretation), meditation, quilting, guerrilla theatre, preaching, drumming, unaccompanied song, silence.

It should be a primary goal for all grassroots leaders and organizers to find and get to know professional and amateur cultural workers; treat them with the deep respect they have earned and deserve; invite them to become allies; and learn to work with them in ways that bring not only their creative abilities but also their full artistic and political sensibilities into play. But it is also critical to call forth and highlight the cultural skills of everyday people, the members and leaders of our groups and organizations — something that many cultural workers and political artists are highly effective at doing.

A remarkable number of people, who in no way consider themselves professional artists, nonetheless paint, draw, sing, play, write, act, quilt, produce pageants, preach, dance. Creating opportunities for them to do so as part of an ongoing initiative, campaign, or organization allows them to voice their rage and hope, to move from being silenced to being outspoken, to strengthen the stories they tell themselves and others. If the worker who says no to the boss from the opposite side of the negotiating table finds power and pride in that act, so does the community person who reads her poetry at the mass meeting before the negotiations begin.

### Integrating Cultural Work & Grassroots Leadership: The "Aunt Molly Jackson" Example Exercise

How do we as grassroots leaders and organizers move towards effective integration of cultural work and workers into everything we do? One answer is to add a set of basic tools to our toolboxes. It may or may not be true that everyone is in some way an artist. But everyone can learn a handful of basic cultural techniques to incorporate into their everyday work. The many options include helping community members and leaders write songs, poetry, and chants (one hint: do it collectively in small groups, rather than individually), and use storytelling and theatre to create strategy.

Here's one example of how to do this. It starts with a story, a piece of oral history told by Aunt Molly Jackson, radical midwife and union organizer from eastern Kentucky. I've memorized it, but it's just as easy to read the script (available at www.sikahn.com). The story takes place in a Kentucky coal camp in the 1930s, where the miners have been locked out, and their children are starving. Aunt Molly borrows an empty sugar sack from a neighbor, robs the company store clerk at gunpoint, distributes the food to the families who need it the most, and goes home:

*My house was the next house*

*and by the time I got inside the door*

*the deputy sheriff was there to arrest me*

*And he said to me, he says,*

*Well, Aunt Molly, what in the world, he says*

*have you turned out, he says, to be a robber?*

I said, Oh, no, Frank, I said

I am no robber

But, I said, it was the last chance

I have heard these little hungry children cry

for something to eat

'til I'm desperate

I'm almost out of my mind

And, I said, I will get out

as I said

and collect that money

just as quick as I can

and pay them

I said, You know

I'm as honest

as the days is long

And the tears come in his eyes

And he said

Well, Aunt Molly, he says

They sent me up here, he says

to arrest you

The coal operator

well, Goodman, sent me here

to arrest you for that

*But, he says*

*if you've got the heart*

*to do that much, he says*

*for other people's children*

*that's not got one drop*

*of your blood in their bodies, he says*

*then I will pay that bill myself, he says*

*and, he says, if they fire me*

*for not arresting you, he says*

*I will be damned glad of it*

*That's just the way he said it*

*He walked out*

*and he didn't arrest me*

Aunt Molly's story makes for a vibrant follow-up discussion, in part because it creates a case study, in which everyone shares the same experience and gets the same amount of information. I started using it when I was looking for a way to make training sessions for grassroots leaders and organizers seem more realistic, more like the actual situations we encountered in our campaigns for justice.

Discussions of potential strategies and tactics, I decided, could best be held in reference to an actual or constructed situation, so all persons participating had approximately the same degree of knowledge about what was going on. This information could be presented to the group by handing out a written document, showing a short film or, as in this case, using a narrative taken from oral history about a real-life situation.

I begin this exercise by telling Aunt Molly Jackson's "Hunger" story in her own words. I then work with the group to analyze the situation:

strategy, tactics, leadership, communication, empowerment, risk. We talk through the complex strategic and ethical questions richly presented by the piece. Is Aunt Molly Jackson an organizer or a grassroots leader? Does she make good strategic choices? Is she acting ethically when she points a gun at the store operator? Does she put people in the community at risk without their knowledge or approval? Is that something grassroots leaders and organizers sometimes just have to do, or is it never acceptable?

At a certain point, the participants begin demanding to know what actually happened, so they can compare their ideas to real life. Given that Aunt Molly's story is about an incident that really did take place, that I'm a historian, and that — from my days as a union organizer with the United Mine Workers of America (UMWA) — I know many people who live and have lived, work and have worked in the coalfields, I could probably find out exactly what happened. But I decided it was better for the group — and for me — if I never knew the answer. Instead, I respond to these questions with: "Well, let's find out," and turn the discussion into improvisational theater.

Since I only know the story as Aunt Molly told it, I ask the participants to treat the story as a half-finished script and to act out the roles as a way of figuring out what might have happened. Members of the workshop become Daisy and Ann, the mothers of the starving children; Frank the good-hearted deputy sheriff; Frank's boss, the "high sheriff"; Goodman the coal operator; Henry Jackson, Aunt Molly's young son; Mr. Martin, the clerk at the company store; other coal camp women and children; and Aunt Molly herself.

I act as the theatre director to keep the action moving. I'll say, for example, "All right, Frank, why don't you go back to the jail now and explain to the sheriff why you decided to let Aunt Molly go free." When (in our extension of the tale) the high sheriff cusses Frank out and strides off to the coal camp to arrest Aunt Molly himself, I'll say, "Wow, it looks like Aunt Molly's going to be in jail for a while. Maybe some of you folks whose children are still alive on account of what she did ought to have a meeting and decide what you're going to do about that. Are you going to let her rot in jail after all she did for you?"

I never know how the scenario is going to play out. Sometimes Aunt Molly gets dragged off to jail after all, despite Frank's attempt at intervention and rescue. Sometimes the women get themselves together, storm the jail waving broomsticks, banging on frying pans, and free her. Sometimes the sheriff fires on the crowd and someone gets killed.

Whatever happens, we talk about it, analyze, strategize. In a short time, we share an experience almost like organizing, made all the more real because it incorporates oral history, storytelling, theater. The cultural content makes the theoretical discussion come alive, pulls it down out of thin air, nails it to the floor.

Sometimes the participants say, "But none of us know anything about coal mining or coal camps." In that case, I try to get them to relate the situation to their own experience. "Okay," I say, "let's assume that instead of the high sheriff in the story we're talking about the local police chief and that Aunt Molly Jackson robbed the all-night convenience store on the corner next to the projects." Once the story is reset locally, in terms of power dynamics that are already familiar, people usually overcome their resistance and jump back into the action.

Sometimes, I just plain get lucky. Once in Spokane, Washington, when someone said they didn't understand what it meant to be in a coal camp, I asked if anyone in the group had ever lived in a company town. I got three hands: a Black woman who had grown up in a coal camp in West Virginia, a Latina woman who had been raised in a copper mining town in Arizona, and a white American man from a hard rock mining camp in northern Idaho. We were able to talk, not just about mines and company towns, but about class differences and commonalities across lines of gender and race.

## Conclusion: The Work of Grassroots Leaders, Organizers, and Cultural Workers

I believe that integrating grassroots leadership, organizing, and cultural work is something everyone can do, at least to some extent, and that the progressive movement would be both more effective and more fun if this happened. But at the same time, we need to recognize that this challenge makes demands on the people and organizations that decide to take it on. Just as culture flourishes best in an open society (although extraordinary and heroic art has been created under the most repressive conditions), cultural work is most at home in a democratic structure.

So, grassroots leaders, organizers, and cultural workers must strive to provide a set of expectations and attitudes that are conducive to creativity in cultural work. We should be proud of our work, but we should always be learning to do it better. We need to be as open and analytical about our failures as we are celebratory about our successes.

Don't be afraid to experiment. Within this intersecting, interdependent world, we need to extend our willingness to risk and to fail. So, don't feel bad if you don't have all the answers. I sure don't, and I try hard not to pretend that I do.

Some people believe that what successful cultural workers, organizers, and grassroots leaders have are good answers. That's wrong. What we have are great questions. We're not there, wherever there is, to *tell* people what to do but to *ask* them. One of the most effective skills someone who is an organizer, a cultural worker, a grassroots leader needs is the ability to frame and ask questions in ways that make people not only want to answer them, but also to think deeply, in unexpected ways, about what the answers might be.

This is how some of the best strategic research takes place, how some of the most effective strategies and tactics are developed. Communities of all kinds have a sophisticated understanding of the problems they confront and often solid, practical ideas about what can be done to solve these problems.

But for the most part, no one person knows even a major part of the answer. Imagine a giant picture puzzle with each person having some of the pieces. Not only are they not sure where those pieces go, they don't even know how to start putting them together — and there's no photograph on the box the puzzle came in to guide them.

That's where grassroots leaders, organizers, and cultural workers come in. They help people work together to assemble the pieces, so what they come up with makes at least reasonable sense to everyone who's been part of the process, and so they feel a sense of ownership over what they have created, what they have built together. At its best, this is not just a political, but a cultural process.

As cultural workers, grassroot leaders, and organizers, we need to be eternally vigilant about recognizing and confronting issues of race, class, gender, sexual orientation, power, and all the issues that can be used to dehumanize and divide people. We need to learn, however, not just how to talk about these principles, but how to incorporate them into the work that we do every day.

How then do we work with people? How do we reach and teach them in ways that transform their understanding of power and their relationship to it, not just individually, but collectively? How do we help them strengthen the story they tell themselves and others, so they have the self-confidence and pride to stand up and struggle for what they want and need?

Combining grassroots leadership with organizing and cultural work is central to the answer. It is at this intersection that the future of all work for justice lies.

And it is at this intersection that the stories told in *A Grassroots Leadership & Arts for Social Change Primer for Educators, Organizers, Activists & Rabble-Rousers* live.

We are, as the great Mississippi Delta blues singer Robert Johnson sang so many years ago, "Standing at the crossroads, trying to flag a ride."

- Si Kahn

Charlotte, North Carolina

*Acknowledgement: Portions of this Foreword first appeared in a modified form in my book,* Creative Community Organizing: A Guide for Rabble-

Rousers, Activists & Quiet Lovers of Justice, *published in 2010 by Berrett-Koehler.*

## About the Author

Si Kahn has worked for 57 years as a professional civil rights, labor and community organizer and musician. He began his organizing career in 1965 in Arkansas with the Student Nonviolent Coordinating Committee, more popularly known as SNCC, the young people's wing of the Southern Civil Rights Movement. During the War on Poverty, he served first as a VISTA Volunteer and later as Deputy Director of an eight-county community action agency in rural Georgia, where he coached the first racially integrated Little League team in that part of the state.

In the 1970s, he worked with the United Mine Workers of America (UMWA) during the Brookside Strike in Harlan County, Kentucky and was an Area Director of the J.P. Stevens Campaign for the Amalgamated Clothing and Textile Workers Union (ACTWU). These historic labor struggles are portrayed in the movies *Harlan County U.S.A.* and *Norma Rae.*

In 1980, Si founded Grassroots Leadership, a national Southern-based progressive organization committed to community, civil rights and labor organizing. He served as its Executive Director for 30 years, stepping down on May Day 2010.

In recent years, Grassroots Leadership has worked to oppose privatization and to defend the public sector. This work has included a campaign to abolish all for-profit private prisons, jails, and detention centers, including immigrant detention centers, as a step towards helping create a prison and criminal justice system that is at least to some extent just and humane.

Si was the initial organizer and founding national board chair of Bend the Arc: A Jewish Partnership for Justice, the largest Jewish social justice organization in the United States. He was one of three co-founders of Musicians United To Protect Bristol Bay, part of the international campaign to help stop the proposed Pebble Mine and to protect permanently the people, jobs, communities, Native languages, cultures, traditions, and wild sockeye salmon of Alaska's Bristol Bay, one of the great remaining wild places in the world (www.Musician-sUnited.info). In 2020 he cofounded folkVOTE to bring the power of music and musicians to the overall campaign to register voters and get out the vote.

Si's musical body of work includes18 albums of his original songs; a collection of traditional labor and civil rights songs recorded with Pete Seeger and Jane Sapp; *Good Times and Bedtimes,* an album of songs for children; five albums of his songs by other artists; and the songs and/or scripts for seven musicals. His musical *Mother Jones in Heaven* is currently touring nationally. He's been inducted into the Blue Ridge Music Hall of Fame, joining such legendary artists as Doc Watson, Etta Baker, Uncle Dave Macon, Emmylou Harris, and Dolly Parton.

His most recent books are *Creative Community Organizing: A Guide for Rabble-Rousers, Activists and Quiet Lovers of Justice* and *The Fox in the Henhouse: How Privatization Threatens Democracy,* the latter co-authored with public philosopher Elizabeth Minnich, his long-time partner and spouse.

# PREFACE

DEBRA DERUYVER

As a multisector, multidisciplinary organization, the International Leadership Association (ILA) supports the many varied practices of leadership undertaken by our members and colleagues as they work to create regenerative futures and make the world a better place.

Grassroots activist-artists, like those present in this book, mobilize and motivate people to create better organizations and communities together. They are leaders doing leadership work.

These artist-leaders interpret and make sense of the world's complexities, struggles, and triumphs in ways that help us better relate to each other and work toward our shared future. They are skilled observers and skilled storytellers, whatever their medium. These are capacities often found in the most effective leaders.

All of us, regardless of the sector in which we work, regardless of if we consider ourselves a business leader, a community organizer or activist, an educator, a public servant, a development professional, or a rabble-rouser, should pay attention.

As you read this book, consider your own leadership practice. What can you learn from these authors that can be applied in your leadership context?

In a recent podcast, Former Canadian Prime Minister, the Right Honorable Kim Campbell, who is Chair of ILA's Global Leadership Project, warned that "future generations will spit on our graves" if we don't make progress on racism, women's rights, climate change, and threats to democracy — just to name a few. She also pointed out that, "We like to create narratives that don't challenge our position, especially if our position is one of privilege" (Metcalf & Campbell, 2022).

In contrast, the art-based narratives created by the grassroots artist-leaders in the following pages challenge us to reconsider what we think we know. They challenge us to reimagine a better future and then encourage us to work to bring it forth. As you read, ask yourself what you can do to accelerate the positive changes needed to meet the daunting problems facing planet and people. How can you use the lessons in this book to contribute to the creation of a flourishing future for everyone?

Today, whether it's the performance art of wrapping a bandage around the bullet-damaged sculpture of a Ukrainian poet outside of Kiev (Detrow, et al., 2022) or one of the many murals in remembrance of George Floyd and Breonna Taylor stating Black Lives Matter (Holowaty Krales & Pavic, 2020), artist-leaders envision and remind us of what we're working towards. They kindle and maintain the fire of our beliefs and support and rejuvenate our actions, encouraging us not to stop until we arrive. They lead — it's that simple.

## References

Detrow, S., Lonsdorf, K., Caldwell, N., Hammer, N. (2022, April 9). This Is What One Town in Ukraine Looks Like After Russian Troops Withdrew. *NPR*. https://www.npr.org/sections/pictureshow/2022/04/09/1091740132/ukraine-russia-borodyanka

Holowaty Krales, A., & Pavic, V. (2020, July 5). 33 Powerful Black Lives Matter Murals. *The Verge*. https://www.theverge.com/2020/7/5/21304985/black-lives-matter-murals-round-up-artists

Metcalf, M. (Host), & Campbell, K. (Guest). (2022, February 1). Reimagining Our Leadership to Be a Good Ancestor (No. 352). [Audio podcast episode]. In *Innovating Leadership, Co-Creating Our Future*. https://ilaglobalnetwork.org/podcasts/reimaging-our-leadership-to-be-a-good-ancestor/

*Acknowledgement. Many thanks to Susan J. Erenrich, "Susie," for her partnership on this project and for her remarkable body of work that expands the leadership literature to include grassroots, collaborative, horizontal leadership and the arts for social change. And to Jasper, Piper, and Everett whose sacrifices made my work on this book possible.*

**About the Author**

Debra DeRuyver is the Communications Director of the International Leadership Association. Previously she was Internet and Information Project Manager, Kellogg Fellows Leadership Alliance and Electronic Communications Coordinator, James MacGregor Burns Academy of Leadership at the University of Maryland. She is ABD in American Studies from the University of Maryland College Park (UMCP). At UMCP, she co-founded the Cyberculture Working Group and taught one of the first web-based distance education classes on campus, a senior seminar on electronic publications and virtual exhibitions. She also designed and taught a junior seminar on online activism and an Intro to American Studies course that used dance to explore identity, culture, and struggle in the United States. In 2001, her website analyzing online public history won the National Council for Public History's graduate student project of the year award and she published on the same topic in *American Quarterly*. Debra served as co-chair of the American Studies Association's Students Committee (1997-1999) and was active in student government when she attended California State University Fullerton (MA, American Studies) and the University of Michigan (BA, English Literature).

# INTRODUCTION

## SUSAN J. ERENRICH

Dear Friends,

Welcome! *A Grassroots Leadership & Arts for Social Change Primer for Educators, Organizers, Activists & Rabble-Rousers* has been several years in the making.

The project started in January of 2018 as a monthly, multi-media guest column published by the International Leadership Association (ILA) in its *Interface* newsletter.

We were thrilled to be embarking on this journey to further explore this important topic. Over the past four years, we engaged with fellow travelers, interested newcomers, and leadership traditionalists in a robust discourse about this developing leadership field.

The practice of grassroots, collective, collaborative, horizontal leadership intersecting with the arts for social change has been around for quite some time. Throughout history, artists have led bottom-up movements of protest and resistance. They have been on the frontlines of campaigns for liberation and emancipation. They have created dangerously, sometimes becoming martyrs for a cause. They faced censorship, black listing, imprisonment, and physical and mental persecution. Their efforts ignited fires, awakened the imagination, and helped mobilize ordinary citizens, culminating in real transformational change. Their art has also served as a form of dissent during times of war, social upheaval, and political unrest. Less forcefully, perhaps, artists have participated in demonstrations, benefit concerts, and have become philanthropists in support of their favorite causes.

Even though they have often been leading the way on the battleground of change initiatives, artists have been given too little attention in the literature on leadership. That is, until the birth of this project.

I launched this form of people's scholarship merging the arts for social change and grassroots leadership with the 2017 publication of my book *Grassroots Leadership & the Arts for Social Change*, coedited with Jon Wergin. The book is part of the ILA's Building Leadership Bridges (BLB) series from Emerald Publishing. The release of this groundbreaking book was the first step in expanding the leadership footprint in this area of inquiry.

Following the success of the book, I partnered with the ILA to continue this work through the establishment of the column. Invited guest authors, like those in the published text, help to shed light on the subject by providing readers with a mechanism to vicariously experience the work of grassroots artists/leaders, to reflect on their commitments and achievements, and to dream a better world full of possibility.

Throughout this process, I encouraged readers to share their thoughts and questions evoked by the material. This was accomplished in university classrooms, in local communities, on Facebook, and through the personal connections of individual contributors. My hope was to create a vigorous platform for ongoing dialogue and debate. I also energetically campaigned for new writers from around the globe to share their stories in an accessible and engaging manner. The experiment has had a favorable outcome. Guest columnists wrote about community engaged theatre; exhibitions of art, politics, and resistance; cultural activists in the fine and performing arts; the role of the arts in social movements; and people power and community building. I also conducted a number of interviews with troubadours of conscience that were published as columns.

In addition to the printed text, multimedia content such as photographs, audio, and video recordings often accompany each article. This material provides another entry point for readers to fully immerse themselves in the published offerings. Many of the audio recordings are from the weekly radio show I produced and hosted for five years, *Wasn't That A Time: Stories & Songs That Moved The Nation* on WERA.FM in Arlington, VA. When appropriate, one of the shows will accompany a particular guest column to provide a more comprehensive view of the topic.

For those readers not familiar with the various grassroots leadership and arts for social change theoretical models, at the heart of this work are the trailblazing ideas and practices of scholars, organizers, and artists like Paulo Freire, Augusto Boal, Ella Baker, Howard Zinn, and Myles and Zilphia Horton, to name a few. They believed in **a people-centered, people-guided, and bottom-up approach to learning called popular education.** This method highlights the participants' life experiences, validates the dignity of everyone in the room, and recognizes each participant as both a teacher and a learner. Or as Ella Baker, a seasoned organizer, Director of Branches of the NAACP in the 1940s, and Executive Director of the Southern Christian Leadership Conference, so eloquently put it: If you "give light, people will find the way" (Grant, 1998).

The research method/philosophy employed in the individual chapters of the book is based upon Portraiture, a form of narrative inquiry. The qualitative approach pioneered by Harvard scholar Sara Lawrence-Lightfoot "combines systematic, empirical description with aesthetic expression, blending art and science, humanistic sensibilities and scientific rigor" (Lawrence-Lightfoot & Davis, 1997, p. 3). Portraiture is "people's scholarship," and it is a storytelling approach. The writing and language are accessible. If members of academic communities want to broaden the audience for their work, then they must "begin to speak in a language that is understandable, not exclusive and esoteric . . . a language that encourages identification, provokes debate, and invites reflection and action" (Lawrence-Lightfoot, 2005, p. 9).

Now, with the publication of this primer, which brings together many of the personal/scholarly/historical accounts that have been collected thus far, we are on to phase three of this campaign to increase the presence of artists in the leadership literature. Before we dive in, however, for folks not acquainted with the concepts of grassroots leadership and the arts for social change, here's a bit of background to begin our conversation and to seek common ground. First, I would like to share some examples of connectivity of the arts with grassroots, social change movements and define a bit of terminology to enhance our mutual understanding.

## Modern Historical Examples of the Arts in Grassroots, Social Change Movements

First and foremost, the intertwining of the arts in grassroots, horizontal, collaborative, collective leadership has historical underpinnings. For example, at the turn of the 20th century, the Industrial Workers of the World (IWW) incorporated songs into its organizing campaigns. It was one of the first modern singing movements, whose roots were firmly planted in a grassroots, horizontally-based infrastructure.

Fred Thompson, an organizer for the IWW and onetime editor of its newspaper, *The Industrial Worker,* discussed horizontal, transformational leadership in a 1957 article, "The Art of Making A [sic] Decent Revolution."

Our hope is that workers will build large and effective unions that are run by the rank and file; that the structure of these unions will correspond to the actual economic ties between workers, so that workers on every job will be in a position to determine more and more what happens on that job; and through a collective class-wide structure, decide what happens in industry as a whole. It is in this way, as we see it, that the working class can reshape its world into something consistent with our better aspirations and with the technical capacities mankind has developed. (Kornbluh, 1998, p. 385)

Thompson also made his case for transformational leadership on a personal and societal level:

If you look to the joint action of yourself and your fellow workers to cope with your problems, you move forward with time into situations where steadily you and they cut a larger role in life, where the decisions about your work are steadily more and more made by you fellows, where the product of your labor steadily redounds more and more to your benefit, where the world more and more becomes as you wish it. (Kornbluh, 1998, p. 387)

Grassroots leadership and horizontal pedagogy are also, for example, at the heart and soul of the Highlander Folk School, now known as the Highlander Research and Education Center. Launched in 1932 in Monteagle, Tennessee, the organization is a place where "average citizens can pool their knowledge, learn from history ... and seek solutions to their social problems" (Dunson, 1965, p. 28).

The integration of cultural expression with a horizontally led leadership development training program has been a component of the school's curriculum since its earliest days. Zilphia Mae Johnson, a singer and musician who joined the Highlander staff in 1935, incorporated the arts into every facet of the program. The daughter of an Arkansas mine owner and graduate of the College of the Ozarks, she was determined "to use her musical and dramatic abilities in some field of radical activity" (Glen, 1996, p. 43); Highlander was the perfect venue. Johnson married Myles Horton, one of the school's founders, in March 1935, about two months after attending her first labor workshop at the adult education center there (Glen, 1996).

Before she died in 1956, Zilphia amassed 1,300 songs from unions, progressive organizations, traditional Appalachian culture, and the South (Dunson, 1965). These songs played a significant role in the decades ahead: "We Shall Overcome," which she co-authored with Pete Seeger, Guy

Carawan, and Frank Hamilton, became the anthem of the American Civil Rights Movement and today is sung around the world. Readers will learn more about Zilphia Horton through the guest column penned by Candie Carawan in this primer.

About three years after Zilphia Horton's death, Guy Carawan, a folksinger from California, officially joined Highlander and revived the cultural program. He first visited the school in the summer of 1953 with encouragement from Seeger and, after hearing one of the Rev. Martin Luther King Jr.'s orations at a Boston church in 1959, was moved to call Myles Horton and volunteer at Highlander. Carawan told Horton that he knew some labor movement songs and could play guitar and banjo. Horton told him, "Come on down. We really miss the work that Zilphia did here" (Carawan & Carawan, 2010).

Highlander pedagogy served as the predominant training model for cultural activists who immersed themselves in civil rights work in the South. The Highlander work continues with the Zilphia Horton Cultural Organizing Project, which was created to "strategically use art and culture to promote progressive policies with marginalized communities across Central and Southern Appalachia and the U.S. South" (Highlander Center, n.d.). Among the goals of the program are to help organizations expand the role of art and culture in their organizing and advocacy efforts, to enrich the work of artists and cultural workers and organizers by providing a strategic opportunity to engage community issues and work with and learn from grassroots organizations, and to inspire people to develop cultural tools — including song, video, or other performances or works of art — that draw on local cultures and address community concerns (Highlander Center, n.d.).

One last example of a grassroots leadership and arts for social change ongoing, global phenomenon is Theatre of the Oppressed and Theatre for Development. Theatre of the Oppressed, pioneered by Augusto Boal, and Theatre for Development, conceived in Botswana in 1973, are highly formed, arts-based systems connected to Paulo Freire, the Brazilian educator and author of *Pedagogy of the Oppressed*. In both instances, Freirean concepts, with lofty goals for personal and societal transformation, utilize the performing arts as a catalyst for social change. Both systems were developed simultaneously in different parts of the world. Several chapters on Theatre of the Oppressed and Augusto Boal are in *Grassroots Leadership & the Arts for Social Change* (Erenrich & Wergin, 2017). Many more are included in this primer.

Here's a story, however, that isn't covered by the various authors in this book but needs to be told. It made quite an impression on me as a budding cultural activist decades ago. Ross Kidd, among the early pioneers of this work, was, at the time, a professor at the University of Botswana; Martin Byam, one of Kidd's colleagues, and Jeppe Kelepile, a Botswana community counselor, were also project architects (Byam, 1999). The Theatre for Development idea sprang from a village colloquium held in partnership with the University of Botswana in which drama was used to elucidate community problems. Previous approaches to generate civic engagement had failed, so Kidd and the others opted to merge Paulo Freire's methods with popular culture.

The Botswana initiative was called Laedza Batanani. Other universities in Africa introduced Theatre for Development projects in the 1970s, with varying degrees of effectiveness. Arguably, the programs' success was limited because they failed to fully include community members in decision-making. These projects also attempted to address local issues without establishing those issues' links to a colonial past, leaving no real possibility for the development of critical thought, which is central to the method (Byam, 1999). Laedza Batanani and the other projects deserve credit, however, for setting the Theatre for Development movement in motion in Africa and for being the first programs of their kind in the region to attempt to implement Freire-based participatory platforms for solving problems. Another highlight of this model was the integration of traditional indigenous art forms into educational practices. Kidd acknowledged shortcomings in these early commissions and recommended that future Freire-based popular theater strategies "dispense with taking plays to the people. The leaders should work to create plays with the community" (Byam, 1999, p. 45).

A few years after the Botswana experiment, the Kenya Kamiriithu Community Education and Cultural Centre did just that. It was the first program to produce plays from the ground up — a radical departure from the programs sponsored by government officials or institutions of higher education. Kidd praised the Kamiriithu Theatre for Development model in a 1982 article, nine years after he and his colleagues carried out the Laedza Batanani in Botswana:

Popular theatre in the Third World often claims to be a tool of protest and struggle and a means of social transformation, but rarely does it challenge the status quo in a significant way. Too often it becomes as marginalized as the peasants and workers it represents, with little real impact on the society as a whole. One significant exception has been the popular theatre work of the Kamiriithu Community Educational and Cultural Centre, a peasant and worker-controlled organization in rural Kenya.... It's a concrete example of what a people's national theatre should be – accessible to and controlled by the masses, performed in their languages, adopting their forms of cultural expression, and addressing their issues. (Kidd, 1982, p. 47-48, 59)

### Getting on the Same Page With Terminology

Now that I've provided a few examples of grassroots leadership and arts for social change initiatives, it is important to define some of the terminology that will be used in the various sections of this primer. Among them are social change, social movement, civic engagement, and community building.

First, social change is defined as a "shift, an alteration, or a reversal in the status quo that brings about institutional or systemic change. Social change is embodied in new laws, procedures, and policies that alter the nature of institutions and, in time, the hearts and minds of people" (Collins et al., 2000, p. 35). Therefore, social-change projects and the artists and cultural activists who spearhead them address "the root causes of problems rather than the alleviation of symptoms. In most cases, the goal is systemic change" (Collins et al., 2000, p. 35).

A social movement, on the other hand, is the shared activity of individuals, nonprofits, and other social organizations to "mobilize citizens at all levels of society to influence politics broadly and, ultimately, to achieve genuine social change as it concerns the rules, processes, and practices of society, the market, or the government" (Riker, 2001, p. 18). As with concepts like cultural activism and social change, scholarly analysis of social movement terminology and praxis is controversial. T. V. Reed (2005) notes that "more than 50 years of scholarly analysis has not generated an agreed upon definition of social movements" (p. xiv). He argues that this is "less of a problem than one might think, since both ordinary folks and ordinary scholars, though they may argue about borderline cases, know a movement when they see one" (p. xiv).

It's important to note the intricate relationship between artists and social movements. They are encased in what French social theorist Pierre Bourdieu coined the "cultural field" — a "social space where cultural texts exist in relation to each other and in relation to texts in other social, political, and economic fields" (Reed, 2005, p. xvii). The artist and the arts are the key force in "shaping, spreading, and sustaining [a] movement's culture and, through culture, its politics" (Reed, 2005, p. 13). The songs, sculpture, poetry, literature, dance, film, theater, and murals become personal and movement narratives, or a "bundle of stories" that "contribute to the construction of a group's 'idioculture' and are among the interpretive materials from which movement narratives are fashioned" (Davis, 2002, p. 54).

Additional vocabulary worth mentioning includes "civic engagement" and "community building." Civic engagement refers to the "commitment to participate in, and contribute to, the improvement of one's neighborhood, community, and nation." There are "many ways in which people participate in civic, community, and political life and, by doing so, express their engaged citizenship [—] from proactively becoming better informed to participating in public dialogue on issues, from volunteering to voting, from community organizing to political advocacy... Civic engagement may be either a measure or a means of social change, depending on the context and intent of efforts" (Korza & Bacon, 2010, p. 11).

Cultural activists spearheading civic engagement initiatives are the ones who instigate, agitate, and serve as allies to indigenous communities. Their victories, no matter how small, culminate in real transformational change.

Furthermore, community building refers to "the process of building relationships that helps community members cohere around common purpose, identity, and a sense of belonging, which may lead to social or community capital" (Korza & Bacon, 2010, p. 11). The strategies and tactics of cultural activists engaged in community building are the cornerstone of civic, social, and community change.

## My Wish for Phase Three of This Project...

My wish for this primer, like the special BLB Volume on *Grassroots Leadership & the Arts for Social Change*, is to go beyond the classical thinking in the field of leadership studies, to expand the boundaries, build bridges, and invite more stakeholders to the table. This is done in a variety of ways.

For instance, at the start of each chapter, I've included a special introduction to the piece that places it in the context of the overall project. This contrasts with traditional introductory approaches to books, where readers become acquainted with the contents of a publication upfront.

Other changes, like language accessibility, people's scholarship, and the egalitarian nature of the primer have been previously discussed. There is no need to repeat the specific changes here.

I hope you are inspired by the written narratives and audio/video companion pieces spotlighted throughout this book. Perhaps you will be motivated to support cultural activists who are doing the work, or possibly, to do a little bit of rabble-rousing yourself to make the world a better place for us all.

## References

Byam, L. D. (1999). *Community in Motion: Theatre for Development in Africa*. Bergin & Garvey.

Carawan, G., & Carawan, C. (2010). [Unpublished manuscript notes].

Collins, C., Rogers, P., & Garner, J. (2000). *Robin Hood Was Right: A Guide to Giving Your Money for Social Change*. W. W. Norton.

Davis, J. (2002). *Stories of Change: Narrative and Social Movements*. State University of New York Press.

Dunson, J. (1965). *Freedom in the Air: Song Movements of the 60s*. International Publishers.

Glen, J. (1996). *Highlander: No Ordinary School*. University of Tennessee Press.

Erenrich, S. & Wergin, J. (2017). *Grassroots Leadership & the Arts for Social Change*. Emerald Publishing

Grant, J. (1998). *Ella Baker: Freedom Bound*. John Wiley & Sons.

Highlander Center. (n.d.). *Programs*. www.highlandercenter.org.

Kidd, R. (1982). Popular Theatre and Popular Struggle in Kenya. *Theaterwork Magazine, 2*(6), 46-61.

Kornbluh, J. (1998). *Rebel Voices: An IWW Anthology*. Charles H. Kerr.

Korza, P., & Bacon, B. S. (2010). *Trend or Tipping Point: Arts & Social Change Grantmaking*. Washington, DC: Americans for the Arts. https://www.giarts.org/sites/default/files/Trend-or-Tipping-Point-Arts-Social-Change-Grantmaking.pdf

Lawrence-Lightfoot, S., & Davis, J. H. (1997). *The art and science of portraiture*. San Francisco, CA: Jossey-Bass.

Lawrence-Lightfoot, S. (2005). Reflections on Portraiture: A Dialogue Between Art and Science. *Qualitative Inquiry, 11*(1), 3–15. https://doi.org/10.1177/1077800404270955

Reed, T. V. (2005). *The Art of Protest: Culture and Activism From the Civil Rights Movement to the Streets of Seattle*. University of Minnesota Press.

Riker, J. (2001). *The Nonprofit Leadership and Democracy Curriculum: A Guide for Strategic Analysis, Participatory Research, Civic Action, and Effective Advocacy*. The Union Institute Center for Public Policy Nonprofit Leadership and Democracy Project Washington D.C.

## About the Author

Susan (Susie) J. Erenrich is a social movement history documentarian. She uses the arts for social change to tell stories about transformational leadership, resilience, and societal shifts as a result of mobilization efforts by ordinary citizens. Her career in nonprofit/arts management, civic engagement, community organizing and community service spans more than four decades. She has diverse teaching experience at universities, public schools, and community-based programs for at-risk, low-income populations; has edited and produced historical audio recordings and anthologies; and has extensive performance, choreography, and production experience. Susie holds a Ph.D. in Leadership and Change from Antioch University. She is the editor of *The Cost of Freedom: Voicing a Movement After Kent State 1970*; *Freedom Is a Constant Struggle: An Anthology of the Mississippi Civil Rights Movement*; *Kent & Jackson State 1970-1990*; co-editor of *Grassroots Leadership & the Arts for Social Change* (a volume in ILA's BLB series); and co-editor of *A Grassroots Leadership & Arts for Social Change Primer for Educators, Organizers, Activists & Rabble-Rousers*. She was the producer/host of *Wasn't That A Time: Stories & Songs That Moved The Nation*, a live community radio broadcast that ran on WERA.FM for five years and is now available on-demand.

# SECTION 1

## COMMUNITY-ENGAGED THEATRE AS GRASSROOTS LEADERSHIP

# CHAPTER 1

# THE WINTER/SUMMER INSTITUTE IN APPLIED THEATRE: CREATING WITH THE COMMUNITY

KATT LISSARD

## INTRODUCTION

By Susan J. Erenrich

This chapter is penned by my dear friend Katt Lissard. Katt and I were colleagues at The World Culture Open, a nonprofit in New York City, whose mission is to "promote and advance a worldwide open culture movement" (World Culture Open, n.d.). At the time of our initial meeting, staff members at the organization were working on the FESPAD dance festival. FESPAD, which was initiated by the African Union in 1998 post-Rwandan genocide, aimed to "bring together Africans and to promote the culture of peace through African traditional dances" (ChinaDaily, 2018). For Rwanda, who was entrusted with its organization, FESPAD was an attempt to bring restoration, healing, and peace back into the country (Mushimiyimana, 2018).

Our time at The World Culture Open, however, was short-lived. After a major philosophical dispute with the CEO over her top-down leadership practices, the entire staff staged a walkout and quit. Contrary to the CEO, we were all firm believers in the pedagogy of Paulo Freire and Katt and I were Theatre of the Oppressed (Augusto

Boal) practitioners. Both Freire and Boal understood that leadership in oppressed communities had to be collaborative, collective, horizontal, and bottom-up in order for change to happen. Allies need to be catalysts for community and movement building. They are there to support the efforts of people indigenous to the area, because they are best at shaping their own destiny.

Prior to our decades-long friendship, Katt had already been involved in best practices in her theatre work in Lesotho, South Africa. Her chapter, *The Winter/Summer Institute in Applied Theatre: Creating With the Community*, is based on her experiences. It is an exemplary model of how friends of those struggling for equality, justice, and human rights should partner with those directly impacted by oppression.

I hope readers are inspired by Katt's piece. It is a salient glance into how art can move mountains – even if they are small ones.

### References

*China Daily*. (2018, July 30). African Traditional Dance Festival Opens in Rwanda. http://global.chinadaily.com.cn/a/201807/30/WS5b5e1f2ea31031a351e90d42.html

Mushimiyimana, D. (2018, July 25). All Set for FESPAD Cultural Festival. *The New Times*. https://www.newtimes.co.rw/news/all-set-fespad-cultural-festival

World Culture Open (n.d.) About. https://www.worldcultureopen.org/about

# THE WINTER/SUMMER INSTITUTE IN APPLIED THEATRE: CREATING WITH THE COMMUNITY

By Katt Lissard

*Chapter 1 Image 1.* Bilingual (Sesotho/English) post show talk-back led by Selloane Mokuku, Lesotho — WSI Malealea Festival 2008. Photo Courtesy, Katt Lissard.

## Prologue – The Contamination Waltz

It's July 2008, the dead of winter in the high mountains of Lesotho, a small landlocked sub-Saharan country surrounded by South Africa. An audience of over 600 people from the seventeen rural villages that make up the stark, stunning Malealea Valley has gathered on this bitter but sunny day for The Winter/Summer Institute's (WSI's) Festival.

We're mid-way through the final performance of *It's Just You and Me ... My Wife and Your Boyfriend* — a collaborative creation between WSI actors and local villagers, the outcome of ten intensive days working together. *The Contamination Waltz* is a comically chilling scene, the pivotal moment of the show where we "perform concurrency" — a network of interconnected lovers coming together, then unraveling in the wake of HIV/AIDS. We've carefully constructed our theatrical concurrent network using immediately recognizable characters suggested by the village performers. The first link in the chain is the sanctimonious married man in the village who claims to be devoted to his wife when everyone knows he's been sleeping with her best friend for years — his wife takes one extended arm, his girlfriend the other.

The audience bursts out laughing, elbowing each other and hooting at the actor playing the sanctimonious man. "That's how it is!" a villager wrapped in a traditional *Seana Marena* patterned Basotho blanket exclaims. "That's just how it is!"

The wife of the sanctimonious man offers her unattached hand and her lover, a retrenched miner sent home from South Africa, comes swaggering forward into the chain to claim it. The miner is followed quickly by his other long-term girlfriend (his childhood sweetheart), who has also been carrying on for several years with her boss at the liquor store. Moments later the miner's girlfriend and her boss and her boss's wife join the chain. Next up, the principal from the primary school comes forward and attaches himself to the boss's wife while extending his free hand to the new intern at his school.

The increasing complexity of the entwined network with its clandestine duplicity has the audience in hysterics. Their comments and laughter grow louder as the chain becomes even more intermeshed. The sense of fun and shared recognition continues to grow until the final link appears — The Visitor, a handsome mysterious traveler from far away, steps forward.

He takes the free hand of the last lover in the chain and introduces HIV — the virus symbolized by yards of brilliant red silk whisked in, out, and around, infecting the entire network of lovers. The audience falls suddenly silent and reflective.

The next scene begins in a graveyard.

*Chapter 1 Image 2.* Arrival of The Visitor — Julius Nkosi, South Africa; Despina Stamos, U.S.A., 2008. Photo Courtesy, Limpho Mokuku.

*Chapter 1 Image 3.* Rehearsing the spread of the virus — WSI & Malealea Community, Lesotho 2008. Photo Courtesy, Limpho Mokuku.

## Entry Point

The midwinter spectacle of *The Contamination Waltz* played out in the mountains of Lesotho as the finale of The Winter/Summer Institute's 2nd International Residency. The Malealea Festival performance was the culminating event of a month of intense collaboration that enabled us to create scenes that were intimate, unsettling, thought-provoking, and entertaining. Our portrayal of this complicated but ordinary pathway for the spread of HIV through a multiple-concurrent-partnership (or MCP) was so thoroughly engaging for the rural community who gathered to witness it because characters captured recognizable nuances of behavior and displayed an insider's ear on local gossip. The characters were suggested and brought to life by village participants in our collaborative process, many of whom we'd been working with for the second time – a reconnection that opened the possibility for increased familiarity and the ability to go deeper into issues, questions, ideas, and contradictions that came up in the work.

The story of how we first came to be in Lesotho creating theatre with participants from the U.S., the U.K., South Africa, and Lesotho, along with villagers from the rural Malealea Valley, was the end result of months of planning, hundreds of international email exchanges, dozens of meetings, weeks of preliminary research by facilitators and students, exhaustive fundraising efforts and painstakingly detailed preparation. But it's a story that began, as many projects do, with a series of chance encounters, unexpected connections, and happenstance.

*Chapter 1 Image 4.* Litšeo Mosenene, Lesotho; Melissa Shetler, U.S. A.; Kim Hess, South Africa; Ufoma Komon, U.K. — WSI Launch, Lesotho, 2006. Photo Courtesy, Rik Walton.

Our launch in July of 2006 involved ten colleagues from three different continents and an initial cohort of 22 students from four universities and 30 villagers. The ten co-founders included community development activists, REFLECT practitioners (An acronym for a community empowerment system developed around Paulo Freire's work: Regenerative Freire Literacy through Empowering Community Techniques ), university professors, adult education advocates, and theatre makers. Pressed to name this new project in the very early days when the offer of a sizable grant suddenly appeared, we became *The Winter/Summer Institute* — signifying our multi-cultural, multi-country and multi-climatic nature: July is winter in Lesotho and South Africa and summer in the U.S.A. and the U.K.

## HIV/AIDS — Gossip & Silence

Our work in Lesotho was motivated by the urgency of the HIV/AIDS pandemic in the sub-Saharan (Lesotho has the 2nd highest infection rate in the world according to UNAIDS "AIDSinfo" [https://aidsinfo. unaids.org/ Accessed June 2019]). It began through a shared desire to find ways to use theatre to make a difference in confronting the virus.

WSI's ten co-founders (Chris Dunton, Rethabile Malibo, Selloane Mokuku, Ntsele Radebe, Moso Ranoosi – Lesotho; Gillian Attwood, Alta Van As — South Africa; Katt Lissard, Lucy Winner — U.S.A.; and Nigel Watson, U.K. ) were already involved in a range of projects related to art and social change — a Theatre for Adolescent Survival project in New York City, choir-building in Gauteng (Johannesburg), people's theatre and REFLECT circles in rural Lesotho, and practical theatre training in the U.K. I was teaching at the National University of Lesotho in 2005, working with students and colleagues in the Theatre Unit there, as well as with the AIDS Outreach office on campus. Asked to create a performance for an all-campus AIDS Day, seven students (all young women) and I began work on a devised piece about getting tested, which quickly brought a powerful contradiction between agency and stigma to the surface expressed in the tension between gossip and silence. The show's echoed taunt: *"Do you want to hear what I heard?"*

When WSI came together the following year for our first international month-long residency, we decided to use the contradiction as a potent theme. Our work took shape through the lens of gossip and silence, a generative frame that allowed us to look at cultural paradox and the way it influences behavior, decision-making, gender inequity, and agency, starting from the complicated entry point of whether or not a person chooses to get tested.

*Chapter 1 Image 5*. The Gossips rehearse — Litšeo Mosenene, Lesotho; Sarah Owen, U.K. Roma, Lesotho 2006. Photo Courtesy, Rik Walton.

Our first international residency was a rollicking, enthusiastic, challenging baptism by fire. Applied theatre projects focused on social change share elements of philosophy and methodology, and many look to the theory and practice of Augusto Boal (a Brazilian theatre practitioner and political activist, Boal was the founder of Theatre of the Oppressed) as a starting place (or one of several starting places). An early strength for us was in having gathered a group of co-founders who were also core facilitators, and who brought multiple modalities, diverse creative aesthetics, and complementary pedagogical experiences to this collaborative experiment. Though Boal was an important foundation for some of us, we didn't start from a single agreed-upon philosophy or one common methodology or a required skill set beyond an eagerness to discover what theatre could bring to the community conversation around HIV / AIDS.

*Chapter 1 Image 6.* Playing AIDS: Condom Candy — Ntombi Khumalo, South Africa; Mohapi Moeketsi, Lesotho; Canedy Knowles, U.S.A. — WSI Malealea Festival 2011. Photo Courtesy, Jussara Santos-Raxlen.

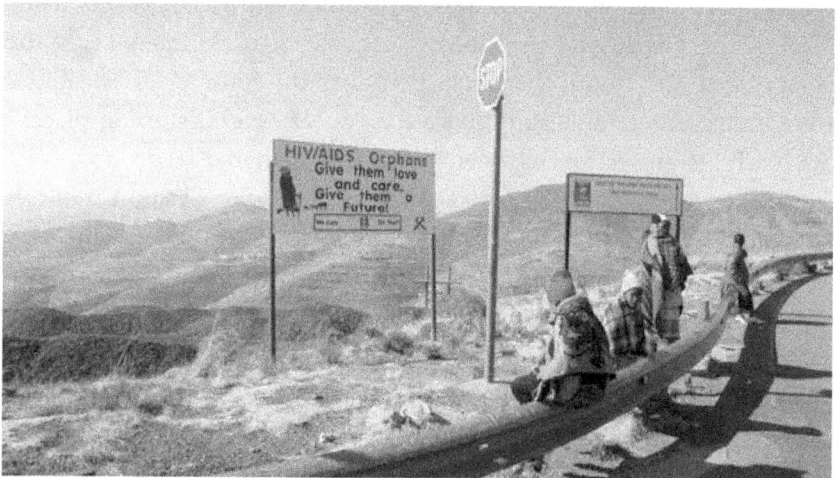

*Chapter 1 Image 7.* HIV/AIDS Orphans sign in English on the route to the Mohale Dam (a tourist destination) next to a Lesotho Highlands Water Project marker — Lesotho 2006. Photo Courtesy, Eric Feinblatt.

From that focused improvisational beginning, we've continued to develop a creative process that shares some methodology with the fields of applied and devised theatre, along with earlier roots in theatre for development, but which also includes elements unique to WSI. We were in the process of finalizing a "Field Guide" for our work scheduled to launch in Spring 2020, when the global pandemic necessitated rethinking and reformulating a tool originally intended for live, on-the-ground community interaction and collaboration. The Guide will still include a collective narrative that traces our history, process, mistakes, learning, methodology, and theatre-making – along with supplemental images, scenes, songs, and resources. But we are reframing and reformatting our exercises, examples, creative tasks, templates, and dialogues to include both virtual and live versions and options. Once published, the Guide will be a layered exploration that presents tools to facilitate using our work for community-building, activism, racial justice, research, conflict resolution, problem-solving, group learning, and artistic expression – all within the context of creating performance.

WSI's work began as a response to the devastating HIV/AIDS pandemic in one very small country on the African continent. We began with the idea that theatre, created collaboratively, could have some kind of impact. We don't have a prescriptive approach to what might constitute change or what, specifically, to change. Our main effort has been to encourage dialogue and to collaborate with communities to discover what might be areas of concern or interest to the community that would be "served" in some way by creating theatre with us about those areas of concern or interest. There are complex social issues surrounding the HIV pandemic – some of them glaring and obvious, others subtle, nuanced, and surprising. Over the years many of those issues have found theatrical expression through our collaborative work.

From the start, our experiences in Lesotho have been built on a combination of synchronicity, intention, and collaboration. Our entry point was a very specific antagonist in a very specific place, but the key to the process we've developed has always been the community.

## Working With the Community — Not Just in or Around It

WSI doesn't just go into a community, do a show, and leave. We do a show, but we present it as the first step in a dialogue with the community. We initiate a conversation with the show we've created and performed, but the next part of the exchange comes from the community.

An example from a recent international iteration of WSI illustrates how this works: The initial WSI performance is created by our cohort of student participants in collaboration with core facilitators. It's the first thing we do when we gather in residency in Lesotho, although the process begins in the months leading up to the residency through shared thematic readings, resources, and ideas between the participating schools. Once in Lesotho, we spend an intense three weeks creating a show based on the issues and concerns of the students. We then use the show as the springboard to doing more collaborative work with the villagers.

In this case, we'd just performed *Would You Still Love Me If You Knew? (Ha U N'u Tseba, Na U N'u Tla 'N'u Nthate?)* in front of the Malealea Valley's small rural mountain health clinic for nearby communities. The show was built around "secrets" and everything that simple word might contain. It included scenes of a young man coming out to his father and refusing to go to Initiation School, a corrupt priest exposed for pocketing most of his congregations' tithes, an accusation of marital rape, and a disturbing trend where children play various AIDS games. The show included a thread of dark comedy facilitated by two Tricksters and a lot of music.

We were in the "gathering" phase of our work, post-show brainstorming in small groups with village participants, asking what had worked for them, what might have rung true, and, more importantly, what might be missing. In other words: What do we keep, what do we get rid of, and what do we need to make together that comes from "here" (i.e., from the village)? We gather these reactions, thoughts, ideas, phrases and then we move on from there to make new scenes with the villagers using WSI's process of improvisation, creative tasks, small group presentation, feedback, and shaping.

There are always unexpected things that come up, things we'd never know or hear about or be given access to if we didn't come into community with people by first sharing something and then asking: What did we get right? What did we get wrong? What should be here that isn't? It's important to note that it's not just the foreigners from the U.S., U.K. and South Africa who wouldn't be privy to these reactions, ideas, and criticisms. The National University of Lesotho students are also seen as "other" by villagers, even if they originally came from a rural area, as most do. Once they enter the university, they become part of a different social class.

We're often provocatively surprised and/or chastened by the gravity of these initial feedback sessions. In this particular session an elder whispered, *"Girls are disappearing from the villages, and no one is talking about it!"* Silence. For a moment no one could speak. His raspy, hushed exclamation touched on so many complicated issues: sex trafficking, poverty, gender inequity, the spread of HIV, the social hierarchy (even in bare-bones villages) of those girls who might be targeted and those not, and the fact that *"no one is talking about it!"* ... for multiple reasons.

In the show we created with the community, his astonished line is whispered in both English and Sesotho (Lesotho's official language) — *Girls are disappearing from the villages, and no one is talking about it! Girls are disappearing from the villages, and no one is talking about it!* — as the transition out of one scene focused on a pregnant teenager and into a new one where a village girl is lured away by a slick procurer with the promise of "a job in town."

*Chapter 1 Image 8*. Sex Trafficker Buying Silence – Sekoai Mahlaka, Lesotho – WSI Malealea Festival 2011. Photo Courtesy, Katt Lissard.

*Chapter 1 Image 9.* Prayer as Power against HIV rehearsal — WSI & Malealea Community — Lesotho 2011. Photo Courtesy, Jussara Santos-Raxlen.

The job proposition includes a wad of cash given by the Trafficker to the girl's family, a "friendly loan" the girl can repay once her fabulous new life begins. The parents are sworn to secrecy.

The more we worked on the scene with the village actors, the more obvious it became that the specifics of what we were creating were drawn from one participant's immediate, shattering loss. Lesotho's villages are often desperately poor. Part of the shame of this particular secret and one of many reasons "no one is talking about it" has to do with poverty and the way people are manipulated because of it. We might all say we understand poverty is a universal ingredient in sex trafficking — but breaking that down at the local level, performed live, was compelling.

That's an example of creating with community members that was fairly straight forward and went well. A more complicated example would be this: Every time we've worked with a rural community a storyline comes up or a scene is proposed about taking a person sick with HIV to the *sangoma* (traditional healer) **and** to the health clinic **and** to the priest or preacher. Also, typically, the clinic usually wins the contest of which of these is the best treatment for the one who is ill. On a recent trip there was a heated debate between those who were "for" the clinic and those who were "for" the *sangoma* and those who were "for" religion and prayer.

On one hand, this was a positive development because we were being brought into the intricacies and nuances of the debate. Instead of village performers appeasing what they presumed were our outsiders' expectations — i.e., someone sick with HIV should go to the health clinic — they insisted on the complexity they experienced in the face of this deadly illness. On the other hand, the scene this all-encompassing approach gave rise to was fraught, tedious, and interminable, an epic tale full of lengthy monologues and sermonizing — there was a lot to work with! And, eventually, we were able to turn it into a sharply comic scene that took all the conflicting solutions (Western medicine, traditional medicine, religion) and presented them in a highly provocative but satiric way, which left the door open to multiple resolutions depending on the needs of the sick person.

In the end, the HIV-positive person was taking ARV's, using herbs prescribed by the *sangoma*, and his mother was praying for him. Which, when you think about it, is exactly what people do everywhere. Rarely does someone only go to the doctor or to the alternative healer or to the minister; we approach illness through multiple routes and seek out multiple paths to a cure.

Advocating for the health clinic is part of advocating for testing and for an approach to the spread of HIV that takes all aspects of community health into account. We wanted to support and encourage people to use the clinic and to access the advantage of knowing their status, but it was crucial to communicate and to perform the multiple avenues of approach the community was negotiating and to present a way to balance those possibilities.

*Chapter 1 Image 10.* Leading Day One Warm-Ups – Molomo Ramothello, Lesotho & Malelea Community – Lesotho 2008. Photo Courtesy, Limpho Mokuku.

## Trusting the Process

As we continue to explore this work, one of the lessons we learn over and over again is the way theatre allows crucial things to be said "creatively" that might not be said otherwise and how exhilarating and empowering that can be, not only for rural villages in places like Lesotho but for participants in WSI who come from big Western cities or university faculties or professional theatre companies. You can put words into the mouths of characters created through our process and those characters can say to a neighbor or a husband or a friend what you, the performer, can't say yourself. You can challenge stigmatizing rumors, expose domestic violence, negotiate condom use, critique corruption, take a stand — finally give confident voice to what you've been thinking.

Through all our work we've continued to "trust the process" — not only the creative process we're developing, but the notion that process itself is fundamental to art and to social change.

## About the Author

Katt Lissard is the artistic director of The Winter/Summer Institute (WSI), an international HIV/AIDS & Theatre for Social Change project based in New York and Lesotho, southern Africa (wsimaketheatre.org). A teacher, writer, and performer, she spent two years in the Theatre Unit at the National University of Lesotho as a Fulbright Scholar (2005, 2012), where she taught, directed, and devised shows — WSI grew out of her early work there. Recent publications on her work in Africa: "Venus in Lesotho: Women, Theatre and the Collapsible Boundaries of Silence," in Palgrave Macmillan's anthology *Feminist Popular Education in Transnational Debates: Building Pedagogies of Possibility* and "Viral Collaboration: Harmonising to defeat AIDS in southern Africa," *in SATJ/South African Theatre Journal*. A longtime faculty member of the Graduate Institute at Goddard College, Katt currently teaches in the Department of Ethnic and Race Studies at City University's BMCC in New York.

# CHAPTER 2
# THE FREEDOM THEATRE IN JENIN REFUGEE CAMP

SHAINA LOW & JEN MARLOWE

## INTRODUCTION

By Susan J. Erenrich

This chapter features a column penned by Jen Marlowe and Shaina Low. It covers an explosive topic that is usually discussed in an impassioned way — the Israeli-Palestinian conflict. This is not an ordinary portrayal of the decades-long struggle in the region. Instead, it is a noteworthy glimpse into the innerworkings of The Freedom Theatre in Jenin and what it means to lead and create dangerously in occupied territory.

The idea that one must create dangerously is certainly not new. On December 14, 1957, at the University of Uppsala in Sweden, four days after accepting the Nobel Prize in Literature, Albert Camus famously challenged artists to immerse themselves in the thick of battle. *Create Dangerously* was the title of his speech. He ended his remarks with a passionate plea to people everywhere:

Great ideas, it has been said, come into the world as gently as doves. Perhaps then, if we listen attentively, we shall hear, amid the uproar of empires and nations, a faint flutter of wings, the gentle stirring of life and hope. Some will say that this hope lies in a nation, others, in a man. I believe rather that it is awakened, revived, nourished by millions of solitary individuals whose deeds and works every day negate frontiers and the crudest implications of history. As a result, there shines forth fleetingly the ever-threatened truth that each and every man, on the foundation of his own sufferings and joys, builds for all (Camus, 1988, p. 272).

Even though Camus never defined what he meant by his charge, throughout history artists involved in movements of protest, resistance, and liberation have taken enormous risks and have placed themselves in perilous situations — just like those participating in The Freedom Theatre, as you'll read below.

My personal interest in *Create Dangerously* as a motif began when I was a doctoral student. Albert Camus's lack of definition in his provocative statement has left room for multiple interpretations and misinterpretations over the years that have taken the speech out of context. As part of my dissertation I established, as follows, seven benchmarks to explore the idea.

Do artists or artist groups *Create Dangerously* when they:

1. Threaten the social, economic, and political status quo?
2. Mobilize for systemic change?
3. Introduce new practices and tactics into a community?
4. Openly express the hidden transcripts of opposing views?
5. Keep the stories of repressive power alive?
6. Assist ordinary people usually locked out of the political process to write their own scripts (i.e., popular education)?
7. Lead without authority?

To answer these questions, I researched two artists and one artist group, crafting portraits to help critically examine these concepts. My inquiry is ongoing and evolving. This chapter assists in furthering the leadership footprint in this area.

I hope readers are intellectually and emotionally stirred by Shaina and Jen's chapter and that the compelling content about creating dangerously and leading dangerously stimulates a deeper conversation about this serious issue.

## References

Camus, A. (1988/1960). *Resistance, Rebellion, and Death.* Vintage International.

Erenrich, S. (2010). *Rhythms of Rebellion: Artists Creating Dangerously for Social Change.* [Unpublished Doctoral Dissertation]. Antioch University, Dayton, Ohio.

## THE FREEDOM THEATRE IN JENIN REFUGEE CAMP

By Shaina Low & Jen Marlowe

A little boy, approximately seven years old, leans against a light blue door embedded in a single-story, cement-block home in Jenin camp, the northern most refugee camp in the West Bank. "Freedom to me is the occupation ending and the army leaving." His political manifesto declared, he then gets down to the real business of defining freedom: "It is also playing snooker, hide and seek, and no one hitting me" (Marlowe, 2010).

The other children of Jenin refugee camp interviewed in the summer of 2008 espoused similar thoughts on freedom. First, an end to Israeli occupation (one boy offered the chilling detail of "being able to sleep in your house and not hiding in hospitals"), followed by more personal desires: one girl wished to travel and learn other languages; another wanted to pursue her hobbies of theatre, circus, and music. But what should have been prosaic desires for these children, were — and continue to be for the next generation — often as far-fetched as imagining a complete and permanent withdrawal of Israeli troops.

And that is why The Freedom Theatre (TFT) exists. Artistic Director Nabil Al-Raee describes TFT as "a safe spot for people to express themselves and to find their own freedom; individually and then, collectively" (The Freedom Theatre, 2015). Understanding and telling your own story, Al-Raee believes, is a necessary first step towards being able to stand and fight against the different levels of occupation that exist.

*Chapter 2 Image 1.* The Freedom Theatre. Photo Courtesy, The Freedom Theatre.

## TFT Background and Context

TFT is situated in Jenin refugee camp, which was established in 1953 to shelter Palestinians who were displaced during the creation of the state of Israel in 1948. At the time of a 2007 census, Jenin camp had a population of 10,000 living on .26 square miles - approximately 42% of them under the age of 15 (Palestinian Central Bureau of Statistics, 2008). According to the United Nations Relief and Works Agency, Jenin camp's rates of poverty, unemployment, and school drop-out are among the highest of the 19 refugee camps throughout the West Bank (United Nations Relief and Works Agency, n.d.).

Jenin is separated from the Palestinian cultural hub of Ramallah by less than 40 miles, yet closures, curfews, checkpoints, and other restrictions on freedom of movement over the years have amplified their distance. The city of Nazareth, which hosts the largest concentration of Palestinian citizens of Israel, is less than 20 miles away, but Israel's Separation Wall and permit regime prevent nearly all of Jenin's residents from reaching it. In recent decades, Palestinian society has grown increasingly religious and conservative, remote areas and refugee camps even more so. The combination of these factors has led to Jenin camp being one of the most religiously conservative areas in the West Bank. It is also one of the most traumatized, having been targeted with especially acute violence in both Palestinian uprisings, or *intifadas*. In 2002, during the second intifada, Israeli forces invaded the camp, in what has been termed "the Battle of Jenin." Israeli forces killed dozens of Palestinians and large swaths of the camp were bulldozed by the Israeli army, rendering 25% of the camp's residents homeless (United Nations, 2002).

It was against this backdrop of death and destruction that Juliano Mer-Khamis, Zakaria Zubeidi, and Jonatan Stanczek co-founded The Freedom Theatre in 2006, as an outgrowth of Mer-Khamis's 2004 documentary, Arna's Children. Mer-Khamis was born to Arna Mer, a Jewish Israeli, and Saliba Khamis, a Palestinian Christian citizen of Israel. The film depicts the Care and Learning Center, an art and theatre program that Arna established for children in Jenin refugee camp in the late 1980s, during the first intifada. Juliano worked with the children briefly, but, following his mother's death in the early '90s, returned to his life as an actor on the Israeli stage. After the 2002 Battle of Jenin, Juliano returned to the camp with a video camera and discovered that nearly all of the children who had been involved in his mother's center were now dead. Several had been part of the resistance against the Israeli invasion. One had undertaken a suicide attack in the Israeli city of Hadera. Of the few that were still alive, one was killed during the course of the filming.

Mer-Khamis had no intention to return to Jenin long-term, but after the release of *Arna's Children*, he felt a renewed responsibility to the community in the camp. "I cannot just do films and go on," he reflected in a 2007 interview (Khalidi & Marlowe, 2011). "You do films with the purpose to change reality, at least to have some influence on it." So, Mer-Khamis partnered with Zubeidi (one of the few surviving youths of Arna's program and a leader of the armed resistance in Jenin) and Stanczek (a Swedish nurse) to launch TFT, in hopes that it would be a venue to "join Palestinian people in struggle for liberation," and yield a third, cultural intifada with poetry, music, theatre, and photography.

The early years of TFT chiefly served children and youth from Jenin refugee camp, focusing to a great extent on drama as a tool for emotional healing. Mer-Khamis observed symptoms of severe trauma exhibited by children in the camp including aggression, inability to concentrate, and bed-wetting by children as old as 11. Petra Barghouti, a drama therapist contracted by the theatre, worked to give youth the space to feel safe and express themselves via theatrical techniques such as storytelling, role-play, movement, and sound work. Rami, a teenaged boy with a pronounced speech impediment, described these drama therapy sessions as "pulling out the fear inside me so I can be free, so this thing inside my mouth will go away" (The Freedom Theatre, 2009).

*Chapter 2 Image 2.* The Little Lantern. Photo Courtesy, The Freedom Theatre.

But Mer-Khamis's vision always went beyond trauma healing. From the start, TFT was grounded in notions of cultural resistance and ideals of freedom on all levels. In an early promotional video for TFT he declared, "We hope that this theatre will generate a political, artistic movement of artists who are going to raise their voice against women discrimination, against children discrimination, against violence." It was also explicitly about leadership. In the same video he says that what is needed is "liberation leadership. We have to build up this leadership from scratch and to do this, the best way is to start an artistic venue" (Marlowe, 2010).

Another unique element to TFT is its political and social diversity. Many of Palestine's civil society institutions are (at least unofficially) affiliated with a particular political party, yet TFT's board and staff run the gambit from conservative, to communist, to everything in between.

**Staging Freedom**

A cultural revolution requires foot soldiers; ones who have nurtured a vision of liberation and developed the skills required to build towards that vision. With that in mind, in 2008 TFT launched its Drama School, the first professional theatre school in the West Bank. The three-year training program is rigorous with its students producing multiple new works each year. TFT productions (both ones that originate in the Drama School and ones that are spearheaded by its graduates and other members of TFT's artistic team) typically perform initially on TFT's modest stage, often followed by a tour in the West Bank, and sometimes, international tours. This enables TFT to actualize another goal: for Palestinian narratives, told by Palestinians, to impact the outside world.

Early TFT productions often took classic theatrical works and adapted them with a uniquely Palestinian twist, such as *Animal Farm* in 2009, in which the oppressive Farmer Jones and other humans were Israeli soldiers, and the pigs who collaborated with them represented the Palestinian Authority — a pointed critique at the perceived corruption of Palestinian leadership. In 2011, the Drama School mounted a production of *Alice in Wonderland* in which Alice embarks on her journey down the rabbit hole in order to escape an arranged marriage. In 2013, two Drama School graduates performed an adaptation of Athol Fugard's, The Island, re-imagining the South African play as a commentary on the experiences of Palestinian political prisoners. According to a 2014 report released by the prisoner advocacy group Addameer, approximately 40% of the adult Palestinian male population has been imprisoned by Israel since the beginning of the occupation in 1967 (Addameer Prisoner Support, 2014).

*Chapter 2 Image 3.* Children's Summer Camp, 2018. Photo Courtesy, The Freedom Theatre.

In recent years, however, TFT has shifted away from adaptions and is more frequently producing entirely original works, sharing Palestinian narratives on their own terms. Perhaps the boldest (and most controversial) of these was the 2015 production *The Siege* (Gardner, 2015; Frazer, 2015). *The Siege* was developed by TFT Artistic Director Nabil Al-Raee and British director (and longtime TFT associate) Zoe Lafferty. The basis of the play is interviews with Palestinian fighters who sought refuge in the Church of Nativity for 39 days in 2002, under siege from the Israeli army. (The siege on the Church was part of the same Israeli offensive as the Battle of Jenin.) The play imagines the siege — and the eventual negotiated settlement that sent the fighters into exile — from the perspectives of six fighters, an amalgamation of the dozen or so Palestinian exiles interviewed by

Al-Raee and Lafferty. The play not only preserves a slice of Palestinian history, made accessible both to Palestinian and international audiences, but offers a human, nuanced, and complex view of resistance in a political context in which Palestinian fighters are usually either glorified or demonized.

*The Siege* initially toured throughout Palestine and then in Europe in 2016. In 2017, a significant ten-day run of the play was mounted at New York University's Skirball Theatre. The significance of the New York run is rooted in a previously scheduled run of *The Siege* at New York's Public Theatre that was cancelled, rescheduled, and cancelled again (Bryan, 2016). These cancellations are part of a history of censorship of Palestinian theatre in the U.S., which includes a 1989 cancellation of a production by El-Hakawati Palestinian Theater Company, also scheduled to perform at the Public, and the production of *My Name is Rachel Corrie* at the New York Theatre Workshop in 2006. Approximately 3,500 people attended the New York run of *The Siege*, signaling that, despite institutional fears and censorship, there is an audience that wants to hear Palestinian stories and support Palestinian art.

## Freedom on Wheels

Productions (and developing the artists who create them) are the cornerstone of TFT's work — but TFT's vision of cultural resistance includes its own versions of deep, ongoing, community organizing. The Freedom Bus, a project that spanned five years, is one such example (The Freedom Theatre, n.d.). The Freedom Bus combined TFT's goals of developing skilled Palestinian artists within a liberatory framework, staging uniquely Palestinian narratives, building solidarity with internationals, reaching remote Palestinian communities who typically have little to no access to the arts, and using theatre as a mechanism to transform pain into power.

Ben Rivers, an Australian theatre artist, based his PhD dissertation research at TFT in 2011 (Rivers, 2015). There, he trained actors in the techniques of Playback Theatre, creating a cadre of young Palestinian actors mastered in the skills of eliciting personal stories from audiences/community members and then improvising theatrical reenactments of those stories. This work became the basis of the multifaceted Freedom Bus program. The concept was grounded in building connections; between TFT and remote, rural, Palestinian communities, and between internationals and Palestinians. A physical bus brought a delegation of foreigners and Playback actors to villages and refugee camps that were largely remote and isolated, yet on the frontier of fighting annexation and occupation. These communities were often in areas of the fragmented West Bank that are difficult to access due to land expropriation, settler violence, and closed military zones.

Days were spent learning about the specific issues, challenges, and needs facing each community, and engaging in service work in partnership with community members. This work included clearing demolished homes and rebuilding a demolished oven in the Bedouin community of Umm al Kheir, making mud bricks in the resource-deprived village of Fasayel, and planting olive trees in the Jordan valley. During the March 2015 ride, visual artist Alaa Albaba painted murals in each community the bus visited, using the motif of fish to illustrate the different challenges each community faced. For example, because the village Fasayel faces severe problems with access to water, the mural there depicted a water tap with fish coming out. In Bil'in the Separation Wall cut through the village's land, so Bil'in's mural was a fish whose scales were a wall.

*Chapter 2 Image 4.* Fish Mural. Photo Courtesy, Shaina Low.

Most days included Playback performances, where community members in the audience were invited to share personal stories. Some told stories of ordinary life, but many related the specific struggles in their community — whether it was the army continually demolishing an unrecognized village's schoolhouse in the Jordan Valley, or settler attacks in the south Hebron Hills. The playback actors re-enacted the story on the spot, giving the storyteller the agency to determine whether the story was portrayed accurately or if they wanted to make any changes — a therapeutic aspect to the process that enables the storyteller to reclaim some modicum of power in a dynamic where all too often, in the lived experience, the person had been stripped of all power.

Internationals were invited to share stories during playback performances, too, cultivating a sense of true exchange with the local community. Internationals' stories varied as much as Palestinians', yet many used the Playback performance as an opportunity to reflect on the violence and oppression they had witnessed in Palestine. The playback helped them to process these experiences and reinforced the solidarity shared between host communities and their visitors.

For internationals on the Freedom Bus, the opportunity to build solidarity with communities marginalized within Palestine was rare — most delegations travel chiefly to the urban centers of Ramallah, Bethlehem, and Hebron. Furthermore, the very act of Palestinians from TFT traveling to remote Palestinian communities to learn about their localized needs and injustices and to collaborate with those communities for their stories to be told was, in and of itself, a challenge to the fragmentation of Palestinian society that is inherent in the occupation. A number of Freedom Bus delegations also included Palestinians from other parts of Palestine, in an effort to challenge this fragmentation.

The south Hebron Hills village of Atuwani is one of the communities who hosted the Freedom Bus. Though only 75 miles from Jenin as the crow flies, Palestinians must drive a circuitous route to reach Atuwani, around settlements, through checkpoints, and bypassing Jerusalem. West Bank Palestinians cannot enter Jerusalem without an Israeli army-issued permit even though the most direct route from the northern to southern West Bank passes directly through Jerusalem. The journey can take hours. The Israeli settlement of Maon looms high on the hill above Atuwani as does the Israeli outpost Havat Ma'on. Since the late 1990s, villagers in Atuwani have experienced violence and harassment from these settlers. For more than a decade, internationals from an Italian NGO, Operation Dove, have accompanied children from neighboring villages to the school in Atuwani in order to protect them from the possibility of violence from the settlers.

Faisal Abu Alhayjaa, a Drama School graduate turned director, playwright, and teacher, and a member of the Freedom Bus Playback troupe, was inspired by the time he spent with the community at Atuwani to create a deeper collaboration. He wrote and directed a play named after the village that was based on the experiences that the community shared during the Freedom Bus tour and fleshed out with further research and interviews. Stories include a woman who blocked the demolition of the village's school with her body and a shepherd who was arrested for grazing his sheep on his own (expropriated) land, which created such a commotion that the police ended up begging *him* to leave the station. The 2014 tour of Abu Alhayjaa's play brought a theatrical rendition of Atuwani's people (particularly women), their struggles, and their creative, nonviolent, highly organized resistance to other West Bank communities enabling the creativity and resilience of the Atuwani villagers to reach and inspire Palestinian villages and refugee camps all over the West Bank.

## The Dangers of Cultural Resistance

The work of the Freedom Theatre — from the Drama School to the original productions to the Freedom Bus (not to mention the different multimedia projects over the years, including photography, filmmaking, writing, and hip-hop) — has been profound and transformative. But the challenges and dangers are also very real and come with the highest stakes imaginable. Much of the danger emanates from the raison d'être of the theatre itself.

Al-Raee has described the theatre's mission as resisting not one, but multiple occupations. "Resistance is, first, against the Israeli occupation. The second occupation, it comes from our own society. The social occupation, and then you have the mental occupation."

Samah Mahmood, a young woman in TFT's drama school in 2015, illustrated Al-Raee's point. "Resistance from my perspective is not just against the occupation, but also for me, a girl in society, there are things I cannot do, because I'm a girl, and because of society and because of norms and traditions, and because I'm in Palestine, and because I'm in Jenin, and because I'm in a refugee camp. There's a lot of pressure. Everything is forbidden, nothing is allowed. A lot, a lot. So, thankfully, I found a place like this where I can express what I want" (The Freedom Theater, 2015).

Abu Alhayjaa put it like this: "When you grow up in Jenin refugee camp, everything will be about killing or death, or about intifadas, or about the army, prison. These are our stories; this is our dialogue. But suddenly in the theatre, there is something more than this.... I start to feel the occupation (is) not only the wall or the checkpoints, or the army or the prison...the occupation is more in the mind, in the dreams, in the thoughts."

Mer-Khamis and his colleagues challenged — and angered — conservative power structures in Jenin camp and beyond from the very start of the project. Girls and boys were on stage together, defying deeply traditional community norms. Critique of Israeli occupation was received enthusiastically; critique of Palestinian leadership and society often was not. Some complained that the lifestyle of some of TFT's staff, students, and international volunteers were corrupting the youth. Opposition to the theatre, which had been vocalized from some quarters all along, took a new, darker form starting in 2009 when the theatre was firebombed during the production of *Animal Farm*. Nobody was hurt — then.

On April 4, 2011, Mer-Khamis was driving his car from TFT's small parking lot when a masked assailant stepped in front of his car and shot seven bullets into his chest. Mer-Khamis died en route to the hospital. Some believe the assailant was sent by power structures in the camp who disapproved of TFT in general and Mer-Khamis in particular; others are convinced that the assassination was directed by Israel. The murder was never solved.

After the assassination, it was not clear how — or if — TFT would continue without its charismatic co-founder while in the midst of the deep grief, turmoil, and fear that followed his murder. It did not help that in the wake of the killing, Israeli attacks on the theatre and its staff intensified. In the months following the killing, staff and board members were arrested in nighttime raids, which continue to the time of this writing. As recently as February 2019, Israeli forces arrested TFT co-founder Zakaria Zubeidi from his Ramallah apartment in a nighttime raid. At the time of this writing, Zubeidi remains in Israeli custody.

*Chapter 2 Image 5.* Us Too. Photo Courtesy, The Freedom Theatre.

Other challenges facing TFT are consistent with the more mundane, structurally oppressive aspects of occupation: actors being unable to receive visas to tour with productions; other actors being unable to even receive permits to travel to either Jerusalem or Jordan to visit consulates, a necessary first step towards obtaining a visa; and all the ways in which the occupation creates barriers and obstructions to travel, life, work, and study. Jenin's isolation means that the TFT also has difficulty attracting talent and audiences from other parts of Palestine. The 2010 refurbishment and reopening of Cinema Jenin in Jenin city offered hope that the two institutions could help Jenin become a vibrant center for the arts in the northern West Bank. Yet, mismanagement and financial problems led to the Cinema's closure within six years. The building was ultimately sold and razed, and a shopping mall built on its lot.

There are other, more deeply embedded challenges as well. TFT as an organization works for full equality between men and women. But in certain ways, elements of the very patriarchy that TFT is seeking to resist is replicated there. The lack of women in leadership positions among TFT's Board of Directors and staff is one example. Both of us have heard some TFT team members profess views supporting women's equality but have observed them personally behaving in ways that contradict those beliefs. Yet, there are team members actively challenging their own internalized misogyny. TFT recently partnered with women community members from Jenin to present stories of oppression faced by women entitled, *Us Too*. One TFT actor/director remarked how hearing the women's stories helped prod his own continuing evolution in this arena.

For all the challenges, the dangers, and the ways in which TFT struggles to live up to its mission, it is providing a critical source of hope and vitality for those seeking to nurture a deep vision of liberation. Abu Alhayjaa said that at TFT he both finds and shows people "new colors of life, of happiness, of joy, of art, and also of a dream. And this is important because I believe we live because we have a dream."

Alia Alrosan, a former coordinator of the Freedom Bus and Drama School student, believes the central importance of TFT lies in this nurturing of dreams. "People can change their reality only if they can imagine the life that they want to live, and the stage is a place to create whatever you want," she said. "So, it's an amazing chance to have this place to create how real life can be, how freedom can be, how love can be…how Palestine can be!"

## References

Addameer Prisoner Support and Human Rights Association. (2014, January). *Palestinian Political Prisoners in Israeli Prisons*.

Bryan, Rob. (2016, February 25). Public Theatre Backed Out of Oral Agreement to Put on 'The Siege'. *Mondoweiss*. https://mondoweiss.net/2016/02/public-theater-backed-out-of-oral-agreement-to-put-on-the-siege/

Frazer, Jenni. (2015, May 2). Palestinian Gunmen Turn Heroes in UK Production of 'The Siege'. *The Times of Israel*. https://www.

timesofisrael.com/palestinian-gunmen-turn-heroes-in-uk-production-of-the-siege/

The Freedom Theatre. (n.d.). *The Freedom Bus*. https://freedombuspalestine.wordpress.com/

The Freedom Theatre. [thefreedomtheatre]. (2009, June 8). *Drama Therapy* [Video]. YouTube. https://www.youtube.com/watch?v=jJJx0Sr5I_Y&t=196s

The Freedom Theatre. [thefreedomtheatre]. (2015, November 16). *The Freedom Theatre* [Video]. YouTube. https://www.youtube.com/watch?v=7t3g9koISf8

Gardner, Lyn. (2015, May 21). The Siege Review - Lives on the Edge in Bethlehem Standoff. *The Guardian*. https://www.theguardian.com/stage/2015/may/21/the-siege-battersea-arts-theatre-review-bethlehem-church-of-the-nativity

Khalidi, I., & Marlowe, J. (2011, April 11). Remembering Juliano Mer-Khamis. *The Nation*. https://www.thenation.com/article/archive/remembering-juliano-mer-khamis/

Marlowe, Jen. (2010, November 11). *The Jenin Freedom Theatre Today!* [Video]. YouTube. https://www.youtube.com/watch?v=pQGqmLyunm0

Palestinian Central Bureau of Statistics. (2008, August). *Population, Housing and Establishment Census 2007: Census Final Results in The West Bank – Summary (Population and Housing). Ramallah - Palestine.* http://www.pcbs.gov.ps/Portals/_PCBS/Downloads/book1487.pdf

Rivers, Ben. (2015). Narrative power: Playback Theatre as Cultural Resistance in Occupied Palestine. *Research in Drama Education: The Journal of Applied Theatre and Performance*, 20(2), pp. 155-172. https://doi.org/10.1080/13569783.2015.1022144

United Nations. (2002, July 30). *Report of the Secretary-General Prepared Pursuant to General Assembly Resolution ES-10/10.* https://unispal.un.org/DPA/DPR/unispal.nsf/0/FD7BDE7666E04F5C85256C08004E63ED

United Nations Relief and Works Agency for Palestine Refugees in the Near East. (n.d.). *Jenin Camp*. https://www.unrwa.org/where-we-work/west-bank/jenin-camp

## About the Authors

Shaina Low is an attorney and works as an advocacy officer at Defense for Children International - Palestine. Her experience with organizations in both the U.S. and Palestine/Israel has included fundraising, working with children, guest lecturing at high schools and colleges, organizing and leading coast-to-coast advocacy tours, and bringing delegations to the region. Her legal research has covered topics ranging from forcible transfer, the international community's obligations under international humanitarian and human rights law, and the rights of prisoners and children. Shaina holds a BA in political science from Columbia University and a J.D. from the City University of New York Law School. She is admitted to practice law in the State of New York. She serves on the American Friends Services Committee's Palestine Advisory Committee and the board of the GRALTA Foundation. She is a former board member of the Friends of the Jenin Freedom Theatre.

Jen Marlowe is an award-winning author, playwright, documentary filmmaker, and journalist. Her books include *I Am Troy Davis*, *The Hour of Sunlight: One Palestinian's Journey from Prisoner to Peacemaker*, and *Darfur Diaries: Stories of Survival*. Her films include *Witness Bahrain*, *Remembering the Gaza War*, *Rebuilding Hope: Sudan's Lost Boys Return Home*. She is the co-producer of Just Vision's *Naila and the Uprising* and the playwright of *There Is a Field*. She identifies first and foremost as a social justice/human rights activist and considers her filming and writing to be tools of her activism. She lives and works on unceded Duwamish territory in what is now known as Seattle. Marlowe serves on the board of the Friends of the Jenin Freedom Theatre and is the founder of Donkeysaddle Projects (http://www.donkeysaddle.org/).

# CHAPTER 3

# UNAFRAID OF UNCERTAINTY: DEVELOPING GRASSROOTS LEADERS USING THEATRE IN AFGHANISTAN

KAYHAN IRANI

## INTRODUCTION

By Susan J. Erenrich

This chapter features my dear friend and Theatre of the Oppressed compatriot Kayhan Irani. I first met Kayhan at The Brecht Forum in New York City. We joined approximately seventy-five others from around the globe to study with Augusto Boal, the founder of Theatre of the Oppressed, and his son Julian. It was my summer ritual back when I resided in the Big Apple. Enrollees from all over the world — Israel, Brazil, France, England, Morocco, Denmark, Lebanon, Canada, Azerbaijan, Ireland, and the United States, to name a few — gathered together during those extraordinary times. Men and women with ages ranging from their 20s to their 70s and from many different ethnicities speaking many different languages attended. Most of the participants were theatre practitioners who worked in a variety of settings. We had one thing in common. We were all there to study with the champion of Theatre of the Oppressed and his son.

The workshops were organized by The Theatre of the Oppressed Laboratory (TOPLAB), which was founded in New York City in 1990 by Marie-Claire Picher. Claire, a good friend of Augusto and Julian, was a founding member responsible for the summer get-togethers. Claire's intention was to create an organization to provide a forum for the practice, performance, and dissemination of the techniques of the Theatre of the Oppressed. Besides Claire, TOPLAB consists of a group of educators, cultural and political activists, and artists whose work is based on extensive training and collaboration with Augusto Boal. Kayhan is an integral part of this group.

For readers not familiar with Theatre of the Oppressed, it is grounded in popular education, a methodology credited to Brazilian educator Paulo Freire. Paulo Freire was a major influence on Brazilian playwright Augusto Boal, who incorporated the principals of popular education into a theatrical practice. Freire and Boal first met in 1960 while Augusto was touring in the poorest region of Brazil. Based on Freire's (1992) principles outlined in *Pedagogy of the Oppressed*, Boal created Theatre of the Oppressed. While Freire talked about learning to "read the world," Boal emphasized the need for participants to "'speak' theatre for themselves, rather than be content to watch plays written and performed by acknowledged experts" (Babbage, 2004, p. 20). Participants in Theatre of the Oppressed workshops "would learn theatrical language based on the need to express their own reality, in order to engage with the contradictions of that reality. Finally, the trainer would be motivated by a genuine desire for dialog — a belief that in this process the 'students' have knowledge which the 'teacher' needs to learn" (Babbage, 2004, p. 20). The approach was similar to Freire's, who had outlined the methods whereby students within the educational process could make the transition from seeing themselves as objects (unconscious and acted upon by others) to subjects (capable of self-conscious action). "Boal had identified stages by which the spectator — in his view fundamentally a passive being — could become an actor. The proposed steps are as follows: (1) knowing the body; (2) making the body expressive; (3) the theatre as language; and (4) the theatre as discourse" (Babbage, 2004, p. 20).

The Theatre of the Oppressed influence has been far reaching. Boal's book, *Theatre of the Oppressed* has been translated into at least 25 different languages. There are Theatre of the Oppressed centers, groups, and organizations on every continent — such as Jana Sanskriti (Calcutta), Headlines Theatre (Vancouver), Giolli (Italy), ATB (Burkina Faso), TOPLAB (New York), Formaat (Rotterdam), and Ashtar (Ramallah) — that use techniques directly or in combination with other strategies. There are Theatre of the Oppressed festivals that take place all over the world. In 2001, as Boal reflected on five decades of work, he put the Theatre of the Oppressed in a global context: "In stable countries, artists know where they stand — serene and unperturbed. They know what they want and what is expected of them. In a Brazil cast adrift, everything was and is possible: we asked where we were, who we were, where we wanted to go" (Babbage, 2004, p. 2).

By a fluke of fate, Paulo Freire and Augusto Boal died on the same day, but years apart. Their teachings live on in the hearts and minds of those of us who had the opportunity to study with these incredible people. I hope you enjoy Kayhan Irani's important story.

**References**

Babbage, F. (2004). *Augusto Boal*. Routledge.

Freire, P. (1992). *Pedagogy of the Oppressed*. Continuum.

# UNAFRAID OF UNCERTAINTY: DEVELOPING GRASSROOTS LEADERS USING THEATRE IN AFGHANISTAN

By Kayhan Irani

*The concept of culture serves the basic need of naming such ineffable and inexplicable features of human existence as "meaning" and "spirit" and living together with others. [Stop thinking] of it as a name for a thing and come to view it instead as a placeholder for a set of inquiries — inquiries which may be destined to never be resolved. – N. M. Stolzenberg (2001, p. 444)*

*When does a session of the Theatre of the Oppressed end? Never — since the objective is not to close a cycle, to generate a catharsis, or to end a development. On the contrary, its objective is to encourage autonomous activity, to set a process in motion, to stimulate transformative creativity, to change spectators into protagonists. And it is precisely for these reasons that the Theatre of the Oppressed should be the initiator of changes the culmination of which is not the aesthetic phenomenon but real life. – Augusto Boal (1992, p. 245)*

Working to develop grassroots leaders within a cultural space, one in which participants use the tools of theatre to critically examine their own lives and explore multiple versions of reality, has allowed me to bear witness as people step into their own power and fight for justice in many parts of the world. As a culture worker and a Theatre of the Oppressed "Joker" (expert trainer/facilitator), I consider myself extremely lucky to be in the position of teaching and sharing intangible, but robust; unremarkable, but life changing, practices and tools with grassroots groups working for social change. The Theatre of the Oppressed methodology provides unique and rewarding tools to surface desires, analyze power relations, and mobilize capacities needed to move through dynamic change processes unique to transforming entrenched social issues and cultural norms. This chapter will go between New York City; Kabul, Afghanistan; and Kuala Lumpur, Malaysia as I recount an eight-year process of developing grassroots leaders in Afghanistan using Theatre of the Oppressed methods and practices, while weathering the larger structural forces of war, political upheaval, and economic strife. It will include the voice and journey of my project assistant and trainee Saleh Sepas, an Afghan theatre-maker and grassroots human rights activist turned refugee and refugee advocate.

Around the world, creative initiatives are making changes on the local level and beyond (Solinger et. al, 2008). People are coming to the arts as hopeful and fresh ways to participate in civic life and create a world they want to see. In Afghanistan, when Taliban rule ended, theatre arts were making a slow and steady comeback due to authentic Afghan efforts. Afghan storytellers organically lean towards telling stories with social and moralistic considerations and most productions are about local problems, social ills, and tragic situations. This community-minded, ethical stance is what gives storytellers a great deal of flexibility in reaching the public and maintaining their activities despite the systematic dismantling of arts and culture throughout the 30-plus years of conflict.

*Chapter 3 Image 1.* Photo Courtesy, by Kayhan Irani.

In 2010 I was brought into a rich community of storytelling for grassroots engagement situated within Afghan Education and Production Organization (AEPO), the largest single media-for-development project for Afghans run by Afghans. Set up in 1994, AEPO provides informative radio programming to refugees, internally displaced people, and the rural population of Afghanistan. Their programs are broadcast on the BBC Persian and Pashto Service, which have been broadcasting to Afghanistan since the 1960s and 1981, respectively. It so happens that AEPO is the home of the most popular radio drama in Afghanistan. In 1993, a group of Afghan radio producers in exile in Peshawar, carrying on the Afghan oral tradition of storytelling, started a radio drama to build community among the displaced Afghans now living in Pakistan. They called the show "New Home, New Life" and used humor and entertainment to reach Afghans of all ages, across borders. Storylines reflected real-life situations in listeners' lives and offered information listeners needed to help improve their own lives.

After returning to Kabul in 2002, the show continues to be popular; 39% of Afghan adults listen to "New Home, New Life." The characters have become household names in Afghanistan and after years of uninterrupted broadcast, the program has become an Afghan institution. In 2010, AEPO producers envisioned possibilities to build on the sincere relationship audiences have with the show in order to develop dialogue on important issues. What could live performance and public dialogue look like? How could they support civic engagement through drama? A theatre project was drawn up, where theatre troupes from select provinces would come to the AEPO offices to be trained in models of participatory theatre as well as in dialogue facilitation in order to generate and tell stories of local importance and to offer a space where everyday people could generate ideas and perspectives about eliminating entrenched social inequity. I was called in to train these provincial theatre troupe members.

From 2010 through 2013 I worked in Kabul (on and off) with AEPO to train ten different groups from provinces such as Balkh, Baghlan, Gazni, Ghor, Herat, Kandahar, Khost, Kunar, and Nangarhar in the

Theatre of the Oppressed tools, popular education methods, and ethical considerations of storytelling for social change. The program provided theoretical and practical training in order to explore the possibility of using live theatre as a location and format for constructing authentic Afghan forms of public discourse. Our work would expand on the operation of regional performance groups, training them to be regional leaders in this format and working with them to track the viability and development of this new approach. The project took on the challenge of improving and enhancing not only their skills as theatre artists but also their skills as dialogue facilitators and leaders of collective discussions. My specific training goals were to help participants develop their cultural organizing skills by:

- Training participants as practitioners of Image Theatre and Forum Theatre — a repertory of group dynamic techniques designed to enhance democratic group process, community-building and solidarity;
- Stimulating reflection on, and discussion of, the structure of local theatrical and non-theatrical participation models and strategies as well as the current practices and potential of theatre work;
- Providing participants with the opportunity to work with other theatre artists in a safe space in order to explore and confront issues of power and oppression that concern them; and
- Providing a collaborative structure designed to enable participants to directly apply and adapt, within the context of future facilitation/performance, elements of the training they will have received in the intensive workshop.

*Chapter 3 Image 2.* Photo Courtesy, by Kayhan Irani.

The training was delivered through the practice of Image Theatre where participants engage in and learn a process-based approach to group-building and dialogue; drama techniques useful for individual and group empowerment; group dynamic structures for analyzing power relations, conflict, and oppression; interactive dialogue models; and group facilitation skills. Sessions were a mixture of facilitated conversation, group work, and participatory theatre activities. We used games, role play, and power analysis to ground the theories of leadership and change as well as to understand local context and cultural perceptions more clearly.

The goals of creating a space where artist/activists can navigate ever-changing dynamics and contradictory points of view, while staying in a dynamic process of inquiry, can be explored through one key exercise called "Complete the Image." This exercise is Augusto Boal's theatrical exploration of Freire's popular education methodology "To See, To Analyze, and To Act." In pairs, and with no discussion or dialogue, participants use frozen body poses to explore telling a story, contending with change, cooperation, leadership, and praxis. One partner takes a pose of any kind to express something. The other partner considers that image, walks around it to "see" the image from all angles, analyzes what she would like to add to this image or transform about the image, and then steps in and takes a pose of her own to "complete." Since there is no discussion, neither partner knows the story the other is trying to tell but has to "act" to continue or change that story in some way. After the second partner enters the image, the first releases their pose and steps out to look at this new image. Then, the first partner steps back into the image, in a brand-new pose, to change the story again. Once she is back in the image, the second partner steps back out, looks, and re-enters in a new pose, making a new story. This process continues in improvised format for 10 minutes or so. The only rule is that you cannot manipulate or move your partner.

The exercise moves participants through an embodied analytic process where they must contend with the image they see, the "real" image, and how the world changes. Each new iteration of the image is made by the participant as well as around the participant. Their own body is the subject and the object of change. There is no right or wrong, only the process of analyzing, creating, and re-creating. What we see in this exercise is what we see in life: images of solidarity, violence, love, disconnect, support, and fun. But while I am asking participants to "complete the image," they are never making a complete image. They are always struggling with change, with perception, with taking a risk. They practice being inside the image, being analyzed by others, and being outside the image, analyzing it, and then taking a step to create something that did not exist before. They are embodying the goals of the Theatre of the Oppressed as a method for leadership development "...its objective is to encourage autonomous activity, to set a process in motion, to stimulate transformative creativity, to change spectators into protagonists" (Boal, 1992, p. 245). In order to gain a sense of comfort with this complex relationship between oneself and society — one needs practice. Instead of throwing the theatre artists into situations of conflict, entrenched power, and rigid social hierarchies, I have them explore themselves, how they act, what they feel, and what they are triggered by within a cultural space and through the aesthetic dimension.

The weaving of theatre, storytelling, and social issue analysis allowed us to develop individual and group insights, create new information, and share creative workarounds that fed into an approach to leadership that was uniquely theirs. In this way, culture as a set of inquiries, allowed us not only to discuss and consider what local conditions would permit but to expand the ways in which we could widen the types of acceptable public interaction. The leadership model then, doesn't hinge only on the dramatic structure of the theatre work but on the manner in which the facilitator and the actors can create a space for change, for dynamic discoveries, for the articulation of desires out from under one's social conditioning while maintaining safe boundaries of participation. The training prepares the theatre workers to carry on the work outside the workshop, with all the complications that may come. A fact reflected in a comment by Neda after she completed a training. She said that the training felt to her like the shopkeeper allowing his young assistant to run the shop after only a short time. I was pleased by the comment because it meant she truly felt the responsibility of the work and the real-life repercussions (good and bad) of what may come of it. Also, because in Afghanistan, hierarchies of power and decision-making are rigidly structured in all realms of society — from the home to the village, to school, even to the local shop. If they can feel the difference of working with horizontal and cooperative leadership development processes, then they will be able to transmit and replicate such processes in their leadership and practice.

My hopes were confirmed as I started getting reports from the field. The troupes were finding ways to innovate and make the format and tools their own. The artists from Kandahar reported back to the staff at AEPO that they hired a "white beard" (a male elder, who literally has a white beard) to travel with them for their shows. They gave him a very small role on stage, but his main purpose was to liaise with the community — to demonstrate that they are a respectable group by speaking with local elders, inviting them to the performances, and holding conversations to gauge whether the content of their show would be received well or with some tension. The participation of an elder within the event signifies to the villagers that this form of "entertainment" is not breaking any taboos or social norms. It helps audience members feel safe to engage and, come discussion time, having elders in the audience, who often have great decision-making power and status, allows space for dialogue that often doesn't happen in traditional decision-making spaces (jirgas). Women's concerns, youth concerns, the claims of the marginalized get to be heard by all strata of the local society. Importantly, the community's thoughts and points of view on these issues are aired in public. Whether any change is made in the moment is not the point. The point is that many perspectives are shared, and the community can take the temperature of its members about a vexing issue. All of this trickles down from the initial innovation of including a white beard in the work of the troupe and preparing him to do the work on stage and off. It is a brilliant way that the artists made these tools and theories their own and exerted their unique Afghan approach to getting the work done.

To keep the work going, the AEPO and I chose a staff member who would be the institutional knowledge keeper and a guide and mentor for the theatre workers to touch base with as they developed their role as Afghan community cultural leaders. Saleh Sepas, a young writer on staff and theatre maker, was identified. Saleh, in fact, was part of the first graduating class of Kabul University's Theatre Department after the Taliban rule ended. I worked closely with Saleh to help him learn all he could — not only about the technical aspects of creating a Forum Theatre piece but about the maieutics of being a Joker and the capacities of being a culture worker who can hold open a space for inquiry and possibility despite volatile and uncertain contexts. To understand his journey as a theatre worker and leader in arts for social change methods, I asked him to share his story.

*Chapter 3 Image 3.* Photo Courtesy, by Kayhan Irani.

### Saleh Sepas' Story

*Translated by Ahmad R. Salim*

The political climate has prevented theatre in Afghanistan from taking its natural course. As a result, at no point in its history has it benefitted from a milieu befitting the social and cultural needs of the population. A general review of theatre in Afghanistan confirms that it has never successfully attracted the attention and appreciation of the public either in the spheres of culture or in art. However, this points to the absence of locating and formulating a place and identity for the population as well. In a traditional society marred by volatility, new ideas and changes are perceived as a danger to the people and their way of life.

I was accepted as a student at Kabul University's Fine Arts & Theatre department in 2001. As I entered the university's grounds for the first time, I never imagined that I would be met with damaged buildings without windows and doors, but the reality was as such. The walls of the buildings were riddled with bullets, and it seemed that no corner was left undamaged. I was clueless as to where my department was located. I finally reached the campus directory with its faded colors and made my way towards the department. A mere 50 meters away from the building a stench overwhelmed the senses. When I came closer, a pack of stray dogs darted out of the building's basement and into the distance in search of food. Half of the building was destroyed as a result of a bomb's explosion and the other half was charred by fire. The repugnant stench emanating from the building's basement was unbearable. I was in a state of shock and disbelief. My mind couldn't make sense of it all and I regretted my decision and my chosen major.

Until 2001 throughout Afghanistan there was only one Fine Arts department in existence. A country of 30 million had no more than 35 students in the department of Fine Arts at Kabul University; the theatre division had 12 of those students. The difficulties of my studies started when my relatives and friends viewed my field of study with ridicule and mockery. They considered theatre a useless pursuit without a stable future. They considered studying theatre as shameful and banned me from pursuing my chosen field. The continuation of such pressure and restrictions forced me to pretend that I was studying literature and to no longer identify as a theatre student. The ridicule and mockery impacted my mental health, and my family was impacted negatively by the gossip and criticism of others. I became disheartened.

Finally, one day, my dad told me: "My dear son, it matters not what people say. Realize that you have a chance to earn a degree! Don't lose this opportunity. Go and pursue whatever you desire!" This was the spark that ignited the fire of hope and determination in me to commit to theatre. Being a university student inspired me to seek out and peruse different sources and familiarize myself with other artistic styles and genres. The first thing I learned from art during my studies was that one must think deeply, creatively, and look at things anew. In reality, art changed my outlook towards life and caused me to awaken to my humanity and civic duty. I discovered that I must not lead a selfish life but rather labor for my oppressed people, tired and exhausted from war, and for my ravaged country.

It was in 2004, after graduation from Kabul University, that I began my work at Radio Kalid in the production of the "Ending Violence Against Women" program. My work was contingent on researching and understanding the realities of the condition of women in Afghanistan. My visits would range from frequenting jails to the Commission for Human Rights to the Department of Women's Affairs. The result of this work familiarized me with the depth of sorrow and calamities that Afghan women faced. I found that the women of my country were brutalized under social difficulties, a culture of toxic masculinity, and archaic traditions. It was impossible to be desensitized to such unbearable pain and tragedy that permeated one's existence. As a result, I continued my work and efforts and decided to work for an organization with a wider audience and impact. I joined the BBC Afghan Education and Production Organization in 2008 as a writer for "New Home, New Life." Concurrently, I continued my involvement in theatre but always felt that in order to bring change in Afghan society there needed to be a stronger apparatus and means in place. I felt that an adherence to the classic method could not change an insular, conservative, and war-ravaged country like Afghanistan. As a result, I always felt that the traditional approach was insufficient.

Fortuitously, a great opportunity presented itself when Ms. Kayhan Irani, a celebrated playwright and theatre instructor, arrived in Kabul on July 12, 2010, to teach theatre companies in collaboration with the BBC/AEPO and familiarize them with the methods of the Theatre of the Oppressed. I attended the workshop, but Augusto Boal's method wasn't comprehensible to me initially. I questioned its effectiveness and, since I was seeking impactful methods, Theatre of the Oppressed did not pique my interest. However, towards the last days of the workshop my assessment and view of Theatre of the Oppressed changed. I was prodded to research and understand deeply and with openness. This in turn led to a gradual discovery that Augusto Boal's approach was exactly what I was after. I then decided to study and research his method further. In addition to Kayhan's expertise, the additional trainings she led in 2011 and 2012 allowed me to expand my skills and practice alongside other individuals. Though time was limited, we benefited greatly from these opportunities.

*Chapter 3 Image 4.* Photo Courtesy, by Kayhan Irani.

This methodology and approach were new and refreshing and led me to apply the medium of theatre to women's rights work being done through the Organization of Fast Relief and Development (OFRD). This project enabled the collection and dissemination of the struggles and narratives of Afghan women within the framework of the Theatre of the Oppressed. What we discovered was, despite the violence and oppression against them, the women had tremendous willpower, determination, and audacity to demand their rights and assert their role in forming their own future. Women entering the arena of public polemics and being willing to debate the basis of their rights was, in fact, a taboo shattering event and something that the theatre plays afforded them. This in turn led to more women critically thinking about the paucity of rights allotted to them and to more women striving to establish a greater voice and role for women in society.

During a performance of "The Other Face" in "Baghe Zanana" [Kabul's main park designated for women] the result was completely beyond our expectations. Following a discussion and input on women's rights, a middle-aged man came to the stage, eyes filled with tears, and vulnerably spoke about how he as a husband was experiencing tremendous difficulties given his wife's refusal to be a supportive partner to him and build their family. This gentleman, Rajab Ali, noted that for 14 years he had been struggling against the burden of keeping up with the Joneses. The audience of almost 200 women fully agreed with and supported him as he bemoaned the pressure to constantly buy jewelry and other material goods. At this time, the park's director approached the stage and noted that in the 14 years Rajab Ali had worked as a groundskeeper there, he had uttered nothing more than hello and goodbye. It was the theatre and the open platform of discussion that inspired him to speak and share his pain.

Sadly, such pressures and issues are all too common in Afghanistan and often lead to tremendous family problems and divorce. Thus, the need and benefit from the Theatre of the Oppressed is that it enables a milieu and safe space to discuss and engage in such conversations amongst the population. It has the potential to transmit values of tolerance, discussion, and openness as crucial components of a healthy society. Theatre groups from other areas were also able to contribute to the growth and reception of theatre in the country by emulating Boal's method and offering platforms for discussion and engagement for the attendees.

Due to the deteriorating security situation in the country, my family and I became refugees and arrived in Malaysia in 2016, and thus I was no longer able to participate in the field of theatre. The condition of other refugees and our own condition was extremely painful for me. The impact of depression, hopelessness, the lack of self-confidence, fear, and isolation are ingrained in the refugee experience and are not easily overcome. In reality, the life of a refugee is akin to the confines of a prison. The difference is that a prisoner must experience this isolation for the crime they've committed while the refugee must experience this isolation as a result of seeking security and safety. The initial six months following our arrival was unbearable. In an attempt to escape the hopelessness and despair I'd at times watch movies. Other times, with the help of my wife, I would plant flowers or turn to reading and writing. Certain days I'd just cry or try laughter to cheer up, but none of these were effective.

I submitted proposals to refugee assistance committees in Malaysia in the hopes of establishing the Theatre of the Oppressed there but never received a response from them. It was during this difficult period that my teacher and friend Kayhan Irani came to my aid and recommended that I start a refugee theatre group. I lacked the financial resources to materialize this vision, but Kayhan's support and online fundraising drive were of great help. This enabled me to begin recruiting Afghan refugees in Malaysia. Twenty young refugees signed up. Though none had any previous experience with theatre, I selected the six best candidates based on three criteria: 1) Belief in theatre as a platform for progress and change; 2) Creative talent; and 3) Time and commitment to the effort.

I chose Parastoo as the group's name. It is the word for swallow, a bird that's present in all seasons and places, associated with journeying and establishing a home nearly anywhere. The actors faced a very real and serious challenge in that their original assumption — that theatre is just mere performance, and they would easily be able to win an audience over — was misplaced. After receiving their parts, they soon realized that a lot of hard work goes into this art. A number of them were overwhelmed and doubtful. We even had a few individuals leave! However, we would spend an hour each day practicing the art through games that would build up the confidence and comfort of the actors. In addition, feedback and discussion were an important part of these activities.

Within a month, they realized that theatre truly is a medium of expression and a voice for them. Refugees are generally silent listeners, but through theatre they not only had a voice but also an audience. On August 11, 2017, refugee assistance organizations held a three-day Refugee Arts Festival in Kuala Lumpur, in which our play, *The Bitter Taste of History*, was showcased. Beyond our wildest imagination, Parastoo's performance left the audience spellbound. Prior to the performance, many doubted that the refugees could truly muster a convincing performance. But the performance spoke for itself and greatly moved people. It received a lot of attention and buzz from the Malaysian press and the social development sector but also from other refugees.

After this project, Roqayyah Yusufi, a 55-year-old woman who had protested against her son Hafeez joining the ranks of Parastoo, joined our subsequent work and brought her daughter-in-law and grandson as participants. She now enjoys theatre, and when I inquired about her change of heart, she noted that theatre gave her the confidence to speak. She recalled how when she had enrolled in English language classes she wouldn't speak in class and felt painfully shy with any attention. Now she wants to express herself, on stage. Then there is the case of a woman who plays a police officer in the play. She had endured a number of difficulties while being a refugee in Iran and had preferred to be secluded and hidden from the public. She is now so committed to her role in the drama and her performance that she doesn't want a break, even during pregnancy. There are numerous other refugee women who were previously barred from participation by their husbands, but who now have the freedom to be a part of our work.

The Afghan refugee community in Malaysia is very isolated and not very active. Through the work of Parastoo many people have been able to experience a more rewarding and hopeful way of life. Z is one such individual who had endured the difficulties and bleakness of being a refugee to such an extent that he almost committed suicide. Theatre has given him a new hope and he focuses his energy into refining his performances. Many of our actors, in general, had struggled with mental health issues and other difficulties. However, they are now sources of inspiration and a positive example for others in the community. Furthermore, our work in theatre has built bridges and understanding between the local communities and the refugee community.

Theatre has allowed for a nuanced and intimate understanding of the refugee population and their lives by the local communities. This includes positive media coverage and building relationships with Malaysian civil society. I think this is just the start of our work and potential. As we continue, we believe that through theatre we can help our refugee community make positive social, cultural, and legal progress; establish trusting and connected relationships with our host country; and offer support to refugees dealing with mental health issues and depression. We're more determined and thoughtful about the future of our work.

## Kayhan's Conclusion

Saleh is writing in Farsi, from Malaysia, where he is now a refugee because of the increasing violence against arts and culture workers in Afghanistan. In fact, one could say this intentional targeting of artists means that the work they are doing is truly powerful and transformative. Using the arts to understand and explore resistance is a powerful force for transformation because of the regenerative properties, the subjunctive action, the imagination, and the visioning process for creating the future. The women Saleh was working with in

Afghanistan identified the resource the Theatre of the Oppressed offered to them. They engaged with and used the tools to develop their own thinking despite all odds. In fact, it created a new space — one in which new social dynamics could emerge. A man no longer felt it was a diminished space, a "women's space," one in which he could lose his social status if he entered. In fact, he opened himself up even more once he engaged with the women in the space. He became vulnerable and offered his story — not to diminish the women's stories, but to say that he recognizes his struggle in theirs. He is also trapped by impossible gender roles and expectations. The women did not boo him off-stage; they recognized his struggle as real and as valid in the larger struggle against rigid gender roles. Theatre as a method of engagement and leadership development allows analytical and aesthetic faculties to work together so that individuals can rehearse and remember the complex weave needed to make a new social order — not simply one group being allowed to dominate the other. In such a space, artists and culture workers can offer hope, build agency, and create a space where dialogue can occur, new possibilities are imagined, and actions are initiated toward change.

*Chapter 3 Image 5.* Photo Courtesy, by Kayhan Irani.

However, Saleh's story reminds us that in a conflict zone, one's daily life is taken over by large, powerful forces. The ability to dream within that storm, to create amidst chaos, is a huge contradiction to the oppressive forces that want us to remain hopeless and confused. Even as a refugee, with no legal personhood or rights, there is power to be claimed. Saleh's hopelessness and depression living as a refugee was transformed into action as he reclaimed the theatre tools he had put to use in Afghanistan. His knowledge and practice of holding space for change, for conflict, for transformation had to be revived, and these tools and practices allowed him to take leadership and activate his Afghan refugee community to fight for themselves. The resilience of those in dynamic struggle is one of their strongest assets and, if activated and organized, is the very weapon that will bring about their own liberation. Any attempt to use theatre as a tool of change must be rooted in the capacity of the oppressed to solve their own problems and must work to strengthen their collective will. Defeat is never permanent and while the oppressed may suffer many setbacks, it is their will to continue that keeps them in the game.

Using the language of theatre, Parastoo has been able to build connections across lines of language, ethnicity, legal status, and gender. The performances are not only for refugee communities but for the Malaysian public to understand the lives that these newcomers have fled, and the lives they would like to make. When one person examines the world she lives in through art, it becomes a prompt for wider reflection. When art is shared, it builds relationships as others are generously invited in to think about and expand on the artist's vision. The exchange starts a process of questioning, analyzing, and processing. We are pulled into participating, whether in our own thoughts or in a discussion with others. Whether or not we find an answer or fully formulate an opinion, we have expanded our thinking. We have spent time engaging with possibility and reflecting on the present. It brings to light different perspectives, an alternative narrative, and it challenges us to acknowledge our limits.

Dialogue and artmaking with diverse populations in Malaysia, through a refugee lens, has led to the "buzz" that Saleh speaks about. But it's not a PR buzz, it's the genuine excitement of local organizations, schools, and development workers to build new relationships. Using theatre, Saleh has created a process of understanding and exchange that has extended out into the "real world." Through an aesthetic frame, one that assists us in performing our own power, he and his troupe members see the struggle but are not bogged down by it. Rather, they create links for continuing to move out of hardship — a process that is filled with imagination, creativity, creation, regeneration, and love. As Freire says, "Thus, nascent hope coincides with an increasingly critical perception of the concrete conditions of reality. Society now reveals itself as something unfinished, not as something inexorably given; it has become a challenge rather than a hopeless limitation" (Freire, 2013, p. 11).

## References

Boal, A. (1992). *Games for Actors and Non-Actors*. (A. Jackson, Trans). Routledge.

Freire, P. (2013/1974). *Education for Critical Consciousness*. Bloomsbury Academic. (Original work published 1974 by Sheed and Ward, Ltd.)

Solinger, R., Fox, M., & Irani, K. (2008). *Telling Stories to Change the World: Global Voices on the Power of Narrative to Build Community and Make Social Justice Claims*. Routledge.

Stolzenberg, N.M. (2001). What We Talk About When We Talk About Culture. In Borofsky, R., Barth, F., Shweder, R. A., Rodseth, L., & Stolzenberg, N. M. (2001). When: A Conversation about Culture. *American Anthropologist*, 103(2), 432–446. http://www.jstor.org/stable/683475

## About the Author

Kayhan Irani is an Emmy-award winning writer, a performer, a cultural activist, and a Theater of the Oppressed trainer. She creates storytelling spaces to build community, offer healing, and to re-connect participants to their innate creative power. She works internationally and in the U.S. with community organizations, social service providers, educational providers, and government agencies to expand what's possible when we deepen our relationships to community through story.

Kayhan was one of ten artists named by President Obama's White House as a 2016 White House Champion of Change for her storytelling work. Her one-woman show, *We've Come Undone* toured nationally and internationally, telling stories of Arab, South Asian and Muslim-American women in the wake of 9/11. She has trained hundreds of groups in Theater of the Oppressed and participatory storytelling tools over the years, both nationally and overseas, in Afghanistan, India, and Iraq.

She is currently building *There is a Portal*, (https://www. thereisaportal.com/) an immersive digital experience, pedagogy, and refugee leadership model which offers creative visioning spaces to build networks of belonging. She is also working day and night to find permanent safety and resettlement pathways for Afghan artists and culture workers at risk.

# CHAPTER 4

# WALK WITH ME: DECOLONIZATION AND RECONCILIATION THROUGH PARTICIPATORY THEATRE

CATHERINE ETMANSKI, WILL WEIGLER, NIELS AGGER-GUPTA, CHERYL HEYKOOP, LISA CORAK, ASMA-NA-HI ANTOINE, KRYSTAL COOK, & SHIRLEY ALPHONSE

## INTRODUCTION

By Susan J. Erenrich

This chapter features eight Indigenous and non-Indigenous authors from Canada. Their piece, *Walk with Me: Decolonization and Reconciliation Through Participatory Theatre* describes the process of creating a deeply engaging dramaturgical experience that more than 100 faculty and staff at their university have since participated in. The design process required diverse synergetic partners within their university and between the university, its Indigenous advisory council, and community members. The article also takes you step-by-step through the actual *Walk with Me* experience.

The purpose of this rare experiment was for the faculty and staff of the university to boldly and courageously begin to confront the legacy of colonization in Canada through an artistic platform. The team wanted to actively engage with and respond to the Calls to Action laid out by the Truth and Reconciliation Commission of Canada (TRCC) in 2015. Taking on a leadership role in this process was especially important to them in light of the fact that educational institutions have often been used as a tool of colonization. Since several members of the team have a background in experiential, adult learning and arts-based leadership, participatory theatre was the perfect approach. Formal experience or training isn't necessary for participatory theatre or Theatre of the Oppressed. The objective of the system, according to its creator, Augusto Boal, is to bring forth fruits, seeds, and flowers, not only to understand reality, "but to transform it to our liking" (Boal, 2006, p. 7).

For folks not familiar with the TRCC and its Calls to Action, it was part of a process of restorative justice in Canada. Its mandate was as follows: "There is an emerging and compelling desire to put the events of the past behind us so that we can work towards a stronger and healthier future. The truth telling and reconciliation process as part of an overall holistic and comprehensive response to the Indian Residential School legacy is a sincere indication and acknowledgement of the injustices and harms experienced by Aboriginal people and the need for continued healing. This is a profound commitment to establishing new relationships embedded in mutual recognition and respect that will forge a brighter future. The truth of our common experiences will help set our spirits free and pave the way to reconciliation" (http://www.residentialschoolsettlement.ca/ SCHEDULE_N.pdf and see https://www.rcaanc-cirnac.gc.ca/eng/ 1450124405592/1529106060525 for more information).

I hope readers are moved by this chapter. It is an important glimpse into how art can help us acknowledge the wrongs of the past and construct a better world for the future.

And, if you're interested, check out the plenary from the 2019 International Leadership Association global conference, which took place in Ottawa and featured keynote speaker Senator/Ànike Nìgànizi Murray Sinclair, the Chair of the TRCC. You can access the video of the plenary, as well as other resources from the conference at https:// ilaglobalnetwork.org/events/21st-global-conference-ottawa-2019/.

## References

Boal, A. (2006). *The Aesthetics of the Oppressed*. Routledge.

# *WALK WITH ME*: DECOLONIZATION AND RECONCILIATION THROUGH PARTICIPATORY THEATRE

By Catherine Etmanski, Will Weigler, Niels Agger-Gupta, Cheryl Heykoop, Lisa Corak, Asma-na-hi Antoine, Krystal Cook, & Shirley Alphonse

This article documents the work of a group of Indigenous and non-Indigenous people who collaborated to create a series of experiential educational events at Royal Roads University (RRU) that began to address the Truth and Reconciliation Commission of Canada's (TRCC) Calls to Action (2015b). This project is understood as a structural and organizational change effort not only toward reconciliation, but also toward bridging silos between community members, staff, and faculty, and building upon the perspectives of the Heron People Circle members and artists who guided us. The theatre-based methods used throughout this project and extensive collaboration across multiple offices throughout the university enabled this project to come into being. This article includes insights from the process itself, as well as a description of the campus events. It concludes with an acknowledgement that this project is but one step in a long journey.

### Context: The Era of Reconciliation and Canada's Colonial History

Indigenous people in Canada have "withstood the near destruction of their populations, social structures, and cultures as a result of colonial interventions" (Ball, 2005, p. 3). In this article, we chose to use the term *Indigenous*. In Canada, this term is frequently used interchangeably in different contexts with the terms *First Nations, First Peoples, Aboriginal, Native*, and *Indian*. Each term has its own nuanced meaning and political context. Wherever possible, it is preferable to use the specific nation or tribe's name. At RRU, the Indigenous advisory council (called the Heron People Circle) prefers the term *Indigenous*.

Colonial interventions in Canada have included violent acts of warfare, exposure to diseases, segregation, and restriction of travel through a system of land reservations, forced sterilization, confinement of Indigenous children in government sponsored Residential Schools, and social policies that promoted the legal adoption of Indigenous children into White families, all as part of a program to explicitly eradicate Indigenous culture (Ball, 2005).

As an outcome of the recent Truth & Reconciliation of Canada (TRCC) process (2015a), the Government of Canada now recognizes that the consequences of colonial interventions, such as the Indian Residential Schools policy, were "profoundly negative and... had a lasting and damaging impact on Aboriginal culture, heritage and language" (Regan, 2010, p. 1). The legacy of these damages — especially in terms of personal and intergenerational trauma, legal discrimination, and other forms of systemic racism — continues to this day. Revealing collective truths (Newman & Etmanski, 2019) about this context is part of the current era of truth and reconciliation in Canada. However, the concept of *reconciliation* is controversial and fraught with multiple, at times conflicting, interpretations.

Nevertheless, the TRCC findings (2015a) call for all Canadians to take action towards reconciliation. Moreover, in light of the above context, it is essential — and urgent — for educational institutions to take a leadership role. Specifically, the TRCC's Calls to Action (2015b) challenged members of institutions of higher education to:

"62. ii. . . . educate teachers on how to integrate Indigenous knowledge and teaching methods into classrooms" (2015b, p. 7); and,

"92. iii. Provide education for management and staff on the history of Aboriginal peoples, including the history and legacy of residential schools, the *United Nations Declaration on the Rights of Indigenous Peoples*, Treaties and Aboriginal rights, Indigenous law, and Aboriginal–Crown relations. This will require skills based training in intercultural competency, conflict resolution, human rights, and anti-racism" (2015b, p.10).

Since education has historically been used as a tool (or some might say weapon) of colonization, these Calls to Action present a genuine challenge, both professionally and personally, to administrators, faculty, and staff in higher education. Integrating Indigenous knowledge into classrooms effectively, for both Indigenous and non-Indigenous learners, is not simply about adding a sprinkling of Indigenous culture, knowledge, and methods to the status quo. It requires, at minimum, that non-Indigenous university staff, faculty, and students learn not only about the legacy of colonization, Eurocentrism, systemic racism, and cultural genocide in Canada, and the unequal impacts of these, but also consider how to take action to create needed changes and long-awaited justice (Lowman & Barker, 2015; Simpson, 2014).

By way of context, faculty in RRU's MA Leadership program (in which three of us teach) deliberately take an experiential, adult learning approach in their courses and seminars. Moreover, several members of the team have a background in arts-based leadership, teaching, and research. As a result, we were excited to apply some of these approaches to the task of reconciliation in our own institution. Since many of us had worked with theatre-based methods, we knew that participatory theatre, or *performative engagement*, could help us enter into new kinds of conversation about reconciliation (see e.g., Weigler, 2016; Weigler, 2015). As Jackson (2002) suggested, "the process of 'thinking with our hands' can short-circuit the censorship of the brain" (p. xxiii), thus creating a powerful and embodied learning and teaching experience and authentic community-building effect.

**Conceptualizing Leadership in This Context**

Although we know that the path to reconciliation will require leadership, the question of what constitutes good leadership, or even leadership per se, is highly contested (Grint, 2005). Our school has been particularly influenced by the leadership factors identified by Kouzes and Posner (2017) in which the leader models the way, inspires a shared vision, challenges the standard or traditional process, enables others to act, and encourages the heart, (i.e., cares about their followers), to accomplish the organization's goals and initiatives by following their own values and building good relationships. Furthermore, Indigenous/non-Indigenous relationships have traditionally suffered under the history of ethnocentric, heroic (Carlyle, 1849), charismatic, and patriarchal leaders and leadership. Yet, a number of positive shifts in the field of leadership studies have built momentum toward needed changes.

A major shift, of course, has been the development of a body of scholarship on Indigenous Leadership (e.g., Kenny & Fraser, 2012; Spiller, Maunganui Wolfgramm, Henry, & Pouwhare, 2020) as well as Indigenous and decolonizing methodologies (Kovach, 2010; Tuhiwai Smith, 2012; Tuhiwai Smith, et al., 2019; Wilson, 2008). Raelin's (2016) understanding of "leadership as a practice" has also been influential among contributors to this project from RRU's School of Leadership Studies. This relates to the notion of organizational citizenship, which is part of the motivation for taking this initiative within our own institution. In addition, we have been inspired by the concept of inclusive leadership, which includes honoring organizational members' needs to be recognized as both belonging to — and able to make a unique contribution to — their organizations (see Agger-Gupta & Harris, 2017 or Stefani & Blessinger, 2017).

A number of additional ideas have been influential in the approach we have taken to this initiative. Experiential learning, for example, as articulated by Kolb and Kolb (2017) and Knowles, (1975) describes adult learning as a cyclical process where the learner proceeds through a cycle of personal experience with a topic; reflecting on this experience; planning some related action on the topic; experiencing the action; and then continuing the cycle by reflecting on the new experience (while linking it to earlier experiences, broader knowledge, and cumulative understanding). In addition, Taylor (2011) suggests that most adult learning takes place in the domain of complexity. Therefore, learning is an emergent process whose outcomes cannot truly be predicted in advance. Freire (2005) and Horton and Freire (1990) describe how adult learning can result in transformative changes at a personal level. Whether dealing with topics involving liberation from bureaucratic or other kinds of oppressions, personal participation is required in order to learn about and understand the larger systems working to maintain the oppressive situation(s). Participation thereby allows for personal breakthroughs in understanding and what Freire (2005) called, conscientização, or coming to critical consciousness. However, the experience of a personal breakthrough, as Tuck and Yang (2012) have argued, while necessary, is still only the very first step of a much larger process that requires systemic actions to move reconciliation forward.

A number of authors, most notably Etmanski, Fulton, Nasmyth, and Page (2014), have described the need for authenticity, being present and aware, and experiencing joy in the working of their team or organization as crucial for successful leadership. This can be especially useful when supporting ourselves and others to develop empathy with the issues faced by Canada's Indigenous populations, rather than experiencing a process that only produces feelings of defensiveness, guilt, or shame. A related influence in the school has been maintaining an "orientation to possibility" (Harris & Agger-Gupta, 2015), which involves seeing what might actually be possible under the circumstances of the current moment. This builds on the notion of appreciative inquiry (Agger-Gupta & Perodeau, 2017; Watkins, Mohr, & Kelly, 2011) as a philosophical orientation toward change as a mystery to be understood through shared stories, rather than as a problem to be fixed. Within the context of forging approaches to contributing to genuine reconciliation, the appreciative inquiry approach and philosophy extends to include recognition of the need for appreciation, care, and even love for every individual (Gray Smith, 2017). All of these ideas coalesce in teaching leadership through a narrative and arts-based approach to adult experiential and emergent learners (see, for example, Bishop, Weigler, Lloyd, & Beare, 2017; Etmanski, 2014; Weigler, 2015; and Weigler, 2016).

Mindful of these aspects of leadership, those of us in RRU's School of Leadership Studies chose to take a lead role in facilitating an organizational dialogue among staff and faculty at the university so that we could all take steps to better understand reconciliation. Although we have engaged in learning about our Indigenous neighbors as part of ongoing professional development in our own school, this was the first occasion where we have responded to the TRC's Final Report and Calls to Action (2015b) by working explicitly on reconciliation at the level of the entire organization. With our team in place, and with guidance from the Heron People Circle, we worked together for several months to design and stage the experiential learning event, *Walk with Me: A Step on the Path Toward Reconciliation at RRU.*

## Coming Together: The Right People at the Right Time in the Right Place

One of our core intentions in designing this experiential learning event was to create an environment where staff and faculty from across the RRU community could come together to engage with the perspectives of Indigenous peoples without requiring Indigenous facilitators to be put in the position of always having to be the authorities on the delivery of cultural content. Instead, we invited participants to engage in an embodied and performative dialogue with a series of writings by a diverse range of Indigenous authors and allies. We hoped that direct personal investment and human connections with these profoundly moving stories would lead participants to a new way of perceiving the lives and perspectives of Indigenous peoples and perhaps stir a renewed commitment to becoming more connected with them, taking steps to forge the kind of relationships that lead to sustained support.

*Walk with Me* was an immersive theatre experience that required multiple collaborative partners within a post-secondary institution that had no history of anything theatrical (outside of student improvisations as part of class assignments in other subject areas). As a small, special-purpose university dedicated to mid-career professionals, RRU has neither a theatre-style auditorium, nor any performance-based programs. Nevertheless, many members of the RRU community are familiar with experiential, arts-based methods, as they are a cornerstone to RRU's learning, teaching, and research model (Harris, Wallinga, & RRU Faculty & Staff, 2019). After a site visit from the artistic team, we set our event in the Quarterdeck, a large rectangular room on the RRU campus.

Given the nature of the activity, one of the needs of this event was privacy. The team also hoped to transport people from the mindset of their daily workday worlds into an alternate mindset, even when it took place in familiar surroundings. After arranging to black out the numerous glass doors surrounding the space, we created a pathway with different stations along the route, lending an air of ritual to the event.

An important aspect of our planning process was ensuring the Heron People Circle members were well looked after during the event and provided with a place for rest and nutrition. For example, our catering team worked with us to bring food and beverages into a room adjacent to the event where food is typically not permitted. This may seem like a small detail, but these details became essential to walking the talk of our work together.

This project could not have been successful without support from the Heron People Circle members. After all, it was their life experiences we were remembering and honoring throughout. Through Asma-na-hi's leadership, her office of Indigenous Education and Student Services hosts a monthly gathering of the Heron People Circle, which provides ongoing opportunities for guidance on any RRU projects related to Indigenous ways of being, doing, and knowing. They enabled us to tether this project to their insights regarding the purpose and intentions behind the spirit of reconciliation. The title of the event was born when team member, and member of the Heron People Circle, Elder Shirley Alphonse suggested that no one could actually "walk in my shoes" if they have not experienced what she or other Indigenous people have experienced. She offered that perhaps they could instead "walk with me" for a little while to develop greater understanding.

## Walking Together: An Overview of the Experiential Learning Workshop

The event was, in essence, a series of one-hour experiential learning workshops, intentionally involving fewer than 20 participants each hour. Each workshop guided participants through a sequence of clearly defined experiential stations where participants would metaphorically and physically walk from one end of the room to the other, taking steps on the path to reconciliation. Members of the Heron People were present throughout the day to offer support, guidance, and wisdom in various capacities, and a team of volunteers (including members of the School of Leadership) offered support in the preparation and execution of the *Walk with Me* event. We are grateful to all those who lent their support.

The event was successfully hosted on October 16, 2018, when 60 people participated, and again on February 19, 2019, with 50 people. Employees from all across campus — e.g., program staff, librarians, gardeners, staff who support educational technology, marketing, recruitment, faculty, and some senior executives — attended both sessions. Because this was intended to enhance organizational learning among staff and faculty, we did not invite students to these events.

Each experiential learning workshop began with a brief orientation outside the event space explaining a little about what would happen inside, the potentially sensitive nature of the topic and experience, and a reminder for participants to be both appreciative and gentle with themselves and others.

Once participants entered into the workshop space they were greeted by members of the team and welcomed to the ancestral lands of the *Xwsepsum* (Esquimalt) and *Lkwungen* (Songhees) families through a video from Songhees' Chief Ron Sam. Only certain knowledge keepers, or those with permission from local chiefs, have permission to welcome people to these ancestral lands. Participants were invited to set an intention for the day, become present in the experience, and get oriented to the five stations or experiences they would walk through together. Through our introduction and through a subsequent welcome to the event from one of the Heron People Circle members in Lkwungen language, the intention was to establish a sense that this was a space set apart from business-as-usual at the university.

**Step One: Grounding in Place.**

The first station focused on the significance of locating oneself as living and working on the traditional lands of Indigenous peoples. Heron People Circle members' presence at the event contributed to the understanding that where we are located was not an issue of the past; Xwsepsum and Lkwungen families continue to live and thrive on this land. At this station, participants were invited to learn more about the Indigenous name of their place of birth or where they currently reside. We brought in various maps of the province of British Columbia, the entire breadth of Canada, and the continent of North America. Each map featured the traditional names and locations of the Indigenous peoples of these lands, and participants were invited to locate the place where they came from, or currently live. An iPad app staffed by a volunteer showed the name of the traditional lands of whatever location (participant's birthplace or current residence) was entered (Native-land, n.d.). Name badges were available for participants to write down these place name(s).

*Chapter 4 Image 1.* Elder Shirley Alphonse and Will Weigler with a map of what is now the province of British Columbia. Photo Credit Brian MacDonald.

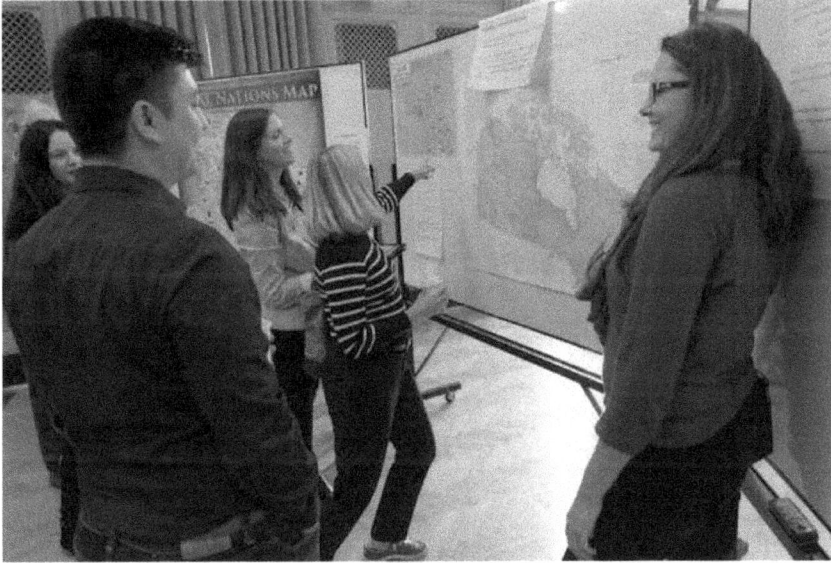

*Chapter 4 Image 2.* Team members interacting with Indigenous place name maps. Foreground: Keil Kodama and Catherine Etmanski; center: Sherry Richards and Beverly deVries; background left corner: Niels Agger-Gupta and Krystal Cook. Photo Credit Brian MacDonald.

## Step Two: Connecting With Stories.

Following the opportunity to explore different orientations to place, participants were invited to take another step on the path and engage with a short reading by an Indigenous author or a non-Indigenous, immigrant-descendant ally, as well as several excerpts from historical documents. Over a dozen short readings — one- to three-page excerpts in the form of memoirs, poetry, fiction, letters to parents from residential schools, song lyrics, and testimonies — were placed on tables. Participants were invited to partner with three or four others to look through the readings on the table, choose one with a title that intrigued them, and discuss the reading together. We explained that the next activity built on these readings was intended as a laboratory experiment of sorts to test the idea of how we might experience empathy for the lived experience of Indigenous peoples through creative engagement with these readings.

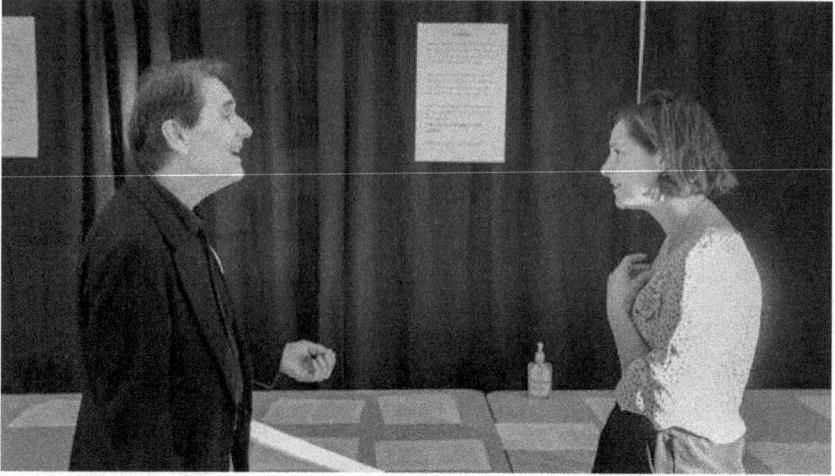

*Chapter 4 Image 3.* Will Weigler and Cheryl Heykoop at the story selection station.
Photo Credit Brian MacDonald.

### Step Three: Embodying the Stories.

Once participants had read their selection, they were invited to set
aside scholarly analysis and, instead, meet what they encountered
from a place of empathy and, perhaps, vulnerability. We supplied each
team with a handout including a list of prompts or guides designed to
encourage them to allow the material to register on an emotional level
and to sit with the feelings that emerged.

In the handout we also laid out the next step in the activity. Although
we wanted the experience to be generative, open-ended, and empathy-
building, we understood that our role as leaders involved carefully
crafting the way the invitation was framed. Specifically, we wanted to
discourage readers from projecting attitudes of pity toward the
Indigenous people in these stories or to perceive them as hopeless or
powerless victims. We found an answer to this challenge by offering
prompts that could contain the powerful paradox of an individual or a
people striving to hold on to their buoyant, resilient, and loving spirits
while experiencing extraordinarily oppressive circumstances. In this
way, by focusing the readers' search parameters (so to speak), we
could direct participants to see what they might not otherwise have
recognized within a story of personal and social trauma. To round out

the prompt, we asked them to find a physical action that quintessentially embodied a particularly significant aspect of what happened in the story — a closing in on proximity, a sudden silence, the placement of an object, etc.

Up until this point we had asked the participants to gather and pool their responses to the readings. Now, while still at the third station, the activity turned performative. The flip side of the handout invited participants to link the physical actions they had developed with a *memory from their own life*. Then, in collaboration with their partners at the table, the handout invited participants to create a short poem, a brief story, a single performed image, a few lyrics of a song, or a simple movement that incorporated the power of the same physical action just developed but now framed in the context of *their own experiences*. Participants were given 10 to 15 minutes to develop and practice their team piece. They were asked to resist the temptation to re-enact the events in the passage (that is, to act out someone else's story) and, instead, to focus on a connection with their own experiences.

Since performance-based work is uncommon in our daily university interactions, we acknowledged that moving into a more performative space could be perceived as a risk for many participants. As such, we described the room as being a Perfection-free Zone (von Koss, 2007), explaining to the participants that no one expected the presentations to be a polished performance. Each group embraced the task with enthusiasm, though some showed more trepidation than others. With just a bit of encouragement, clarification of the task, and time-keeping announcements from the facilitators, everyone had soon created a short performative response to their readings.

*Chapter 4 Image 4.* Sherry Richards, Keil Kodama, and Catherine Etmanski discussing a story. Photo Credit Brian MacDonald.

## Step Four: Performing Our Empathetic Response to the Stories.

We then gathered again in one large group and moved to the fourth station: a collection of chairs arranged in a semicircle all facing a slightly raised stage. It was at this station that we were joined by several of the Heron People Circle members, whom we had invited to share in the presentations of the work. Each group took turns moving up to the stage, first telling us their names and what they did at the university, then offering their brief performances based on the elements in their readings that had moved them and had resonated with something in their own lives. Hanging above the stage where we could all see it was a long paper banner emblazoned with a quotation from Thomas King, used repeatedly throughout his (2003) book The Truth About Stories, written in large letters: "Don't say in the years to come that you would have lived your life differently if only you had heard this story. You've heard it now."

After each group's presentation, their audience of co-participants, facilitators, and Heron People Circle members reflected on what they heard and saw. The performers then shared their own thoughts on the links between the performed piece they had created and the story they had read. When all the presentations had been offered and discussion had come to a close, we invited everyone to move to the fifth and final station, which was set up near the exit.

*Chapter 4 Image 5.* Will Weigler and Krystal Cook demonstrate an embodiment of story. Photo Credit Brian MacDonald.

*Chapter 4 Image 6.* Kathy Bishop and Cheryl Heykoop demonstrate an embodiment of story. Photo Credit Brian MacDonald.

## Step Five: Closure Through Smudging and Encouraging Humble Allyship.

As they exited the room, participants found several large wall posters identifying specific actions one can take to build respectful, sustainable relationships with Indigenous people and their communities and to support their aspirations for social justice. We also set up tables with a wide array of books by Indigenous authors and by immigrant-descendant authors who have written about the legacy of colonialism. On the tables, notepads and pens encouraged participants to jot down (or photograph) intriguing book titles, or names of authors, so that in the days and weeks ahead they could seek out copies at bookstores and libraries to read. Team member Elder Shirley Alphonse then invited people to engage in a smudging ceremony, if participants were interested. Lastly, participants filled out feedback forms and made their way out the exit, leaving the facilitators time to reset the room before the next scheduled group arrived.

*Chapter 4 Image 7*. Elder Shirley Alphonse's smudging altar. Photo Credit Brian MacDonald.

*Chapter 4 Image 8*. Members of the team reviewing resources on being an ally. Photo Credit Brian MacDonald.

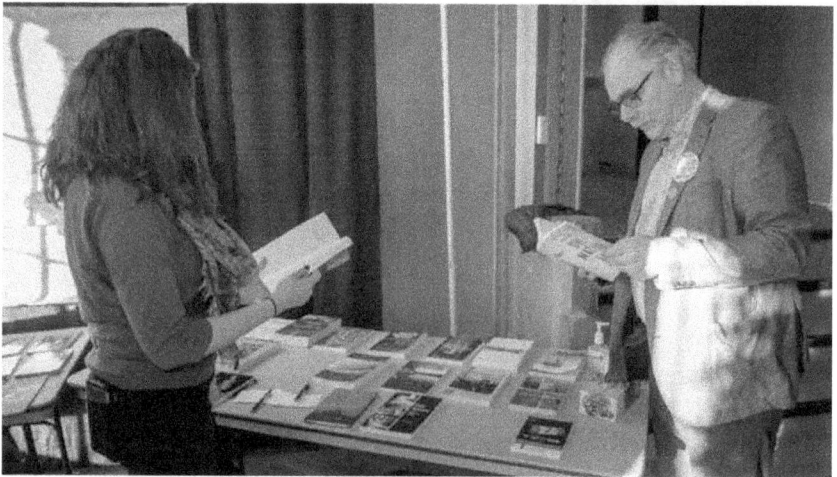

*Chapter 4 Image 9*. Catherine Etmanski and Niels Agger-Gupta browsing books on decolonization. Photo Credit Brian MacDonald.

## Closing Thoughts

In this article, we have described several elements of our work on the path to reconciliation at RRU. As guided by the Heron People Circle members and as mentioned at the outset, we acknowledged that this project is but one step in a long journey. Yet, for us, it was an important step in coming together to learn from one another as we endeavored to lead within our own organization and define the process of leadership, "whereby an individual influences a group of individuals to achieve a common goal" (Northouse, 2018, p.4). With two successful events behind us, our intention now is to host follow-up learning circles to move ourselves and our university community into deeper dialogue about what it means to truly decolonize our minds as well as our institution. In our team's writing process through this article, we have already begun to coalesce our learning. One parallel development has been that the university has begun to take seriously the practice, at the beginning of meetings, to acknowledge the traditional lands of the Lekwungen and Xwsepsum families (the Indigenous peoples where RRU is located) (RRU, 2019). It is our hope that the seeds of peacebuilding, empathy, decolonization, and reconciliation we have collectively planted will take root and grow strong in the years ahead — within ourselves, at this university, and beyond.

## References

Agger-Gupta, N., & Harris, B. (2017). Chapter 17: Dialogic change and the practice of inclusive leadership. In A. Boitano & H. E. Schockman (Eds.), *Breaking the Zero-Sum Game: Transforming Societies Through Inclusive Leadership* (pp. 303–320). Emerald.

Agger-Gupta, N., & Perodeau, A. (2017). Chapter 11: Appreciative Inquiry in RRU Mid-Career Student Life. In D. Hamilton, P. Márquez, N. Agger-Gupta, S. Grundy, G. Veletsianos, & V. Forssmann, (Eds.), *Engaging Students in Life-Changing Learning: The Royal Roads University Learning and Teaching Model in Practice* (Revised ed., pp. 237–253). Royal Roads University. https://learningandteachingmodel.pressbooks.com/chapter/appreciative-inquiry-in-rru-mid-career-student-life/

Ball, J. (2005). 'Nothing About Us Without Us': Restorative Research Partnerships Involving Indigenous Children and Communities in Canada. In A. Farrell (Ed.) *Exploring Ethical Research With Children* (pp. 81–96). Open University Press/McGraw Hill Education.

Bishop, K., Weigler, W., Lloyd, T., & Beare, D. (2017). Fostering Collaborative Leadership Through Playbuilding. In C. Etmanski, K. Bishop, & M. B. Page (Eds.), *Adult learning Through Collaborative Leadership*. New Directions in Adult and Continuing Education No. 156, Winter 2017. Jossey-Bass Quarterly Sourcebooks.

Carlyle. (1849). The Hero and the Printer. *Scientific American*, 5(8), 59–59. http://www.jstor.org/stable/26130423

Etmanski, C., Fulton, M., Nasmyth, G., & Page, M. B. (2014). The Dance of Joyful Leadership. In K. Goldman Schuyler, J. E. Baugher, K. Jironet, and L. Lid-Falkman (Eds.), *Leading With Spirit, Presence, and Authenticity* (pp. 91–108). Jossey-Bass.

Etmanski, C., Weigler, W., Agger-Gupta, N., Heykoop, C., Corak, L., Antoine, A., Cook, K., & Alphonse, S. (forthcoming). Walk With Me: Engaging in Participatory Theatre to Walk the Path to Reconciliation in a Canadian University Context. In C. McGregor & S. Bedi (Eds.), *Diverse Leadership Landscapes: Exploring the Terrain*. McGill-Queen's University Press.

Freire, P. (2005). *Education for Critical Consciousness*. London, UK: Continuum.

Grint, K. (2005). Problems, Problems, Problems: The Social Construction of 'Leadership.' *Human Relations*, 58(11), 1467–1494. https://doi.org/10.1177/0018726705061314

Harris, B., & Agger-Gupta, N. (2015). The Long and Winding Road: Leadership and Learning Principles That Transform. *Integral Leadership Review*, (January–February). http://integralleadershipreview.com/12569-115-long-winding-road-leadership-learning-principles-transform/

Harris, B., Wallinga, J., & RRU Faculty & Staff. (2019, October). Learning, Teaching, & Research Model. RRU Centre for Teaching & Educational Technologies. http://ctet.royalroads.ca/learning-teaching-research-model

Horton, M., & Freire, P. (1990). *We Make the Road by Walking: Conversations on Education and Social Change.* (B. Bell, J. Gaventa, & J. Peters, Eds.). Temple University Press.

Jackson, A. (2002). Translator's Introduction to the First Edition. In Boal, A. *Games for Actors and Non-Actors* (2nd ed, A. Jackson, Trans.) (pp.xxii–xxix). Routledge.

Kenny, Carolyn., & Fraser, T. N. (2012). *Living Indigenous Leadership: Native Narratives on Building Strong Communities.* UBC Press.

King, T. (2003). *The Truth About Stories* (6th ed). House of Anansi Press.

Kolb, A. Y., & Kolb, D. A. (2017). *The Experiential Educator: Principles and Practices of Experiential Learning.* Experience Based Learning Systems.

Kovach, M. E. (2010). Indigenous Methodologies: Characteristics, Conversations, and Contexts (Reprint). University of Toronto Press, Scholarly Publishing Division.

Kouzes, J. M., & Posner, B. Z. (2017). *The Leadership Challenge: How to Make Extraordinary Things Happen in Organizations.* John Wiley & Sons, Incorporated.

Knowles, M. S. (1975). *Self-Directed Learning: A Guide for Learners and Teachers.* Cambridge Adult Education Company.

Lowman, E. B., & Barker, A. J. (2015). *Settler: Identity and Colonialism in 21st Century Canada.* Fernwood.

Native-land (n.d.) [website]. https://native-land.ca/

Hayalthkin'geme, C. N., & Etmanski, C. (2019). Truthful Engagement: Making the Witness Blanket, an Ongoing Process of Reconciliation. *Engaged Scholar Journal: Community-Engaged Research, Teaching, and Learning, 5*(2), 237-243. https://doi.org/10.15402/esj.v5i2.68347

Northouse, P. G. (2018). *Leadership: Theory and Practice* (8th edition). Sage Publications.

Raelin, J. A. (Ed.). (2016). *Leadership-as-Practice: Theory and Application*. Routledge.

Regan, P. (2010). *Unsettling the Settler Within: Indian Residential Schools, Truth Telling, and Reconciliation in Canada*. University of British Columbia Press.

Royal Roads University. (2019). *Acknowledgement of Traditional Land*. http://www.royalroads.ca/about/aboriginal-relations/aboriginal-relations

Simpson, L. B. (2014). Land as Pedagogy: Nishnaabeg Intelligence and Rebellious Transformation. *Decolonization: Indigeneity, Education & Society* 3(3), 1–25. https://jps.library.utoronto.ca/index.php/des/article/view/22170

Spiller, C., Maunganui Wolfgramm, R., Henry, E., & Pouwhare, R. (2020). Paradigm Warriors: Advancing a Radical Ecosystems View of Collective Leadership From an Indigenous Māori Perspective. *Human Relations*, 73(4), 516–543. https://doi.org/10.1177/0018726719893753

Smith, M. G. (2017). *Speaking Our Truth: A Journey of Reconciliation*. Orca Book Publishers.

Stefani, L., & Blessinger, P. (Eds.). (2017). Inclusive Leadership in Higher Education: International Perspectives and Approaches. Routledge.

Taylor, M. M. (2011). *Emergent Learning for Wisdom*. Palgrave Macmillan.

Truth and Reconciliation Commission of Canada. (2015a). *Honouring the Truth, Reconciling for the Future: Summary of the Final Report of the Truth and Reconciliation Commission of Canada*. https://ehprnh2mwo3.exactdn.com/wp-content/uploads/2021/01/Executive_Summary_English_Web.pdf

Truth and Reconciliation Commission of Canada. (2015b). *Truth and Reconciliation Commission of Canada: Calls to action*. Winnipeg, Canada: Truth and Reconciliation Commission of Canada. https://www2.gov.bc.ca/assets/gov/british-columbians-our-governments/

indigenous-people/aboriginal-peoples-documents/
calls_to_action_english2.pdf

Tuck, E., & Yang, K. W. (2012). Decolonization Is Not a Metaphor. *Decolonization: Indigeneity, Education & Society, 1*(1), 1–40. https://jps.library.utoronto.ca/index.php/des/article/view/18630

Tuhiwai Smith, L., Tuck, E., Yang, K. W., John, K. D., Goodyear-Ka'ōpua, N., Batz, G., Mays, K. T., Whalen, K., Gaudry, A., Picton, C., Lorenz, D. E., Tufue-Dolgoy, R., Newberry, T., Trujillo, O. V., Xemŧoltw, N., & Karyn Recollet. (2019). *Indigenous and Decolonizing Studies in Education: Mapping the Long View* (L. T. Smith, E. Tuck, & K. W. Yang, Eds.). Routledge. https://doi.org/10.4324/9780429505010.

Tuhiwai Smith, L. (2012). *Decolonizing Methodologies: Research and Indigenous Peoples* (2nd Revised edition). Zed Books.

von Koss, D. (2007). *Doug von Koss – On the Good Enough Elder*. https://dougvonkoss.com/elder.htm

Watkins, J. M., Mohr, B. J., & Kelly, R. (2011). *Appreciative Inquiry: Change at the Speed of Imagination* (2nd ed.). Pfeiffer.

Weigler, W. (2015). *From the Heart: How 100 Canadians Created an Unconventional Theatre Performance About Reconciliation*. Victoria International Development Education Association.

Weigler, W. (2016). *The Alchemy of Astonishment: Engaging the Power of Theatre*. University of Victoria.

Wilson, S. (2009). *Research Is Ceremony: Indigenous Research Methods*. Fernwood Publishing.

**About the Authors**

Asma-na-hi Antoine. Asma-na-hi translates as "Caring for Precious Ones." It comes from my late mother Vera Thompson of the Toquaht Nation, Nuu-chah-nulth lands. My last name comes from my late father Eugene Antoine from the Saik'uz Nation, Carrier Sekani lands. I am the Director of Indigenous Engagement at RRU.

Catherine Etmanski's heritage is from the Kasubian region of Poland, Clanranald in Scotland as well as Dutch, British, and Irish-American. She is a professor and director of the School of Leadership Studies (SoLS) at RRU.

Cheryl Heykoop. I grew up in Ontario on the ancestral lands of Anishinabewaki and Huron-Wendat Peoples. I am of Dutch and English origin. I am an associate professor with the School of Leadership Studies at RRU.

Krystal Cook. I am a Kwakwaka'wakw Woman from the Namgis First Nation. I am a graduate of the En'owkin International School of Writing at the University of Victoria and the Centre for Indigenous Theatre's Native Theatre School Program. I am a theatrical performer, facilitator, and poet. I work with Aboriginal Nations Education Division in School District 61.

Lisa Corak. I was born on the traditional lands of the Tsleil-Waututh people. I worked professionally in theatre, primarily as a production stage manager, for over 15 years. I now enjoy supporting the leadership programs at RRU, especially the experiential learning activities.

Niels Agger-Gupta's heritage is multicultural: German-Norwegian-Indian. He is an associate professor with SoLS at RRU.

Shirley Alphonse. I am from the Cowichan Tribes and a member of the Heron People Circle. I serve as a spiritual representative of the T'Souke Nation and I am the Elder in Residence for BC Premier, John Horgan. I work with people of all ages, including children and youth, to share my teachings to preserve cultural knowledge.

Will Weigler. I was born and raised on the lands of the Multnomah peoples in Portland, Oregon. I am a theatre director, playwright, producer, and professional storyteller, and have written five books on different aspects of co-creating theatre with people in communities about the issues that matter to them.

# SECTION 2

## INTERVIEWS WITH TROUBADOURS OF CONSCIENCE

# CHAPTER 5

# A VOICE FOR INTEGRITY, JUSTICE, AND PEACE

## AN INTERVIEW WITH HOLLY NEAR

## INTRODUCTION

By Susan J. Erenrich

Holly Near joined me for an informal chat on July 9, 2018, at the WERA.FM audio suite in Arlington, Virginia. For folks not familiar with Holly, you are in for a real treat. For more than five decades Holly has been a strong voice for integrity, justice, and peace influenced by social change movements around the globe. She writes and sings songs that look at the world through the lens of feminism, anti-racism, and peace. She was born in rural Northern California. Holly has a powerful performance style that rings true whether from a stage like Carnegie Hall or from a makeshift platform in war-torn El Salvador.

**Listen**

You can listen to our conversation, interspersed with songs she recorded throughout her career, at the following links:

https://www.mixcloud.com/WasntThatATime/wasnt-that-a-time-episode-79-a-conversation-with-singer-cultural-activist-holly-near-pt-1/

https://www.mixcloud.com/WasntThatATime/wasnt-that-a-time-episode-82-a-conversation-with-singer-cultural-activist-holly-near-part-2/

https://www.mixcloud.com/WasntThatATime/wasnt-that-a-time-episode-84-a-conversation-with-singer-cultural-activist-holly-near-part-3/

## A VOICE FOR INTEGRITY, JUSTICE, AND PEACE - AN INTERVIEW WITH HOLLY NEAR

### Susan J. Erenrich

You are tuned in to *Wasn't That A Time: Stories & Songs That Moved The Nation* on WERA-LP Arlington, Virginia 96.7 FM. I'm Susie Erenrich, your host for the hour. I'd like to welcome my special in-house studio guest Holly Near. Holly was in Washington, D.C. for Sisterfire. Thank you for coming.

### Holly Near

It's my pleasure. I'm glad you invited me because I know that there are a lot of people who listen to your show who like folk music and political music and historic music. So, it's nice to be part of that.

### Susan J. Erenrich

Well, it's an honor to have you here. And just so listeners know, Holly has a fantastic new album that you can learn about on her website called *Holly Near 2018*. So, we're going to dive right in. I saw you at the Kennedy Center [John F. Kennedy Center for the Performing Arts] on the evening of July 7th for a fantastic gathering. Holly was in the District of Columbia on July 7th and 8th to celebrate the 40th anniversary of Sisterfire at the Smithsonian Folklife Festival in Washington, D.C. Why don't you tell listeners about some of the origins of Sisterfire and your involvement in this amazing experiment?

### Holly Near

Sisterfire was one of many women's music festivals that happened over the last 40 years, and this particular one was an urban festival held in metro Washington, D.C. There were others that were more out in the land and/or in smaller communities, but this is the first one, I think, that was really in the middle of a city. It was also intentionally designed and organized from the bottom up to be multicultural. So, this is an anniversary of Sisterfire, but prior to Sisterfire was a group that was formed called Roadwork, and Roadwork was an organization also completely committed to multicultural music by women —

women identified music, music that spoke to women's lives from a multicultural point of view. And the point of it, and the title of the organization, Roadwork, was to put women on the road — to make it possible for feminist and outspoken women artists to have the organizational capacity to actually tour in the United States predominantly but also to some other countries.

This was before cell phones. This was before fax machines. I know it sounds like I'm speaking as if I'm a dinosaur, but it was quite extraordinary to try to find one another and to make this music accessible to people. It was also music that wasn't being recorded by mainstream record companies. So not only did we have to create our own production companies, we started our own record companies, and we opened up our own book and record stores. If we didn't know how to do something, we trained ourselves. When I first started my record company in 1972, we didn't know any women engineers in the whole country, in the whole world. And we found one artist, I think it was Chris Williamson, who found an engineer up in Oregon, Joan Lowe. And then up popped Leslie Ann Jones, the extraordinary engineer who's now the chief engineer at Skywalker Sound. So back then none of this was accessible. Women weren't taught these skills. So, we just said, "Well, well, well, if we don't teach ourselves, nobody else will."

**Susan J. Erenrich**

Let's go a little further back. Let's take a walk down memory lane in 1970. You were a cast member in the Broadway production of *Hair*. This year marks the 50<sup>th</sup> anniversary of the first performance. 1968 was also a major turning point in the Vietnam War. What was it like to be a cast member in *Hair* during that volatile time in history?

**Holly Near**

I wasn't as politically engaged, so I probably had less of a response to it than I would have now. I probably know more about my response now than I did then. I had been working in film and television in Hollywood and doing sitcoms, and I came East to be in a film. And after that film was done, my agent said, "Do you want to stay in New

York for a while? Because I can hook you up to a Broadway show." And I had always thought being on Broadway would be really fun. I knew how to sing and dance and act. I trained for that. I just sort of had gotten stuck in LA and never came East. So here I was in New York. My agent put the word out, and there was an opening in the cast of *Hair*.

So, I went. It wasn't at the beginning. It was close to two years into the production. It had started at the Public Theatre and then it had moved to Broadway. And being two years in, they didn't even stop to really have rehearsals at that point. If you were new, you worked with a choreographer in a little room. You worked with a music director in a little room — but not with the other dancers or the other singers. And then the day came when they said, "Okay, stand in the wings, and when you feel like it, jump in." It was really as broad as that. And the stage manager would say, "You're ready." And I said, "Yeah, here I go." And eventually I knew the whole show. And I could stay in it for the whole time.

One day I arrived at the theatre in the greenroom, and everyone was very solemn. I asked what was happening and they said the national guard has just opened fire on students at Kent State for their protests against the invasion into Cambodia. I didn't know where Kent State was. And I didn't know where Cambodia was. So, part of my recollection of *Hair* was that it forced me, in a way, to begin my knowledge, to become educated about what was going on in Indochina and the way the U.S. was waging war, not only against the Indochinese people, but against the protesters in the United States.

**Susan J. Erenrich**

Do you feel that moment politicized you?

**Holly Near**

It took me to the next step. I grew up in a family that was political. My morning conversations with my mother and father over coffee were all political. It wasn't Republican and Democrat. It was pacifism versus armed struggle. They were pretty sophisticated conversations. And the music we listened to was political — Paul Robeson, The Weavers, Woody Guthrie, Odetta, Harry Belafonte. We grieved the execution of the Rosenbergs [Julius and Ethel]. We knew that we were meant to be antiracist. We were in school with Indigenous children and were given an education about the Pomo Nation right from the beginning. So, I can't say that I was politically naïve. I probably had been to an anti-war demonstration even before going to *Hair*.

It's not like I wasn't aware of social change and activism. It was more that I hadn't gone into it deep. And the moment it started coming into my work, I began to look at it deeper. At first it was kind of like, yeah, I'm against war. I'm against racism. I'm against class discrimination. All of those things. It was pretty generic. I was 17, 18, 19 years old. But I think being in *Hair*, and seeing what happened at Kent State, invited me to step up and kick into a higher gear. I became more aware of the military industrial complex and how it works.

**Susan J. Erenrich**

Following your *Hair* debut, you went on to join the Free The Army tour — known by another name, which we can't say on the air — with Jane Fonda, Tom Hayden, Donald Sutherland, and a host of others. Some of our listeners might not be familiar with this group. Could you talk a bit about the goals of the tour and your particular role?

**Holly Near**

I had come back to California after being on the East Coast and was having lunch with an African American choreographer that I had gone to school with. I was really interested in what he was doing in his life. And he said, "By the way, have you heard of the show FTA?" And in military terms, just so people know, FTA also stands for fun, travel, and adventure. There's a variety of ways those initials have been used within the military. It's in their promotional packets. "Come and join the military - There'll be fun, travel, and adventure." So, the tour was named FTA, but the words were changed to Free The Army. This was a tour that was the total opposite of the Bob Hope tour.

Bob Hope was the most famous entertainer that went out to entertain the troops, and he was very patriotic. He was very pro war. He usually had scantily dressed women on stage with him. His show was directed towards that part of the male consciousness in the military. But this show, FTA, was written by soldiers who had fought in Vietnam and started writing about what they had seen from a soldier's point of view. They started newspapers, and they started an internal movement of soldiers who were resisting war and racism from within the military. And based on their writings, a group of entertainers got together and started creating sketches, songs, and materials to go out and voice what these soldiers were saying. So, we weren't making up stories for them. They had already created the information and we put it into an entertainment format.

The show had been done around the United States a bit, and then this decision was made that the show was going to go to the Pacific, where the wars were happening, and to countries where soldiers were sent for rest and recuperation. Someone from the company had dropped out and they were very quickly trying to find somebody to take that person's place. And for some reason, this friend of mine knew about it. So, I ran over, and I got an audition. And the audition, basically, was spending most of the afternoon filling envelopes and doing fundraising pitches and other things. It had nothing to do with an audition. And finally, they took a lunch break and said, "Okay, where's that woman who came in?"

So, I read a sketch and I did a little dance step. And then I sang a song and they said, "Do you have a passport?" And off I went into probably the most extraordinary university of my life. It changed everything for me. I was going and seeing from an emotional point of view of being opposed to the war. And all of a sudden, I saw it from a military and a financial point of view — and thus the military industrial complex. And as I later learned from Tom Hayden, you follow the money; you have to follow the money. And even today, with what's going on with the caging of children at the borders, if you follow the money, you know what's going on there. Some people will see it from a completely emotional point of view. And how can we not. I sob reading about these children being locked in cages at the border. But if one wants to have a strategy to confront it, I keep coming back to: You follow the money.

**Susan J. Erenrich**

Were you all connected with the GI Coffee Houses coordinated by Barbara Dane and Irwin Silber?

**Holly Near**

I knew about them. I came in later. Barbara had been doing this work already. She had been doing soldier work. She was in front of me on this. And when I got back from the FTA tour, it would've made sense to go and do the coffee house circuit and meet up with the soldiers. But pretty quickly after that, Tom Hayden and Jane Fonda moved to organize in the States. They developed a campaign, along with some brilliant organizers, called the Indochina Peace Campaign. And that, again, was about money. How do you cut off the funds that taxpayers are paying for this slaughter as well as for this destruction? And I was working at Dan Ellsberg's office during his trial. I just walked in there and volunteered and was answering telephones just to try to do something.

And they walked in and said, "Do you want to be the musical arm of this trio that's going out across country?" And I picked up my shoulder bag and walked out. I said, "Yes, it makes a lot more sense for me to be singing than answering telephones." And it really was extraordinary work. Jane Fonda is an amazing person. And I attribute to her all the beginnings of this work that I went on to do. She was really a key starting point in that regard.

**Susan J. Erenrich**

Well, moving a couple years down the road, after the September 11, 1973, coup in Chile you wrote *Hay Una Mujer Desaparecida*. The song is a haunting eulogy.

**Holly Near**

Yes, it's for women who disappeared after the Chilean coup. The Wallflower Order Dance Collective choreographed a piece utilizing the tune.

**Susan J. Erenrich**

What was it about the overthrow of Salvador Allende and the execution of Víctor Jara that made you gravitate towards that cause?

**Holly Near**

Well, I was actually in an anti-war meeting in [Washington,] D.C. and someone burst into the room and said: "Allende has been killed." So, this was 1973, a year and a half, two years after being in all of this. I was very, very young. So just as before — when I was in *Hair* and they killed the students at Kent State, and I said, "Where is Cambodia?" — I sat there in this meeting, watching everybody be horrified that Allende was dead. Again, I didn't know who they were talking about. I wasn't sure I could even find Chile on the globe if somebody had put it in front of me.

So, my education from the get-go was around these traumatic and historic events. And while they were happening, I had no idea that I would look back and go, "Oh, I was there." It wasn't like I went there on purpose. I guess I say this because I want, in particular, young listeners — and everybody, no matter what your age is — to know, if you put yourself out there somewhere, anywhere, and pay attention, chances are something's going to come along that will invite you into the world, that will invite you to life. And if I were going to say anything about my career, it was that I kept saying, "Yes." I kept showing up and saying, "Oh. Well, I want to learn about that. Yeah, I'll go there." And 45 years later, I wrote a song called *I Am Willing*, which starts "I am open, and I am willing."

And that is the key to my career. It was just being willing. And I digressed. So, I did learn where Chile was. I started to listen to the music. And I went back to California, and there were all of these musicians who had escaped the dictatorship that was put in place after a democratic socialist country had been overthrown. There was a military coup and Pinochet took over and there was incredible violence — people being killed, people being thrown in jail or disappearing. That was the first time that I had heard disappearing become a noun. It was no longer a verb.

I met all of these musicians in the [San Francisco] Bay area, who started a club called La Peña in Oakland. We were all social change activists, artists, including Wallflower Order Dance Collective. We were touched and educated by the exiled musicians. And then later, when I was traveling internationally to, I think it was a disarmament festival in Europe, I met Mercedes Sosa, who is not from Chile but from Argentina. I was living in LA [Los Angeles]. My landlady was from Cuba, and we never talked politics because I assumed that she had left to get away from the revolution. I knew that she spoke Spanish and I didn't. And I went to her, and I said, "How do you say in Spanish that there is a woman missing in Chile?" And her eyes got very big.

Like, why didn't this little White, red-headed kid living upstairs ask me this question before. But she was very polite. And I went back upstairs and looked at this packet of material that had been sent to me by a group in San Francisco — a group of women who were organizing around Chile. And it was many, many pages thick, but the front page was a list of names that they knew of women who had disappeared. And they were in small print, and it just went on and on and on and on. So, I started calling out and singing these names. Because that was the most that I could do at the time — just personalize these people. So, in the same way that I wrote a song for Kent State that said *It Could Have Been Me, But Instead It Was You*, about the students killed, that's how I felt about these women. They could have been me that disappeared. So, I thought it through, and I just started singing these names. I had no idea it would become a prayer and anthem in the solidarity movement in the United States of trying to bring attention to the fact that the United States had seriously and actively participated in the coup.

**Susan J. Erenrich**

You mentioned Kent State. In 1974, you were invited to sing at the fourth commemoration of the Kent State shootings. My former housemate and dear friend, Dean Kahler, who was paralyzed from an M-1 rifle bullet after being fired upon by the Ohio National Guard, asked you to write a song. Could you tell listeners some of the story behind the song, *It Could Have Been Me*? I remember you talking to me about it at the Ash Grove's 50th Anniversary Celebration at UCLA in 2008, saying that you didn't know what you were going to sing. You were on the airplane, and all of a sudden it came to you. Can you elaborate on that a little bit?

**Holly Near**

For folks who don't know, the Ash Grove was a club in Los Angeles that had a lot of political music. An interesting man ran the place, and he would put artists together that were unusual. Like, he had me play on the same night as Sonny Terry and Brownie McGhee. It wasn't your most obvious duo concert, but it was great because the audience got to hear very diverse music. So, I met Dean Kahler in Los Angeles. He was moving himself about in a wheelchair because he had been shot by the national guard at the protest at Kent State. He was one of the ones that survived and lived, and he was very generous.

I thought it was generous of him to ask me if I would write a song about Kent State, because I didn't feel like I was well known at the time. There were other people he could have asked. I was very moved by that. And I set out the intention in my mind to write a really meaningful and powerful tribute for this moment that could be not only about those who perished, but also include some kind of criticism of those who killed the students — and not only that but those who paid the people to kill. I wanted to try to write a big picture and a small picture song. My songwriting has always been about either starting with something really tiny and then the camera lens pulls back and you see something larger, or the reverse, you're looking at something universal, and then you move in and see the details.

I've always felt like that was the essence of good storytelling for my particular songwriting. So, the weeks went by, and nothing was coming. I was just devastated that I hadn't been able to pull this out of a hat. And I was on the plane headed for Ohio and still didn't have a song. And I was saying to myself, what is it that's in your way? Why can't you personalize this? You're being far too rhetorical. Okay. So here are these protests happening. People got randomly shot at one of them — it could have been you. And then I had it. It could have been me. And from then on, I used craft, which I always depend on, to realize that if you have a chorus, then for decades after that, people can keep adding new verses as long as it can come back around to a chorus and it connects those verses.

So, there was that moment where there were the verses about Kent State. But after that, a verse came around about Víctor Jara in Chile and women organizing in Africa. Another verse came around when there were women mass slaughtered up in Montréal. I just wrote recently about the people killed in the dance hall [Pulse Nightclub] down in Florida. It becomes a useful song as well as an emotional one and it doesn't get stuck in time. If one can have a chorus, it keeps coming back around. So, it actually turned out to be one of my better songs.

**Susan J. Erenrich**

For those just tuning in, we are chatting with our studio guest Holly Near. So, we brushed by the Ash Grove. I want to revisit a moment during the April 2008 gathering in Los Angeles to celebrate the 50th anniversary of the Ash Grove at UCLA. You shared the stage with Civil Rights Movement cultural activist Len Chandler during a special afternoon session on protest music. I remember you commenting on your Free The Army tour together in the early 1970s. Would you mind talking about the connection you had with Len during some of those travels?

**Holly Near**

I had never met Len Chandler before. In hindsight, I looked back and realized how involved he had been in the Civil Rights Movement and what a powerful voice he was. I was so grateful that he was on the FTA tour because he knew how to lead a large crowd in song, and he had the material. When I went on that tour, I hadn't started writing the material that I needed. Len had a toolbox. He had a repertoire. He could pull out this song for this moment and this song for that moment. It could be a quiet tender song, or it could be a rousing song. He would get five, 10,000 people on their feet singing. I think that skill came out of the work he did in the Civil Rights Movement. The singing in the Movement, that came out of the church, was not just a form of entertainment that one listened to. It was part of the culture — the bringing together of people spiritually, energetically, politically, and giving people courage to do what was going to be really hard — like walk out of that church and know that the Ku Klux Klan might be standing out there, or there might be dogs barking, or water.

And so, the music was enriched by his knowledge of that work in the same way that I have felt when I worked with Sweet Honey In The Rock. I constantly learned from Dr. Bernice Johnson Reagon, who was in the original Freedom Singers. So, that was another lesson. There I was, what, 20, 21 years old and watching the way in which music could be infused by a lot of other things besides melody, rhythm, and lyric. I learned a lot from Len Chandler. Another thing I learned was that I didn't have any songs about the war that were from a woman's point of view. All the songs that I had been assigned to sing or invited to bring to the table were either labor songs from the past, Civil Rights songs from the past, songs that had been written by Phil Ochs or by Country Joe McDonald or by Bob Dylan.

These songs were beautiful anti-war songs, but they were all pretty much from a man's point of view. And I was just learning at that time what it meant to have a woman's point of view in a song. So, for those weeks on that trip, I was 24-seven trying to connect the dots, trying to put it all together. We had one moment where some soldiers who were clearly drunk — and we found out later they were Marines — had come to one of the shows. A lot of the shows were outside. This one was in Japan. It was inside a big hall, and they started coming around the side to come up on the stage to confront us. At that point, Donald Sutherland was reading a piece from *Johnny Got His Gun*. It was an extraordinary piece about a soldier who'd been blown up, but these Marines were mad.

They were really mad. They saw what we were doing as not being patriotic and of being critical of the military. Now the other 5,000 people in the hall weren't hearing it that way, but they were. And they started coming up and it was interesting how all the people on the stage took a different stance in preparation for the attack. Some people started getting really rational — "Now, calm down," — using words, being very verbal. Another person very quietly picked up a Coke bottle. And another person and Len, just sort of stood there going, "I don't even know what my choice is. I'll go kiss them. I don't know." Len started singing and he just led the whole house in a song — probably *Move on Over*.

Another song was *We Shall Not Be Moved*. He said something like, "You cannot come up here and displace us." And at the same time about a dozen soldiers from the audience got up and walked around and very quietly moved and stepped right between us and the Marines. And they didn't take a fighting stance. They just put their bodies there. And there were a few verbal exchanges and a little bit of huff and puff, but the Marines turned around and left. I was just amazed. It reminded me that a soldier is just a little boy who grew up and found himself in the military. It was just one more lesson that I was learning on that trip.

**Susan J. Erenrich**

So, you talked about women a couple of minutes ago. You're a women's music pioneer. You recently penned a beautiful chapter for a book I co-edited titled, *Grassroots Leadership & the Arts for Social Change*. Can you say something about the women's song movement? Could you talk about it and what it was like in those early years?

**Holly Near**

I think every social change movement has music. I can't think of any social change movement that doesn't. In fact, I can't think of any culture that doesn't. So, it would make sense that, as women, we're starting to move away from the movements that were keeping us in the kitchen, making the coffee, and running the mimeograph machines, as Gloria Steinem says. Well, mimeograph machine — that's a word from the past.

But it's true. That's what we were doing. Women wanted to be part and were a part of these other movements. But there was bound to be a moment where I said, "Well, if I can't speak out and be in the front lines of this, I need to go somewhere else where I can do that." And I think that's really kind of how the women's movement unfolded itself. Now, it wasn't the first one. There had been women's movements back into the 1800s and before. It was just a continuation. But then, I wasn't born in the 1800s. So, I can only talk about the one I was part of. And I think feminism and the women's movement led to a lot of filmmaking, books, literature, poetry, and some song.

But I think the major song explosion came from lesbian feminists. I couldn't tell you why, except maybe they just got tired of translating, having to change gender pronouns in every song that they heard. It might've been something as simple as that. Women started writing songs in the privacy of their homes and singing them to each other. And then those living rooms got crowded, and they moved to the basements of Unitarian Churches or any other place that would have them. And hundreds of women started coming. Hundreds of lesbians started coming to these concerts because it was an invitation to get out of the bars. The bars had been a place where lesbians could meet, but they were oftentimes owned by the mafia. They were oftentimes dangerous. If you parked your car in front of the bar, your tires could get slashed.

So, all of a sudden there was a place to come to meet, to socialize, to express ideas, to hear beautiful music in a safe environment where you didn't have to hide or pretend. And that took off like a wildfire. And because the artists doing it were such good artists, it expanded so that people who weren't identified as lesbians were coming to the concerts. And singers, women singers, who weren't identified as lesbians, were starting to be part of that women's music circuit. And in order to have it work, we had to start our own record companies. We had to start our own production companies. We had to start our own distribution networks. At one point, I think there were 123 women in their little station wagons driving around with records, LPs. We didn't have cassettes. That was heavy stuff to carry around, and you couldn't let it get warped in the car. We walked into mainstream record stores saying, "Would you be willing?"

I mean, how brave back then in the early seventies to walk into a record store and say, "Would you be willing to sell?" One of the records was called *Lesbian Concentrate*. Can't be much more out than that, right? And it was in response to a woman in Florida who was a spokesperson for orange juice. What was her name? Anita Bryant. It took a lot of courage to walk into a record store and ask that they be displayed. And then of course cassettes came along. That made it easier. And ultimately CDs. But if you listen back to some of those early recordings, they're not well recorded. They're not nearly as sonically well recorded as they would have been with other platforms.

We could have worked with all men at a record company, because those guys knew more than we did. But it was just part of saying, well, if we don't start now, it'll just never happen. And at some point, women of color stepped forward and said, "You're calling this women's music, but I don't see myself there." And that confrontation of racism within the context of being able to unite around feminism — unite around lesbian feminism — unite around women identified issues —for us, provided a space to struggle around issues of class, race, and disability. That was very unique because it wasn't like this stranger coming to that stranger. We already had things we had in common. And since there was commonality, there should be love and respect. That should be the essence of what we do as feminists to fight and struggle with each other around class and race and ability.

It was an experiment, I guess. One could call it an amazing time that maybe never had that kind of an opportunity in the past. It was an amazing Petri dish. Let's see if we can find out what is in these cells. It was sometimes terrible — absolutely horrific — because when you love someone, the capacity to hurt them is greater than it is when you hurt someone you don't love. And women loved each other, but they also were fighting. We were struggling over things. I think the festival that I was part of in D.C. this summer [2018] celebrating Sisterfire and Roadwork was very cathartic for me. I saw women who I had known and been in struggle with when I was 25 and now, we're 65 and 70. To greet each other again, after not seeing them in a long time, and realize that we had actually been friends and working together for 40 or 50 years as a result of coming together around feminism and lesbian feminism was very moving, very moving.

**Susan J. Erenrich**

Can you say a bit about Redwood Records?

**Holly Near**

Well, Redwood Records was the record label that I started when I discovered that there was no place for me in the music industry. It was probably the first label that was started by a woman — except I did hear there was a woman in the thirties, an African American woman, who started her label, maybe in Pennsylvania. But in terms of contemporary feminism there wasn't anything. I created Redwood Records mainly because when I went to audition at the record companies, they either didn't like the words, or they didn't like the quality of my voice, or they didn't like this, or they didn't like that.

And I just thought, "I don't think I want to twist myself into the noodle that they want to sell." So, I thought I was just making a record. It was when I had come back from the tour with Jane Fonda and had written a bunch of songs that I realized they didn't have the right songs, and I wanted to be prepared for the next time. And I thought, well, I'll just go into a studio and record them. Then I found out in order to sell, I had to have a label. And in order to have a label, I had to have a business license. One thing led to another, which is kind of how my life goes. I made a record and I thought that was going to be the end of it. I had recorded the songs I'd written.

I went on the second tour, traveling with Jane Fonda and Tom Hayden in the Indochina Peace Campaign. Thousands of people were coming to hear them because they were famous. And so, I would be singing to 5,000 people. And that introduced me to the tour, to the audience that I would have in the future. I don't know how people do it when they don't have that. I mean, that was just handed to me on a silver platter. And when people were busy wanting to talk to Jane or interviewing them, I would go over to a phone book or whatever and pull up the record store pages out of the yellow pages. Or I would meet a community organizer. And I'd say, "Well, you want to invite me back sometime and we'll do a fundraiser for your group?" I was a busy body in that way. I just kept taking notes. They'd say, "There's Mary Brown over in this town and there's John Webb over there." And when I got home, I put it all together. I called everybody. And then my pianist and co-writer Jeff Langley and I went out and started touring.

**Susan J. Erenrich**

What happened to the label?

**Holly Near**

The label lasted for about 18 years. I left it, probably after about 10 or 12 years. But it went on. It became a nonprofit, which maybe was a good idea. The main problem was that it had a really hard time surviving the Reagan years. Reaganomics just slapped it down, and it struggled to stay ahead of that. And then, eventually, the debt became too great, and it was headed to a sad ending. I was sorry to see that it ended up that way. But I keep being reminded by my peers — when I fall into a state of despair around it — that there were a lot of external conditions going on that I had no control over.

**Susan J. Erenrich**

So, this show's called *Wasn't That A Time*. It's named after a song composed by Lee Hayes, a member of the musical group, The Weavers. You make an appearance in the documentary with the same name. Subsequently you went on the road with Ronnie Gilbert. I attended many of those performances. How did all this come about?

**Holly Near**

Well, Ronnie was the female singer in The Weavers, along with Pete Seeger, Lee Hayes, Fred Hellerman and, I guess at one point, Eric

Darling was in there. There are a couple other singers who came and went from The Weavers, but they were the original four. And growing up, I listened to them a lot.

I lived on a farm away from everything, and I had my first music teacher when I was about eight or nine. So, it's not as if I didn't have a singing teacher, but these singers really brought the world into my living room. To hear somebody like Lena Horne or Julie Andrews or Patsy Cline — they were all such different singers that it gave me a sense of what the possibilities of a female voice could be. But hearing Ronnie sing with The Weavers got my attention because it wasn't like she was fighting to be heard above the men. There were three men's voices, and a guitar, and a banjo, and sometimes some percussion, but she just soared over the top. Like there was no problem — just like an airplane, right over the top. And I just thought, "Okay, how does she do that?" Because it doesn't sound forced. It sounds joyful. It sounds big, but it doesn't sound pushy. There was a lot for me to learn from her voice.

So, my second album, I dedicated to Ronnie. I didn't even know if she was still alive. She teased me about that. Her daughter saw the record and said to Ronnie, "Do you know this Holly Near person?" She said, "No." "Well, she's gone and dedicated a record to you." It made Ronnie mad: "How dare she? What if I don't like her music? I don't want her to dedicate something." So, in her kind of snarky way, she put the record on while she was vacuuming. But at some point, she heard enough of it that she turned off the vacuum cleaner. She loved the record and she called me. And that was kinda how it all got started.

And then I said, "Why don't you come sing?" "Oh, no, I don't sing anymore." She'd become an actor. She was working with Joe Chaikin in New York City. She was working in a theater company in Vancouver, and she'd become a therapist. And she really walked away from the music when The Weavers got hit pretty big-time during McCarthyism. They were accused of being communists and rabble-rousers. So, she had taken her daughter and went to try to create some safety for them.

So, I said, "Oh, you don't have to come back to singing. Why don't you just come to this event and sing a song with me? People would love to see you and say hello to you again in the audience." And so, we did that. And from that time on, all we got were calls saying, "When are you going on tour? When are you going on tour? Is there a record? Did you record that?" So, we kinda got pushed into it. And as Ronnie says, "Wasn't that a good idea?"

**Susan J. Erenrich**

So, you have a new album out titled, *Holly Near 2018*. Tell listeners about the album and some of the songs. Tell us why you wrote them.

**Holly Near**

Well, I got breast cancer a few years ago. When something like that comes in and interferes with the life of a busy person, that person doesn't have to feel guilty about resting. It was not my fault. I'm resting. I had to. My doctor told me I had to. I'm doing fine. I didn't have to have chemo. I had radiation, and I'm still on a cancer drug. My road was easy compared to a lot of people. I want to send a shout out to all of you who are survivors of cancer, and to those of you who have lost people to it. It's a mean and ugly diva.

It did slow me down. The radiation made me so tired. All I could do is lay around in a chair. I ended up not liking the cancer but liking the resting. It wasn't something I was used to doing. So, I thought, well, maybe I've done enough. I started so early in my life. Maybe I could take some time to put to bed my career. That is an interesting phrase, given how tired I was. I was really headed in that direction. I felt, I live on an extraordinary planet. I haven't seen that much of it. Maybe what I really want to do is tie up some loose ends and go see the world. Cause when I've toured, it's from the airplane to the hotel, to the concert hall, to the hotel, to the airplane. It's not as if we have time to go see anything.

So that was the plan. I was heading in that direction. And then, as I've said throughout this interview, sometimes something comes along and gets in my way. Instead of going around it, I just say, "Okay, who are you? What's up?" And I sat down and wrote 12 or 13 songs. Just kaboom, boom, boom, boom, boom, boom, boom, and went in and recorded them. We were going to record in the fall of 2017, but my county caught on fire, and I was evacuated from my home. And I said to all the players, "I need to get out of California. I can't breathe. Let's postpone until the spring." So, we recorded it in spring, and it came out in June.

I couldn't think of anything to call it. I looked at all of the names of the songs. None of them were representational of the body of work as a whole. And I thought, "Well, we'll call it Holly Near 2018." That's when it happened. That's what it is. And it is a series of songs that are about what is going on in my mind now in this particular time of my life. And in this world that we're in right now in 2018 with a fascist president in the United States. It's not surprising to me, some of the things that are going on, because some of the things that are going on were always going on. They were done in secret, and he [President Trump] just doesn't keep secrets. He comes right out and is boldly offensive. There might've been some other more civil, dignified people who were doing the same thing, but they were just polite about it.

I'm never surprised. And when they're talking about the children in cages at the border, I want to go, "Well, this has been part of U.S. policy for a long time." We sold children away from their parents when slavery happened. We kidnapped Indian children [Indigenous Americans] from their parents and sent them off to Indian schools to de-Indianize them. This is just another version of that. So, it's hard for me to be surprised by what the United States will do, because it's been doing it for so long. But the songs all come out of the Trump era — what is happening in this time, in this world, and in my particular life.

I'm always frustrated by recording because at the moment I sing a song, I know it better than I did three minutes before. So, I'm recording, and I want to go, "Oh, well, let's do that again, cause now I know how to sing it better." But at some point, you just have to say stop. You know this is just an idea. You're recording a moment in time simultaneously. Jim Brown, who made the film, *Wasn't That a Time* about The Weavers — as well as films about Harry Belafonte; Peter,

Paul and Mary; Arlo Guthrie; and Woody Guthrie — was an incredible filmmaker. He decided he wanted to make a film about my life and work. He wanted to come west of the Mississippi and come out to California. He was fascinated by women's music and feminism. I think it will be out in spring 2019. I'm also writing a book. And so, this is me, who was going to stop working.

**Susan J. Erenrich**

It's your second memoir, and I read the first one decades ago, which was fantastic. I remember when we were sharing a house at the Rowe Camp & Conference Center — because I took your wonderful writing workshop in Rowe, Massachusetts — I asked you if you were sorry that you put out your first memoir so soon. Now you're working on another one. So, I'm wondering what people can expect in this updated version.

**Holly Near**

Well, I remember Tom Hayden saying to me, "You're only 45. Why are you writing a memoir?" He thought it was a little early. He said, "You can write a book, but not a memoir." But I'm so glad I did it because it was raw and unsophisticated, and it was not in hindsight. Now I might read it and be horrified. I wrote it the way I was feeling at the time. And if I had waited until now, especially since I'm losing some memory, I would have remembered it differently. So, there's something kind of wonderful. And I would say this to young people who are listening: Start writing your memoir. Don't release it. Keep writing those chapters and putting them in a notebook somewhere because we don't remember in hindsight the same way we feel it at the moment.

Margaret Randall, who's a writer and a poet, told me that she wrote about an experience she had in Mexico during the student revolts there, the student revolution. And she was, I think, in a basement trying not to be deported back into the United States. I can't remember exactly the conditions. But she found a journal that she was writing, and she opened it up and she compared it to what she had written in memory of that time. And she said it was astounding. They were not the same. It was the same person, the same experience, but really different. So, the book I'm writing now is not so much a memoir — this happened and that happened —the premise of it is more, what did I need to learn to write that song? So, by the time you're through the essays, which are not necessarily in any timely order, it feels like a memoir. Because there's been a journey through the creative process — how I learn, how I think, how I teach, and how I create — I try to write it in such a way that it's not just about me.

It is about me, but I wanted to write it in such a way that it was useful to other people, useful to other artists, useful to other writers and teachers. I hope that I have achieved that. I'm not quite done yet, but it has drained me in a way that I didn't expect. I'm pretty exhausted by it. I have two or three readers right now who are sending me their feedback, and I'll enter that into the book. Then I'll start working with a professional editor. I think the reason it's exhausted me is that I have always understood the power of art and of music, and it takes a lot of work to tell the truth. It takes a huge amount of work to write about something or create something where I'm not glossing over material and, at the same time, I'm not being accusatory, not gossiping, not doing harm. It's that place where you can be profoundly honest and, at the same time, not let your ego take somebody down.

How do you write about racism from the point of view of a White person where you don't speak for someone else, don't represent somebody else's culture, but yet be very, very clear about where you come from in your own unlearning of racism? My journey might not be the same for someone else. Every single sentence has to be put through these lenses of clarity. And it's a wonderful process. I lean on craft a lot. I'm a great believer in craft. But it is tiring.

**Susan J. Erenrich**

As we wind down, I'm wondering if you have any pearls of wisdom for current and budding cultural activists?

**Holly Near**

I feel that anybody, whether you're a basketball player or whether you're a song writer, can be an activist. My activist voice has probably been my best friend, so I keep putting information into my instrument. And that's true for an athlete, and it's true for a songwriter. It's true for a parent. And the more we bring in, the more we allow ourselves to remain teachable, the more we have to work with when the time comes for us to speak up. I've actually been really impressed by some of the athletes who have been speaking up and the political work they're doing within their field. And the way to do that with the most confidence, I think, is to have done one's homework. And that homework is never over.

For example, I can be sitting in traffic, and I can just decide to be bored or rageful — road rage — or whatever they call that. Or I might look across the street and there's a tennis court and there's an African American person playing tennis. Maybe I just see the tennis court. Maybe I see the players. Or maybe I think about what happened in our country that allowed that to be possible. Because there was a time when that person was not allowed on that court or not allowed in a tennis club. And by taking a moment to think about history, my boredom turns in to something else — an extraordinary way of connecting with that history and with activism. It allows me, in that moment, to not take for granted that which I am looking at now. Some people would say, "Oh my God, that's exhausting if you're doing that all the time."

Well, not all the time. I'll go see a bad movie sometimes. Or watch a "chick flick." I like to have light-hearted things in my life. I said "chick flick" by the way with quotes around it — you can't see that on the radio. But I find it more interesting to be engaged like that. I don't like being bored and I don't see that there's any reason to be. So, in terms of young artists, if you're paying attention, if you're noticing, if you're sitting in a circle and you're waiting for somebody to come in instead of going, look around and see the difference between the shoes that people are wearing. I mean, there is no situation — unless you're in solitary confinement in a prison —where there's not a lot to notice. And when we notice details, as opposed to generalities, we become better teachers, better critical thinkers.

I think that's what I would say to young artists, whether they want to go and work in Hollywood, on the Broadway stage, or whether they want to become a political activist artist. And they're not mutually exclusive. My career shows that I was able to do lots of different things. And the thing I would say is to respect theatre. The artists that I see who have a knowledge of theatre — look at someone like Toshi Reagon who has a real understanding of theatricality. She can curate an event, and she has the flow. She knows what follows next, what goes well, what sounds catch people's attention. And that's all a kind of theatricality.

I remember speaking with a young man who came to one of my workshops about theatricality, folk music, and political music. And he said, "Well, I don't want to be theatrical. I want to be like Pete Seeger." And I said, "Well, what do you mean?" You can be at one of his concerts, and he makes you feel like you're in his living room. And I told him this. I've been in his living room, and it doesn't hold 3000 people. It feels that way because Pete was one of the most theatrical presenters ever. And if you saw more than one concert of his, sometimes he'd have the same introduction to a song because he'd worked on it. He'd lift his banjo at a particular place in it because he knew that was where he was wanting to say to the crowd: "Come on." It was not all casual. It upset this boy so much. He left the workshop. He just didn't want to leave his image of Pete being just a regular old guy with no feet, no game playing. It's not natural to walk on stage. You have to want to be part of the theatre of performance. When you walk on stage, it's a stage. Even the back of a flatbed truck with a megaphone singing to striking nurses in the rain requires a certain amount of understanding of theatre. Why else would you be there but to move people into a place in the way that art does. So good luck to all you young writers.

**Susan J. Erenrich**

Final thoughts for our listeners?

**Holly Near**

I get asked to speak a lot about hope lately. People ask, "How do you keep hopeful?" I'm not always hopeful, but that's a big word. Am I hopeful? I'm hopeful that the president [President Trump] won't push the wrong button out of his stupidity and ignorance. I hope that more young Black men won't be shot by police. I hope the babies will all be released from the cages. But that hope is void and empty unless it's connected to activism. So, my hope is that we, on this planet, in whatever way it is — maybe we're delivering Meals on Wheels, but whatever it is — that all of us turn a world that could just be Pollyanna into something that's real — that we take it seriously. As Alice Walker says, activism is how we pay rent for the right to be here and how we take care of this home. So, I would hope for all of us that we can find our place in this time. Every generation, every century has had a rough time, whether it was a potato famine or whether it was in the Middle Ages. You're born into a time. This is your time. What are you going to do with it?

**Susan J. Erenrich**

Well, I want to thank our special guest Holly Near for taking time out of her busy schedule and touring to come in to be my special guest in a conversation.

**Holly Near**

Thank you for having me. I have a new website up. We are adding more information about art and activism. Please visit it from time to time so you can see what we're up to.

**Susan J. Erenrich**

Do you want to tell folks where they can find your website?

**Holly Near**

It's www.hollynear.com. I tried to keep it simple so I can remember it. It's where you will find my discography and my music. It's also a place where I have a historic photo gallery. I'm building a timeline of what happened over the last 50 years. It's a process. There's a place where people can write letters, see my papers or lessons. Every one of us out there has a story. And as long as I'm in the story, somewhere, it can legitimately go into my archive. We want to leave a trail for the next generation of researchers to go in there. And they may go and look and say, well, who is this Holly Near person? When they open up the collection, they will find social change activists and artists from all over the country and throughout the world. Because those stories are not going to be in mainstream history books. So, we need to create our own trail of history. I hope people will feel encouraged to do that. There's a space on the website where you can send the notes.

**Susan J. Erenrich**

I want to thank you for tuning in to *Wasn't That A Time: Stories & Songs That Moved The Nation* on WERA-LP Arlington, Virginia 96.7 FM. The fabulous Rusty Roberts is the On Air engineer. He sits by my side every week to ensure the success of this show. A special shout out to Holly Near for granting me the July 9, 2018, interview. I'm thrilled that she was able to share a part of her story with all of us during her busy Sisterfire weekend.

**About the Author**

Holly Near has been a strong voice for integrity, justice, and peace for almost five decades. Influenced by social change movements around the globe, she writes and sings songs that look at the world through the lens of feminism, anti-racism, and peace. Born in rural northern California, Holly has a powerful performance style that rings true whether on the stage at Carnegie Hall or a make-shift platform in war-torn El Salvador. To learn more about Holly, please visit http://www.hollynear.com.

# CHAPTER 6
# ALLIES OF THE CIVIL RIGHTS MOVEMENT: A HORIZONTAL LEADERSHIP MODEL FOR SOCIAL CHANGE & WE BUILT A FORTRESS OF FOLK

## AN INTERVIEW WITH CAROLYN HESTER

## INTRODUCTION

By Susan J. Erenrich

This chapter features a reflection from my longtime friend Carolyn Hester and an interview I conducted with her in 2019. In 1964, Carolyn was a member of the Mississippi Caravan of Music, a cultural arm of the Freedom Summer Project. She toured the Magnolia State for a short stint, along with other troubadours of conscience, supporting a dangerous frontline operation to break the back of the Jim Crow South. The caravan's job was to support movement foot soldiers and draw attention to the racist modus operandi perpetuated by Southern Whites throughout the Black Belt region. Following Carolyn's pilgrimage to Mississippi, she, along with other caravan artists, educated audiences through their lyrics and raised money for the Student Nonviolent Coordinating Committee (SNCC), Council of Federated Organizations (COFO), and other groups that were fighting institutionalized segregation. They accompanied the freedom struggle in vital ways. Carolyn and the other members of the caravan were allies to movement activists.

They played an important role. However, it was the day-to-day grueling, laborious work by local grassroots leaders involved with SNCC, CORE, and COFO, that was responsible for the passage of the Civil Rights Act in 1964 and the Voting Rights Act in 1965, with assistance from their Northern friends. Local Civil Rights warriors were the decision makers. They were the strategists and tacticians. They encountered the routine ill-treatment and torment. They were in Mississippi for the long haul. Allies like Carolyn were there to bear witness to the cause.

Staughton Lynd (1997), the renowned historian and labor lawyer, called the alliance between the protagonist and the "professional" associate, accompaniment. Important in the concept of accompaniment is speaking out against injustice and sharing the journey with the protagonist wherever it may lead. It's also important to note that the person being accompanied decides when the work is complete, not the associate doing the accompaniment. The concept of accompaniment originated with Archbishop Oscar Romero, a social justice worker who was assassinated in 1980 in El Salvador. It is a political theory, with roots in liberation theology, that empowers ordinary people to speak for themselves (Lynd, 1997, p. 6).

Carolyn, who hails from Texas, tells part of her story in this chapter. She reflects upon those salient childhood moments that catapulted her into a life of cultural activism.

Carolyn's chapter is accompanied by an episode of my radio show, *Wasn't That A Time, Stories & Songs That Moved The Nation*, that originally aired on September 29, 2017. A few weeks before the broadcast went live, on September 16, 2017, Carolyn, her daughters, and many of her friends, gathered at the Peoples' Voice Cafe in New York City for her 80th birthday bash. In typical Carolyn fashion, she didn't want a party — she wanted to sing. So, after a bit of convincing, she allowed me to produce the show on one condition — that it would be a regular PVC performance that she shared with her daughters,

Amy and Karla Blume. I agreed. Behind the scenes, however, I went about collecting tributes from longtime compatriots to read intermittently throughout the night. There was also one surprise guest. Listen to find out who!

I hope readers and listeners are moved by Carolyn's piece and interview below and the companion *Wasn't That A Time* tributes. It is a modest glimpse into the life of a longtime advocate for social change.

**Listen**

*Wasn't That A Time - Episode 38: Celebrating A Woman Pioneer From The 1960's Folk Scene*

This show recreates part of the 80th birthday bash for Carolyn Hester at the Peoples' Voice Cafe for those who weren't able to attend the event.

https://www.mixcloud.com/WasntThatATime/wasnt-that-a-time-episode-39-celebrating-a-woman-pioneer-from-the-1960s-folk-scene/

**References**

Lynd, S. (1997). *Living Inside Our Hope: A Steadfast Radical's Thoughts on Rebuilding the Movement*. ILR Press.

Lynd S. (2012). *Accompanying: Pathways to Social Change*. PM Press.

## ALLIES OF THE CIVIL RIGHTS MOVEMENT: A HORIZONTAL LEADERSHIP MODEL FOR SOCIAL CHANGE

By Carolyn Hester

There are few books that I cling to as much as Susie Erenrich's *Freedom Is a Constant Struggle: An Anthology of the Mississippi Civil Rights Movement*. It has proven to be a treasure to thousands of activists, professors, and students who have marched together to strengthen the United States' stride towards freedom. You would think that the issuance of the Emancipation Proclamation would have guaranteed the end of slavery, but President Lincoln was assassinated, and his momentum was thwarted. You would think that the North winning the American Civil War would have guaranteed the end of slavery, but it took many decades for Blacks to simply be granted the right to vote. As for me, I left home at eighteen to sing folk music, but it took me years to join the movement even though I was called to the cause early in life.

My parents, Gordon and Ruth, scooped me up when I was two and a half and we rode the train from Texas to Washington, D.C. as my dad had been accepted at Georgetown University Law School. We lived at 641 I Street, not far from the Library of Congress. Eventually the house became part of the RFK Freeway, but then it was in Southeast D.C., and I attended Friendship House for preschool. My schoolmates and I were from everywhere.

Looking back, I realize I was an inner-city kid. My neighborhood playmates and I met after school at the Salvation Army Shelter to play, dance, and sing. When my mom saw me singing Christmas carols in the Salvation Army Choir, she was proud. One day I wasn't there when she came to pick me up and was told that I had gone around the corner to my friend Berniece's house.

When Mom got there, she discovered that lots of people were there, and they were all dressed up. Mom might have been surprised to find that the family was Black and that they were having a wake due to the death of Berniece's aunt. She was a lovely young woman laid out right there in a white silk-lined coffin. Instead of taking me and leaving, my mom sat down with us. Then Berniece asked her if I could stay a while because they were about to have cake and coffee.

Mom said, "Yes, of course. I'll come back after I check on Carolyn's baby brother."

My brother Dean had recently been born at Providence Hospital. Then it was on the corner, but now there is no more than a plaque commemorating its past existence. When Mom returned, she had Dean with her and so did not stay for coffee even though they invited her. As we walked home, I needed Mom to answer all my questions about what was "wrong" with Berniece's aunt. It was my first knowledge of death.

As I grew up, I realized that some parents would have fussed at me for going home with someone else or for making friends with Black children. Or they might have disapproved of my being near a dead person. Mother's calm attitude, I'm sure, reinforced the open-mindedness I had towards all my schoolmates.

World War II was underway when my parents decided that my mother's younger sister would take Dean and I home to Texas. So, our Aunt Lynette carried six-month-old Dean and a suitcase, while I carried my own small suitcase and scrambled to keep up with her. I was up for adventure and for riding the train again, but I did not fully realize the deep sadness Dean and I would experience without Mom and Dad.

Soldiers and sailors swarmed the trains. On each train we got on, they would stand up and make a place for "Aunt Nettie" to sit with Dean on her lap. I might get a seat occasionally, but I was quite content to sit or sleep on the luggage rack, which was always located to your left as you boarded. It took up the space where a few seats might have been.

Dean and I loved our grandparents dearly. However, Dean developed asthma, which Grandma told me was because he missed Mama. Being part of the war effort like everyone else, Mom worked the night shift at the Bureau of Engraving in Washington, printing serial numbers on ten-dollar bills. Dad had his Georgetown studies as well as a job running and maintaining printing presses at the Navy Yard not far from I Street, N.E.

Grandpa and I were busy teaching Dean how to walk. My preschool was just across the street. I enjoyed my new friends, but they all looked just like me. While in Cameron, I saw the damage from a tornado, but it was another first that floored me. Since Grandpa was the County Surveyor of Milam County, Texas, they had enough money to hire a maid once a week. She was a wonderful Black woman named Jo.

Dean and I would have lunch with Jo in the kitchen. One day Grandpa appeared home early for lunch so both of my grandparents sat down at the dining room table. "We could all go sit together for lunch in the dining room today, okay?" I asked Jo. "No, little Miss. I can't eat with the White folks," she said.

It still hurts thinking about it.

Then she explained, "White folks won't allow me to eat at the same table."

Silence.

I was just not understanding, but the look in Jo's eyes communicated her message as if to say, "Believe me, little Miss, I am telling you the way it really is."

And that is how a five-year-old came to be committed to the cause.

The Navy drafted my dad, even though he was married with two children and in law school. The Navy just needed him the most and pronto. He was assigned to the Officer Training School located at Harvard Yard in Cambridge. Mom came and got us, and we lived in Brookline for six months. Then he was sent to more Signal Corps training at Alameda in the Bay Area. We lived in a San Francisco hotel for a while.

Then came the day Dad was to be shipped out. We went by train once more, this time to San Diego. My brother, Mom, and I went to the dock. Dad said he could take us small fry on the ship, but Mom would have to wait on the dock. Seems that as a grown-up she might be a spy. I was torn. Stay or go? But Dad prevailed. The other sailors and officers also had their children with them. The ship was battleship gray and had bulkheads that could be sealed off in case she was to sink or have a fire. I'll always be grateful I saw it. After Dad and his Signal Corps team unloaded in Hawaii, the ship was loaded with the injured. However, they never made it home with that precious cargo as she was sunk somewhere between Pearl Harbor and San Diego.

Much later, in 1955, I arrived in Greenwich Village, which was to be my home on and off for eighteen years. I finally connected with the Civil Rights Movement through the Vietnam Anti-War Peace Marches. Pete Seeger was my hero. I had already traveled quite a lot, so I was not afraid to go places by myself, just me and my guitar. In 1957 I made my first album, and it was released in 1958. My Dad had taught me how to type and if I had no club, coffeehouse, or concert to play, I could "play" the typewriter. I performed at college concerts and, hopefully, helped spur the questions of the day.

In 1964 came the offer from folksinger/songwriter Gil Turner to go with him to play in the Mississippi Summer Caravan of Music. The Caravan was operated by The Council of Federated Organizations (COFO), as part of the Voter Registration Drive. By that time, thanks to reading countless copies of *The Village Voice*, *The New York Times*, *Time Magazine*, and *Newsweek*, I realized my main function as an ally was to be a witness.

That same summer I stood next to Doctor Martin Luther King, Jr. in Atlantic City as he encouraged the Mississippi Freedom Democratic Party in their attempt to be seated at the Democratic Convention. I enjoyed seeing MLK smiling for those gathered around him. Some of the party were with Fannie Lou Hamer. None of them could get a hotel room in Atlantic City during the convention. The party could only find shelter under the Atlantic City Boardwalk. That's where they slept and organized. My great friend Patricia Mathis, who was producing the nighttime television performances at the convention, made it her business to locate food and deliver it to them.

My role at the convention was to sing for The Young Democrats, for Johnson & Humphrey — "Which Side Are You On, Boys, Which Side Are You On?" I met Dr. King's associate, the great Aaron Henry there. Senator Birch Bayh was the featured speaker after I warmed them up with songs of the Movement.

In 2018, as we still endure an "Age of Uncertainty, Where Freedom Doesn't Feel So Free," I want to say to you, that I treasure you so much and want to help you keep the magnificent flame of freedom alive.

To allies everywhere, Dr. King's lighting of the flame is never to be forgotten. There is nothing greater we can offer each other and humankind than to be vigilant in keeping that flame alive. Let neither circumstance nor negativity divide us in this "fierce emergency of now."

# PART II. WE BUILT A FORTRESS OF FOLK — AN INTERVIEW WITH CAROLYN HESTER

## PART II. INTRODUCTION

By Susan J. Erenrich

On May 15, 2019, Carolyn Hester and her daughters, Amy and Karla Blume, were my special guests at the WERA.FM audio suite in Arlington, Virginia. Carolyn generously granted me an interview for my weekly radio broadcast *Wasn't That A Time: Stories & Songs That Moved The Nation.* Several days later, I met them at the Peoples' Voice Cafe in New York City for the venues' last show of the season. What follows is an edited transcript of our interview.

**Listen**

*Wasn't That A Time Episode 117: A Conversation with Carolyn Hester - 1960s Folk Music Pioneer*

https://www.mixcloud.com/WasntThatATime/wasnt-that-a-time-episode-117-a-conversation-with-carolyn-hester-1960s-folk-music-pioneer/

## PART II. WE BUILT A FORTRESS OF FOLK — AN INTERVIEW WITH CAROLYN HESTER

**Susan J. Erenrich**

Welcome to *Wasn't That A Time: Stories & Songs That Moved The Nation* on WERA-LP Arlington, Virginia 96.7 FM. I'm in the audio suite with Carolyn Hester and her daughters, Amy and Carla Blume. I am so excited that you're here. Thank you.

**Carolyn Hester**

We've really been looking forward to this Susie. It's special. You've touched me and my life so many times. So, thank you for this. We've had a visit already and we've had a lot of green tea. That sounds just so calm, doesn't it?

**Susan J. Erenrich**

For folks who aren't familiar with Carolyn, she was a woman pioneer and trailblazer back in the heyday of the 1960s Greenwich Village scene in New York City. Carolyn, you often refer to yourself as a "chick singer." Talk about what it was like to be a female performer during the folk revival.

**Carolyn Hester**

It's complicated. I wanted to be nowhere else. Yeah, that was the thing. The idea of living alone was a little tough, but there was really no alternative. In 1960, I married Richard Fariña. We were married about a year and a half and after that I was happy to be alone again. With the first marriage you just do it too fast, you know what I mean? Right now, I'm working on my memoir and trying to write about that. Often, I get questions about my life in the Village but also the people that I knew.

One person I got to know was Bob Dylan, and then he recorded on my first Columbia album. But I really started back even before then, because that Columbia album — where Bob Dylan was discovered — was my third album. First, when I was 20 years old, I recorded for a man named Norman Petty in Clovis, New Mexico. He had hits with Bo Diddley and Buddy Holly. So, I think it was that Buddy Holly connection that drew Dylan my way. That's sort of an interesting thing, trying to put all that together, because, of course, Bob Dylan ultimately became one of the biggest rock stars this country has ever had. He'd say that I was his connection to Buddy Holly, which is really a very nice thing to say. I don't know who knows, but on my first Columbia album I had a band that, in addition to having Bob Dylan in it, had Bruce Langhorne, who ended up playing on many albums for Dylan. Billy Lee was my bass player because he'd been Odetta's bass player. Billy Lee is the father of Spike Lee, the great filmmaker.

We were all trying to rise to the top, like the good cream does. I had been blessed getting an early start. Because of Buddy Holly's great success, I got to have a nationally distributed album on Coral Records, which was part of the Decca family. And then I started getting bookings by people who were, more or less, show business bookers. But I, myself, was not drawn really to show business. I was much more drawn to the Civil Rights Movement and the anti-war question of the Vietnam War. It just was so important to me. Other people who felt like me came to the Village — people like Phil Ochs; of course, Dylan; and then Judy Collins came.

And we kind of became known as the children of Woody [Guthrie] and Pete [Seeger], which is a great compliment. So that was the guts of it, the heart of it. I feel like we built a fortress of folk. We weren't afraid to consider these questions about society. I remember we were just heartbroken when Pete Seeger got banned from the *Hootenanny* show. So, we started a protest against that show. Apparently, just the fact that he had been called up before the [U.S. House of Representatives] Un-American Activities Committee scared television enough to ban him from the air. Why doesn't he have freedom of speech like Americans are supposed to have? That really inflamed us. I had done two of the shows, but I immediately announced that I wouldn't be doing any more. I had the producers calling me. I met one at the Village Gate one night and he wanted to know why I wouldn't be coming on. I said, "I wouldn't be me exactly the way I am without Pete Seeger. If there's no

Pete, then there's no me for real." So, I told him, "I can't stand him getting blacklisted by ABC." You know, I just wasn't going to stand for it. Well, others joined in, and some fell away from the protest, but it lasted for like two years. And the show did finally end. Our protest was a success... I suppose I don't even know if we had anything to do with that, but I do know that we have a satisfaction in that we did what we knew we must do.

### Susan J. Erenrich

Continuing along those lines, several years later, in 1964, Gil Turner convinced you to join the Mississippi Caravan of Music, a group of troubadour-allies who went South to help break the back of Jim Crow. Could you tell folks what it was like to be in Mississippi during the Freedom Summer Project?

### Carolyn Hester

I really think we were totally frightened the whole time. Especially because — by the time we got there — three Civil Rights workers, Goodman, Schwerner, and Chaney, had gone missing. While we were there, they discovered the bodies. And it was something I didn't want to look at. I didn't want to be there. We went because it was one of these things where I can't be an American if I don't go witness. And that was what we felt we could contribute. It was to be a witness. They were young people, college age kids — 10 years younger than we were. They were out there signing up people in the voter registration drive, "One Man-One Vote," through the COFO — the Council of Federated Organizations.

They organized the Caravan of Music. We were sent to all kinds of locations in Mississippi — to churches, to places where we started to sing some songs, freedom songs, or whatever kind of songs that would help people. It would hopefully energize them and take their minds off their fear for a little while. That's one of the great things that Pete Seeger has left us — marching goes better with singing. And that was it. That was what Pete called the living folk process. In Mississippi, that's where we saw it. I want to try to talk about that in my memoir as much as I can. I'm so grateful that I got invited to go.

Jackie Washington, Len Chandler, and so many others were there. I think it was different for them. Some of them had done more marching than I had. But believe me, that situation was a stark contrast. I had noticed in some of the towns, I saw things that I would have never seen. And I'm so glad I did, because some of the communities were just lost. They owed their soul to the company store. You know, the rich plantation owners had given them credit or whatever, and they were never going to pay it off. And the little kids were wandering around. They looked like they were living in a third world country and not in America. And I just want to say, I don't want us to create that again.

**Susan J. Erenrich**

While you were in Mississippi in 1964 with the Caravan of Music, you had a scary hotel experience. You were sharing a room with Alix Dobkin. Can you talk about the incident?

**Carolyn Hester**

Yeah. Alix is a great, great musician and soul. She and I shared a room in Jackson, Mississippi. Gil Turner was right next door on the same floor. We had arrived in Jackson the night before. This was around early August of 1964. We asked the hotel to give us a wakeup call at six o'clock the next morning. We were going to have breakfast, and then we were going to go to downtown Jackson to meet Bob Cohen, who headed up the Mississippi Caravan of Music. Bob was a very close friend of Gil Turner, and they were in a group together called the New World Singers.

So, what happened was, at 5:30 the phone rang. And I thought, "Oh gosh, I hope nothing's wrong." So, I answered it. And the voice on the other end said, "Okay, n****r lover, it's time to get up." And that just exploded us, you know? And we quickly got down to breakfast. We came back and when we walked out of the elevator to our floor, there on our doors, scrawled in black, was "KKK" [Ku Klux Klan]. And wow. We didn't sleep too well the whole time we were there. A lot of people had the same experience. Fortunately, our guitars were okay. Nobody had bothered them. We let Bob Cohen know what had transpired. And as we were standing across the street from the COFO office, he said,

"Before we go in, I want you to know that your pictures are going to be taken. See that car over there — that's the local police. And this car over here — that's the local sheriff. And that car over there — fortunately, that's somebody from the Justice Department. They know we're here."

**Susan J. Erenrich**

As we wind down our time together, I want to ask you one more question. As you're currently writing your memoir, can you provide a sneak peek for our audience?

**Carolyn Hester**

Before we came here, I asked my daughter Amy, "Well, if I talk about the book, what should I say?" Amy is here — Amy, say hello. So, what was it you thought I should talk about?

**Amy Blume**

Well, one of the things that is interesting to me, as someone who wasn't there, is that through most of the book you discuss a lot of folk singers who were really important to the movement but who are now forgotten, because things get lost to time. And so, part of the memoir is a family tree of folk musicians. Hopefully, one of the things this book will do is remind people of the who and what and where and how. Key puzzle pieces that will fill in the gaps. It's not just about Bob Dylan. It's *all* of the people who came before, who were there behind the scenes and who were singing in the coffee shops and marching.

**Carolyn Hester**

You're right. And so, we hope that in the book, we'll actually have a family tree. We'll show the names of all these people who belong and who would enjoy being seen on that family tree. That was really an important kind of a revelation and connection for me. Folks in the Village at that time were a family. And it hasn't been discussed in that way. So that's one of the things that's different in this book. I don't know when the memoir will come out. I haven't approached any publishers, and I've still got things to work on. Who knows if I'm going to finish it this year or next year. New things keep happening. As long as I'm alive, I'm going to have more chapters.

**Susan J. Erenrich**

I want to thank you for tuning in to *Wasn't That A Time: Stories & Songs That Moved The Nation* on WERA-LP Arlington, VA 96.7 FM. The fabulous Rusty Roberts is the on-air engineer. He sits by my side every week to ensure the success of this show. My gratitude to David Lamb, who recorded the session for this episode. And of course, a special shout-out to Carolyn Hester and her daughters, Amy and Karla Blume, who graciously spent part of the afternoon with me at the WERA.FM audio suite.

**About the Author**

Carolyn Hester is a noted singer from the 60s Greenwich Village folk scene. She appeared on the cover of the *Saturday Evening Post* (May 30, 1964) and has been remembered in many books including *Chronicles*, Bob Dylan's autobiography, as being the person who was most instrumental in Dylan's signing to Columbia records — the label that took an unknown singer-songwriter and elevated him to super-stardom. *The* Los Angeles Times requested Carolyn Hester to contribute an Op-Ed piece for their October 23, 2016, Sunday edition, asking her reaction to Bob Dylan's Nobel Prize for Literature. (Read the Op-Ed here: http://www.latimes.com/opinion/op-ed/la-oe-hester-dylan-nobel-early-days-20161023-snap-story.html).

The "Texas Songbird," has an expanded audience these days due to her steady re-emergence as a torchbearer of the '60s folk movement. In 2009, Carolyn had her own BBC show, consisting of highlights from her BBC concert performance at London's Barbican Theatre, co-starring Hester, Judy Collins, Roger McGuinn, Eric Andersen, and Billy Bragg titled, the Folk America Series. In 2010, Hester was included in the 90th Birthday Celebration for Ravi Shankar on Radio France. She also was featured in the documentary, *For the Love of the Song,* that debuted at the South by Southwest Film Festival in March of that same year.

Besides her beautiful, expressive voice, she is known for her repertoire of original contemporary folk and traditional English ballads. She has recorded more than nineteen albums in her fifty years of performing. Hester was signed to the Decca-Coral label in 1957 by her manager and producer, Norman Petty. Also under Petty's influence at that time, was a hip entertainer and friend of Hester's, Buddy Holly, and to this day, she answers many requests to play the song he taught her, "Lonesome Tears." Throughout the '60s, Hester was well established in the Greenwich Village folk scene where she met a young, Bob Dylan. Her two-album set, *Carolyn Hester at Town Hall*, is one of the few live recordings of female folk singers in the 1960s. In that same time frame Carolyn was one of the leaders of the ABC-TV *Hootenanny Show* boycott by American folksingers due to ABC banning Pete Seeger. Her deeply rooted passion for the Civil Rights Movement came to fruition in her participation in the 60s Mississippi Caravan of Music, joining the fight for Voter Registration in that State, and in the songs she presented at the August 1964 Democratic Convention in Atlantic City when the effort to seat the Freedom Democratic Party was attempted.

Since 1972, Hester has played, almost annually, at the Kerrville Folk Festival in Kerrville, Texas and served as a member of the board of directors for most of that time. In 1992, Hester was asked to perform at the Bob Dylan tribute at Madison Square Garden that celebrated Dylan's 30 years recording for Columbia with Bob himself performing with an international, all-star cast. Hester has appeared as a guest artist on many albums including the Grammy-Award winning album by Nanci Griffith, *Other Voices, Other Rooms*, recorded in 1993.

In 2002, Hester was remembered as a major player in David Hajdu's, *Positively 4th Street*, due to her ties with Dylan, the folk scene in general, and her first marriage to Richard Fariña. Carolyn is the first artist to record a "Tom Paxton Tribute" album, celebrating the music of her friend from her Greenwich Village days. Professional record collectors are often seeking out a song called, "Majhires" written specifically for her by the great Indian Sitarist, Ravi Shankar, who also directed the session when Hester recorded it.

Her second husband, jazz pianist David Blume wrote the hit-song "Turn Down Day" by the Cyrkle and played as Hester's sideman for more than 30 years before his passing in March of 2006. Blume and Hester's two children, Amy and Karla Blume, are both musicians and have taken over the role of Hester's musical accompanists and songwriting partners. Hester and the Blume sisters are currently recording a new album and its release may coincide with that of a memoir being written by Hester.

For more about Carolyn Hester, visit http://www.carolynhester.com.

# CHAPTER 7

# GUITAR PLAYER FOR THE ALL-MALE GROUP OF THE SNCC FREEDOM SINGERS

## AN INTERVIEW WITH BILL PERLMAN

## INTRODUCTION

By Susan J. Erenrich

On September 9, 2020, I joined Bill Perlman on Zoom to discuss his time as a guitarist with the all-male group of SNCC Freedom Singers. For readers unfamiliar with Bill — he was born in 1947 in Brooklyn, NY. His mother, Lucille Perlman, was already an active member of the Student Nonviolent Coordinating Committee (SNCC) when Bill got involved in 1965. He was eighteen and had just graduated from high school. He performed with the troupe for almost two years. He was the only White affiliate of the all-Black musical ensemble.

Following his stint with the SNCC Freedom Singers, he performed as a solo guitarist and worked in theater, film, and video. Bill has a bachelor's degree in electrical engineering and a master's degree in computer science. He resides in Ashfield, MA, where he continues to be politically active at both the local and county level of government. Over the years, he has also reunited with his musical compatriots in the SNCC Freedom Singers at various U.S. Civil Rights Movement events.

I first met Bill in late 1997 when I produced the *Songs of Dissent Live!* concert at the Holton-Arms School in Bethesda, MD. The musical performance featured professional singer-songwriters who have dedicated their lives to social change. Some of them have passed on, but the ones who took the stage that evening lent their voices to the ongoing struggle for a just world until they took their last breath. Their names, like Bill Perlman's, might not be widely known, but they are unsung heroes and heroines that deserve recognition.

In the early and mid-1960s, the all-male assemblage of SNCC Freedom Singers educated audiences through their lyrics about segregation in the South and the brutality committed against those who tried to dismantle the system. Four of them participated in the *Songs of Dissent Live!* gathering and were included in the companion CD that was released in 1998. Bill Perlman, Emory Harris, and Marshall & Matthew Jones were among the troubadours that were featured that night. Wazir Peacock, one of the original SNCC Song Leaders also graced the stage. Wazir lived in Mississippi and directly confronted the Klan. These men were soldiers in a domestic war. Music was their most powerful weapon.

Following the 1997 event, Bill and I stayed in touch. Over the years, he participated in numerous programs that I produced and hosted. We saw each other during SNCC conferences and meetings. Our paths crossed during sad occasions as well. Unfortunately, with so many Civil Rights Movement freedom fighters aging and near the end of their life, we have been in each other's company far too often.

The interview below, however, was a happy moment — an opportunity to chat and catch up. I am thrilled that Bill was willing to share part of his remarkable story here. He helped pave the way for the continuing battle for racial equality in the United States and beyond.

Enjoy!

**Listen**

In this episode, celebrating the Martin Luther King, Jr. holiday, listen to songs by two of the SNCC Freedom Singers who have passed on — Matt & Marshall Jones. Compositions performed by SNCC Freedom Singers, Matthew Jones, Marshall Jones, Magpie, and Kim and Reggie Harris are featured.

*Wasn't That A Time Episode 167 - Remembering SNCC Freedom Singers Matthew & Marshall Jones*

https://www.mixcloud.com/WasntThatATime/wasnt-that-a-time-episode-167-remembering-sncc-freedom-singers-matthew-marshall-jones/

# GUITAR PLAYER FOR THE ALL-MALE GROUP OF THE SNCC FREEDOM SINGERS - AN INTERVIEW WITH BILL PERLMAN

**Susan J. Erenrich**

I'm here on Zoom with my friend and pal Bill Perlman. Today we are going to talk about his involvement with the U.S. Civil Rights Movement and the SNCC ["Snick"] Freedom Singers. Bill, for readers who aren't familiar with the group, why don't we first inform them about the different configurations of SNCC Freedom Singers, like the original ensemble from Albany, Georgia; the men's group; The Freedom Voices; and the SNCC Song Leaders. Could you say a little bit about what each of those groups did?

**Bill Perlman**

Okay. But people have to understand first the importance of music and singing in the Civil Rights Movement. It was inspirational. It brought people together. It gave people courage. They would sing in jail and on marches. They would sing on the picket line. And most of the songs were variations on gospel songs. Words were changed to fit the situation.

Now a brief history of the groups. In 1961, a group of youngsters in Albany, Georgia started the SNCC Freedom Singers. Originally, they were three women and two men: Bernice Johnson [now Bernice Johnson Reagon], Rutha Mae Harris, Bertha Gober, Cordell Reagon, and Charles Neblett. There were others from time to time, but this was the original makeup of the Albany ensemble.

They traveled throughout the country. They had a dual purpose. They would raise money for the Student Nonviolent Coordinating Committee (SNCC), and they would educate people about racial inequity. They also participated in mass meetings in the South. Their voices tended to uplift the spirits of everyone in the room. They served an important role. With concert ticket sales and donations, they brought a lot of money into the SNCC organization.

The first group, however, split up after about nine months. Being on the road constantly is exhausting. There was a limit to how long anybody would stay in and do it. There were a couple of attempts to create something new, but it never amounted to much. Then in 1963, a guy by the name of Matthew Jones put together an all-male group with his brother Marshall Jones, Chuck Neblett from the original troupe along with his brother Chico Neblett (who is now living in Ghana), and Cordell Reagon. And there was a guitar player there for a short period of time. Then, I was asked to join. I was the first and only White person ever in the SNCC Freedom Singers.

I was recruited by Jim Forman. He was the Executive Secretary of SNCC. He met me and heard me play and sing at a fundraiser out on Long Island that my parents were involved in. They didn't have a movement person up there to do any singing. So, I did it. And after that, he asked me to consider joining. He introduced me to Matthew Jones. I went to his house. We spent several hours talking. We both agreed that I would join. Then I met up with the rest of the guys in the early summer of 1965. Things were very busy during that time. It was right after the Selma to Montgomery March and right after the Mississippi Summer of 1964. We jumped right into it. We rehearsed some and did a small concert in someone's living room out on Fire Island, NY.

The next stop was Carnegie Hall, which for me, was not a great place to start cause the rest of my career had to go down from there. But we performed all over the place from Massachusetts down to Atlanta in January, I guess, of 1966. We did a tour through Canada, by cars, starting in Nova Scotia and working our way to Windsor, which is near Detroit. And later we performed in all kinds of venues, stretching anywhere from people's living rooms to rallies. I remember one rally in front of the UN where there must have been 200,000 people.

I was 18 turning 19 in the group. The next youngest person was Cordell. He was 23 at the time. Cordell and I became fast friends. We were traveling with two other sets of brothers. We spent a lot of time together. It was just an amazing experience. It wasn't without its difficulties. There were people in SNCC and in the movement who objected to having a White person as part of the group. But for the most part, it worked out very well.

We stopped touring in the fall of 1966, but we still got together occasionally. It wasn't until Whites were asked to leave SNCC as an organization that we finally fell apart. I continued playing with Matthew and Marshall separately and with Cordell separately. There were always requests for something. One of the most memorable moments that I have was being asked to perform at a fundraiser at NYU because there was nobody else in town. So, I was leading it and, about halfway through the set, somebody handed me a note and I had to announce to the audience that Martin Luther King had been killed. That was a frightening experience. I had everybody stand singing *We Shall Overcome*. And then everybody went home. There was fear of riots, which happened in some areas.

During those heady days in the 1960s, we learned a lot about each other and what life was like. I came from a nice, middle-class, very far left, and radical family. The makeup of the rest of the group ranged from quite poor to middle class. None of it mattered. There was a dedication that we all had, and we respected each other. And that helped to overcome a lot of the other problems. For instance, there was one concert that we did in New York where one of the speakers asked all the Whites to leave the meeting before he spoke. At the time, he was a playwright named Leroy Jones. All of the Freedom Singers left following that request. We all walked out. So, we defended each other. We were defending Jim Forman's concept of an integrated face and I stayed with the group.

The places we went and the people that we met were outstanding and very dedicated. You had to be, to be in that movement. It was not a safe place to be. I was 18. Now I'm 73. It has been a lifelong commitment.

**Susan J. Erenrich**

Talk about some of the stories from the road. What was a typical scenario?

## Bill Perlman

It looked like six large guys in a single station wagon driving for sometimes 10 or 12 hours to get to where we were going. It was crowded. It got a little smelly after a while. It was kind of cramped. We got on each other's nerves. But by the time we got out of the car and walked on stage, everybody transformed. And if I may say so, we were very good. We were well-rehearsed. And unlike the movement song leaders, who were out on the picket lines and in the fields, who sang the songs and people sang with them, we were a professional singing group. And the harmonies were out of the church. And it was just amazing. It's one of the better things that I have ever done in my life. One of the most satisfying.

There's very little in life that compares to being on stage and getting the kinds of reactions that we did — the applause, the appreciation. And to combine it with the fact that we were spreading the word of the Civil Rights Movement, telling the stories, just made it that much more extraordinary. I've done many other things in my life from working in a shoe store to being a charter pilot. Nothing compares to the time I spent with the SNCC Freedom Singers. And over the years, of the six people in our group, three of them have passed away — both Matthew and Marshall Jones and Cordell Reagon. The rest of us keep in very close touch. They are some of the oldest and closest friends I have, and we are as dedicated today as we were then. And as upset now as we were back then with what is happening now.

## Susan J. Erenrich

I met you in 1997, for the first time, when we had a reunion concert at the Holton-Arms School in Bethesda, MD. The show featured you, Matt and Marshall Jones, Emory Harris, Wazir Peacock, and Magpie (Terry Leonino & Greg Artzner). After that, our paths crossed many times at SNCC reunions. And then we had the tribute concert for Jim Forman at the Peoples' Voice Cafe in New York City. And sadly, Matt's Celebration of Life in the main hall at the Community Church of New York. And of late, too many funerals. Say a bit more about your current status with the SNCC Freedom Singers.

**Bill Perlman**

Yes — my time with the SNCC Freedom Singers has been a lifelong journey. People always asked me how I got into the movement. My response was that I was sort of going into the family business. Initially, they wouldn't let me sing. I just played the guitar. I'm singing now cause we're losing personnel. So, they need the voice.

For the last 10 years or so, we've been going to Selma every year. It was the last trip I took before the pandemic hit. We went to Mississippi every year for a number of years for the Veterans of the Mississippi Civil Rights Movement Conference. We performed at the Smithsonian Folklife Festival one year. We were in demand before the pandemic hit. It wasn't expensive to get us to where we had to go even though we lived all across the country. But as money became hard to get, we performed less. There were other things we did for a number of years. We went to the Children's Defense Fund's training outside of Knoxville, Tennessee. The organization trained people to create a freedom school prototype modeled after the freedom schools of the 1960s.

**Susan J. Erenrich**

Talk about some of the lessons that can be learned from the Civil Rights Movement, SNCC, and the SNCC Freedom Singers. What can this generation of movement folks gain from your experiences?

**Bill Perlman**

Well, the underlying issue has been around since 1619, which is when the first enslaved Africans were brought to this country. And racism has been with us ever since. So, there's been a common theme. It has changed its appearance over time, but the overarching problem is still present and affecting people of color across the world. It has taken different forms. It has taken different shapes. It's been worse at some points in history than others. But it has never gone away.

For instance, when I first joined the group in 1965, the word integration was used everywhere. And for some time, that was the goal. But by 1967 or 1968, that concept appeared to be impossible. The general population was not ready for a fully integrated society. And so, the movement switched its emphasis to the vote. It's the one thing that would give us the power that we needed to get people elected, to unseat some of the hardcore segregationists and racists from the local government up to the federal government.

The Civil Rights Act and the Voting Rights Act seemed like victories at the time. Unfortunately, a lot of the teeth that they both had have been removed by the courts in the last number of years — in the Southern States in particular. The Northern Midwest States have reverted back to voter suppression. They're trying to do it through voter ID laws, gerrymandering, and whatever other techniques they can find to decrease the number of people of color who are voting. It's a constant battle. It is very frustrating and infuriating, but this is still with us.

**Susan J. Erenrich**

Do you see change on the horizon?

**Bill Perlman**

Yeah, I see change on the horizon. I don't know which way it's going. In the sixties, we had two very well known, identifiable leaders in the movement. There was Malcolm X on one side and Martin Luther King on the other. These were people we could identify with. They were the charismatic leaders that appeared at exactly the right time.

No one, as far as I am concerned, has replaced either one of those two leaders. They were known, respected, and listened to. Today, there are groups everywhere. There are things going on, but there certainly isn't the sort of aggregating force — the person, or people, who hold everybody together.

In SNCC, we had Ella Baker, the Executive Director of the Southern Christian Leadership Conference (SCLC), and an advisor to SNCC. She believed in a group centered leadership approach. She believed we are all leaders. We also had Fannie Lou Hamer, a great indigenous community organizer in Mississippi, and Jim Forman, the Executive Secretary of SNCC. They played a vital role.

In terms of the general population, however, people didn't know who Ella Baker was. She worked behind the scenes. The people in the movement knew the people in the movement. The general population did know who Fannie Lou Hamer was. She was out there singing at places like the Newport Folk Festival. And she made national news during the 1964 National Democratic Convention when her testimony about the state of affairs in Mississippi was broadcast throughout the country. And they did know who Jim Forman was. They weren't people who showed up in the newspapers very often. But they were the people who defined the movement — who helped us get going — who taught us how to work together nonviolently. The philosophy of nonviolence was a key part of the movement at the time.

And there were people in the movement who truly believed in nonviolence, not just as a strategy or tactic. It was a lifestyle and a life philosophy to them. For instance, Bernard Lafayette — he is still teaching courses in nonviolence and working in that way. There were others who accepted nonviolence as a tactic, but were not necessarily themselves, nonviolent people. It was a tactic that worked to some extent. It worked a lot better when there were press cameras present.

I think the use of nonviolence held people in the movement together during that time. We were so outnumbered. There was no point to any kind of violence. You would just be asking to get killed.

Things were a little different out in California with the Black Panther Party. They armed themselves as a matter of self-defense. They were not willing to take the kind of abuse that was inflicted upon them year after year. And the level of abuse that's going on now, I think, is pushing us in the same direction. That's one of the things I worry about.

In the sixties, we also had known enemies. There was Governor George Wallace from Alabama, who was one of the faces of the South, and Senator James Eastland from Mississippi. These were people who were identifiable and were the living definition of racist. It's easier to fight when you have something and someone that you can visualize.

So as far as today is concerned, there are groups that are doing a lot of community organizing. There's a lot of stuff happening separately and in pockets. Black Lives Matter is not a unified organization. It's an umbrella for lots of individual efforts. And they're all good. But when you're looking for an enemy or you're looking for a friend, it helps to have something tangible.

I've always described it as a face that I can put on a dart board. During the Vietnam War, it was Nixon. It was McNamara. It was the people who were leading the war. In the Civil Rights Movement, it was Wallace and various sheriffs and governors. But today, I don't know of anybody who can name the CEO of a large bank. And they are part of the reason that people are being abused.

Lives lost and threatened. So many now with this virus. And the United States is perhaps the most irresponsible government in the world — both in terms of the pandemic and in terms of foreign policy. And everything else that you can think of. So, it's a very frustrating time for me.

**Susan J. Erenrich**

What is your legacy? What do you want people to know about you?

**Bill Perlman**

Oh, hell, I don't know. I got involved in the antinuclear movement in the sixties when I was in high school — going on marches and running benefit concerts. My parents, going back to the 1930s, were always active, and my great grandfather was an anarchist. So, I just grew up in movements, unions, civil liberties groups, and steeped in first amendment issues. I grew up knowing a lot of the people in those movements. Like Alger Hiss — I met him a number of times. He was the American official accused of spying for the Soviet Union in the 1930s. That is just one example.

I met many people who made sacrifices and went to jail. They had been discriminated against and blacklisted. I grew up around them and was inspired by them. Then came the Freedom Singers and a variety of other things through the years. And then finally, when I moved to where I am now, which is a very small town in Western Massachusetts, I ran the local select board. The board is made up of three people, who kind of administer and run the town. I was on the board for 15 years. I have also been a County Commissioner now for over 20 years. So, I've worked outside the government and am still working hard from within the government to deal with problems of poverty and a lack of education.

The County that I live in is the poorest in the state of Massachusetts. We have the highest domestic abuse rate. We have one of the highest rates of alcoholism. It's a constant battle to get government resources out here. We need programs — treatment centers, safe housing for abused women. And this is a fairly racist area. There are a lot of good Progressives up here, but there are very few people of color. The ones that are here are viewed with suspicion. Everybody knows my background. It flies in the face of a lot of them. But we've gotten to know each other on a personal basis, and that's how I try to convince them that there are other people who are left-wingers that are also okay.

Some of my left-wing friends ask me how I can hang out with right-wingers. I say, I can hang out with them because they're good people. They have a bad view of politics, but they have many, many good qualities. And I get to talk to them. I get to argue with them without coming to blows. It's a way of working more one on one. The county government has become quite active. I've been pushing them on some social causes like trying to get resources and people into Franklin County who can help build the county economically and socially. It's important. We're not far from Springfield, MA, which is more urban. And they have all of the problems of every other urban area up here. We have similar problems in this rural area. We still have the drugs. We still have the racism.

Then there are a few of us who happen to be good people and who are trying to change things. I'm not sure if we're fighting human nature. I hope not. But there are days that I think we are.

**Susan J. Erenrich**

So, as we wind down our chat, do you have any final thoughts about the SNCC Freedom Singers or the Civil Rights Movement?

**Bill Perlman**

It was an exciting time. There are a few more stories I'd like to tell.

So, I guess it was June of 1966. I was on the Meredith March Against Fear. It was a major movement event in the South. It was the first time I got beaten in jail. And in a way, it was sort of a Rite of Passage that virtually everybody else around me in the movement had gone through.

Others had been beaten up numerous times, jailed numerous times. But because I was young and small, I was protected a lot of the time by the other guys in the group. But that time, the group was not together. I just went down to the March. It was terrifying while it was happening, but in some ways, it was gratifying after it was over. I wasn't sure how I would react to the situation, but I think I did fairly well.

You see, I was still a kid. The rest of the group raised me into a world that I didn't really know. The first time I had gone South was with the Freedom Singers. It was a whole different world down there.

It was surprising, not to them, but to me, that there could be that level of hatred. People were willing to kill you on a whim and it didn't make any difference. There was no getting into conversations. There was no point that you could find in common. The beliefs were so different, and the hate was palpable. And I began to learn a little bit about what it feels like not to be treated as a human being. I just became more and more impressed with people who have managed to live their lives under this kind of society.

People in the movement fought back, and now many more are fighting back. They are not accepting this as their lot in life. And that's encouraging.

It's frustrating because we're not making the kind of progress that we need to make. Matthew Jones wrote a song titled, *When I Was Young.* Some of the words are: *"Who [would have] thought I'd still be fighting 30 or 40 years down the line."* But it turned out to be 50 or 60 years down the line. Who would have thought that we would have these huge successes like the Civil Rights Act and the Voting Rights Act. Then we had the election of Barack Obama, who became President, and I really wanted to hang my hat up and say, "We've done it." But we haven't. We haven't even come close.

I don't have the energy to do what I did back then. Being in a station wagon for three months at a time. Not being home. It would kill me now. But I wouldn't have given that experience up for anything. To be invited to participate in the movement was an honor. To meet and be accepted into the group was not easy. But again, it's something that I treasure. And the friendships. It was hard to go through some of the experiences that we went through and not create this extraordinary bond that all SNCC people have.

Of course, we fought among ourselves. I remember being at a rest stop and walking back from the building to the car with Cordell. We saw Chico and Matthew trading blows with each other. Cordell and I just stopped, turned around, and walked back to the building. As I said before, we had two sets of brothers lined up in mortal battle and we figured this was the time not to get into the fray. The fights were always over something really stupid. It would pass. Then, we would get back into the car, and off we'd go to do our concert. I suspect that being in close proximity with that number of people for that many hours at a time, is bound to try anybody's patience. Nobody ever wavered on our purpose. Nobody ever wavered on the reason we were doing it. We knew what that was, and we stayed with it.

It's important to keep this history alive. People aren't really learning about the Civil Rights Movement.

Last September, in 2019, we performed in a lot of schools in Denmark. The children and the adults knew there had been a Civil Rights

Movement in the United States, but they didn't know much else about it. They knew a couple of names. They had no idea what the chronology looked like. They didn't know the difference between the Freedom Riders and SNCC. And when I talk to people who are younger — in their twenties, thirties — it is amazing to me how little they know of what went on other than MLK giving a great speech in Washington, D.C. in 1963.

There's very little education about the history of the movement. It's important. And it's getting harder to get primary resources because we're dying at an alarming rate. A lot of the performances that the Freedom Singers have been doing in the last number of years have been at funerals.

That's a hard thing. It's very hard. People who I've grown up with, loved and respected, have passed on. It is difficult. We are all aging. I leave a conference and wonder: How many of these same people will be back next year? That was the fear when they canceled the 60th anniversary of the SNCC gathering because of the pandemic. There are people who haven't made it, and won't make it, to June of 2021. That is when the conference has been rescheduled for Washington, D.C.

I would have hoped that those people would have at least seen some of the progress that they helped create in their lifetime. But it's not going to happen. I don't see this centuries-long struggle with racism changing.

People made lots of sacrifices by joining the movement. Some had to leave home, having to rebel against their parents. I didn't have any of those problems. If anything, the family encouraged me and was supportive all the way. And that was a tremendous help. I was a good guitarist. They were a great singing group, and we had a purpose. You can't get much more out of life than that.

There were other experiences that made it magical.

I remember being up in Nova Scotia. It was the middle of winter. Whoever decided that we were going to do concerts in January in

Nova Scotia had to be out of their mind. I remember trying to get to one of those auditoriums. We had a government plow truck in front of us. Otherwise, there was no way we were driving a car through that weather. We had a small enough audience that we called them all up onto the stage. We all sat in chairs on the stage. We closed the curtains, and we all sang. I think that was in 1966.

We had other weather-related incidents. One time, when we were driving along, we thought we were on Route One in Maine. That's when Chico drove us off the road into a huge snowbank. It turns out that we were barely on the road at all. It was an unused logging road. It was the middle of the night. We couldn't get the car out. One member of the group thought that he was freezing to death. He had that feeling right before you freeze to death. You feel warm. Another member was terrified of bears. He was convinced that we were going to be eaten by a bear. We walked up the road and found a little hunting cabin. We broke in. We ate the popcorn that was left there and made in a fire. The next morning a logging truck pulled us out of the snowbank. I think the most dangerous thing that I did while I was in the movement was to be a passenger while Chico was driving!

No one in our group died as a result of the singing and marching.

As for being the only White member of the group — at the time, I was never really made aware of the pushback by some members of SNCC against my being in the group. I was shielded from that. I'm glad I was. I don't know how I would have reacted. It might have been the end. It wasn't my place to stand up to that decision. And personally, I think that the integrated look was the correct one for SNCC. There were a lot of White people who were involved with SNCC from the beginning. It worked.

There were other conflicts. Some people didn't like the idea that we were doing some songs that were not gospel. We sang a Beatles song. We did a Phil Ochs song. And some of Matthew's songs were not in the same traditional movement genre. That bothered some people musically. And the fact that there was an instrument, my guitar, also bothered some people musically. So, we had those smaller battles to fight and issues to work around.

SNCC was a consensus organization. This means that if you were going to make a decision, everybody had to agree on it. It was not a majority vote. This is why staff meetings sometimes took two weeks. One meeting, in 1967, was held in a resort in upstate New York. The resort was called Peg Leg Bates. It was the meeting where the vote asking all White members of SNCC to leave the organization took place.

About four or five years later, I was traveling in New York, and I see a guy on the side of the road who seems to be having trouble changing a tire. So, I pulled over behind him. I saw the license. It said Peg Leg. I helped him change his tire. And I said to him, after I got done, "I'm sort of familiar with your resort." He said, "Have you been there?" I told him that I was in SNCC at the time that the notorious meeting took place. He was beside himself. He said, "I can't tell you how sad I am to have my name connected with that."

I guess in some way, it was the natural progression. And today, to some extent, a lot of these protests are very integrated with more and more people being horrified at what's going on.

**Susan J. Erenrich**

We are out of time, so we are going to have to end it there. I'm thrilled, my friend, that you agreed to share part of your story this afternoon. I always thought that your story was an important one and that it should be told.

**About the Author**

Bill Perlman was born in 1947 in Brooklyn, New York. He began playing with the Freedom Singers at the age of 18, following his graduation from high school. His mother, Lucille Perlman, was already an active member of the Student Nonviolent Coordinating Committee, SNCC. Bill performed with the group for almost two years. He later performed as a solo guitarist and worked in theatre, film, and video. After many years of being a "child of the 60s", Perlman earned his Bachelor's degree in Electrical Engineering and his Master's in Computer Science. He has worked in that field for the last 30 years. But he has rejoined the Freedom Singers whenever the opportunity arose. He now resides in Ashfield, Massachusetts, where he continues to be politically active at both the local and county level of government.

# CHAPTER 8
# CARRY IT ON
## A STUDIO SESSION WITH SINGER-SONGWRITER REGGIE HARRIS

### INTRODUCTION

By Susan J. Erenrich

On February 1, 2019, singer-songwriter/storyteller/cultural ambassador Reggie Harris stopped by the WERA.FM Audio Suite in Arlington, VA to play some music and chat. For folks not familiar with Reggie, you are in for a real treat. For more than 40 years, Reggie's mission has been to educate, entertain, and inspire. He is a teaching artist for the John F. Kennedy Center's Changing Education Through the Arts program, a Woodrow Wilson Scholar, and the Director of Music Education for the Unitarian Universalist Living Legacy Project. His work has taken him throughout the United States, Canada, and across Europe where he has averaged 250 dates per year. Some readers/listeners might know Reggie previously as one-half of the acclaimed folk acoustic duo Kim and Reggie Harris. What follows is an edited transcript of our session featuring our conversation. You can listen to the interview, which features some of Reggie's songs, by clicking on the radio show link below. Enjoy!

**Listen**

*Wasn't That A Time Episode 104: A Studio Session With Singer-Songwriter Reggie Harris*

https://www.mixcloud.com/WasntThatATime/wasnt-that-a-time-episode-104-a-studio-session-with-singer-songwriter-reggie-harris/

## CARRY IT ON: A STUDIO SESSION WITH SINGER-SONGWRITER REGGIE HARRIS

### Susan J. Erenrich

Welcome to *Wasn't That A Time: Stories & Songs That Moved The Nation* on WERA-L P Arlington, Virginia 96.7 FM. We're going to spend the next 55 minutes, give or take a few, with my dear friend, Reggie Harris. I'm Susie Erenrich, your host for the hour. I'll kick off the afternoon's conversation by asking you about your involvement with the music of the underground railroad.

### Reggie Harris

Well, the underground railroad has been part of my life for years and years and years. When I started out, I wanted to be rich and famous like everybody else. My partner Kim and I were doing love songs and we were writing and doing songs by mirroring other people - some, that we heard on the radio. But as I traveled around the country, it became very difficult finding work. Part of it was just the climate of the time. Part of it was that people were reacting to the fact that we were African Americans touring around the country doing love songs. Even though I grew up in Philadelphia and faced segregation and racism my entire life, I wasn't really ready for what the impact of being an African American out and around the country was going to bring.

It just began to dawn on us. People didn't want to hear Black people singing love songs, at least not in terms of the folk music community we were part of. Obviously, there are lots of African Americans who sing love songs, but within the small community colleges and what have you, we were finding it difficult to get work. So, we began to look around for a topic that we could actually do to make ourselves more palatable to the audiences. Obviously, they were responding to our race. The anger that came from that time period was channeled into a discovery that if we were going to represent people around America, to our mostly White audiences, we needed to represent the positive nature of what it was we brought to the table.

In looking around, we found this topic called the underground railroad. It came out of our childhood of singing spirituals - spirituals that were used as code songs, mapping songs, and songs of encouragement during slavery. They were also secret code songs. Here was a topic that we could use to introduce the audience to a whole other side of African American life. Then we found out that schools actually were interested in the historical subject of the underground railroad. So that's actually how we sort of took a little break from trying to promote all these songs we were writing and just settled into performing songs that had this historical meaning and context.

People didn't necessarily have to like us to book us. They were booking the topic. It opened up a new opportunity to do performances - not only for the public, but also in schools. So really, it was a very pragmatic thing to try to get work. But what that set off in me was a desire to know more about myself and my history and, to really seize on this topic of the spirituals, what they really mean to the overall American experience. After discovering this, my love of history and my knowledge of the way music connects history and social movements just led to the Civil Rights Movement. The same songs that were used on the underground railroad to get people out of slavery were the songs that people began to sing as they began to work towards voting rights and voter registration.

So, it was a very natural progression. I love how one thing often leads to another. And besides, the songs, not only were part of my past, but there were songs that I love to sing: *Wade in the Water* and *Oh Freedom* and *Steal Away*. They lead very naturally into songs like *Been Down Into the South* and, *Keep Your Eyes on The Prize* and *We Shall Overcome*. The connectivity of that really got me excited about myself as a musician and myself as an advocate for peace and justice.

**Susan J. Erenrich**

Reggie, I first met you around 1992, when I developed the *Freedom Is A Constant Struggle* Project, a major multimedia undertaking spotlighting the Mississippi Civil Rights Movement. Since then, you have participated in a multitude of educational ventures centered around the struggles of racial inequality in this country. Tell us about your commitment to learn, teach, and engage in courageous conversations about the topic of race.

**Reggie Harris**

I love looking back and seeing the ways in which our connection has really brought so much of what I'm doing today into being. When Kim and I first met you, we were deeply involved in publicizing and promoting the story and the message of the underground railroad. It was a Civil Rights Movement in America, in the 1700s and 1800s, where you had people of different races, different religions, and different backgrounds coming together. You were doing all of this extensive material on the Civil Rights Movement, and we had just begun to really tag into those songs. So, it was really an opportunity to expand the frame. I didn't realize at that time that a lot of my future activity would be based on connecting people with those songs.

Certainly, the work I'm doing today is a direct result of that. I have had the opportunity to be in the room and on the streets and in the schools talking about the Birmingham Children's March and the March on Washington. Teaching about the Civil Rights Movement is the work that I do now with the Living Legacy Project — an organization that takes people on Civil Rights tours. We take people to Alabama and Mississippi and Tennessee and Georgia. I have a particular love of connecting people with those songs. The Civil Rights Movement was framed and fueled by songs. So, when you brought Matt Jones into my life and Marshall Jones and then I met Chuck Neblett and Hollis Watkins, figures I read about suddenly came alive.

Now I'm doing that music. I saw Hollis this very year, in January. He is now a feature on one of the tours that I lead. We take people to Jackson, Mississippi, and we have Hollis talk to our group for about an hour and a half. One of my highlights this year was he and I standing in the middle of the street singing to 23 college kids. Getting them interested in why the music of the underground railroad and the Civil Rights Movement is such a powerful vehicle for change. I've taken these songs around the world, Germany, Italy, and other places in Europe. Singing these songs has become an everyday thing.

They were also very much connected with my writing around the time that we got acquainted with you. My writing started to change. The songs that I began to write really had much more of an issue-oriented frame. Most of the CDs I've produced over the years have really connected with the human frame of how music makes change possible. I have to say thank you to you for that introduction and for helping to frame out a way of life that has felt very fulfilling to me because I've continued to make this connection both personally and globally.

**Susan J. Erenrich**

As I mentioned at the top of the hour, Reggie has recently released a new album titled, *Ready to Go*, which is his first solo recording. Reggie, tell us about your new CD.

**Reggie Harris**

Well, the album came about because in 2015, Kim and I decided to separate - at least as working partners and as married partners. We still do a few concerts every year together, but I needed to branch out and do a frame album from myself - an album that really showed some of the things that I kept under wraps for all those years as a partner in the duo. When you're in a duo, you compromise, you collaborate, you don't always get the chance to bring your best self to the fore. This was an opportunity for me to unleash myself and have fun with it.

And so, I called my friend, Greg Greenway. I've sung on his albums a lot. I always appreciate the way he records albums. He helped me coproduce it. We went in the studio and spent about nine months framing out a CD. This album is uniquely me. And I think it's resonating with people. When they come back with reviews and comments it is positive. They hear my voice in a different way. They hear my experience coming out of the songs. Seven original songs were written for this CD. They encapsulate the experience that I've been living all these years.

Of course, I could not do a CD without including some spirituals. So, I put on songs like *Sheep, Sheep*, which is one of my favorites of the Georgia Sea Island Singers, and *Been Down Into The South*, which I actually learned from Hollis Watkins. I had a great time revisiting Phil Ochs material. His song, *Another Age*, is on the album along with a remake of a Bob Dylan tune, *The Times They Are A-Changin'*, and they certainly are. So, it's been a great statement to put out in the world. When you put these things out, you don't know how they're going to be received. I've been really gratified by the reception. It ended up being the number five album for the year of 2018 on the Folk DJ chart. A little bit of a push but, the great thing is — if all of those things hadn't happened, if the accolades hadn't come in, I'd still feel great just making the statement. It is who I am. It is what I meant to say. It is me at my best in that moment. And that feels pretty good.

**Susan J. Erenrich**

Reggie, you're currently doing a show with singer songwriter Greg Greenway titled *Deeper Than the Skin*.

**Reggie Harris**

Well, Greg Greenway has been an important figure in my life. We've been friends for 30 years. We met through the Phil Ochs Song Nights. For those who know Greg's work, he's a literary writer. He's a passionate Civil Rights writer. He has written some of the best songs, I think, that have been commentaries on social issues. Our friendship has been framed around music, sports, and race. About four years ago, we started talking about doing a show together. Greg and I are presently doing that show. It's called, *Deeper Than the Skin*, which describes both our friendship and our approach to living in the world as artists. It's a show that is story and song based. It's a show where we share our individual stories about how we came to be in this world.

Greg's a White man growing up in Richmond, Virginia, and I was born three days earlier — growing up as a Black man in Philadelphia, Pennsylvania with roots in Virginia. We talk about how we came together and how music forged our vision of the world. But then we also talk about some of the joys and difficulties of framing a friendship in a very racist country and how our coming of age as artists and as people has given us an opportunity to mirror for the world a way to come together. The show encompasses all of that. And the neat thing is, at the end of the show we open it up to the audience. We ask them to comment on what they're seeing and maybe on what they're working on within their lives. It's a particularly poignant time to be doing this show in America. We didn't plan it that way. It is just something we had to do. We took a trip South into Louisiana to visit a slave plantation. After that, we made a commitment to speak out about the racial climate in this country. We decided to do it from a positive standpoint of sharing stories that hopefully open windows of opportunity.

**Susan J. Erenrich**

You mentioned the Phil Ochs Song Nights.

**Reggie Harris**

Phil Ochs Song Nights — I met Sonny Ochs at a Philadelphia Folk Song gathering and she invited Kim and I to be part of a Song Night about 30 or 32 years ago. It was in New York City at the Bottom Line. We learned a Phil Ochs tune. I think it was *That's the Way It's Going to Be*. And since then, I fell in love with his music. I didn't really hear Phil growing up. I seem to remember hearing *Changes* on the radio, and I heard maybe a couple of other songs, but I got introduced to his music through his sister and through these Song Nights that she put on where people come and they perform his music. I'm very grateful for the fact that in midstream, about 20 years ago, she decided to change the frame. Instead of just coming and singing all of his songs, she opened it up so that we do some of his music and some of our music. That way, each of us who are topical songwriters get to share our own music. We can show that the continuum of writing is going forward into the future.

It has been a particular joy of mine because I have a real affinity with the way that Phil wrote. And, even though I'm not always as in your face as he could be, it's been an education for me. It's a conduit into other ways in which you can make your point. I've had a lot of fun playing around with his songs. They provide a very melodic and chordal frame for my chordal structures. We continue to have Phil Ochs Song Nights a few times a year. We get together - Greg Greenway, Pat Wictor, Tom Prasada-Rao and lots of others are part of the line-up. Magpie, Emma's Revolution, and many others have been part of the bill. The tradition has been very long. Each of us is really committed, not only to the singing of the songs, but to living the principles of social change. Phil's been a very good foil for me to learn about being an activist in the world. I'm very grateful to Sonny for that frame, and I'm very grateful to the artists who have come in because they've actually changed my music as well.

**Susan J. Erenrich**

It's near the end of our time together. Tell me about your relationship with SNCC Freedom Singer, Matt Jones.

**Reggie Harris**

Well, Matt Jones came into my life because we were doing a concert with you. I didn't really know anything about Matt Jones before walking into that room. And I am happy to say that during the last years of his life, I got an education from Matt. What an incredible writer and incredible activist. Matt and I, we kind of danced around each other for years. As a Black man in folk music, I didn't know much about his history. I'm happy to say that we invited him to come and perform two of his songs on an album. It gave me an opportunity to sit down with Matt and have a heart-to-heart about some of the experiences of being African American males in the arts community.

I'm deeply grateful, not only for Matt's work as a Civil Rights activist and a Civil Rights artist, but as a songwriter. I think Matt typifies for me, not only the tenacity, but also the fact that at the very last stages of his life, Matt still had hope for the world. That was very clear and very evident from his writing. And that is one thing that I, as a writer, try to always continue to show in my writing. I have to thank Matt for a piece of that. It is a very vibrant part of my education.

**Susan J. Erenrich**

Thank you, Reggie, for joining me on *Wasn't That A Time: Stories &
Songs That Moved The Nation* on WERA-LP Arlington, VA 96.7 FM. The
fabulous Rusty Roberts is the on-air engineer. He sits by my side every
week to ensure the success of this show. My gratitude to Antonio
Vilaronga — who recorded and prepared the mix for this episode.

**About the Author**

Reggie Harris is a singer-songwriter, storyteller, and cultural
ambassador on a mission to educate, entertain, and inspire. For over 40
years, he has captivated audiences in the U.S., Canada, and across
Europe. Reggie combines spirituals, roots music, historic inspiration,
and moving original songs, often wrapped in the themes of unity and
social justice. He is a teaching artist for the John F Kennedy Center's
CETA program, a Woodrow Wilson Scholar, and the Director of Music
Education for the UU Living Legacy Project. He is a master song leader
who deeply values the power of song and the dignity of every human
being. Previously known as one-half of the acclaimed folk acoustic duo
Kim and Reggie Harris, this natural collaborator, also invigorates his
solo touring with occasional partnerships, most notably with Greg
Greenway, (Deeper Than the Skin) Alastair Moock, (Race and Song)
and Pat Wictor (In Concert Improv) . Reggie leads workshops and
seminars on songwriting, race relations, and performance at colleges
and universities, retreat centers, and festivals. A partial list includes the
Kennedy Center Summer Education Institute, The Swannanoa
Gathering, Boston's Summer Acoustic Music Week (SAMW), the
People's Music Network, and the Southeastern Unitarian Universalist
Summer Institute (SUUSI).

# CHAPTER 9
# A STUDIO SESSION FOR HIS 100TH BIRTHDAY
## MAGPIE SINGS PETE SEEGER

## INTRODUCTION

By Susan J. Erenrich

May 3, 2019, marked Pete Seeger's 100th birthday. Magpie (Terry Leonino & Greg Artzner) joined me in the WERA.FM audio suite on March 29, 2019, to create this celebratory program for Pete's special day. The husband-and-wife duo, who had a long-term personal and musical relationship with the man, performed Pete's songs and chatted about the legendary singer-songwriter-folklorist-cultural activist. During our time together, they also paid tribute to Pete's life and legacy with a composition of their own, "I Call Them All Love Songs." For folks not familiar with Magpie, their career, as troubadours of conscience, spans more than forty-seven years. They are award-winning recording artists, songwriters, musical historians, and social activists. What follows is an edited transcript of our conversation. You can listen to the interview, which features songs written by Pete Seeger, and performed by Magpie, as well as Pete, by clicking on the radio show link below. Enjoy.

**Listen**

*Wasn't That A Time Episode 114 - Magpie Sings Pete Seeger: A Studio Session For His 100th Birthday*

https://www.mixcloud.com/WasntThatATime/wasnt-that-a-time-episode-114-magpie-sings-pete-seeger-a-studio-session-for-his-100th-birthday/

## A STUDIO SESSION FOR HIS 100TH BIRTHDAY - MAGPIE SINGS PETE SEEGER

### I Call Them All Love Songs

Words & music by Terry Leonino & Greg Artzner, based on a comment by Pete Seeger

I call them all love songs, 'cause that is what they are

Love, though the road be smooth or rough

Love for this crazy world and all humanity

Still we know love alone is not enough


It's about the workers in solidarity

And about their singing on the line

A song about their dream to make a better world

Like a beacon through the night, we let it shine

A hope for the planet, the home that we all share

That we may strive to heal the damage we have done

A lament about wrong of war, and standing to defy

Or a song about the peace that we have won.


It's the struggle of poor people just fighting to get by

And the greedy who take more than their share

It is sung for the ones who help to feed body and mind

Of their brothers and their sisters anywhere

A song about walkin' not just talkin' as we go

Remembering the good things that we do

A song about standing with and for each other now

For we know love is not enough to see us through


A song about searching, searching for the truth

And about the things that are unknown

A song about freedom and the struggle that goes on

A story of the place you call home

A song about the river ever flowing to the sea

From the mountains in the north, forever tall

A dream of Clearwater and the wind that fills her sails

It's a song about a song about us all


*January 28, 2014*

*for Pete Seeger, May 3, 1919-January 27, 2014*


**Susan J. Erenrich**

You just heard, "I Call Them All Love Songs," a tune performed by Magpie during our special studio session on March 29, 2019. The composition is a tribute to their long-time mentor, comrade, and musical compatriot Pete Seeger. Today, May 3rd, 2019, marks Pete's one hundredth birthday.

So, during this episode of *Wasn't That a Time: Stories & Songs That Moved the Nation* on WERA-LP Arlington, VA 96.7 FM we are going to celebrate Pete's life and legacy with Magpie, my afternoon guests. I'm Susie Erenrich, your host for the hour.

After welcoming Magpie to the WERA.FM audio suite, I kicked off the afternoon's conversation by asking them about their relationship with Pete Seeger.

**Magpie**

Pete's been gone for, geez — What is it now? Five years? He's not really gone because his music lives on.

**Susan J. Erenrich**

Talk to me about your relationship with Pete.

**Magpie**

We got to be pretty good friends with Pete over the years. We met in 1984 in Philadelphia. Terry and I both grew up with Pete's music. He was a major influence on us in a lot of different ways, but we didn't actually meet him until 1984. There was a conference in Philadelphia of the People's Music Network (PMN) and Pete was there. It was a political songs conference.

It was a gathering of people who write and perform political songs and do music for political action. That was Pete's wheelhouse for sure. So, he was there on the opening night. There was a great big concert and he performed at the concert. We were introduced to him. We didn't make a great impression on him because we didn't actually perform. We were just introduced. But a couple of years later, at another PMN gathering, this time in Brooklyn, New York, we met him again. It is a very interesting little story.

We were sitting in the registration room at the conference — sitting off to one side on a couple of stools. We were just playing a song of his that he had written many years before. Pete had set the tune to the words of Nicola Sacco — the last letter that Sacco wrote to his son, Dante, on the night that he was executed back in 1927. We had learned the song from an album of Woody Guthrie songs about Sacco and Vanzetti. Moses Asch put out the album. He put this one track that Pete wrote at the end of the album. It's the best track on the album. Pete wrote this absolutely beautiful tune.

So, we were sitting in that registration room entertaining none other than Sonny Ochs, who was filling out everybody's information as they came in. Pete arrived. We were off to one side, so he didn't really see us at first when he walked into the room. We were playing "Sacco's Letter to His Son," actually replaying it for the second time. It was the first time we got through it. We were going to perform it at the plenary concert that night. We didn't even get eight bars into the song when Pete came into the room to register for the weekend. He's down there and he's leaning over at the table, writing his name down on the book, and he hears us singing off in the corner.

And he says to Sonny, "I wrote that song 30 years ago. It was probably more than 30 years ago, but 30 years ago." And she just sort of pointed him over in our direction. So, he came over. We were sitting there on the stools singing, facing each other, and he came up real close. He stood right next to us, listening to us sing his song, and we could feel him right there. We saw him out the corner of our eyes. We knew he was there, but we didn't stop. We just kept singing. And then when we got done singing, we turned and looked up at him and he was standing there with tears streaming down his face. And he just grabbed the both of us and gave us a great big three-way hug. And we were friends from that moment on.

**Susan J. Erenrich**

Pete Seeger was a legendary musician, singer-songwriter, folklorist, activist, environmentalist, and peace advocate. He founded Clearwater. According to the official Clearwater site, in 1966, in despair over the pollution of his beloved Hudson River, Pete announced plans to "build a boat to save the river."

At the time, the Hudson was rank with raw sewage, toxic chemicals, and oil pollution. Fish had disappeared over many miles of its length. Pete, along with many other concerned individuals, believed a majestic replica of the sloops that sailed the Hudson in the 18th and 19th centuries would bring people to the river where they could experience its beauty and be moved to preserve it. Inspired by that vision, the organization began with the launch of the sloop *Clearwater* in 1969 — a majestic, 106-foot-long, replica vessel.

What can you tell our listeners about Clearwater?

**Magpie**

Well, as you said, the *Clearwater* is a boat. It's been cleaning up the Hudson River for many, many years. This year is the 50th year. There were a lot of PCBs in the river. It was poisoning the river to the point where there were no more sturgeon. There were no more fish. Everything was really bad. And it was unsafe to swim in the water. Pete had just finished reading *Silent Spring* again, and he said, "You know, the environment is really a political issue." He was really the first environmental political singer. He decided to start this boat to clean up the river. So, he got a bunch of friends together and he said, "We're going to go up and down this river on this boat. We're going to sing. And we're going to tell everybody what's going on. We're going to clean up this river. And we're going to have to advocate for legislative action in the state of New York and the federal government." So, the boat became the environmental flagship of the Hudson Valley, and it still is.

Here's how it worked. The boat would sail and then it would stop at all of these places. We would get off. And then we would set up a whole festival environment for the kids. We'd haul water out on the boat from the Hudson River and pour it into a tank. No matter what was in the water — whether it was a tire tube, whether it was a beer can, whether it was a keg of beer (there were a lot of things we pulled out that we couldn't even talk about) — we would let the kids see it, and we'd discuss it. Then they would go through these little stations where they would learn about how to clean up the rivers, and we sang songs. And then at the end, we all made stone soup. That was the big finale. And kids from schools would come with bags and bags of food — carrots, and potatoes, things that they wanted to put in the stone soup. And at the end, we would have this big soup that we would all make and eat.

This year is the 50th year of the Clearwater Festival, so we're going to participate. The festival is an offshoot of Pete's work. It started as a series of small fundraisers to build the boat. Now it's one of this country's largest environmental celebrations.

**Susan J. Erenrich**

Pete Seeger believed in grassroots leadership. Tell us about Pete's philosophy.

**Magpie**

Pete was very much on a diet of egalitarianism. He believed in the power of collective action and grassroots leadership. He hated that people put him on a pedestal. He would say, "Yeah, idols have feet of clay." Every time we had any kind of interaction with Pete, there was always that element of collective action. He always encouraged everybody to participate and get involved. And yes, he would be there to sing for you if you needed. He was famous. And he knew that he could use his fame that way, that people would come out, and they could raise money for the cause.

He could help to raise money for you just by appearing there. But that wasn't the important thing. The important thing was that you and your community came together to do what needed to be done. And if you could sing in the process of doing that, then all the better.

He was involved in the 1960s Civil Rights Movement. It was there that he really learned, even more, about the power of song and the power of music. Of course, he'd known about the power of song many, many years before — largely because of the labor movement. But the Civil Rights Movement was absolutely the pinnacle — I think probably the greatest musical, sociopolitical movement that there ever was.

**Susan J. Erenrich**

We should talk a little bit about the songs. When we originally discussed you coming to the studio, you sent me a list of around 50 songs. You narrowed them down to about six for today's session. Talk about your selection process.

**Magpie**

The songs that we sent you are the ones that we are most comfortable with. Although, there's definitely at least a handful more that we're comfortable enough to do. There are four that are prerecorded. There are some repeat Pete songs that are recorded on our albums. And then, of course, there is "Old Devil Time."

**Susan J. Erenrich**

Ah yes, "Old Devil Time." It is a Pete Seeger staple in the Magpie repertoire. Say a few words about the origins of the song.

**Magpie**

There is a special story about "Old Devil Time." In the Weaver's, Ronnie Gilbert sang "Old Devil Time." It was not one of her favorite Pete songs. We had lunch with Ronnie out in California and she told us that she never really liked the song. And the reason was because of this 12/8 thing — that 12/8 time that people do.

Pete had kind of an obsession with 12/8 time, which is basically a 4/1 — like 4/4 time except each one of the four beats has a triplet. So, it's one, two, three, one, two, three, one, two, three, one, two, three. Pete really got into that. And in fact, when he was doing "We Shall Overcome," for years and years — the early years when that song came out into the Civil Rights Movement — he would always sing it very, very much emphasizing the 12/8 time. So, when Pete did "Old Devil Time," he did the song the same way. You can hear it, if you listen to his older recordings.

And we did. And we learned it that way. And we did it that way for quite a while. But after recording it with Kim and Reggie Harris — they arranged it as a 4/4 kind of bossa nova thing, which was kind of fun — we just changed it up a little bit. Terry took the lead on it, and we put it up in E-flat. We took out the triplets. But every now and then, we'll sort of throw in a little bit of a triplet effect into the accompaniment. It's beautiful. It's just a beautiful song,

**Susan J. Erenrich**

"The Hammer Song" has been featured at concerts, rallies, demonstrations, and marches around the globe. What did this tune mean to Pete?

**Magpie**

Well, "The Hammer Song" is a mega famous song all around the world. I remember singing that song when I was in the fifth grade, but it was the Peter, Paul and Mary version. Now, the song was originally written by Lee Hays and Pete Seeger back in the early fifties, when The Weavers were popular.

It was the very first song printed in the very first issue of *People's Songs*. In fact, it was on the cover of the very first issue of *Sing Out!* magazine. So, if you want to find out what the original song was like, you can always just find that somewhere. You can actually find it in Pete Seeger's book, *Where Have All the Flowers Gone?*, which is the book about Pete's song-writing process.

It's basically the title page on this whole section of songs. It's all there in black and white. So, Terry and I, you know, it was just typical of us. We went back and learned Pete's original version of the tune, which is great. It's really kind of Peter, Peter, Paul and Mary. It's very folky. Peter, Paul and Mary's version is very driving and owes a lot to popular rock and roll. The way that they adapted the chord progression is very much the way that a lot of popular rock and roll songs were done. Only it's much more driving than most rock and roll. Rock and roll is sort of meant to be upbeat and danceable. Pete and Lee's original song was really kind of upbeat and bouncy. It's a really great tune. Their original melody had a lot of really neat stuff in it that Peter, Paul and Mary kind of homogenized. Pete wasn't keen on that at first.

But he came around, because he realized that it was good, and they did it really, really well. And it was a tremendous song. Peter, Paul and Mary always ended their shows with it. It just brought the house down. And when Pete saw that — and saw that the song was getting out to millions and millions of people — he came around. He ended up loving it so much that it's the version that takes up all the pages in his book.

**Susan J. Erenrich**

I want to thank you for tuning in to *Wasn't That a Time: Stories & Songs That Moved the Nation* on WERA-LP Arlington, VA 96.7 FM. The fabulous Rusty Roberts is the on-air engineer. He sits by my side every week to ensure the success of this show. My gratitude to Antonio Villaronga who recorded and prepared the mix for this episode.

And of course, a special shout-out to Magpie who stopped by the studio to help me celebrate Pete Seeger's one hundredth birthday. Please continue to support community radio by checking out all of the wonderful programming that 96.7 FM has to offer. To hear more episodes of *Wasn't That a Time* – follow us on Facebook at https://www.facebook.com/serenrich1970.

I'm Susie Erenrich signing out with one last tune from Magpie, "Quite Early Morning," from *Raise Your Voice*. Then I'm going to give Pete Seeger the last word with the *Wasn't That a Time* theme song from *Headlines and Footnotes: A Collection of Topical Songs*. Happy Birthday Pete!

**About the Authors**

Since 1973 Terry Leonino & Greg Artzner, MAGPIE, have entertained, uplifted, and inspired audiences around the world with their music, with their amazing versatility, powerful voices in harmony, and their provocative, captivating and moving songs, many of their own compositions, on guitars, harmonica, mandolin, and dulcimer. They have performed on stages from major folk festivals to intimate folk clubs and small concert settings, to school auditoriums and classrooms, to demonstrations, rallies, picket lines, and other venues too numerous to mention. They have toured the length and breadth of North America and toured internationally, including numerous tours of England & Scotland. They have many recordings to their credit, including collections and song cycles on special themes, and tracks on notable anthologies including songs of Civil Rights, and tributes to Phil Ochs, Utah Phillips, and Pete Seeger. Greg & Terry are also actors and playwrights, scholars of the life and legacy of abolitionist John Brown and his wife Mary, whom they have portrayed in their own stage play since 2000, and the many people associated with his revolutionary fight to end slavery in America. They have been educators and activists, never passing an opportunity to lend their voices and instruments to the causes of peace, liberation, justice, and responsibility for the Earth.

# CHAPTER 10
# SOCIAL CONSCIOUSNESS AND CULTURAL ACTIVISM
## A CONVERSATION WITH SINGER-SONGWRITER JOE JENCKS

## INTRODUCTION

By Susan J. Erenrich

On September 18, 2018, singer-songwriter Joe Jencks came to the WERA.FM studio in Arlington, Virginia. During our time together, Joe played songs from his recently released albums — *The Forgotten: Recovered Treasures From the Pen of Si Kahn* and *Poets, Philosophers, Workers & Wanderers*. He also laid down a few tracks that had never previously been recorded. In addition to his music, we chatted about his cultural activism, his relationship with Si Kahn and Pete Seeger, the current political landscape, and his work with veterans. For folks not familiar with Joe, he is an award-winning songwriter and vocalist based in Chicago. He merges conservatory training with his Irish roots and working-class upbringing. Joe is also co-founder of the harmony trio, Brother Sun. He has performed at festivals like Falcon Ridge, Kerrville, Mariposa, and Old Songs as well as in world-class performance venues like Lincoln Center and Carnegie Hall. Joe has enthralled diverse audiences with his approachable style. He is noted for his unique merging of musical beauty, social consciousness, and spiritual exploration, blending well-crafted instrumentals and vivid songwriting. Joe serves it all up with a "lyric baritone voice that has the edgy richness of a good sea salt caramel."

In addition to the reading below, you can listen to the interview, which features songs composed by Si Kahn and Joe, performed by Joe Jencks. Just click on the radio show link below. The broadcast aired on October 26, 2018. Enjoy.

**Listen**

*Wasn't That A Time - Episode 93: A Studio Session With Singer-Songwriter Joe Jencks*

https://www.mixcloud.com/WasntThatATime/wasnt-that-a-time-episode-93-a-studio-session-with-singer-songwriter-joe-jencks/

## SOCIAL CONSCIOUSNESS AND CULTURAL ACTIVISM — A CONVERSATION WITH SINGER-SONGWRITER JOE JENCKS

**Why Are the Guns Still Firing?**

Along the battery in Charleston, South Carolina

The ancient silent cannon point to sea

In 1861 they fired on Fort Sumter

The dead and wounded still cry out to you and me

Why are the guns still firing

Why are the innocent laid low

Why is this war still raging

That should have ended long ago

That war was fought in part to put an end to slavery

The nation's shame we never should forget

One hundred fifty years ago the gunners finally rested

Yet shameless violence enslaves us yet

Now nine new souls are added to the millions

Who've lost their lives in this uncivil war

And it remains for us the living

To spike the guns of hate forever more


Reprinted with Permission. © Si Kahn, Joe Hill Music ASCAP.


**Susan J. Erenrich**

Today on *Wasn't That A Time: Stories & Songs That Moved The Nation* on WERA-LP Arlington, Virginia 96.7 FM, we're going to spend the next 55 minutes, give or take a few, with Joe Jencks. I'm Susie Erenrich, your host for the hour. You just heard, *Why Are the Guns Still Firing* — a song composed by Si Kahn and recorded and performed by Joe Jencks. Joe sang the song during our special studio session on September 18, 2018.

I kicked off the afternoon's conversation by asking Joe about his early cultural activism roots.

**Joe Jencks**

First off, let me just say thanks so much for having me on your show. What a pleasure it is to be here with you. I'm so glad that you're doing this work on radio and in the community. The songs that we sing as artists, as activists — the songs that we write — they all have a history. They come out of a context. It's such a joy to have an opportunity to share these songs in a place where there's room to give some of the context. So, thanks for the work you're doing here.

I'm the youngest of seven children in my family of origin. I was raised in an Irish Catholic family. When I was growing up in the seventies and eighties and early nineties, there was a very strong community doing social justice work. It was moving through the Catholic Church. The idea of social justice was very pervasive. I would say, some of the theoretical concepts of liberation theology had trickled down to the congregational level.

And there were people who were leading strong movements in Eastern Europe — like Lech Wałęsa, the Polish union activist, statesman, dissident, and Nobel Peace Prize winner, who ushered in the Solidarity Movement. He eventually became the president of Poland. He was held up as a hero. During my childhood, there were clergy who were in Central America. They were teaching people to read, setting up schools and hospitals. They were nuns and priests. Many of them were killed for standing up to the military dictatorships. Those were some of the activists and martyrs who were held up in my community as people doing good work — social justice work in the world. So, I think my early childhood was very steeped in that practice.

Plus, I think having an Irish heritage also contributed. My mom, much to the chagrin of my Republican father, taught us a great deal about revolutionary politics. She taught it to us through the lens of Irish culture. So, it was not an immediate threat to the status quo here in the States, because we were learning about a different place. But the core lessons of collaborative effort and people working together in community to better their own condition or to better the condition of others in solidarity was an idea that was very present in my childhood. I don't know anybody who grew up in a large family that didn't grow up engaged in cooperative work in order to make the family system work.

I jokingly say — being the youngest of seven — I had a keen sense of systems of oppression. That's tongue in cheek. I have extraordinary siblings and they're all incredibly engaged human beings. And they were very encouraging as well when I started to show a sense of curiosity about the world around me.

**Susan J. Erenrich**

Your most recent album is called *The Forgotten: Recovered Treasures From the Pen of Si Kahn*. Tell our audience a bit about your relationship with Si.

**Joe Jencks**

I met Si Kahn almost 20 years ago at a Folk Alliance International Conference. We both participated in a song circle and became fast friends. And we were both members of Local 1000, The Traveling Musicians Union. After that initial meeting, we kept in touch. We played a few concerts together over the years in different parts of the country. Then about five or six years ago, Si approached me with about 60 or 70 songs that he had written and never recorded. He asked me if I would be interested in recording some of them. I said, "Well, I'd love to, but I have a lot on my plate." I listened to all of the songs and flagged about 25 of them — the ones that really spoke to me in one form or another. Then I got really busy with my band and my solo work.

But in November of 2016, I was ready to record a new album. I dug out all of the songs that Si sent me and listened again. I never consulted my original notes. I picked my favorite 14 — the ones that best represented Si and the folks he wrote about.

**Susan J. Erenrich**

You were friends with Pete Seeger. Talk about your association with the American folk singer-songwriter and activist.

**Joe Jencks**

Like I mentioned previously, I grew up in a family that had very strong Irish roots — and strong roots in Québec. There were fiddling traditions from both. It is an ethnic culture that I was very familiar with. A couple of my siblings played strings. My sister Jen was a great Fiddler. And my Uncle Louie, who we used to visit up in Minnesota — he used to do the thing that the Québécois artists do where they tapped their feet and kind of tap danced along with the fiddle playing. I have very fond memories of that time. And by the age of eight, I felt like I had a pretty strong handle on what folk music was. Then one of my oldest sisters came home from college with a gift for me. It was Pete Seeger and Arlo Guthrie live at Carnegie Hall.

It was a record that changed the direction of my life. I memorized every song on that record. I learned to play each tune. But I never would have imagined that I would get to know Pete Seeger — or call him a friend — or call him a mentor in a very direct way. In 1998, Pete and I met at the Seattle Folklife Festival and then in 2000 again at the Folk Alliance Conference. I got to perform with Pete at that conference. After that, I started going to the People's Music Network gatherings and got to know Pete much more through those gatherings. And then — I think it was Father's Day of 2002 — Pete and I had about a two-and-a-half-hour conversation, just the two of us one-on-one, about what it meant to be men, what it meant to be husbands, what it meant to be brothers, what the role of fatherhood is, and what it is to be a son.

It was around the 10th anniversary of my father's death. It was a very powerful experience. And I think he shared some ideas with me that he'd been sitting on for a long time but hadn't had an occasion to share with anyone. And so, it was from that moment forward that we became genuine friends.

I had the privilege of being on stage with him a few other times. On the morning that he passed away I got a call from Reggie Harris. He wanted me to hear it from a friend and not from some anonymous news source. My immediate response to finding out that Pete had passed was to hop out of bed and grab my computer. I looked up Pete's testimony from 1955 before the [U.S. House of Representative] House Un-American Activities Committee. Pete gave such an eloquent and impassioned testimony of resistance without being petulant, without being unkind.

He was just direct and firm in his views. At one point he offered to sing one of the songs, though he noted, "I don't know how well I can do it without my banjo." One of the congressmen stomped his foot and said, Mr. Seeger are you pleading the fifth amendment? And Seeger said, "No, I am not, sir." Instead, he pled the first amendment saying, it was improper for them to ask him about his associations and opinions. That was in fact his legal defense, which was very dangerous, and he was later convicted of contempt of Congress. If he had pleaded the fifth amendment and refused to offer testimony that could incriminate himself, he may have avoided prosecution. There were only about six or eight people after the Hollywood Ten pleaded the first and were imprisoned for up to a year that went before HUAC who chose the first amendment as their defense.

[Note: The exact quotes from Seeger's testimony were taken from a partial transcript. See: http://historymatters.gmu.edu/d/6457. For a detailed look in Seeger's own words regarding his choice to plead the first, see this video clip that includes footage take in April 1961, the day of sentencing. https://www.rollingstone.com/music/music-news/watch-10-minutes-of-recently-unearthed-and-rare-pete-seeger-footage-121479/]

And those folks who pleaded the first amendment eventually prevailed. Pete's conviction was overturned. So, I thought — there are going to be a lot of people writing songs about Pete —about his great works. Pete, the famous guy who traveled all over the world. Pete, the superstar. I really wanted to write about a moment that defined Pete Seeger in my life. That moment was when he said NO. I'm not going to sell out my friends. I'm not going to sell out my community. I'm not going to sell out my beliefs, my religious perspectives, my political views. I'm allowed to have those beliefs and views in this country. And you don't get to punish me for them just because they make you uncomfortable. The constitution guarantees that I have the right to speak these ideas and associate with whom I want. And that courage, I think, more than anything, is what I wanted to celebrate in this song. That's what I saw in Pete. He was a man who sang songs that helped to lessen the distance between people. He was both courageous and kind.

[Joe proceeds to sing the song. The lyrics are below]


**Let Me Sing You a Song**

*For Pete Seeger - Inspired by his HUAC Testimony in 1955*

You've asked me here to tell you

About my neighbors and my friends

To talk about the who and what

The where and how and when

Well I won't give you anything

You don't already know

But if you'd like

I'll sing that list of songs before I go


Let me sing you a song

About the people that I love

The poets and philosophers

The workers and the wanderers

The ones who walk the picket lines

Who dare to stand and fight

And the ones who hold their babies close

And rock them through the night


Now you say it's un-American

To do the things I do

Well I sing for justice, liberty

And Civil Rights it's true

But I say it's un-American

To ask me how I vote

How I pray or what I believe

But here's a song I wrote


Let me sing you a song

About the people that I love

The poets and philosophers

The workers and the wanderers

The ones who walk the picket lines

Who dare to stand and fight

And the ones who hold their babies close

And rock them through the night

If you want to send me to prison

I guess that's the way it'll be

'Cause I won't feed you fodder

For your paranoid machine

If the price of my silence is shackles

Well then fellas, take me away

For I will live to sing again

And rise with a brand new day


Let me sing you a song

About the people that I love

The poets and philosophers

The workers and the wanderers

The ones who walk the picket lines

Who dare to stand and fight

And the ones who hold their babies close

And rock them through the night

Reprinted with permission. © 1/28/14 - Joe Jencks, Turtle Bear Music, ASCAP.


## Joe Jencks

I never saw Pete be unkind when it was not necessary. I saw him be direct. I saw him be blunt at times. But I never saw him dehumanize another person in order to make a point. I think that's so needed right now in civil discourse. I think we have to find a way to speak about the things that concern us and do so in a way that does not dehumanize another person or make them less than fully human. We can only change the things we want to change in the world if we see each other as having reasons for our belief systems. Then we can meet somewhere. If we just resort to name calling, we lose the opportunity to learn from each other.

**Susan J. Erenrich**

How do you feel about the current state of affairs in this country [The USA]?

**Joe Jencks**

As we head into the 2018 midterms [elections] — as people are making decisions about who they want to put in charge of our nation — I think it is so important that people get out and vote. I would say more than anything, people have got to get out and vote and participate. Democracy hinges on the idea that literate, intelligent, engaged people will participate in the process. And if we don't know something, it's our responsibility as citizens to go out and learn it. If we're unclear about where a candidate stands, it's our job to figure that out. And I would say most of all, it's incredibly important that we use art and music and poetry and songwriting and storytelling as vehicles for social change. With the arts, we can humanize the conversation and gently caress people's hearts into an open place where there can be an actual exchange of information.

If you ask people to cite 10 speeches from the [U.S.] Civil Rights Movement, I'm not sure you would find anybody who could give you 10. If you ask them to sing you 10 songs from the movement, many people could give you a list of 15 or 20. So I think music does carry a power. Art carries a power. I hope that your listeners understand that. I hope that people continue to use art as a tool for positive and progressive change in our country.

**Susan J. Erenrich**

We are nearing the end of our time together. Before you go, can you comment on one of your projects, the work you do with veterans?

## Joe Jencks

For the last seven years, I've been the songwriter in residence for a retreat program in Spokane, Washington. The program is called Warriors: Heart to Art. It's a standalone program in Spokane that specifically serves the Spokane Valley and parts of the Pacific Northwest. In the program we bring together expressive art therapy, visual arts, songwriting, and storytelling. We invite veterans to tell their stories. So, a song I wrote, *One Piece at a Time*, is a compilation of some of the veterans' ideas. The veterans gave me permission to turn some of their stories into a song. This way, I am able to share their ideas with the world through the chorus:

Does anybody see me?

Does anybody know what I've been through?

Some folks gave their lives all at once

But I've given up my life

One piece at a time

And that really is the experience of many veterans who integrate back into society. They don't have the option of really sharing their story with people that they interact with on a daily basis. There's a sense of being disappeared, lost, invisible within our society.

The vets have taught me a lot about honor, love, and adoration. Personally, I don't believe we need soldiers to go out and die or to kill others. But they are just doing their duty by serving our country. It's our job as activists to make sure that we keep working for a just society and that we don't vilify our soldiers. They volunteer to put themselves in harm's way. We can honor their sacrifice. We can honor their intent to serve. And we can work for a nonviolent society all at once.

## Susan J. Erenrich

For folks who are interested in listening to *One Piece at a Time*, you can find it on Joe's album, *Poets, Philosophers, Workers & Wanderers*.

I want to thank you for tuning in to *Wasn't That A Time: Stories & Songs That Moved The Nation* on WERA-LP Arlington, VA 96.7 FM. The fabulous Rusty Roberts is the on-air engineer. He sits by my side every week to ensure the success of this show. My gratitude to Antonio Villaronga — who recorded and prepared the mix for this episode.

And of course — a special shout-out to Joe Jencks, who stopped by the studio to play some music and chat.

## About the Author

Joe Jencks is a 22-year veteran of the international Folk circuit, an award-winning songwriter and a celebrated vocalist based in the Chicago area. He is known for his performances of musical beauty, social consciousness, and spiritual exploration. Joe delivers engaged musical narratives filled with heart, soul, groove, and grit. Blending well-crafted instrumentals and vivid songwriting, Jencks serves it all up with a lyric baritone voice that has the edgy richness of a good sea-salt caramel. Co-founder of the harmony trio Brother Sun, Jencks has penned several #1 Folksongs including the ever-relevant Lady of The Harbor. From Carnegie Hall to Lincoln Center to Festivals across the US and Canada, Jencks has become a fan favorite throughout North America and beyond. Joe is also a dual U.S.-Irish citizen and has served as a Cultural Ambassador with the U.S. State Department. For more info, please visit: www.joejencks.com.

# SECTION 3

## EXHIBITIONS: ART, POLITICS, & RESISTANCE

# IMAGINING AND STORYING WOMEN'S ACTIVIST-LEADERSHIP THROUGH THE DISOBEDIENT WOMEN EXHIBITION

## DARLENE E. CLOVER

## INTRODUCTION

By Susan J. Erenrich

This chapter features the work of Darlene Clover. She is an activist-leadership-scholar and a chapter author in my co-edited volume, *Grassroots Leadership and the Arts for Social Change* (Emerald, 2017). This chapter on the *Disobedient Women Exhibition* is a continuation of her exploration into gender misrepresentation in the world of museums, which she wrote about in her chapter, "In Case of Emergency, Break Convention: Popular Education, Cultural Leadership and Public Museums."

In a larger context, Darlene's piece illustrates how important it is to have safe, radical, open spaces for participatory democracy. It is within these open spaces for democracy, such as the one created by Darlene in Canada, that we can inquire, engage, and dissent. We can also "become a dynamic citizenry, unafraid to exercise our shared knowledge and power" (Williams, 2004, p. 86).

I hope readers enjoy Darlene's chapter and the companion *Wasn't That A Time* radio broadcast, *Taking It to the Street*, listed below. The episode aired after the massive January 21, 2017, Women's March. The program is a retrospective on the long battle for women's equality. Throughout the show you will hear songs performed by Peter, Paul & Mary; Nettie Metcalf; Jane Sapp; Judy Gorman; Judy Collins; Holly Near; Kristin Lems; Emma's Revolution; and Jefferson Airplane.

**Listen**

*Wasn't That A Time Episode 3: Taking it to the Streets. Sights and Sounds From the 2017 Women's March.*

https://www.mixcloud.com/WasntThatATime/wasnt-that-a-time-episode-3-taking-it-to-the-streets-sights-and-sounds-from-2017-womens-march/

**Reference**

Williams, T. (2004). *The Open Space of Democracy*. The Orion Society.

## IMAGINING AND STORYING WOMEN'S ACTIVIST-LEADERSHIP THROUGH THE DISOBEDIENT WOMEN EXHIBITION

By Darlene E. Clover

"History that comes not from the lofty perspective of 'great men', conquest and capital, but rather from below, the everyday, is always difficult to perceive. Its protagonists are rarely documented; theirs is all too frequently the untold story...To 'disobey' in order to take social action is a byword for the creative spirit... We have captured through this exhibition snapshots of women's 'Promethean acts' — highly visible activities of resilience and imagination — and less visible acts, small disobediences that are part of the daily workings of women's lives in an unjust world. Together they are clever, well thought out, patiently pursued with an essence of what Bachelard (1961) called 'the spark behind all knowledge' (cited in Flood & Grindon, 2014, p. 7). Together, they are activist-leadership, a counter power of perseverance that places women squarely in the making of a more robust and just Canada." - Exhibition Curatorial Statement

*Chapter 11 Image 1. "Sisterhood Is Powerful Eh!"* Photo Courtesy Darlene Clover.

In 2017-2018 I guest curated, in collaboration with colleagues and students at the University of Victoria (UVic), Canada, a multimedia feminist exhibition titled *Disobedient Women: Defiance, Resilience, and Creativity Past and Present.* The exhibition was curated first in a Victoria Arts Council gallery in central Victoria where it remained for three weeks. It then moved, and expanded in size, to the Maltwood Gallery on the UVic campus. It was to show at Maltwood for three months but, due to popularity, was held over for one month.

Although the idea for this type of exhibition had percolated in my years of work as an activist-scholar of pedagogical aesthetics and leadership in community and later in museums and art galleries, its curation was galvanized by two inter-connected and unsatisfying conditions (Obrist & Raza, 2015). One was the positioning by the then Tory (Conservative) federal government of the Sesquicentenary of Canadian Confederation (2017) — the process by which the different provinces of Canada were united into the Dominion of Canada (a nation) in 1867 — as a story of white male heroism, war, ice hockey, discovery, and conquest. The imposition of this imperial masculine memory aimed to forestall any heresies that might suggest women had played a role in Canadian history, sexism and colonialism were deep imperfections in the national narrative, or that this narrative had been met with creative and vigorous forms of resistance by women. The second and related unsatisfying condition was findings from my research into museums and art gallery exhibitions that painted a similarly problematic male heroic picture of Canada including altogether too many sanitized historical tales that erased, stereotyped, and/or marginalized women and "the other" to the masculine norm.

Yet Obrist and Raza (2014) also remind us that unsatisfying conditions can be catalysts to "incite the imagination of new possibility" (p. 2). *Disobedient Women* was just such an act of imagination, an aesthetic coming together of art and politics. The exhibition spotlighted women's activist-leadership, both in the past and the present, through images, stories, poems, and a variety of other creative practices. In this chapter, I share images and stories of the exhibition and its pedagogical impact.

*Chapter 11 Image 2.* Photo Courtesy Darlene Clover.

## Exhibitions as Public Pedagogy

We chose to use an exhibition format for reasons that relate to its power both visually and pedagogically. Cultural scholars Macleod, Hourston Hanks, and Hale (2012), for example, describe exhibitions as narrative environments, storytellers that in visual and textual form, narrate stories about society, culture, art, history, and people to mobilize certain memories. Indeed, we can say that exhibitions are both the messenger (the storyteller) and the message (the story). Telling stories matter because this is how meaning and sense are made of our complex, complicated, and lived realities and even of ourselves. Exhibition stories matter because they lend an authority and significance that deeply influence and convince the audience of the permanence and stability of something about history and reality (Bartlett, 2016; Steeds, 2014). Building on this, exhibitions act as knowledge shapers and mobilizers. Through carefully choreographed representations — images, objects, explanatory texts, and even positioning and lighting — they activate the "seen," and as this is often our most commanding sense, "what we see is considered evidence, truth and factual" (Carson & Pajaczkowska, 2001, p. 1). In other words, what we see (and of course what we do not see) narrated through highly visual stories plays a pivotal role in what we come to know as reality, and what we therefore believe to have merit and legitimacy. Given this, when we query whether it matters if a subject is seen or represented in the stories exhibitions tell, the response has to be a resounding, yes. But we must also consider how a subject or story is represented and who tells the story because the storyteller (which exhibitions are as I noted above) is equally important. All too frequently exhibitions continue to marginalize or stereotype the stories of women and "the other." Without the power to see or represent themselves, women and those who fall outside the masculine norm will be left to the envisioning and storying (or not) of men (Bergsdóttir, 2016; Marshment, 1993).

Another element that drew us to use an exhibition format is its power to evoke the imagination (Bedford, 2014). Aesthetic exhibitions — those that use and include artforms — are visionary spaces that imagine and story other worlds, encouraging us through creativity to venture into things known yet unknown, familiar yet strange. This imagination, however, is never disconnected from the political values and ideologies and pedagogical aspirations of those who create the exhibitions, and this is certainly true of *Disobedient Women*. Our intent was specifically to encourage what is often called the radical and subversive imagination. The subversive imagination acts as a rebellion against the normative by creating alternative narratives that illustrate how, in our case, women's resistance, resilience, and creative practices were being ignored in the national historical discourse surrounding the Sesquicentenary. These rebellious acts of subversive imagination that dare to state and render visible that which has been strategically obscured shock, but they can also, according to Becker (1994, p. xiii), "be an object of outrage," which I will speak to below. The radical imagination, I argue, is similar, albeit perhaps more pedagogical. It is the mobilization of a collective, conscious, creative force aimed intentionally to not only expose but also challenge the root causes of inequality and injustice. The radical imagination is "the capacity to think critically, reflexively and innovatively about the social world" and to act upon it (Haiven & Khasnabish, 2014, p. 2). What both types of imagination have is central to feminist exhibitions — a practice of interruption and disruption. *Disobedient Women*, in particular, intentionally aimed to interrupt the silencing and erasure of women's stories and lives and disrupt the complacency of the national historical narrative espoused by the Tory government.

In summary, the exhibition format combines the power of storytelling, visualization, and imagination in ways that we felt could help us, as feminist adult educators and activists, to re-invigorate the public sphere and to engulf visitors cognitively, emotionally, and politically in a rebellious, radical, and intentionally feminist imagination — a defiant, colorful, resistive, and creative world made by the women of British Columbia who stitched, painted, drummed, recited, protested, or patiently knitted a different historical narrative.

## Constructing Disobedient Women as a Space of Feminist Public Pedagogy

Up to now, curating a feminist exhibition sounded easy. I had read all the right literature, I had seen hundreds of exhibitions, and I was a feminist adult educator. The reality of course was quite different. When I proposed the exhibition, I assumed the gallery curators would simply take the items and, well, curate them. They soon disabused me of this misconception. They would hang the exhibition, but I was to curate it — which meant I was to envision and imagine it into being. This included a great deal of "maths" and working off blue prints to ensure that everything fit the available wall and floor space or glass cases. As feminists remind us, the imagination is a means of possibility, but it is also a pragmatist in terms of what can be given current restrictions (Manicom & Walters, 2012). Imagining and slotting into place the exhibition was made more complex because we had sent out a *Call for items, objects, and narratives* to women around the province, and we had no idea what we would actually receive. We also commissioned eight artists to produce artworks on the theme of women's disobedience and creativity, and there too, we had little idea what they would create, as we gave no stipulations of genre, size, and so forth.

*Chapter 11 Image 3.* Photo Courtesy Darlene Clover.

**What It Looked Like**

*Disobedient Women* turned out to be a multimedia exhibition characterized by beauty, grace, color, courage, vibrancy, expressive power, and vividness in both content and representation. While it is not possible in this limited space to describe everything, I sketch out below some of its main features. The images I've included tell their own stories. The exhibition included two video creations, one a story told through women's bodies and slam poetry and the other an animated illustration of defiance. These required monitors, headphones, and electricity, so that was a bit of a scramble. Also included in the exhibition were two sets of hand puppets, one, of women leaders from around the world, such as Wangarĩ Maathai of the Green Belt Movement, and another, of creatures that represented four aspects of Earth dwelling women. We also had received a series of contemporary protest buttons, which we set against a blanket from the 1970s that had a number of protest buttons attached. While there were differences, the similarities in challenges and issues remain astounding. The exhibition also included one installation, a bedside table loaded with bricks as a metaphor for violence, and a diorama of a woman's bedroom from the 1960s era complete with feminist magazines, books, old phonographic records, tee-shirts, and posters. Other inclusions were single or multiple (a series) paintings, newspaper clippings of arrests at protest sites, activist quilts of varying sizes, poems, and even two decorated hard hats to accompany a story of a woman who worked for years in the trades — *Hammering in a Man's World*.

The exhibition also contained four photographs from *(Mis)Interpretation: Sikh Feminisms in Representation, Texts and Lived Realities*, a critical Sikh feminist ethnographic exhibition that had been curated the previous year. Another photographic series was of the ACHoRd performance art piece that had been co-created by a group of 13 Indigenous and non-Indigenous women. The piece was performed on the steps of the British Columbia Legislature as part of the lead-up to Canada's Sesquicentenary to provoke thought and to challenge, rather than celebrate. *Disobedient Women* also included life size mannequins in the costumes of the West Coast League of Lady Wrestlers, a women's group that "wrestles" with social and ecological issues such as oil pipeline expansion. The Raging Grannies, a robust group of older women who dress in costume and sing off key to raise awareness of issues relating to peace, the environment, and social justice, were also featured. They had arrived at my office with green garbage bags full of everything — from books they had written to a photograph of them heading naked into a freezing lake for the cause, from the lyrics of satirical songs to a full size cut out of them complete with feathered boa.

To ensure we had the greatest breadth possible and filled historical gaps, we also drew items from the Royal British Columbia Museum and University of Victoria archives. We therefore integrated into the exhibition a photograph of a Women's Institute with artist Emily Carr in the front row, a photograph of the First Chinese Women's Auxiliary circa 1900, and copies of *Zenith Digest*, a newsletter edited by transgender woman Stephanie Castle. We wrote up stories to highlight women figures from the past that ranged from Rosemary Brown, the first Black woman in the British Columbia Legislature (parliament), and Jill Carter, a homeless woman who worked tirelessly as an advocate for women living on the streets and who was an amazing poet. We also interviewed women like Indigenous Elder May Sam, who keeps the Cowichan sweater knitting practice alive by teaching it to youth. Extraordinary Indigenous artists such as Val Napoleon and Francis Dick submitted astonishingly beautiful paintings to the exhibition.

We organized an official opening for each exhibition, which included artists talking about their works, slam poetry, drumming, and songs by the Raging Grannies. In addition, we hosted two arts-based workshops (puppetry and photography) around the theme "women, power and disobedience" for students and community members.

*Chapter 11 Image 4.* Photo Courtesy Darlene Clover.

## How Did the Exhibition Work Pedagogically?

It is one thing to create a dynamic, feminist space of public engagement that aims to initiate reflection and dialogue and imaginatively illustrate political acts and stories, and it's another to understand what learning actually took place for visitors as a result of this engagement. Indeed, how did the *Disobedient Women* exhibition function as a collective space of feminist public pedagogy? To find out, we left comment cards and research forms at the exhibition site upon which visitors could record ideas and reflections. We were astonished to find, at the time of dismantling the exhibition, that 322 people had taken the time to complete a card or a form.

There were six types of comment cards, each one with an image from the exhibition and one of the following six questions:

1. Which piece in the exhibition speaks to you most and why?
2. What ideas does this exhibition suggest about gender justice?
3. What does "feminism" mean to you?
4. What connections does this exhibition make between creativity, art and gender struggle?
5. What is the most interesting thing you learned from this exhibition?
6. What new ideas does this exhibition provoke about gender injustice, past and present?

The comment cards actually became part of the exhibition, as one of the students — an artist — had the idea of creating a clothesline installation on which visitors could pin the cards. The more detailed research form consisted of ten questions. The aim was to gather demographic information (age, gender identity, professional and educational background) and qualitative data in terms of why they had visited the exhibition, what they had hoped to learn, and their thoughts about gender, feminism, activism, and art. We also asked what images and/or stories stood out for them and why. The Master's and PhD students and I also spent a number of hours each day at the exhibition site, noting down our visitor conversations and observations. We also did follow-up interviews with those visitors who had agreed to be interviewed as well as with students from two classes who visited the exhibition as part of their courses.

*Chapter 11 Image 5.* Photo Courtesy Darlene Clover.

## What Did People Say?

The interplay of the representations of the past, the performance of memory, and the production of the present were key cultural, pedagogical, and political features of the exhibition and they had an extraordinary impact. I conclude this article by illustrating this through their words.

**Resonating and Remembering:** Trinidad Galván (2010) reminds us that what structures and shapes our worldviews as women "is intricately tied to the 'living' past" (p. 347). This was manifest by the frequency of the term "resonance" and its centrality to why so many had visited the exhibition and returned at least once or lingered: "It resonated so I stayed for over two hours"; "I went around fairly methodically." Data showed many visitors had been involved in public actions as women or as the children of feminist mothers. Remembering, for many older visitors, "evoked for me a lot of feelings that I had early on in my life. I am 77 now."

**Connecting**: For one participant, the exhibition gave her the sense of being "part of a larger struggle that matters as much today as it did then." For another, it came from her feelings of exclusion and injustice and the need to re-connect: "[I came] because I was discriminated against as a young, university student — honours chemistry and [I am] enraged at the continuing domination of powerful...men...and [I am] delighted to be with women [who are] speaking truth to power." Another visitor spoke to the power of the exhibition as a means to re-connect with her lost culture: "As an Indigenous woman disconnected from her culture, it was particularly meaningful to see elements here that spoke to female's Indigenous strengths — sort of promising that I could be part of that too."

**Inspiring**: Biesta (2012) believes critical interruptions through art can "prepare the terrain for political action" (p. 694). We saw this in the frequency of the word "inspiration": "I was hoping to feel a sense of belonging, but I got much more than that, I found inspiration." Finding inspiration was often linked to hope: "I came to get inspired. And I was. This exhibition has given me hope and strength. It is amazing to see these "bad-ass" women." Eight visitors wrote about how the exhibition had inspired them to think about how they could, in fact, use their own arts practice toward gender justice: "Art has such political power. I see that for the first time. I have never thought about art together with politics. I can do this with my own art." Other participants wrote about how the exhibition had given them courage and a renewed faith in women's power to make change.

**Engulfing and Reflecting**: Ellsworth (2005) reminds us that public displays such as exhibitions are important pedagogically when they draw the audience into other realities and experiences. This was exemplified in a number of visitor comments but particularly this one: "It takes you beyond the two-dimensionality of most exhibitions...it kind of came out at the viewer and brought you in." The potential of being drawn into other worlds by the exhibition was also manifest in challenges to past assumptions.

People often talked about remaining at the exhibition for extended periods of time and even returning a second time to peruse the narratives. As one visitor noted of *Disobedient Women* "it is a place where one could take time to learn, to spend time on things that drew you in and return to them without anyone moving you along." Another added: "you have the space here; you have the time. You [the curators] allow us to study things at our own pace." As Harris (2014) reminds us, "slowing down doesn't in itself promise a better kind of education, or an increased opportunity for creative exploration and productive risk-taking, but it sets the condition for doing so" (p. 71). Other visitors also used the term "immersion" and often linked it to the power of seeing things "represented so visually all around you in bright colours and beautiful stories." This illustrates how *Disobedient Women* became, to borrow from Siegesmund (2013), a form of "playful aesthetic education," "an open and fluid imagining" that allowed simple "delight" to be outcome (p. 303).

**Realizing**: One visitor admitted to a previous notion of activism as violent and how *Disobedient Women* had opened their eyes to the diversity of ways women act/ed in public, its power, and "the need for this." For another visitor, "this exhibition showed me how speaking out and choosing not to follow the rules can be liberating." And there were other teaching worlds into which participants were drawn. One was a new awareness of colonialism and its before unseen connections to gender. This is, of course, something Indigenous feminists have been drawing our attention to for decades, and this visually powerful medium contributed to that struggle. For others, it was astonishment at just how many historical injustices, protested against by women in the past, remained today: "I never would have believed it. I was one of the women who thought equality was pretty much fixed. Geez."

**Understanding**: Over 60 visitors filled out the *What does feminism now mean to you?* comment card. While many were clearly familiar with feminism, others, most of whom were younger or male, not surprisingly, were not, but they held forth about their new and exciting understandings: "Many different women exist under 'feminism.' That is not what I had heard. But that is what I now see"; "That it [feminism] is fun and creative, inclusive and fierce and has a long legacy." The term "fun" actually appeared 47 times in the data.

Recognizing feminism's historical and contemporary creative and playful political inventiveness is important to stem refrains that feminism is a relic of the past that is "implicitly unattractive and embittered" (McRobbie, 2009, p. 157).

**Challenging**: There were of course challenges to the exhibition. Some visitors walked out immediately once they realized it was a "political" art show. As one visitor explained, "I only like *nice* art." One comment card argued the term "disobedient" was offensive because it referred to the misbehavior of children. This is, of course, not what the term means at all, and this was articulated beautifully by another visitor: "For me it [disobedience] is a refusal to obey rules, to keep quiet as women have been taught to do." However, this negative comment speaks to the power of language and its multiple meanings which, like images, are read differently. Our readings of exhibitions are, of course, informed ideologically and by where we are positioned. Another challenge was the behavior of a father with his son. Upon entry, the father began to instruct his son on what he called the "amateurishness" of the works and therefore on their creators as "so-called artists." When his assumptions were challenged, he quit the exhibition in anger. Two other comments expressed concern that men would not feel welcome in the space. Yet, many men visited the exhibition, left comments (often adding their names to comment cards), and agreed to be interviewed. Of course, what is far more important is the fact, and I have said this before, that literally hundreds of exhibitions across Canada and worldwide exclude women's artworks or histories yet this, for the most part, is accepted.

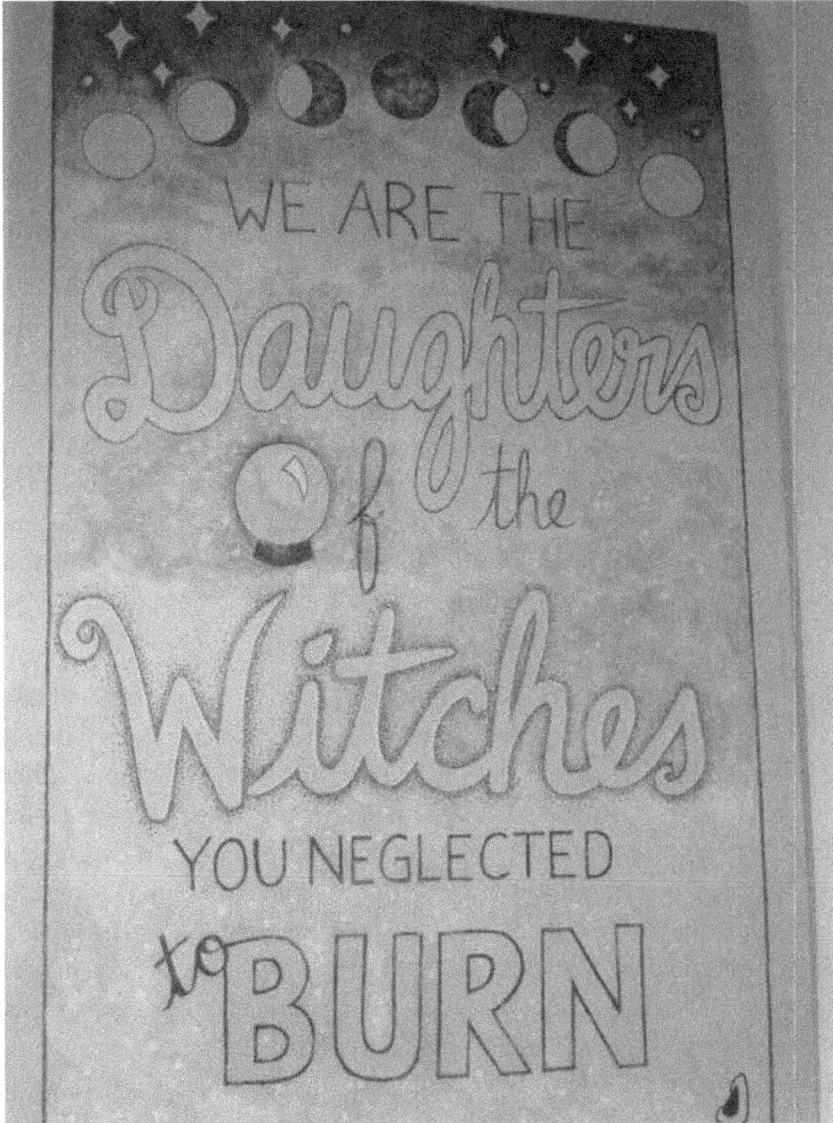

*Chapter 11 Image 6.* Photo Courtesy Darlene Clover.

## Final Thoughts

For Bartlett (2016), feminist exhibitions are important when they act in "the service of remembering feminist activism" (p. 310). For many visitors, as this study illustrates, the exhibition was a powerfully affirming space of remembrance, a place where they could reflect on the past and why speaking out matters (and continues to matter) so much. But it was also a space of remembering/connecting with culture, with a past that had been taken away, a voice that had been silenced. Remembering past activism is important because it reveals that gender and colonial injustices remain with us and that we need to continue efforts for change.

If encouraging activist-leadership is a critical element of feminist exhibitions, then *Disobedient Women* acted as an uplifting source of inspiration to activism, as visitors reflected on how the possibilities of their own artwork could become forms of aesthetic activism.

Importantly as well, the exhibition created a critical conscious about gender issues in the form of new understanding of women's contributions to community and about feminism and activism. Rendered visible was feminism's simultaneous capacity to engage in deep critique as well as its capacity for humor, satire, and fun. The issues are critical, the forms of disruption inspiringly imaginative.

In so many ways, this exhibition was a space of possibility that reinvigorated women's sense of self and agency — the personal and the collective. It also angered, but galvanizing strong emotions either way makes it an important public pedagogical vehicle. Having said this, it is important to note that as a non-permanent exhibition, *Disobedient Women* would not be able to maintain its impact. However, the same can be said of any short duration educational activities such as community workshops and even three-month university courses. The potential of an exhibition like this lies in its ability to make connections, inspire, and encourage remembering and reflection. *Disobedient Women* did not change the world, but it constituted an important public arena in which people could learn, test, examine, imagine, reflect, and quite possibly come to act in the interests of the public good, what Biesta (2012) calls "publicness."

# References

Bartlett, A. (2016). Sites of Feminist Activism. Remembering Pine Gap. Continuum. *Journal of Media and Cultural Studies*, 30(3), 307-315.

Becker, C. (1994). *The Subversive Imagination*. Routledge.

Bedford, L. (2014). *The Art of Museum Exhibitions: How Story and Imagination Create Aesthetic Experience*. Left Coast Press, Inc.

Bergsdóttir, A. (2016). Museums and Feminist Matters: Considerations of a Feminist Museology. *Nordic Journal of Feminist and Gender Research*, 24(2), 126-139.

Biesta, G. (2012). Becoming Public: Public Pedagogy, Citizenship and the Public Sphere. *Social & Cultural Geography*, 13, 683–697.

Carson F. & C. Pajaczkowska (Eds.) (2001). *Feminist Visual Culture*. New York, NY: Routledge

Ellsworth, E. (2005). *Places of Learning: Media, Architecture, Pedagogy*. Routledge.

Flood, C. & Grindon, G. (2015). *Disobedient Objects*. V&A Publishing.

Haiven, M. & Khasnabish, A. (2014). *The Radical Imagination*. Zed Books.

Macleod, S., Hourston Hanks, L. & Hale, J. (Eds.) (2012). Narrative Environments and the Paradigm of Embodiment. *In Museum Making: Narratives, Architectures, Exhibitions*. Routledge.

Harris, A. (2014). *The Creative Turn. Toward a New Aesthetic Imaginary*. Sense. DOI 10.1007/978-94-6209-551-9

Manicom, L. & Walters S. (Eds.) (2012). *Feminist Popular Education in Transnational Debates: Building Pedagogies of Possibility*. Palgrave Macmillan.

Marshment, M. (1993). The Picture Is Political: Representation of Women in Contemporary Popular Culture. In D. Richardson & V. Robinson (Eds.), *Thinking Feminist* (pp. 123-150). The Guildford Press.

McRobbie, A. (2009). *The Aftermath of Feminism: Gender, Culture and Social Change*. Sage.

Obrist, H. & Raza, A. (2015). *Ways of Curating*. Penguin Random House.

Siegesmund, R. (2013). Art Education and Democratic Citizenry. *International Journal of Art and Design Education*, 32(3), 300-308.

Steeds, L. (2014). *Exhibition*. Whitechapel Gallery.

Trinidad Galván, R. (2016). Collective Memory of Violence of the Female Brown Body: A Decolonial Feminist Public Pedagogy Engagement With the Femicides. *Pedagogy, Culture & Society*, 24(3), 343-357, DOI: 10.1080/14681366.2016.1166149

**About the Author**

Darlene E. Clover is Professor of adult education and community engagement in the Faculty of Education, University of Victoria. She is also Co-President of the Society of Friends of St Ann's Academy. This organization, based in a women's heritage site, hosts gender and decolonizing seminars and workshops and a bi-yearly conference on women and leadership. Darlene's research areas are museums and art galleries, exhibition praxis and feminist arts based adult education and research. Her most recent co-edited volumes are *Feminist critique and the museum: Educating for a critical consciousness* (Sense, 2020) and the open access *Feminist adult educators guide to aesthetic, creative and disruptive practice in museums and communities* (2020). https://onlineacademiccommunity.uvic.ca/comarts/feminist-adult-educators-guide/.

# CHAPTER 12

# HISTORY UNFOLDED: US NEWSPAPERS AND THE HOLOCAUST AT AMERICAN UNIVERSITY

ERIC SCHMALZ

## INTRODUCTION

By Susan J. Erenrich

On July 20<sup>th</sup> and 21<sup>st</sup> of 2020, and July 28<sup>th</sup> and 29<sup>th</sup> of 2021, I attended the virtual Belfer National Conference for Educators hosted by the United States Holocaust Memorial Museum in Washington, D.C. The various two-day gatherings introduced participants to the institution's pedagogical approach to classroom instruction about the Holocaust and familiarized those assembled with museum resources.

During our time together, we were provided with an array of thought-provoking sessions by scholars and content facilitators who shared their expertise, blueprints, and justification for learning about this salient time in history. Additionally, enrollees were afforded the opportunity to watch an introductory film and visit a museum exhibition online.

One of the featured speakers during the Belfer conference was Eric Schmalz. Eric is the Citizen History Community Manager at the Holocaust Museum and the author of this chapter.

I initially met Eric in the summer of 2017. Eric and I discussed the prospect of a special partnership between the museum and my Introduction to College Inquiry course at American University. I wanted students in my first-year class to have an experiential research adventure and to be able to contribute to something bigger than themselves.

Our collaboration with the Holocaust Museum was fruitful. For the next three fall semesters, students worked closely with Eric on the museum's *History Unfolded* project. Throughout the term, students examined local newspapers around the United States for information and attitudes about the Holocaust. The reporting had to fall within one of approximately thirty-eight categories established by the museum. Once a student found a relevant article, they would submit it to a national database. Students were asked to submit one entry every week for fifteen weeks to assist the museum with its data collection. If they ran into problems, Eric was virtually on-hand to help. He also visited with the students face-to-face three times during each semester.

The purpose of this endeavor was to see how much Americans actually knew about the Holocaust in real time and how they responded. As a result of our alliance, students in the Introduction to College Inquiry course were able to participate in an important exploration. They helped scholars build upon an existing body of knowledge, learned about community service and reciprocal relationships, and got a taste of what the future could hold.

I hope readers are emboldened by Eric's piece. It illustrates how students can genuinely make a difference and help change the world one article at a time.

## HISTORY UNFOLDED: US NEWSPAPERS AND THE HOLOCAUST AT AMERICAN UNIVERSITY

By Eric Schmalz

As a high school social studies teacher in Charlottesville, Virginia, I wanted students to understand that history is a discipline and not simply a subject consisting of memorizing facts about people in the past. At the end of the year for most of my classes, I required students to craft their own definition of history after reading how some historians defined the word. In addition, students had to create their own "museums," selecting a topic and making an argument about their topic to prospective museum visitors.

I gave the students near free reign on selecting their topics. And for most of them, this part was easy. They created museums about their favorite sport, athlete, business, musical instrument or musician, and more. But students could rarely articulate what argument they were making about their museum. Many students equated the argument with the topic. They likewise struggled to define history as anything more than a series of facts about the past. To them, that was still all history appeared to be.

Teaching in the classroom at that time in my life turned out not to be my calling, so after a long period of reflection, I decided to change careers. During my search, an acquaintance shared with me a posting for a position at the United States Holocaust Memorial Museum (USHMM). The description was for a citizen history community manager for a digital project. While I had been to the museum a few times before as a kid, and all of my grandparents were born in Europe and have stories associated with the same time period, I did not have any connections to the institution and had no idea what a citizen history community manager was.

The museum was seeking an individual with experience teaching, conducting historical research in archives and libraries, and in building and maintaining an authentic community online. The selected candidate's responsibilities would include overseeing the "citizen historians" or project volunteers for a soon to be launched website, History Unfolded: US Newspapers and the Holocaust (https://newspapers.ushmm.org/). History Unfolded was to be the first program associated with a new initiative on *Americans and the Holocaust*. The initiative set out to look at what Americans could have known about the Nazi persecution of Jews from 1933 to 1945 and to tell the history of how Americans did and did not respond. Local newspapers would be a rich historical source for the museum to continue to investigate, as there were some 2,000 local newspapers published in 1933 and a large percentage of America's population received their news from such publications at the time.

Staff at the museum realized that, while they could conduct some of this research on their own, their time and resources were limited. Therefore, they decided that History Unfolded would be the museum's first nationwide citizen history project. Students would research how newspapers reported on various Holocaust-era events by investigating the papers on microfilm or in digitized archives in their area and then submit relevant findings to the project's new database. The project's community manager would assist teachers and students with the research, review the submissions, market the project, and help nurture the community for long-term engagement.

By inviting students to do the research, History Unfolded would address authentic institutional needs and promote student learning. After all, students would have access to local newspapers on microfilm or via online archives that museum staff members would not. Newspapers also would provide students with a glimpse into the history and culture of the area at the time, so students would gain a much deeper understanding of historical context and the various events or factors that may have competed for reader attention. As students study history by actually doing history, they would have their own misconceptions about the Holocaust challenged. And the data participants collected would ideally be used to support other aspects of the initiative in the coming years including a special exhibition, online exhibition, traveling exhibition, teaching materials, and more. Big questions loomed though: Would such a large-scale experiment work? Would teachers invest the time? Could students be trusted to do authentic historical research? Or would the results be of such low or unreliable quality to not be worth the trouble?

I was fortunate enough to secure an interview and then a job offer. And I am very pleased to say that the History Unfolded project has been a great success overall to date. Since the museum began collecting articles in late 2015, the database has grown to include (as of January 2022), over 50,000 published newspaper submissions from every state, the District of Columbia, Puerto Rico, and the U.S. Virgin Islands. Articles in the database are in about a dozen languages and the collection includes submissions from Jewish, Catholic, Black, university, labor, and communist papers. Over 200 different classes from nearly 40 states, D.C., and Puerto Rico have participated. At first, the project's lead and I handled the review of all of the submissions. Now, the project team includes about a dozen back-end reviewers (contractors and volunteers) who handle the majority of the weekly submissions.

History Unfolded played an important role in the research for the *Americans and the Holocaust* exhibition at USHMM. The exhibition's curators included 18 submissions found by students and adult volunteers as part of a large interactive map display at the beginning of the special exhibition, which opened to the public on the museum's 25th anniversary in 2018. The interactive map features newspaper coverage of the Nazi persecution of Jews from 1933 and 1935. In addition, contributions from project volunteers were included in a later section on the Wagner-Rogers child refugee bill. The curators chose to reproduce portions of letters-to-the-editor about the bill, both in favor and against the proposal in Congress to admit 10,000 child refugees per year over two years to the United States that would not be counted against the existing immigration quota laws. (The bill was never put to a vote in Congress.) Material from History Unfolded has been included in the online version of the *Americans and the Holocaust* exhibition as well as lesson plan materials. Finally, the museum has used articles from the project for various public programs, including its popular Facebook Live series.

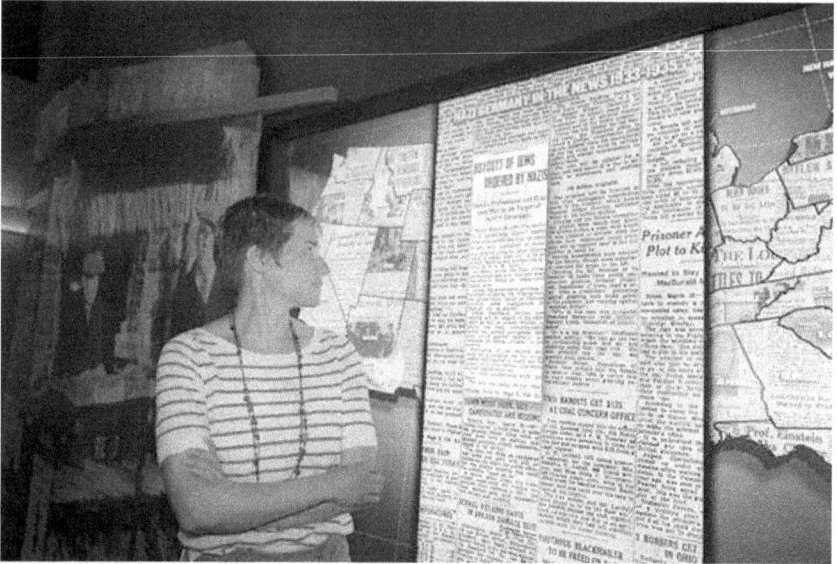

Chapter 12 Image 1. High school social studies teacher Katie Murr views the interactive map in the Americans and the Holocaust special exhibition at the United States Holocaust Memorial Museum. Curators selected one of the articles her students contributed to History Unfolded for the display. Photo Courtesy Eric Schmalz.

Some of the project's most active school groups have been those led by Susie Erenrich at American University. She has incorporated History Unfolded into her courses for several years, and her students have submitted hundreds of articles to the database. Part of the success can be attributed to how fully Susie invested in the project and how she coordinated with me to make this a major assignment for her students. She invited me to come physically to her classes to meet the students, introduce the program, and check in with the student citizen historians as they worked over the semester. Among other things, she wanted students to understand that History Unfolded is not busy work but real research. By having me come and share the ways USHMM has been using the student work, Susie has been able to help the students remain excited and motivated to be a part of something much larger than the classroom.

The student research has been impressive. One of the students during the Fall 2017 semester accepted my invitation to the class to go to the Library of Congress and look up Spanish-language newspapers on microfilm. He found articles about the 1936 Olympic Games in *La Correspondencia de Puerto Rico*. During the Fall 2019 semester, American University students in Susie's Introduction to College Inquiry course used the school library's newspapers.com subscription to submit hundreds of articles from local newspapers all over the country. More than 260 of these articles are now published to the History Unfolded website.

Adding data to the History Unfolded database is arguably the greatest long-term contribution a volunteer can make to the project. At the time of writing, published submissions typically consist only of article metadata (newspaper name, issue date, page number, headline information, etc.) and possibly a small thumbnail image. Eventually, the museum hopes to gain copyright permission to display the full images and perhaps additional details about the newspapers.

*Chapter 12 Image 2.* American University students added over 260 new articles to the database during the Fall 2019 semester. Dr. Susan Erenrich has incorporated History Unfolded into her classes for several years. Since this chapter was written, Dr. Erenrich's students have continued to contribute, submitting hundreds more articles in the past several years. Photo Courtesy Eric Schmalz.

The metadata alone will be of interest to Holocaust historians and digital humanities scholars wishing to gain a better understanding of how newspapers reported on the Holocaust during this time. Such researchers may be able to learn, for example, how many newspapers in the dataset used the word "Jews" in article headlines to describe the primary victims of the Holocaust, whether particular events were commonly front-page news, and to what extent residents of small towns could have learned about the events compared to residents of large metropolitan areas. And as the museum clears copyright to display the full images, the submissions in the database will be of increasing value to students in the classroom as well as other researchers for decades to come.

Beyond that, I was very pleased to be able to share with some of the Fall 2019 students that the curators for the traveling version of the *Americans and the Holocaust* exhibition selected their articles for inclusion as part of a tablet interactive. Five different students contributed at least one article that made the interactive. One student had three of his articles included. This is all the more impressive in that the interactive only includes 153 total articles, three from each state and the District of Columbia.

When I started the job as community manager in late November 2015, the then project lead impressed upon me the essence of my purpose at the museum. I was not only to help the museum collect useful data but also ensure that all project participants, especially students, had as good of an experience as possible conducting the research and learning. To this day, I tell myself that if participating teachers, students, and lifelong learners are not having a good experience or learning more about historical research and the Holocaust, I have failed. Along these lines, our project team made it a goal from the start to test if students were, in fact, making gains in their motivation, knowledge of Holocaust history, and historical skills.

One of the joys of my job is hearing from project participants and leaders, including teachers, who are often very excited to try out the project and tell me about their successes after. As a result, I have collected a plethora of anecdotes that support our hypothesis that citizen history is an engaging and effective methodology for student learning. Students regularly comment on how unexpectedly fun microfilm research is, how surprised they were by what they did and did not find, and how much else they learned about history — such as the "low" cost of food and clothing in the advertisements on the newspaper pages. However, our team wanted to see if we could confirm these initial qualitative findings with a more formal evaluation process.

After conducting a series of teacher interviews in the 2017-2018 school year, the team hired an external evaluator to create and administer a post-then-pre survey of student motivation, content knowledge of the Holocaust, and development of skills associated with historical research and analysis. The evaluator then selected some students to follow up with in more detailed student interviews. Some American University students completed the post-then-pre survey. In total, more than 100 high school and university students took the survey. Nearly 40 high school and university students from various classes across the country completed follow up interviews.

Overall, the evaluation results were extremely encouraging. The evaluator noted significant gains in student motivation, content knowledge of the Holocaust, and familiarity with using historical research tools. Students explained something larger than themselves. Some students even suggested that they would continue to do this kind of research into the future. Since these results emerged, the History Unfolded team has been sharing their findings at conferences and in publications in an effort to help others who are considering similar crowd projects learn both the potential and the challenges to doing a citizen history type project successfully.

Susie's students at American University have helped put many towns "on the map" through their work on this project. They have directly contributed to museum exhibitions. Their survey feedback helped us gain a better understanding of student motivation and learning. The History Unfolded project team sincerely hopes that members of the AU community and anyone else reading this article will contribute to History Unfolded by going to the project website, creating an account, and uploading material that we have not collected before. And along the way, students and lifelong learners will hopefully find history to be, rather than a collection of facts about people long ago, an exciting, engaging discipline where evidence and data lead to informed arguments about the past.

**About the Author**

Eric Schmalz is the Citizen History Community Manager at the United States Holocaust Memorial Museum. He has been the community manager for the History Unfolded: US Newspapers and the Holocaust project (https://newspapers.ushmm.org/) since November 2015. He oversees the review of newspaper submissions to the project website, assists participants with their questions, and helps educators effectively incorporate History Unfolded into various learning environments. Eric specializes in developing and deepening authentic human connection through his work. Before taking on his current position at the United States Holocaust Memorial Museum, Eric taught high school social studies in Charlottesville, VA. He earned his bachelor's degree in History at the College of William and Mary and his master's degree in Teaching (Secondary Social Studies) at the University of Virginia.

# CHAPTER 13

# THE LONG SIXTIES: WASHINGTON PAINTINGS IN THE WATKINS AND CORCORAN LEGACY COLLECTIONS, 1957 – 1982

JACK RASMUSSEN

## INTRODUCTION

By Susan J. Erenrich

This chapter features an article penned by Jack Rasmussen. Jack is the Director and Curator of American University's Museum. The three-story public gallery and sculpture garden that Jack oversees is located in the Katzen Arts Center on the American University campus. It is open to the public all year round.

Jack's chapter, *The Long Sixties: Washington Paintings in the Watkins and Corcoran Legacy Collections, 1957 – 1982*, highlights the museum's commitment to political art as it relates to human rights, social justice, and political engagement. His piece also accentuates the role that the museum plays in supporting artists in the local community. Through the telling of his own story, meticulously intertwined with examples from the creative class in the Washington, D.C. Metropolitan area, Jack builds a framework for the "Long Sixties" that goes far beyond the borders of the District of Columbia.

I first met Jack when I started teaching at American University around 2013. Throughout my years at the institution, Jack generously served as a guide for students in my Intercultural Understanding class. He carved time out of his hectic schedule, pre-selected exhibits most pertinent to course content, and patiently led tours and answered questions. It was a rewarding experience for all the participants. Now Jack has an opportunity to share his work with a global audience.

I hope readers enjoy Jack's personal reflections interspersed with the rich aesthetic landscape presented here.

## THE LONG SIXTIES: WASHINGTON PAINTINGS IN THE WATKINS AND CORCORAN LEGACY COLLECTIONS, 1957 – 1982

By Jack Rasmussen

The American University Museum recently acquired 9,000 works from the Corcoran Gallery of Art, a Washington, D.C. institution that closed its doors to the public in 2014. Together with our Watkins Collection we have an especially strong cache of works by Washington, D.C. regional artists. While curating a show of Washington, D.C. paintings drawn from our growing collections, I became interested in how my memories of a formative time in my life might be affecting my choice of artwork for this exhibition.

This most influential time for baby boomers like me has been referred to as "the long sixties" by both National Gallery of Art curator James Meyer (2019), and sixties radical Tom Hayden (2009). Meyer references Tom Hayden's book, *The Long Sixties: From 1960 to Barack Obama* (2011), as one source for his use of the term. I have identified my personal "long sixties" as the years between 1957 and 1982. My intention is to foreground the effect of my experiences and memories of this important time in my life in my selections for this exhibition and to present interpretation of paintings from that period.

I hope to add transparency to my curatorial process. Every exhibition necessarily presents the intersection of the curator's memories, knowledge, and experiences with the available artwork, limitations on physical space and financial resources, and their understanding of contemporary contexts. The intersection of these elements affects what is exhibited as well as how it is experienced and interpreted by the viewer.

I began my curatorial process by limiting my selection to paintings in our Watkins and Corcoran Legacy Collections. Months into the process, it became clear that these limitations were creating absences in the exhibition. My choice of medium, together with choices made by those who collected and contributed art, and what works our institutions eventually decided to accession, were pre-determining the exhibition's shape and content. Of course, every exhibition has its absences. Every exhibition involves making choices and compromises. But when I finally opened the exhibition to works outside of the museum's collections, I was able to address a few of the more egregious under-representations.

It is the curator's job to deliver an aesthetic, emotional, meaningful experience — one that illuminates for engaged viewers how their own lives and times are intertwined with, and shaped by, their experience of the past and their perception of the present. Every exhibition is an opportunity to address what we can see of the past from our contemporary perspective, and vice versa. My perspective includes the acknowledgement of persistent, systemic, gender and racial injustice, bias, and violence that was present in the fifties, laid bare in the sixties, and continues to the present day. It is clear to me that the defining characteristic of Washington, D.C. art in our collections made during "the long sixties," and still its operative tendency, is an adherence to aesthetic and commercial constraints that encourage artists to remain silent when their voices are most needed in the face of bias and violence that has not gone away.

*Chapter 13 Image 1.* Image credit: AP Photo.

## 1957 – 1959

"The long sixties" began, for me, in Appleton, Wisconsin in 1957. I was in the third grade, watching the funeral of Wisconsin Senator Joseph McCarthy. He had been on our black and white television screen as much as Howdy Doody. McCarthy is seen here with his Chief Counsel and "fixer," Roy Cohn. Even then, I knew in a vague way that the term "McCarthyism" referred to their "Red Scare" interrogations, their practice of making unfounded accusations against federal employees, artists, and others they suspected of being communist sympathizers, and the skillful fanning of our fears of a nuclear nightmare. I well remember "duck and cover" drills were a part of every morning in my elementary school, right after the Pledge of Allegiance.

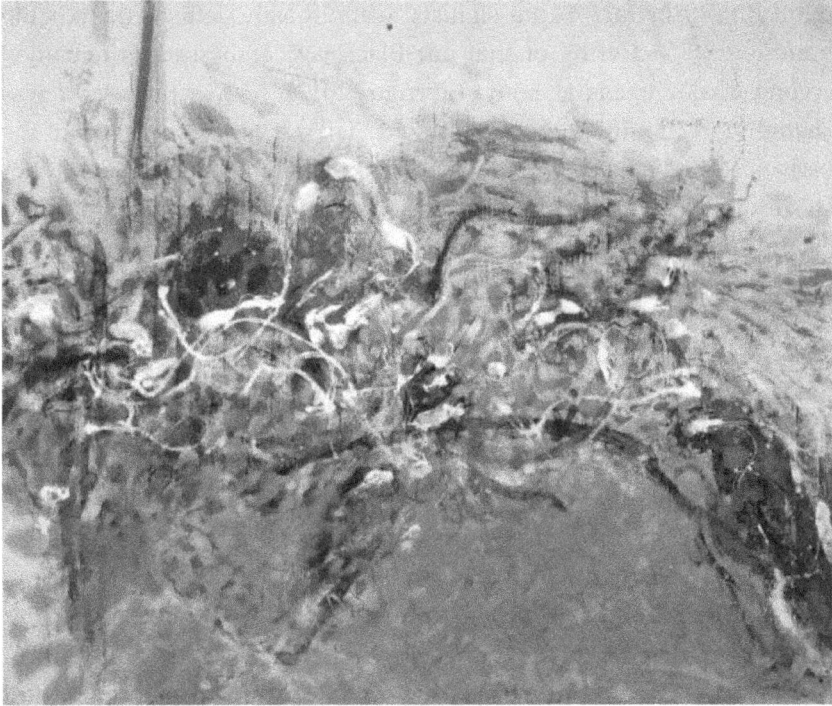

*Chapter 13 Image 2.* Kenneth Noland (1924-2010), *Lavender Blue*, 1957. Oil on canvas, 88 × 106 in. Anonymous Gift, 2016.13.1.

In 1957, Abstract Expressionism was the dominant art movement in the United States, characterized by huge canvases, strong gestures, and emotional content. All these elements are present in Kenneth Noland's (1924-2010) *Lavender Blue* (1957). It is the very embodiment of the turbulent times that produced it. One can even entertain the possibility that Noland's title was inspired by the efforts of Joseph McCarthy and Roy Cohn to "out" federal employees suspected of being gay — the "Lavender Scare" that paralleled and reinforced their "Red Scare."

We now know that Abstract Expressionism, as well as jazz, was employed as a Cold War weapon by the CIA in our country's ongoing fight against communism (Stoner Saunders, 1999). Communist governments were directing their own artists to work in the style of Socialist Realism to promote the ideals of their societies. Our government believed our music and art would demonstrate to the world how free we were, how open we were to self-expression. Never mind that Abstract Expressionists were mostly leftists then being hounded by McCarthy or that our Black jazz ambassadors remained second-class citizens at home (Perrigo, 2017). Just as the world was changing in the fifties, so, too, was art. The art historical canon of the early fifties tells us of artist Helen Frankenthaler's experiments in her studio and her discovery that thinned oil paint would soak into and "stain" unprimed canvas. There was no need any more for a brush manipulated by the artist's hand; thinned paint flowed where directed by the artist's manipulation of gravity. At the urging of art critic Clement Greenberg, Noland visited Frankenthaler's studio, saw her painting *Mountains and Sea* (1952), and was profoundly influenced by her new techniques.

"Advanced" painting was soon declared by critics and dealers alike to be stained painting, making possible Color Field painting and the rise of the Washington Color School. Frankenthaler later remarked to the National Gallery of Art's former Curator of Modern Art, E.A. Carmean, "Yes, I was 'a bridge' and they walked over me," (Carmean, 2017, p. 9). As Washington, D.C. arts and culture activist Melvin Hardy recently observed, "The professional and personal angst of Helen Frankenthaler presages the oppressions, micro and macro, that beset both women and African American fine art producers..." (M. Hardy, email communication, December 15, 2020). Greenberg was the leading formalist art critic. He was involved in the creation of the Washington Color School, fashioning it out of the local practitioners of Color Field Painting in Washington, D.C. The Color School was, and still is, the only instance where a group of Washington, D.C. artists achieved critical and financial success either inside or outside of the city. It was acclaimed as the climax of modernism in the first half of the twentieth century, while others saw it as modernism's dead end, disconnected from the socio-political disorder of the sixties.

Greenberg's brand of formalism imposed very strict limitations on the artist. Only art's purely visible aspects were important. The artist's intentions had no place, nor did gestures of the artist's hand, drawing, subject matter, pictorial illusion, narrative content of any kind, or any relationship at all to the visible world, let alone its social and political context.

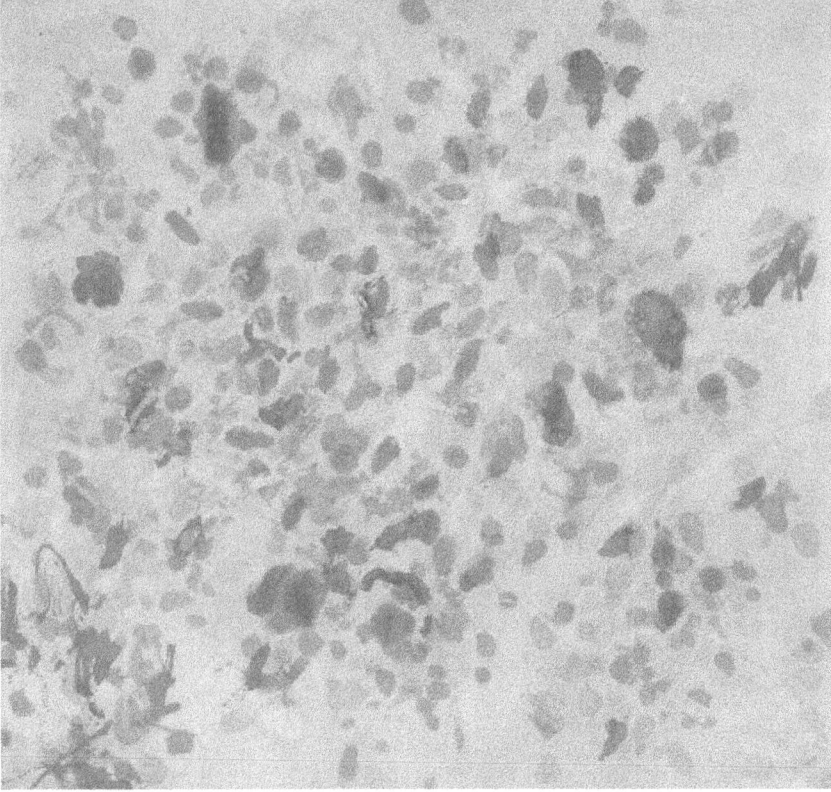

*Chapter 13 Image 3.* Howard Mehring (1931-1978), *Playground*, 1958. Acrylic on canvas, unframed: 106 x 111 in. Gift of the Trustees of the Corcoran Gallery of Art (Museum purchase, Gallery Fund), 2018.15.2170.

Howard Mehring (1931-1978) was a student of Noland's at Catholic University in Washington, D.C. and had also made a pilgrimage to meet Frankenthaler with fellow student Tom Downing (1928-1985). The size and "over all" composition of Mehring's *Playground* (1958) shows its debt to Abstract Expressionism. The relatively measured coolness of his application showed he was moving towards what became the Washington Color School, but it still retains the lyricism and subtle tonal adjustments that distinguished Mehring as such a beautiful painter throughout his short life, Color School or no.

Chapter 13 Image 4. Robert Franklin Gates (1906-1982), *Figure Abstraction*, 1958. Oil on canvas, framed: 47 1/4 × 53 3/8 × 2 in. 1991.1.10.

At the same time Noland and Mehring were abandoning personal, gestural expression for cooler, more formal abstractions, Robert Franklin Gates (1906-1982) and other Washington, D.C. artists were moving in the opposite direction, turning back towards figuration, still enthralled by vigorous expressionist brushwork. They were part of a larger resistance that included artists associated with the Bay Area Figurative School coming out of San Francisco in the mid-fifties. David Park is credited with the origination of the "school" when he took all his Abstract Expressionist paintings and deposited them in the Berkeley dump. Park was soon joined by other artists, including Elmer Bischoff and Richard Diebenkorn (Albright, 1985, p. 57).

Both Gates and Diebenkorn were greatly influenced by The Phillips Collection, the United States' first museum for modern art, from the collection of Duncan Phillips. Gates was a student at the Phillips

Gallery Art School and then taught and exhibited there until the U.S. entered into World War II. Diebenkorn was a marine stationed in Quantico and spent much of his free time during the war in The Phillips looking at Bonnard and Matisse. After the war, Diebenkorn returned to the Bay Area to teach at the California College of Arts and Crafts, where he fell under the influence of fellow teachers Mark Rothko and Clyfford Still, and soon embraced Abstract Expressionism. Around the same time Diebenkorn was undergoing his conversion, Gates' work was also becoming more abstract through the influence of his early teaching colleagues at The Phillips, John Marin and Jack Tworkov. Then, by the mid-fifties, Diebenkorn and Gates both began to pivot back to a more naturalistic figuration, countering the prevailing taste of the critical and commercial art worlds.

Gates was teaching at American University when its art department returned to American University's campus from The Phillips Gallery School, where it had been housed during World War II. Diebenkorn and Gates' figurative work was collected in depth by Duncan Phillips, and it remained a significant influence on American University's Art Department. Another determining influence was Philip Guston, whose work had undergone a similar transition from figuration to Abstract Expressionism, and back again, though to a very personal and idiosyncratic figurative style. The decidedly politicized content of his work, featuring cartoonishly devastating portraits of Richard Nixon and Ku Klux Klan members, remains controversial today.

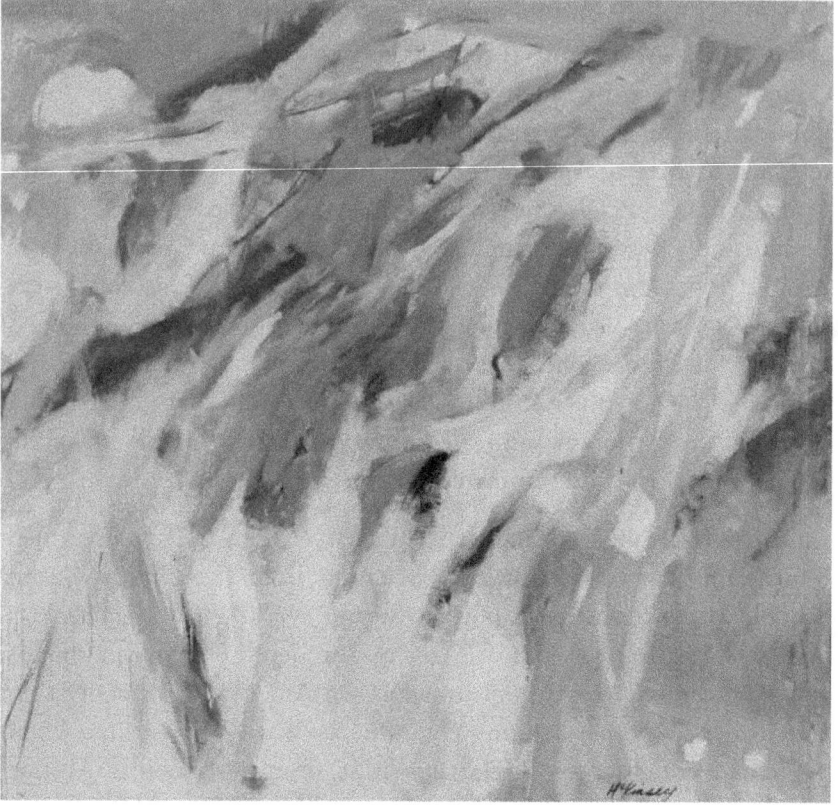

*Chapter 13 Image 5.* Helene McKinsey Herzbrun, (1922–1984), *Flowering*, 1956. Oil on canvas, framed: 39 x 41 in. Gift of James M. and Betty H. Pickett, 1989.1.1.

Helene McKinsey Herzbrun (1922-1984) was one of Gates' students who was also heavily influenced by Jack Tworkov. She, herself, would become an American University professor. Herzbrun was immediately drawn to Abstract Expressionism and never did abandon strong gesture and emotional content. She resisted the pull of the Washington Color School, though she would experiment with thin washes of color, à la Helen Frankenthaler, in her later works. Gates, Herzbrun, and American University's Art Department were largely responsible for the continued relevance of figurative and expressionist painting in Washington, D.C. for the next three decades. They kept it alive, though it was clear figurative and expressionist painting was at cross purposes with what mainstream paintings by most White male artists looked like in the sixties and into the seventies.

## 1960 – 1969

The sixties started for me with John F. Kennedy's campaign and election. In the summer of 1959, my family took a summer trip to Washington, D.C., where I saw Senator Kennedy on the floor of the Senate chamber. A few months later he was running for president, and I was his campaign manager in my elementary school, complete with hats, buttons, and speeches. I would spend four more summers in D.C., 1964-1967, working as a page in the U.S. Senate for Washington Senator Warren G. Magnuson, and falling in love with this city of great museums and its great spectator sport, politics.

Kennedy's assassination in 1963 changed the course of the decade. The Civil Rights Movement finally reached national consciousness with the passage of the Civil Rights Act of 1964, but within months of becoming law, the Gulf of Tonkin resolution, passed under false pretenses, committed the United States to a full-scale war in Vietnam. Despite the passage of major Civil Rights legislation, systemic racism, combined with the Vietnam War and the unsustainable living conditions of the poor in our cities, exposed our country's mistaken priorities — fighting overseas while our neighborhoods were on fire.

1968 is the pivotal year in "the long sixties." It began with two contrasting events: the assassination of Martin Luther King, Jr. on April 4, and the opening of *Hair* on Broadway on April 29. The day after the assassination, violence erupted in downtown Washington, D.C., leaving hundreds of burnt-out buildings in commercial districts and residential areas that would not be rebuilt for a decade. Shortly after the assassination of Robert Kennedy and the cataclysmic 1968 Democratic Convention, where demonstrators were assaulted by police officers on live television, President Richard Nixon and Vice President Spiro T. Agnew were elected. Appealing to the anxious "silent majority," they succeeded in recapturing the White House for the Republicans by promising to restore "law and order."

Campus disturbances spread to every major school. Hundreds of thousands gathered to demonstrate against the war and university polices allowing military recruiters on campus. Soon after the 1968 presidential election, the "Peace" movement began to turn violent out of deep frustration over its inability to effect change. The violence came to a head in 1970 with the killing of students at Kent State University by National Guard troops.

It became clear in the late sixties that all attempts to bring peaceful change would fail. Mainstream artists began to embrace the counterculture and its invocation to "turn on, tune in, and drop out." Most chose to depoliticize their art, exploring form instead of content. But a few, notably feminist artists and many African American artists, had already committed to using their art as instruments of change. They had been systematically excluded from the commercial gallery-museum system. Partly in reaction to their exclusion, they chose, instead, to work outside the system in unorthodox, non-traditional, or collaborative art forms to pursue socio-political engagement. But the more critically and financially successful, predominantly White male artists in Washington, D.C. and across the country continued their disengagement from socio-political realities. This ceding of the institutional battlefield by the mainstream, and the exclusion of other artists from the exhibition system, had consequences. We are still paying the price for this disengagement and segregation of so many creative minds from the town square and the marketplace.

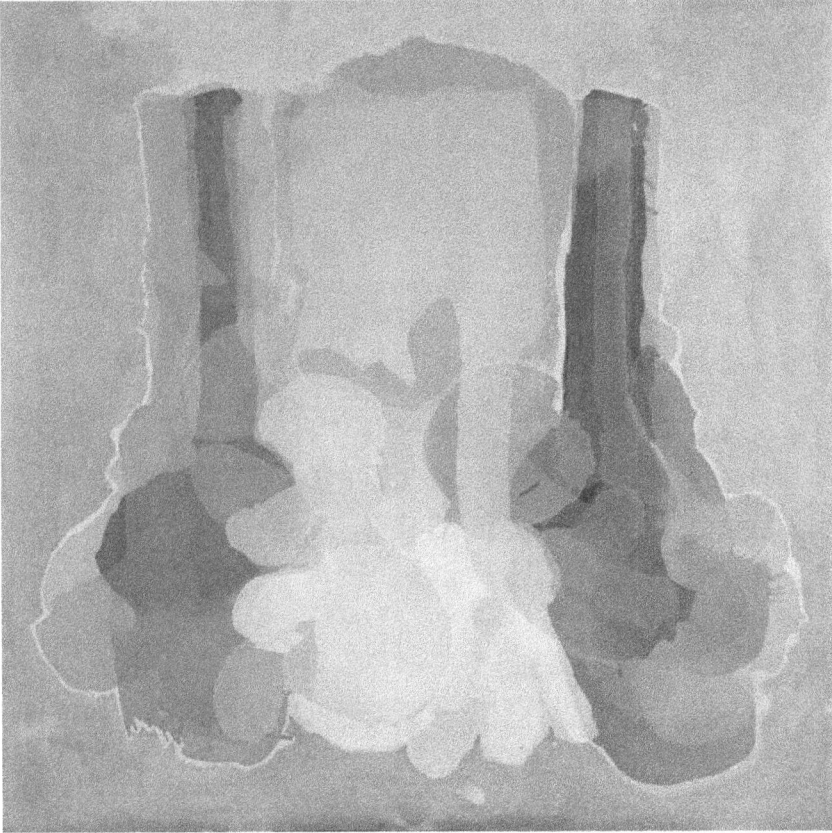

*Chapter 13 Image 6.* Cynthia Bickley-Green (b. 1942), *Hansa*, 1968-1969. Acrylic on canvas, canvas size: 66 3/4 × 67 5/8 in. Gift from the Trustees of the Corcoran Gallery of Art (Anonymous gift), 2018.15.2610.

Cynthia Bickley-Green (b. 1942), initially one of Frankenthaler's artistic progeny, was part of a younger generation of painters coming out of the University of Maryland Art Department in the sixties producing convincing work early in her career that followed the path worn by the Color School. But after successfully establishing herself with stained paintings like *Hansa* (1968-1969), Bickley-Green's art took a left turn in the seventies and became associated with the Pattern and Decoration Movement led by Miriam Schapiro and Joyce Kozloff, coinciding with her involvement in the emerging Women's Movement. This more politicized work was not collected by American University or the Corcoran.

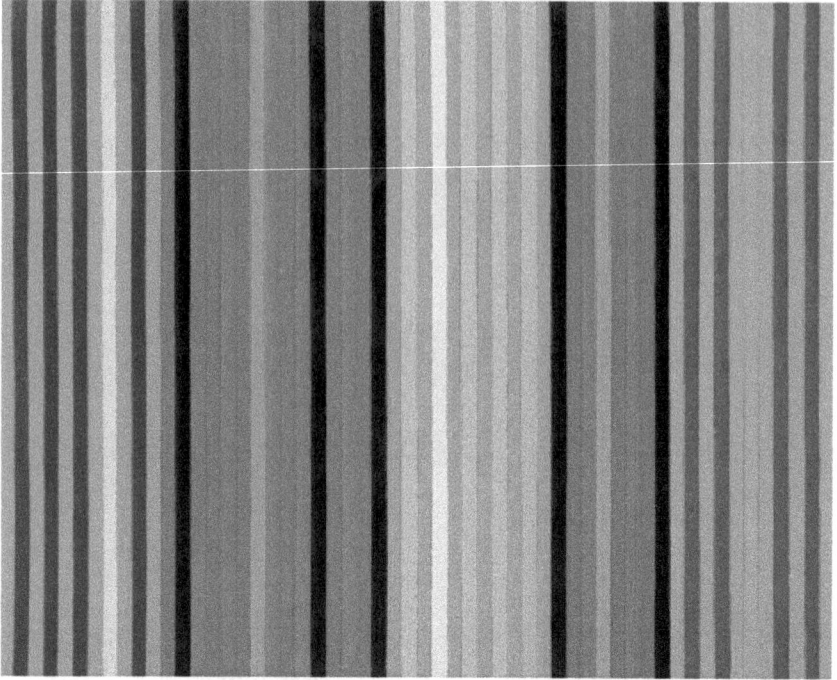

*Chapter 13 Image 7.* Gene Davis (1920-1985), *Untitled*, 1966. Acrylic on canvas, 45 1/8 × 56 1/8 in. Gift of Linda Lichtenberg Kaplan, Washington, DC, 1994.4. © 2021 Estate of Gene Davis / Artists Rights Society (ARS), New York.

Women artists like Bickley-Green first embraced the direction set by Frankenthaler and then found their voices in the feminist movement. White male artists, for the most part, would remain disconnected to what was happening around them. Gene Davis (1920-1985) made this painting in 1966, appropriately titled *Untitled.* Davis' art is the perfect expression of Washington Color School painting in the sixties and through the seventies. The commercial and critical success of the Color School may have had more to do with its separation from politics than its strictly decorative qualities. Here was the perfect corporate art, born of an art movement whose content did not have to be explained because it had none. It avoided controversy by being only about itself and could be shown without risk of embarrassment or, more importantly, risk of defunding the venue that gave it space.

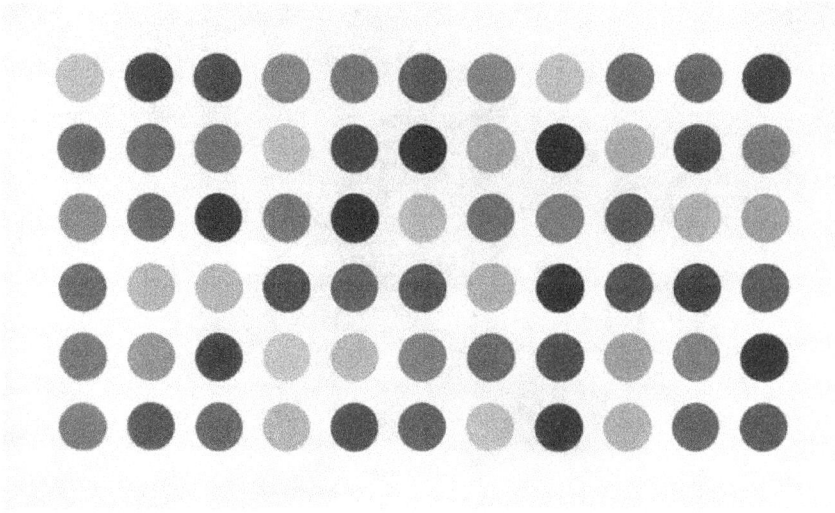

*Chapter 13 Image 8.* Thomas Downing (1928-1985), *Grid #6*, 1969. Acrylic on canvas, 78 × 130 in. Gift of Hortensia Anillo, 2014.43.1.

To really understand the great divide that existed in sixties Washington, D.C. art between the White male mainstream and between women and artists of color, one need only compare two paintings made in 1969. This is *Grid #6* (1969) by Tom Downing. What started as a liberating moment for artists under the sway of the Washington Color School ended in an aesthetic lockdown exemplified by Downing's work.

Chapter 13 Image 9. Joseph Shannon (b. 1933), Freud's Dog, 1969. Polymer, framed: 44 3/4 x 48 1/2 x 3 3/4 in. Gift from the Trustees of the Corcoran Gallery of Art (Gift of the Friends of the Corcoran), 2018.15.2657.

In contrast to Downing's work, *Freud's Dog* (1969) by Joseph "Joe" Shannon (b. 1933) explodes out of the times in which it was made. Born in Lares, Puerto Rico, Shannon's work is impolite and impolitic. He has no problem challenging Washington, D.C.'s dominant sensibilities. Championed early on by then-Corcoran curator Walter Hopps, Shannon was given an important one-person show in the Corcoran in 1969. Shannon's challenging figurative work addressed social, political, and professional ills, and the action in the paintings often took place at the Hirshhorn Museum where he worked as an exhibition designer. In a city so dedicated to the buttoned-up and uncontroversial, it is not surprising Shannon's painting was not a big influence on the figurative art just then beginning to flower in

Washington, D.C. Both figurative art and formalism became sanitized, toned down, in the hands of mainstream White artists.

## 1970 –1979

In the sixties, many in my generation "dropped out" rather than take their politics to its logical conclusion: the streets. The counterculture had arrived with its free love, medications, and great music. It was to be a very different kind of revolution, producing very mixed results. We now know that LSD was developed by the CIA and used in mind control experiments between 1953 and 1964 (Kinzer, 2019). Hayden (2009) argues that the drug-fueled counterculture "...overtook, competed with, and weakened the idea of radical political reform" (p. 44). His argument has merit. It helps explain why there was so little socially or politically engaged painting by White male artists in the sixties and early seventies in the Washington, D.C. region and little political reform.

In the seventies, successful mainstream artists continued to ignore current events, but more exciting abstractions were then being made, most impressively by three African American artists: Alma Thomas (1891-1978), Carroll Sockwell (1943-1992), and Kenneth Victor Young (1933-2017). Each took from the Color School what they wanted and moved off in their own direction. Perhaps guided by the Color School's first generation, all three avoided race, gender, and politics in their art. They may have also observed what was and was not well-received by critics and the marketplace.

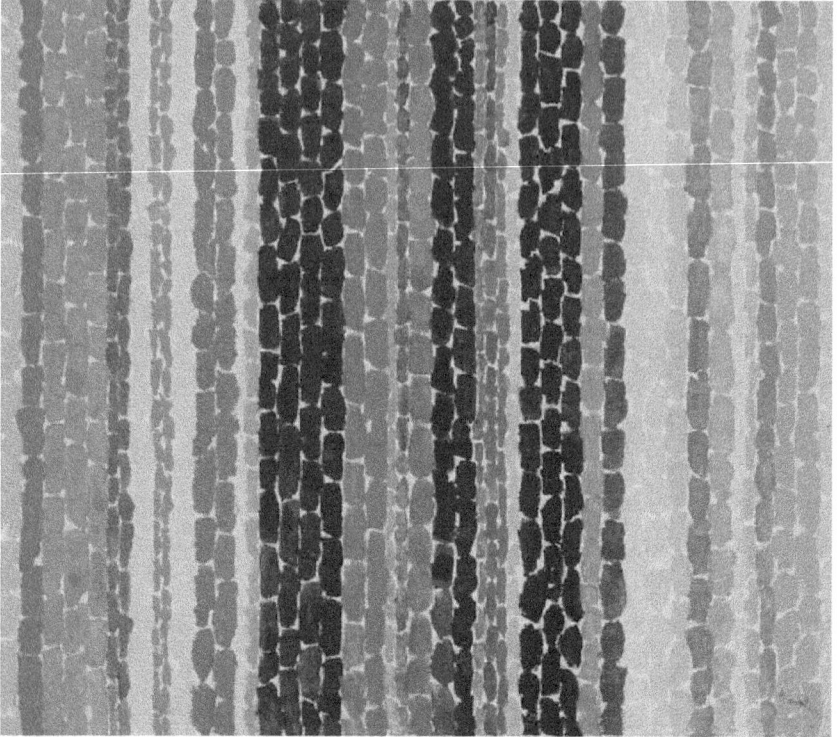

*Chapter 13 Image 10.* Alma Thomas (1891-1978), *Lunar Surface,* 1970. Acrylic on canvas, framed: 34 5/8 × 39 3/4 in. Gift of the Artist, 1975.5.

Thomas was the first graduate of Howard University's Fine Arts program in 1924. She taught in D.C. Public Schools for thirty-eight years while taking painting classes at American University. Her American University professors were Gates and Ben Summerford. In the 1960s, when she finally retired from teaching, she came under the influence of Washington Color School artists Noland and Davis. Thomas went on to achieve great critical success with paintings like *Lunar Surface* (1970). Her dynamic, rhythmic, geometric compositions of thickly applied strokes of color against white backgrounds eventually earned her a one-person show at the Whitney Museum of American Art, the first Black woman so honored.

Thomas' paintings were often lumped in with the Washington Color School and *Lunar Surface*, on its face, appears to owe much to Gene Davis's stripes. But she has clearly departed from the Color School through her expressive, gestural application of paint. The artist and curator Jacob Kainen described her painting process as "… Cyclopean Masonry — put a slab here, a slab there" (Cohen, J.L., 2013, p. 59). Thomas is building something, handmade and solid, patterned and saturated with color like a feminist quilt, but using paint and canvas, not appliques and thread.

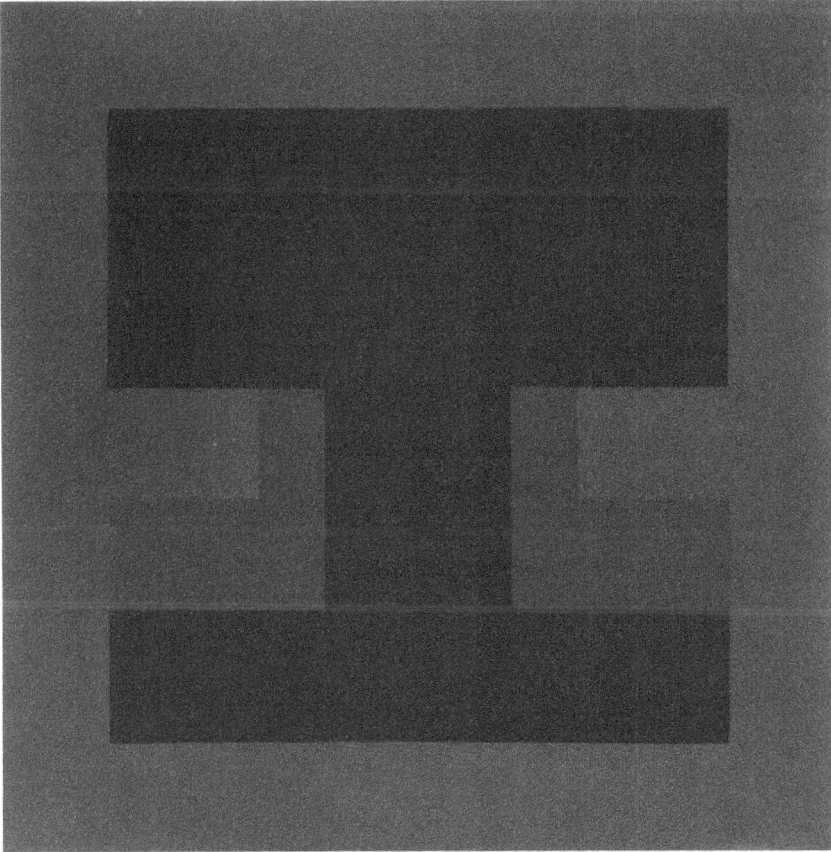

Chapter 13 Image 11. Carroll Sockwell (1943-1992), Untitled II, 1970. Acrylic on canvas, unframed: 48 x 48 in. Gift from the Trustees of the Corcoran Gallery of Art (Gift of Robert Scott Wiles), 2018.15.2679.

Sockwell's Untitled II (1970), is an early work that owes a great debt to Minimalism, a developing movement parallel to Color Field Painting. There was plenty of crossover between the two. Minimal art was abstract, large-scale, and exhibited an extreme simplicity of form, and was made primarily by White male artists. Sockwell would soon abandon Minimalism, traveling back in time to gestural abstraction, creating work for which he is much better known today. Beginning around 1973, Sockwell worked only on paper, creating his highly individualized, signature, lyrical and elegant works with charcoal, pencil, and pastel, until his suicide after his well-reviewed opening at the Washington Project for the Arts in 1992.

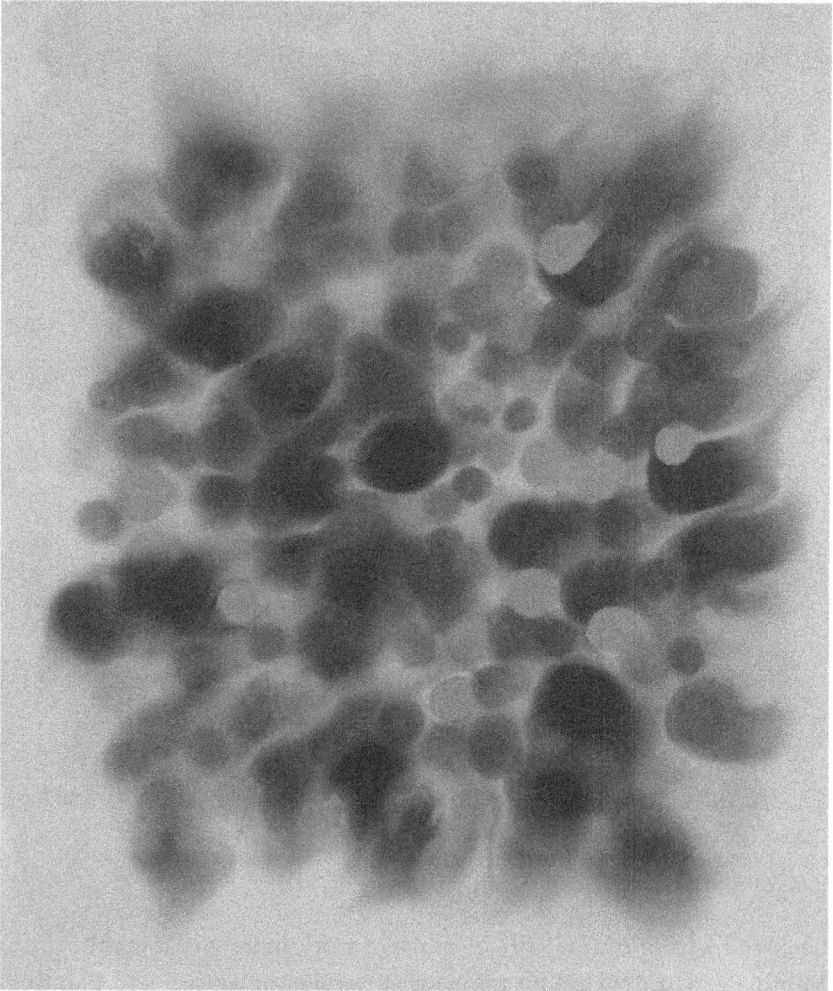

*Chapter 13 Image 12.* Kenneth Victor Young (1933-2017), *Untitled,* 1972. Acrylic on unprimed canvas, 55 x 47 in. Courtesy of Margot Stein.

Young similarly avoided mixing race and art, saying: "An artist is an artist, and his color has nothing to do with it. I don't like labeling a man a 'black artist'" (Capps, 2017). Young said he argued frequently with Jeff Donaldson (1932-2004), one of the pioneers of the Black Arts Movement of the sixties and seventies and the chair of the Howard University Art Department, which was producing much more socially and politically active artists than the region's other educational institutions. Dexter Wimberly, writing in the catalog for *Continuum*, a one-person exhibition he curated for Young at the American University Museum in 2019, allows that "It took courage, focus, self-awareness, and ambition to be a black artist making abstract paintings at that time" (Wimberly, 2019, pp. 6-7). The Black Arts Movement had a manifesto that, according to Valerie Cassel Oliver, expected you to do "work that reflected the beauty of that community in no uncertain terms" (Wimberly, 2019, p. 7).

*Chapter 13 Image 13.* Jeff Donaldson (1932-2004), *Patriot*, 1975. Mixed media, 24 x 20 in. Private Collection, New York, The Estate of Jeff Donaldson, Courtesy Kravets Wehby Gallery.

Donaldson had founded a radical group called AfriCOBRA (the African Commune of Bad Relevant Artists) that is still active today, but Young wanted nothing to do with the group. It speaks volumes about the continued dominance of mainstream White male artists that no works by Donaldson or other AfriCOBRA artists like Frank Anthony Smith (b. 1939) made their way into American University's collections over the past forty years. I borrowed their works for *The Long Sixties* because they provide a more accurate and comprehensive vision of the D.C. arts scene than the Washington Color School allows.

*Chapter 13 Image 14.* Frank Anthony Smith (b. 1939), *Santaquin*, 1980. Acrylic on canvas, 67 x 84 1/2 in. Courtesy of Pazo Fine Art, LLC.

Smith was an original member of AfriCOBRA, as well as a longtime faculty member at Howard University. His paintings, on first sight, give the impression of expressionist brush work and three-dimensional objects making aggressive attacks on the picture plane. Rather, they are amazing demonstrations of trompe l'oeil still life, though not very still. Donaldson and Smith introduced provocative ideas in their art, but it just wasn't being collected by major art museums. Even the Howard University Museum does not have a Jeff Donaldson in its collection. And, with a few notable exceptions, neither were the works of less political African American abstract artists, like Young, being collected at the time. Without work by AfriCOBRA artists or other Howard University faculty or alumni in general, this exhibition would have presented a very skewed survey of Washington, D.C. art.

*Chapter 13 Image 15.* Allen Carter (1947-2008), *Duck*, c. 1979. Enamel and plywood, unframed: 36 1/4 x 33 in. Gift from the Trustees of the Corcoran Gallery of Art (Gift of Mary H.D. Swift), 2018.15.2662.

Two African American artists whose work managed to be somewhat figurative, non-political, and find homes in museums were Allen "Big Al" Carter (1947-2008) and Franklin White (b. 1943). I was the graduate teaching assistant in 1975 for William Calfee when "Big Al" was his student. Calfee was one of the founding professors of the American University Art Department after World War II. He was quite a bit older, very soft-spoken, very intellectual, and tended to be somewhat mystical in his teaching and conversations.

"Big Al" was big; he was a one-man band. He broke all the rules and decibel levels with his voice and his music and his all-embracing good humor. Calfee eventually moved "Big Al" out of the classroom and into his own studio, so as to mute his "disruptions" to studio decorum. The interaction between "Big Al" and Calfee was something to behold. Carter's three-dimensional *Duck* (c. 1979) gives a taste of this irrepressible, barely controlled, cartoon-influenced artist clearly challenging the American University figurative style. Carter taught for thirty years in alternative schools in Arlington County and set a powerful model for creativity in the community. His work eventually made its way into both the Watkins and Corcoran Legacy Collections.

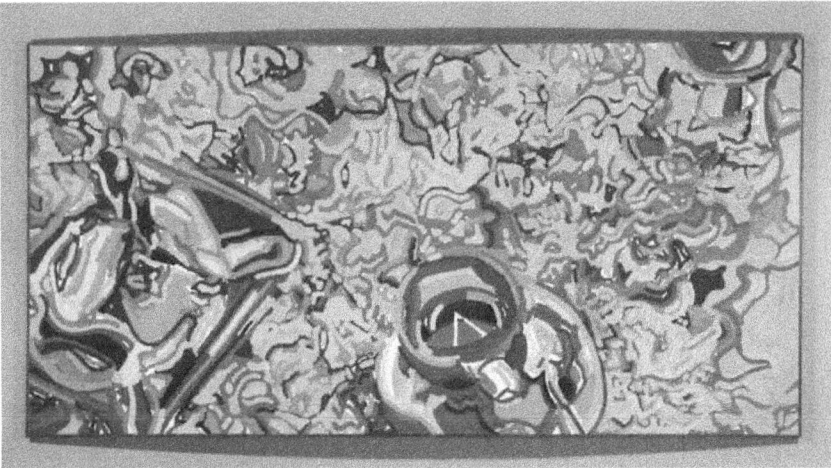

*Chapter 13 Image 16.* Franklin White (b. 1943), *Ashtray,* 1973. Oil on canvas, canvas size: 84 × 168 in. Gift from the Trustees of the Corcoran Gallery of Art (Gift of Gray Martin), 2018.15.2304.

Franklin White received his BFA and MFA at Howard University and taught at the Corcoran School of Art for thirty years. This 7 x 14 ft. oil still life is so large it had to be painted in the Corcoran's Hemicycle Gallery in advance of his one-person exhibition there in 1973. His paintings did not overtly engage in social or political commentary. Instead, he gave us this immense, bold, vibrant, beautiful still life celebrating the mundane familiar life around him in a most dramatic, transcendent, and ultimately political fashion.

*Chapter 13 Image 17.* Carol Brown Goldberg (b. 1940), *Blue Bricks*, 1968-1978. Acrylic on canvas, framed: 73 × 85 1/2 in. Gift of Linda and Howard Sterling, 2020.1.

Other artists associated with the Corcoran at this time were Carol Brown Goldberg (b. 1940), Michael Clark (b. 1946), Lisa Brotman (b. 1947), William Newman (b. 1948), and William S. Dutterer (1943–2007). Goldberg's primary influences as a Corcoran student were Gene Davis and Tom Green who, along with Nicholas Krushenick at the University of Maryland, encouraged her signature technique of outlining color saturated shapes in black. Goldberg also credits Corcoran faculty members Franklin White and Chris Muhlert for introducing her to the work of William H. Johnson, her direct inspiration for *Blue Bricks* (1968-1978). Like Johnson and White, she found transcendence and provocation hiding in a seemingly ordinary domestic scene.

*Chapter 13 Image 18.* Michael Clark (b. 1946), *Grey, Black and Grey George Washington*, 1969-1971. Acrylic on linen, 28 3/4 × 28 3/4 in. Gift of Barrett Linde, 2013.15.20.

Other figurative painters like Michael Clark (aka Clark Fox) seem to have spun off from the Color School experience. After his Color School apprenticeship, Clark displayed the early influence of his forays into Pop Art with this portrait of *Green, Black and Grey George Washington* (1969-1971). Like early American portrait painter Gilbert Stuart before him, Clark painted perhaps one hundred portraits of George Washington. Clark often painted popular icons, dematerializing his subjects through his flawless pointillist execution. Dematerialized as they were, his portraits achieved the formality and stillness of a Piero Della Francesca. Two other figurative artists associated with the Corcoran Gallery and School acknowledged Color

School influence, then went in the opposite direction, following their own surrealist muse. They formed the "Washington Color Pencil School" and exhibited together in 1973. The "School" consisted of William Newman, Lisa Montag Brotman, and several others. According to Brotman: "The Washington Color Pencil School was truly a rebellious act. Color painting was conceptually not enough for us. I think our work had a sense of escapism, fantasy, and social commentary as a result of events in the sixties and seventies" (L. Brotman, email communication, July 4, 2020).

*Chapter 13 Image 19*. Lisa Montag Brotman (b. 1947), *Playing for Keeps*, 1980. Oil on canvas, framed: 49 1/2 × 49 1/2 in. Gift of the Artist, 2020.6.

Brotman's painting, *Playing for Keeps* (1980), was one of her series of female figures in surreal settings. Here, Brotman appropriated the figure of a masked prostitute in a brothel from a vintage black and white photograph and transplanted her to a fantasy setting, at once both splendid and threatening. Masked, she confronts the viewer directly, with strength and vulnerability, knowledge and innocence.

*Chapter 13 Image 20.* William Newman (b. 1948), *Boiling in Mental Water,* 1974. Oil and acrylic on canvas, framed: 48 1/4 × 56 1/4 in. Gift of the Artist, 2020.8.

Look carefully at Newman's painting *Boiling in Mental Water* (1974), and you can just see Walter Hopps in the window to the left, rendered to the left of the large black and white face. Hopps, the most influential curator in Washington, D.C. from 1967 to 1985, can be seen here pulling a woman in a blanket. He figures in most of Newman's paintings at this time. The painting is a testament to the omnipresence of Hopps' independent, if erratic, curatorial spirit, and to the extraordinary skill and provocative subject matter of Washington, D.C.'s ascendant figurative painters.

*Chapter 13 Image 21.* William S. Dutterer (1943-2007), Grrrrr, 1979. Acrylic on canvas, canvas size: 76 1/4 × 60 1/2 × 1 3/4 in. Gift of the William S. Dutterer Trust, 2020.7.

William Dutterer taught with Newman at the Corcoran School of Art for twenty years during its golden age of amazing faculty before moving to New York. Early on in his career he made the dramatic transition from a successful maker of exquisite minimalist abstractions to an early proponent of funky new image painting. *Grrrrr* (1979), part of Dutterer's "Mask" series, has taken on new metaphorical possibilities as we suffer through the COVID-19 pandemic.

*Chapter 13 Image 22.* Willem de Looper (1932-2009), *Untitled*, 1973. Acrylic on canvas, 86 × 93 in. Gift of the Frauke and Willem de Looper Foundation for the Arts, 2020.5.

Willem de Looper (1932-2009) was a student of figurative artists Gates and Summerford at American University and then achieved early success with atmospheric paintings very much in line with the Color School orthodoxy of the time. His work did depart from the Color School because he still employed brushes and canvases primed with gesso, rather than leaving them raw and more absorbent for staining. Beginning in 1972, de Looper experimented with different paint applications and materials and discovered rollers used by commercial house painters. His experimentation with paint rollers made the application of paint and the construction of his compositions one action or gesture.

In *Untitled* (1973), de Looper found the perfect balance between freedom and structure, building up layers as he rolled paint horizontally across the canvas, revealing shimmering patterns left visible from his previous passes and peeking out at the edges. As in Mehring's paintings, de Looper often went back into the painting with a brush to make subtle adjustments here and there. He violated many Color School strictures, while maintaining its thematic disengagement.

I enrolled in American University's MFA program in 1973. For art history, I took every course offered by the pioneering feminist Art Historian Mary Garrard. She and her colleague Norma Broude offered a definition of feminist art in their catalog essay for the 2007-2008 American University Museum exhibition, *Claiming Space: Some American Feminist Originators:*

Feminism… is the spirit and instrument of change. It advocates for equal rights for women and more, for it involves challenging masculinist political and cultural hegemony. Feminist Art… challenges and rewrites the visual language through which gendered identity has been psychically inscribed and the oppression of women has been culturally institutionalized, and it aims to construct a new visual vocabulary for female empowerment and gender equality (Broude & Garrard, 2008, p. 4).

Strictly following this definition, which calls for images explicitly directed towards achieving female liberation and empowerment, I could find very few feminist painters represented in our collections, and almost no self-identified feminists.

The lack of feminist artists in *The Long Sixties* is partly a function of my decision to limit the exhibition to paintings. I became aware that my preference for painting distorted my initial purpose — to create a straightforward survey of art from our collections made during a specific period. Most feminist artists preferred the newer, then-unorthodox methods of performance art, conceptual art, and body art, as well as preferring to work "in such previously subordinated genres as film and photography, or the collaborative arts and crafts..." (Broude & Garrard, 2008, p. 5).

The absence of feminist artists from our collection is also a function of what was being shown in commercial galleries and purchased by collectors at the time, and what would eventually be accessioned by museums from those collectors. The seventies coincided with the rise of women-run co-op galleries, as well as non-profit spaces, which provided alternatives to the commercial gallery-museum system that women were excluded from. There was demonstrable sexism in the marketplace and, unfortunately, only rarely did co-ops and non-profits in Washington, D.C. make sales to "important" collectors and collections.

As was the case with the AfriCOBRA artists missing from our collections, feminist art and activism also redefines our understanding of Washington, D.C. art in "the long sixties," beyond the Washington Color School. And, as I also found with non-political African American painters, work by women artists in general was under-represented in our collection. It became necessary to solicit gifts from collectors of three women artists to achieve anything close to their adequate representation in *The Long Sixties*. Clearly, there is a need for future exhibitions to address the different priorities of feminist and African American artists in this era and remedy the inadequacies of museum collections in general.

While most women painters in Washington, D.C. were not self-identified feminist artists at the time, they were clearly influenced by artists who did self-identify and the Women's Movement that inspired them. Many of the women whose works are included in *The Long Sixties* present strong, confrontational, women-centered subject matter. As Brotman describes her somewhat complicated relationship to feminist art: "...my women paintings in the eighties were definitely a reaction to the Women's Movement, as well as my personal feelings about the inherently conflicting messages coming from our culture for a young artist/mother with small children" (L. Brotman, email communication, July 4, 2020).

*Chapter 13 Image 23.* William Woodward (b. 1935), *Kimono*, 1972. Oil on canvas, 69 × 60 in. Gift of Donna Keller, 2015.10.1.

While feminist artists were hard to find in our collections, "masculinist" painters of women seen through a decidedly male gaze were in abundant supply. William Woodward (b. 1935), like de Looper, studied under Gates and Summerford and retained their painterly touch while producing sensual realist works like *Kimono* (1972). Woodward carried on the American University painterly figurative tradition, training several generations of artists as a professor at George Washington University.

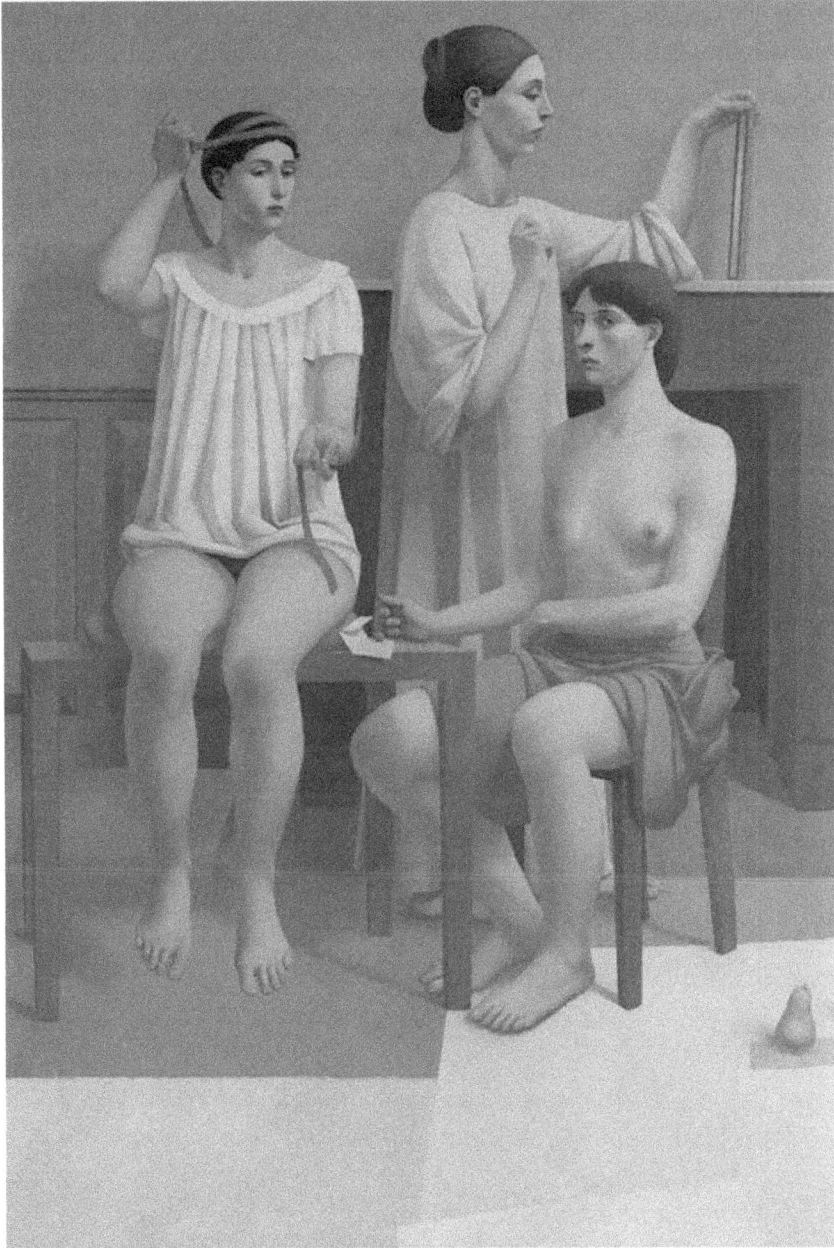

*Chapter 13 Image 24.* Alan Feltus (b. 1943), *Three Women with Pear*, 1981. Oil on canvas, 70 × 48 in. Gift of Robert P. and Arlene R. Kogod, 2005.14.10.

Alan Feltus (b. 1943) was also a faculty member in American University's Art Department. His gorgeously painted, often unclothed nudes with their flawless surfaces and brooding androgyny are now exhibited internationally. One can be seen here in *Three Women with Pear* (1981). By the mid-1970s, figurative art was on the ascendency in Washington, D.C. Paul Richard's 1997 article in *The Washington Post*, "The Museum is their Muse," explained why he thought there were so many superb realist figurative painters in our city. He called them "National Gallery School" painters (Richard, 1997). Three of the best are Rebecca Davenport (b. 1943), Manon Cleary (1942-2011), and Michal Hunter (b. 1950). Among their subjects, all three made portraits of Washington, D.C.'s most influential artworld tastemakers.

*Chapter 13 Image 25.* Rebecca Davenport (b. 1943), *Rebecca Cooper*, 1976. Oil on canvas, 72 × 60 in. Gift of Richard and Sondra Schoenfeld, 2017.9.1.

Rebecca Davenport's portrait of *Rebecca Cooper* (1976) was spot-on in portraying her P-Street art dealer's well-known eccentricities, topping off her portrait with Cooper's famously spacey countenance, décolletage, and very seventies bell-bottoms.

*Chapter 13 Image 26.* Manon Cleary (1942-2011), *Ramon After Lunch,* n.d. Acrylic on canvas, 30 × 72 in. Gift of Ramon Osuna, 2012.3.1.

Manon Cleary's portrait of her art dealer Ramon Osuna, titled *Ramon After Lunch* (n.d.), shows him asleep on the ground after what I am sure was a very nice lunch. He is wrapped in an art-moving blanket, while one of Cleary's trademark giant white rats strolls by just beyond his dreaming head.

*Chapter 13 Image 27*. Michal Hunter (b. 1950), *Walter at the Ambassador Grill, 3:31 am*, 2018 after 1978 original. Oil on canvas, 72 × 54 in. Gift of Wilfred Brunner and Joyce Jewell, 2020.9.

Michal Hunter's portrait of legendary night owl, curator Walter Hopps, titled *Walter at the Ambassador Grill, 3:31 am*, repainted in 2018, was originally painted in 1978. The artist was fresh out of graduate school and new to Washington, D.C. Hopps saw Hunter's work and sought her out for a portrait, choosing how he wanted to be portrayed and remembered — in front of a neon sign in an all-night diner. The original portrait was purchased by a collector and then disappeared when, it is believed, the collector went to prison.

## 1980–1982

The idealism of the sixties gradually wore away during the seventies with the Vietnam War and subsequent draft, political scandals, addiction, inflation, rising poverty, and malaise, culminating in 1980 with the presidential election of Ronald Reagan. Reagan's Inaugural Ball in January 1981 featured Donny and Marie Osmond as the entertainment, which was fairly emblematic of the Reagan era's repudiation of the counterculture.

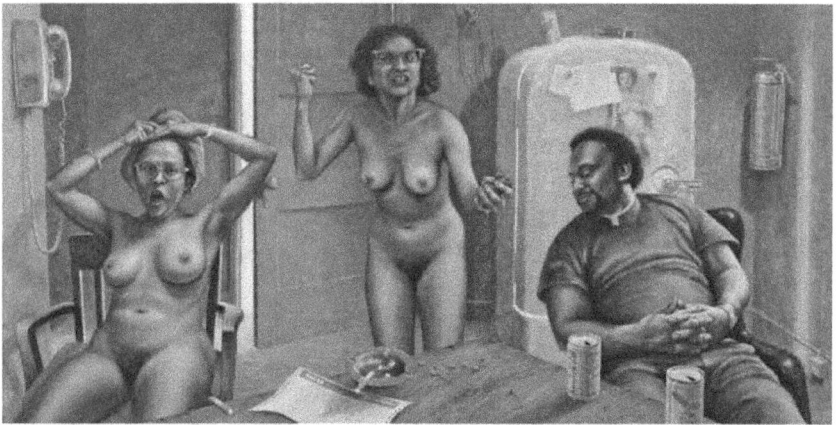

*Chapter 13 Image 28.* Fred Folsom (b. 1945), *Sisters*, 1981. Oil on board, 36 × 48 in. Gift of Amy Ross Loeserman, 2018.20.1.

Pop culture aside, by the eighties, Washington, D.C.'s White male artists had caught up with women and African American artists in returning to subject matter and engagement with the world. Fred Folsom (b. 1945) used his "National Gallery School" talents to tell stories about the seedy side of society, the leftovers, and, perhaps, the victims of the drug-fueled counterculture. The drunks, druggies, bikers, and strippers who inhabit his paintings have hit bottom, but it becomes clear, as one views the iconography woven through his compositions, that there exists the potential for redemption. We are all sinners, and we can rise, just as Folsom himself had risen. At long last, overt social content from a White male artist.

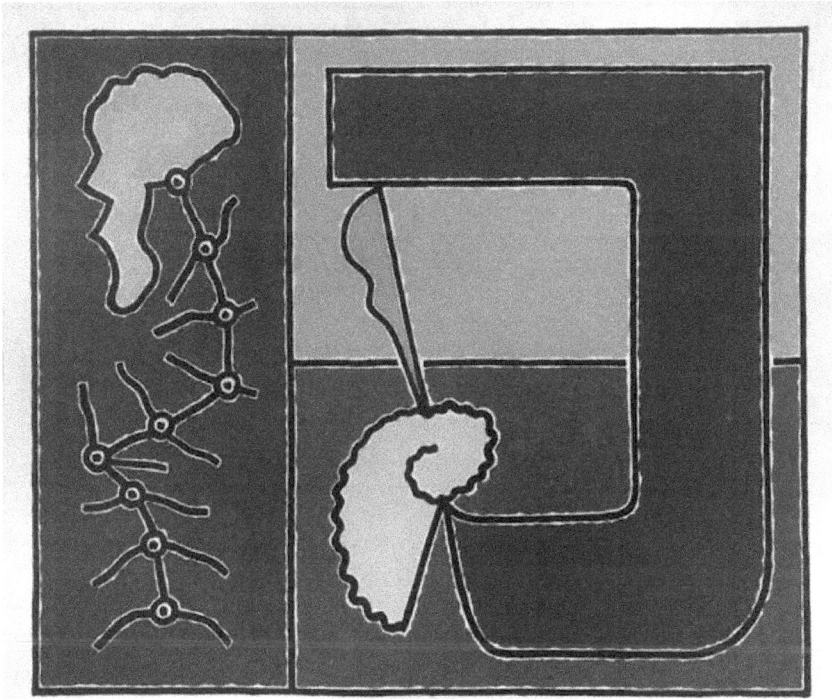

*Chapter 13 Image 29.* Tom Green (1942-2012), *Beirut*, 1982. Acrylic on canvas, 72 x 74 1/4 in. Courtesy of Paul Feinberg and Wendelin White.

Tom Green (1942-2012) began his career as an abstract artist coming out of the University of Maryland in the sixties. He never became a figurative artist, but he did develop his own iconography, and, as non-objective as Green's paintings are, one can sense his firm grasp of reality and tragedy as he frequently addressed overtly political and social conditions in his hybrid abstractions. *Beirut* (1982) brings the geographically remote human tragedy, the Siege of Beirut, then reported nightly on our television screens, into our consciousness today. It asks us to consider our culpability in this and future tragedies, to bear witness.

*Chapter 13 Image 30.* Val Lewton (1937-2015), *Arlington Cabs*, 1982. Acrylic on canvas, framed: 37 1/4 × 49 1/4 × 1 3/4 in. Gift of Joseph L. and Lisa W. Kirk, 1995.1.

Val Lewton (1937-2015) and Robin Rose (b. 1946) show two other approaches to what we might now call reality. Both are masters of their medium. Lewton is best known for chronicling the downward spiral of downtown Washington, D.C. after the 1968 Civil Rights Movement unrest by painting the empty lots where burnt-out buildings were razed and never rebuilt. He also lovingly painted the rise of suburbia in Washington, D.C.'s Virginia suburbs, as in *Arlington Cabs* (1982). His career as an exhibition designer for the Smithsonian certainly makes him an honorary member of Richard's "National Gallery School," though greater influence came from the car culture of Southern California and Northern California Realists Ralph Goings and Robert Bechtel.

*Chapter 13 Image 31.* Robin Rose (b. 1946), *Rapture,* 1981. Encaustic on aluminum laminate, framed: 48 5/8 x 73 1/2 x 1 1/2 in. Gift from the Trustees of the Corcoran Gallery of Art (Gift of Dr. Jerome Canter), 2018.15.2669.

Rose's color-saturated, formal, minimal abstractions indicate that he is an heir to the Washington Color School, though his mastery of the encaustic technique and the numinous play of light and texture he achieves makes him his own one-man "School." His title, *Rapture,* (1981), directs our attention to the mysteries and spiritual possibilities made visible in his art in a way that makes Color School paintings appear stuck in the ground, flat, unable to fly. Upon receiving my MFA, I went to work for Alice Denney's newly opened Washington Project for the Arts in summer 1975. Between then and when I closed my own commercial gallery in downtown Washington, D.C. in 1982, I was fortunate to have exhibited the work of hundreds of Washington, D.C. artists, including Sam Gilliam (b. 1933) and Robert D'Arista (1929-1987). Gilliam and D'Arista defined for me the opposite ends of the D.C. art world in "the long sixties."

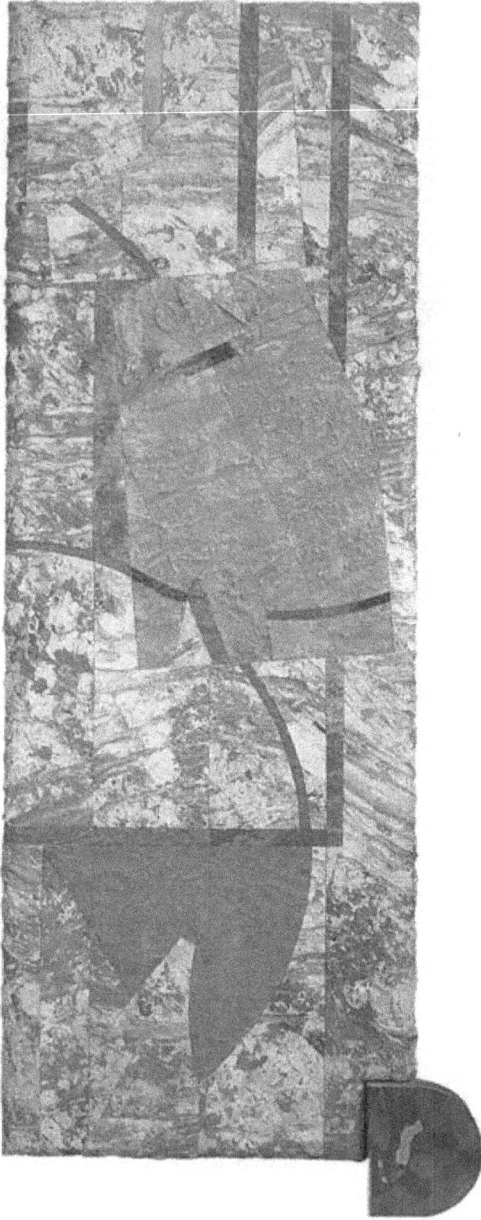

*Chapter 13 Image 32.* Sam Gilliam (b. 1933), *Muse III*, 1982. Acrylic on canvas with collage, enamel on aluminum, 73 × 25 × 2 in. Gift of Stanley and Barbara Tempchin, 1992.16.

Gilliam broke all the rules by innovating, experimenting, looking forward. He took the Color School as his jumping-off point and kept pushing and expanding the medium. *Muse III* is one of a four-painting series he completed in 1982. Gilliam describes the series as like "a musical composition played multiple times by a musician... repeated but nuanced and never exactly the same" (Feinberg, 2012, p. 10). *Muse III* displays his experimental collaging of thick layers of color-saturated acrylic polymer on a shaped canvas, recalling the color patterns and shapes of African American quilt-making traditions from slavery through the present. He broke out of the rectangle b shaped enameled aluminum object to the lower right-hand corner. Gilliam made his own rules. They surprised, and they worked. He disrupted the cool of the Color School.

*Chapter 13 Image 33.* Robert D'Arista (1929-1987), *Figure,* 1982. Oil on panel, framed:
22 1/8 × 19 1/2 × 1 1/2 in. X1669.

Robert D'Arista represents the opposite end of the artistic spectrum. He was a major influence at American University when he arrived from Boston University, freshly mentored by Philip Guston. D'Arista's art looked back, past Alberto Giacometti and Giorgio Morandi, all the way back to the Italian Renaissance. A comparison of D'Arista's *Figure* (1982) and Gilliam's *Muse III* says a lot about where we were in Washington, D.C. then, and where we are today. Though differing wildly in scale, medium, and subject matter, both embraced the physicality of paint and the expressive gesture of the brush or, in Gilliam's case, the rake and the knife. We've shown, beginning in 1957, the White (mostly male) mainstream's slow departure from these qualities of painting towards flat, decorative abstraction in Washington, D.C. and observed the painterly and expressive pushback through the seventies and into the eighties led by the growing recognition of the centrality of women and African American artists.

*Chapter 13 Image 34.* Image credit: Marilynn K. Yee/ The New York Times/Redux.

## THE END OF THE LONG SIXTIES

The end of "the long sixties" came for me in 1982. I closed my art gallery in downtown Washington, D.C. after surviving four long, lean years, until the recession took a double dip and rents began increasing. Artists' studios, galleries, and museums relocated and flourished in downtown Washington, D.C. in the seventies, but as the city's redevelopment proceeded, spurred by the opening of the Metro in

1976, all but museums would soon be priced out of downtown real estate. By the mid-eighties, the D.C. art world had become uncentered. It is still without a center today, and it lacks a significant collector base to support a small but healthy gallery scene that managed to flourish for some artists here in the sixties, seventies, and early eighties.

I came of age during a turbulent time, as turbulent as now. We began with an image of Senator McCarthy and his "fixer" Roy Cohn. We can also end *The Long Sixties* with another strikingly similar image of Roy Cohn, this time with Donald Trump. Before he died of AIDS, Cohn served as Donald Trump's "fixer" in the early eighties, defending his real estate company against charges it had systematically discriminated against Black tenants. The photograph provides, in retrospect following Trump's presidency even more than at the moment it was taken, another piece of proof that progress is just an illusion, that battles can be won, but the war is long. As I write, there is unrest again on the streets of Washington, D.C. and across the country over the denial of civil rights and the persistence of racism and systemic social and economic inequality. The Black Lives Matter movement appears to be having a transformational impact on the way the U.S. is confronting its past and present. It remains to be seen how long it will hold our attention. In the present context, I looked in our collections for Washington, D.C. art that in some way mirrored my time or might help me to interpret my experience of "the long sixties," but it is clear I was looking in all the wrong places.

Art History is replete with great artists fully engaged with their world. During the two world wars there were movements (Dada, Surrealism, Expressionism) and great artists (Max Ernst, George Grosz, Otto Dix, Pablo Picasso) who spoke clearly, sometimes elegantly, sometimes brutally, about the times they were living through. Between the wars, Social Realism produced Ben Shahn, Jacob Lawrence, Romare Bearden, Raphael Soyer, and many others protesting injustice and inequality. We now understand that many artists were systematically excluded from galleries and museums and were thereby left out of the canon and out of our collections. Since World War II, there have been plenty more wars and much human suffering. Where were the artists who would stand up and make us confront uncomfortable, sometimes tragic, truths about ourselves? Most art that was made during "the long sixties" addressing civil rights, women's rights, LGBTQ rights, environmental degradation, and the waste of war was excluded from commercial galleries and museums. Many were not painted at all, but installed rather than hung, displayed on monitors or projected on walls, or performed in public spaces

Consequently, my initial selection of paintings from the American University Museum's collections represented less of what artists did as we lived through "the long sixties," and more about which White (mostly male) artists were still making paintings in those years, whose work was given wall space in commercial galleries, who was buying what art between 1957 and 1982, and what American University and the Corcoran had been purchasing or accepting as gifts in the ensuing years.

After deciding to supplement work from our collections by borrowing and soliciting gifts, 25% of the artists in *The Long Sixties* are women and 25% are African American. As women and African Americans both make up about 50% of Washington, D.C.'s population, the exhibition falls far short of offering a balanced view. What inclusivity there is results from reaching outside our collections to find loans or gifts that could disrupt the standard White art historical narrative.

There have been occasions when White mainstream artists felt they had the freedom and support to make art that reflected their time. Women and Black artists had neither the freedom nor the support, and yet they persevered and made great contributions. The Works Progress Administration (WPA), operating during the Depression between the world wars, provided jobs for artists and enabled Social Realism to flourish. The opposite happened at the beginning of "the long sixties." Artists of all media were subjected to accusations of subversion or treason and sometimes threatened with the loss of livelihoods if their subject matter was perceived to be to the left of Senator McCarthy. This had a chilling effect on the socio-political engagement of mainstream White artists that extended well into the seventies.

The sixties were a very tumultuous time, but its social movements and struggles eventually allowed for some progress towards ending discrimination, securing rights, protecting the environment, and creating awareness of the constant warfare we are engaged in around the world. It took a generation to recover from the repressive climate of the fifties. We are again living in dangerous times. Federal funding for the arts is threatened whenever difficult or controversial subjects are addressed. The culture wars never really ended. Now, more than ever, we need all artists free to engage with today's problems, to reach an audience, to offer resolution and to inspire us with hope.

We also need our arts institutions, our curators, donors, directors, and boards to be transformed by new efforts to balance and share power in the art world. As D.C.-based writer and literary activist E. Ethelbert Miller sees our way forward: "It is vital that when future generations walk into galleries or museums that there is no 'echo of absence' but instead the sweet song of representation—the beauty of paintings hung in a way that all are lifted up—all have a place on the wall and in each passing heart" (E. Miller, email communication, December 12, 2020).

*All images courtesy American University Museum unless otherwise noted.*

## References

Albright, T. (1985). *Art in the San Francisco Bay Area, 1945 – 1980.* University of California Press.

Broude, N., & Garrard, M. (2008). *Claiming Space: Some American Feminist Originators.* American University Museum. https://dra. american.edu/islandora/object/auislandora%3A68156/datastream/ PDF/view

Carmean, E.A. (2017). *Mehring/Wellspring: The Early Color Field Paintings of Howard Mehring.* American University Museum.

Cohen, J.L., Forgey, B., Tebow, E., Lawrence, S., & Bussolati, E. (2013). *Washington Art Matters: Art Life in the Capital 1940-1990.* Washington Arts Museum

Capps, K. (2017 June 1). Late Artist Kenneth Young Is Finally Getting His Due. *Washington City Paper.* https://washingtoncitypaper.com/article/190708/late-artist-kenneth-young-is-finally-getting-his-due/

Feinberg, P. (2012). *The Constant Artist.* American University Museum.

Hayden, T. (2009). *The Long Sixties: From 1960 to Barack Obama.* Routledge.

Kinzer, S. (2019). *Poisoner in Chief: Sidney Gottlieb and the CIA Search for Mind Control.* Henry Holt and Company.

Meyer, J. (2019). *The Art of Return: The Sixties and Contemporary Culture.* The University of Chicago Press.

Perrigo, B. (2017 December). How the U.S. Used Jazz as a Cold War Secret Weapon. *Time Magazine.* https://time.com/5056351/cold-war-jazz-ambassadors/

Richard, P. (1997 November 7). The Museum Is Their Muse. *The Washington Post.* https://www.washingtonpost.com/archive/lifestyle/style/1997/11/09/the-museum-is-their-muse/540148de-6579-431e-b385-320fab76dca7/

Saunders, F.S. (1999). *The Cultural Cold Warrior: The CIA and the World of Arts and Letters.* The New Press.

Wimberly, D. (2019). *Kenneth Victor Young: Continuum.* American University Museum.

## About the Author

Jack Rasmussen earned his BA in Art from Whitman College in Walla Walla, WA, before completing an MFA in Painting, MA in Arts Management, and MA and PhD in Anthropology at American University. He worked in the Education Department of the National

Gallery of Art and became Assistant Director of the Washington Project for the Arts when it opened in 1975. He left this position to open the Jack Rasmussen Gallery, helped launch Rockville Arts Place (VisArts), served ten years as Executive Director of Maryland Art Place, and three years as Executive Director of di Rosa in Napa, California. Rasmussen has been Director and Curator of the American University Museum since it opened in 2005. He currently serves on the board of the Maryland State Arts Council.

# CHAPTER 14

# CULTURAL MEMORY AS SOCIAL JUSTICE: THE CRITICAL ORAL HISTORY METHODOLOGY

## DANITA MASON-HOGANS, WESLEY HOGAN, & GERI AUGUSTO

## INTRODUCTION

By Susan J. Erenrich

This chapter features an article penned by Donita Mason-Hogans, Wesley Hogan, and Geri Augusto. Their piece, "Cultural Memory as Social Justice: The Critical Oral History Methodology," emphasizes the power of storytelling within social movements. Storytelling is vital to social movements because it builds agency, shapes identity, and inspires action (Ganz, 2001). Through the assemblage of an array of personal and collective movement narratives, meaningful and cogent accounts of struggle, hope, strategic analysis, and a vision for a new world order come to life. Stories also provide a critical lens to examine historical and contemporary phenomenon from marginalized communities whose stories have been ignored, hidden, and expunged from the dominant culture. Through storytelling, these same communities have an opportunity to come together to challenge, reconstruct, and transform the conversation.

As a social movement history documentarian, I know how impactful storytelling can be. All too often, the trials and tribulations of ordinary citizens are third, fourth, or fifth hand accounts. The messenger doesn't even have a stake in the community. By the time an explanation of an event appears, the lifeblood of what actually happened is lost or is discovered years later by researchers who try to reconstruct the scene.

By reclaiming history through storytelling, as illustrated by the authors here, social movement participants are able to capture, preserve, and provide missing links. Consequently, lessons learned can be utilized by generations of current and future activists.

## Reference

Ganz, M. (2001). The Power of Story in Social Movements. In the Proceedings of the Annual Meeting of the American Sociological Association, Anaheim, California, August 18-21, 2001. http://nrs. harvard.edu/urn-3:HUL.InstRepos:27306251

# CULTURAL MEMORY AS SOCIAL JUSTICE: THE CRITICAL ORAL HISTORY METHODOLOGY

By Danita Mason-Hogans, Wesley Hogan, and Geri Augusto

People's understanding of what is important in history is often driven more by what is *left out* than by biased history writing, filmmaking, or museum curation. This is true not only for public history's audiences, but for curators, filmmakers, and historians. We only make films, exhibits, and books about what we can find evidence of — what we can find through archives, oral histories, museum collections, and big data.

Sometimes this means a massive loss of information. The Student Nonviolent Coordinating Committee, or SNCC ("Snick"), dismantled large parts of legalized segregation in the United States in just eight years, between 1960-68. These young people took action in the very places in which segregation was most deeply rooted. Despite ferocious violence from White supremacists, they themselves acted nonviolently. Here were youth who defied all odds, who attempted the seemingly impossible.

Fifty years later, at a reunion in 2010, SNCC veterans realized that very few U.S. school children or citizens knew anything about their work. It was as if the entire team that made the first successful moon landing, Apollo 11, possible was simply dismissed after the mission landing with no one asking what they had learned or what conditions created the desire to attempt such a journey in the first place. Imagine how peculiar — and dangerous to future missions — it would have been if the hard-won knowledge of these astronauts and their support team had been ignored. In response to this realization, the SNCC veterans formed a nonprofit organization, the SNCC Legacy Project (SLP) to preserve and share this history that is so vital to people's pursuit of democracy and equality.

In 2013, SLP joined together with Duke University's Center for Documentary Studies (CDS) and Duke University Libraries (DUL) in a new partnership to build a free and accessible-to-all archive chronicling the history of SNCC **from the perspective of the activists themselves** and to pass on the essential whys and how-tos of the freedom movement to subsequent generations. See the note at the end of this chapter for more details on this partnership. Working to center the perspectives of the activists themselves was a major point of departure, transitioning from the traditional university norms of interaction to a more equitable one that explicitly acknowledged that expertise does not come only from the university. In fact, university-based scholars in the project recognized that without such a partnership, they would have reached the outer-limits of their knowledge.

The collaboration's **goals** were

- to change the normative story of the Civil Rights Movement;
- to tell the story of SNCC's organizing from the *bottom up* but also from the *inside out*, exploring how affected people organized to change history; and
- to make SNCC materials more widely accessible to our **primary audiences**: students, teachers, activists, cultural workers, and citizens.

SLP and Duke also sought to create a replicable model for partnerships between activists and cultural workers/scholars in which the former would have the primary voice in assembling archival materials and shaping the historical narrative (see the list of major participants in building the SNCC Digital Gateway at the end of this chapter).

The resulting SNCC Digital Gateway (SDG) (http://snccdigital.org/) unveils the inner workings of SNCC as an organization, examining *how* it coordinated sit-ins and freedom schools, voter registration and economic cooperatives, anti-draft protests and international solidarity struggles (*Inside SNCC* https://snccdigital.org/inside-sncc/). The SNCC partners worked collaboratively with historians of the movement, archivists, and students to weave together grassroots stories. The SDG digitized primary source material to create new multimedia assets that illuminate this history for new generations (e.g., *People* https://snccdigital.org/category/people/ and *Our Voices* https://snccdigital.org/our-voices/). A section called *Today* (https://snccdigital.org/today/) highlights how the actions and strategies of SNCC are being adapted for use in the organizing work of today's young activists. Other sections allow visitors to explore the site through events (*Timeline* https://snccdigital.org/category/timeline/1943-1960/), and geographic locations (*Map* https://snccdigital.org/map/). The *Resources* (https://snccdigital.org/resources) section connects to primary sources, recordings from events sponsored by the project, lessons learned, and cultural works by SNCC veterans. Links within each section allow users to follow their interests by clicking on names, events, places, and topics. The search box on each page allows for more targeted discovery.

**Critical Oral History: An Overview**

While working on the SNCC Digital Gateway, we realized that we couldn't find and did not have evidence to answer many of the questions people still had about SNCC's work. It also became clear that there were multiple perspectives on the most important moments, developments, and ideas among movement folks themselves. At the urging of scholar-activists and SLP board members Geri Augusto and Charlie Cobb, SNCC veterans in the Legacy Project determined that the critical oral history methodology, first developed by James Blight and Janet Lang (https://www.choices.edu/video/why-did-you-do-a-critical-oral-history-project-on-the-vietnam-war/) to study the Cuban Missile Crisis and the Vietnam War, might be adapted to study SNCC's legacy. The Center for Documentary Studies, with its own rich history of innovative oral history work starting with the Behind the Veil (https://library.duke.edu/digitalcollections/behindtheveil/about/) project, eagerly partnered with Augusto and Cobb.

Together, we agreed that the critical oral history methodology was a way to develop a richer, more complex set of questions to ask, with the possibility of generating a far more nuanced body of evidence about critical, unanswered questions. It would facilitate a telling not of a monolithic, unreflective story, but rather one of many voices in retrospect. As one SNCC veteran has noted, "Most of the stories important to understanding SNCC and its legacy have not yet been told." Our goal was to develop the methodology to elicit from SNCC veterans a new wealth of information that allowed a clearer understanding of how SNCC activists engaged and resolved the tensions that inevitably developed as they fought for freedom. What made it possible for them to transform an entire region captive to White supremacy and strive to make it into a model of citizen democracy? "What if a way were found," another SNCC veteran asked, "to reflect, in carefully put together small groups, the thinking, concepts, and strategies pursued. . . by SNCC?"

The SLP-Duke team garnered funding from the Andrew W. Mellon Foundation and the National Endowment for the Humanities to develop the critical oral history approach to explore the sometimes contentious and conflicting memories of former SNCC activists, their opponents, and people like journalists, government agents, and other "adjacent actors." Our goal was to understand better, discover, and explain, just how multi-layered and complex the activism of the 1960s-era really was.

What exactly does "critical oral history" mean? There are multiple kinds of oral history. The most typical is the **interview,** which essentially asks the person being interviewed to recount her or his experience. These interviews are often biographical in nature. The interviewer may not have done extensive prior research on the individual or the issues under discussion. These conversations, therefore, are largely controlled by the person being interviewed.

**Critical oral history's conferences or forums**, by contrast, involve extensive research by trusted facilitators and carefully chosen scholars, both new and mature. As opposed to the relative freedom traditional oral history interviews provides the person being interviewed, critical oral history sessions are triggered by a collective reading of existing documentation — text and images alike — and a commitment to asking hard questions that will zero in on exact details. In the revised SLP methodology, each critical oral history forum evolves by juxtaposing, in real time-conversation, three key elements. First, a curated archive — a dossier of primary documents, images, and even sounds, prepared in advance and circulated to all participants well before the gathering. Second, a fairly small group of movement veterans who had firsthand participation in the main events, concepts or turning points to be discussed. And third, a smaller set of adjacent actors, whether allies or opponents during the time period under consideration, whose memories and viewpoints can offer a useful counterpoint.

The sessions are structured to dig into conflicts that may have occurred as part of a person's civil rights activism. For instance: How did SNCC members overcome the obstacles they faced? What were the divisions within the movement over how to proceed? How did Black Southerners view Northerners? Was there a difference in their attitude towards Black Northerners and White Northerners? How did activists keep lines of communication open in an era before long-distance phones were routine, and there was no e-mail? What were the competing forces — family, employer, faith leaders, friends, political ideology — that shaped the decisions activists made? How did initiatives such as freedom schools, citizenship classes, and new political parties such as the Mississippi Freedom Democratic Party (MFDP) and the Lowndes County Freedom Organization (LCFO) emerge and evolve over time?

As is clear, *critical oral history* demands far more preparation than traditional oral history and brings together, in the same room, people with different perceptions and experience. The result is that the questions (and answers) are much more precise. But, at the same time, they are also more nuanced and hence more likely to yield more complex reconstructions and retrospectives — the result of multiple voices and outlooks. We think that this is an important mode of research when what is needed is to more fully understand the causes and interworking of some of the movements on a national and global stage. In addition, critical oral history (COH) forums have the potential to produce far more detailed evidence as well as provoke a fresh approach to issues where disagreement exists.

Based on all the previous work done to build the SNCC Digital Gateway between 2013-2015 and the abundant sources we gathered as part of that work, the SNCC Legacy Project (SLP) helped us focus on two principal sets of **unanswered questions** for these critical oral history forums:

First, in July 2016, (https://snccdigital.org/our-voices/emergence-black-power/roots/) we held a three-day forum that worked to clarify the organization's shift in the 1960s from "One Person, One Vote" through the creation of the MFDP and the movement toward **Black Power and self-determination**. This forum allowed SNCC people to contextualize this shift on multiple levels and on their own terms, which was vital given the way those outside the organization had characterized the Black Power movement in the fifty years following its first articulation in June 1966.

Second, in June 2018, (https://snccdigital.org/our-voices/dealing-with-power/) we held a three-day forum on the Mississippi Summer Project in 1964 and its aftermath. How did it become a pivotal turning point in the movement? What were the issues of controversy that had to be addressed before embarking on such a grand venture? What went into the decisions to develop Freedom Schools, create agricultural cooperatives, and build a Mississippi Freedom Democratic Party (MFDP)? How did Southern activists handle the influx of Northerners, and how did Blacks and Whites handle the racial tensions that inevitably appeared? What were the consequences of the 1964 Summer Project and, in particular, the experience of the MFDP? What happened when the MFDP went to the Democratic National Convention in Atlantic City to ask for equal representation in the Mississippi delegation? How did Lyndon Johnson's insistence that the MFDP **not** be recognized affect the attitude of SNCC activists toward White liberals? What role did the experience of the MFDP have in the emergence of the Black Power movement and the development of new political parties like the Lowndes County Freedom Organization?

Each critical oral history forum (COH) involved ten or so SNCC activists, several adjacent actors, two of the SLP scholar-activists we have been working with since 2013, two civil rights historians from outside of Duke, and two civil rights historians from the Duke faculty. At the first COH in 2016, we also invited five to eight youth activists to campus to observe and ask questions. The participation of youth activists was so successful that we extended and **formalized** this as part of the process in 2018, so that at the end of **each** morning or afternoon session in 2018, the young people had 30-45 minutes to set the agenda, frame queries, and make critical observations.

Youth activist participation had several beneficial impacts. The young people raised questions that had not yet been addressed and thus expanded our knowledge-building. It also allowed substantive relationships to build between youth and elders and expanded already-existing relationships. Over shared meals and informal time during the COH forum, these intergenerational ties allowed for significant new insights to emerge that then found their way back into the formal sessions. The presence of young people also placed the SNCC veterans in a different mindset than simply talking to "history." They were talking with flesh-and-blood youth who were right in front of them trying to make a change now. This allowed for a more thoughtful and instructive accounting of the events that brought an additional layer of power to the COH experience.

All the participants in these critical oral history forums were sent extensive documentation on the issues under discussion — a dossier that sometimes included their own words, as well as those of others; writings on the issues of controversy that were already out there; and lists of potential questions to be addressed. The dossier-creation process was led by Danita Mason-Hogans, guided by the SNCC veterans' memories of particular events and knowledge of existing literature on the movement. Mason-Hogans then assigned students to do the research to find documents. We expected all participants to be grounded in these materials and to come ready to address, in detail and in collective deliberation, the pivotal issues under examination.

Geri Augusto **acted as a key facilitator** and innovator of the COH, bringing the COH methodology to the attention of the SLP-Duke working group, guiding the intellectual framework as we set it up, making sure the logistics reflected the tone we needed to generate, and setting the ambience for the sessions as they unfolded in real time.

"Remembering is a moral act," Augusto stated at the beginning of the first SLP COH in 2016 at Duke. "Each of you saw the emergence of Black Power as an idea in its early practice in a different way," she shared with those gathered. "I think of it like this: Each of you came into the same room, but at a different point, you left on a different note. You might have stayed in the same house, but with a different set of people. We were all reading, many of you were reading, the very same books, but you were not necessarily reading them in common. Or the way you came across them or interpreted them might have been different. We want to bring out all those different ways and different paths by which people came to them." SNCC's own understanding of Black Power's origin and development had not been well-documented except through individual interviews, scattered in archives around the country. So, Augusto asked people in the room to recognize "the kind of knowledge production that this calls for," and suggested that the session might build on the ideas of Māori activist-scholar Linda Tuhiwai Smith, author of *Decolonizing Methodologies: Research and Indigenous Peoples*. Augusto invoked Tuhiwai Smith's notion of research created by Indigenous and marginalized communities as "reframing, claiming testimonies, storytelling, celebrating survival, remembering, intervening, revitalizing, connecting, writing back." Augusto stated: "You've been written *about*; this is about writing *back*." She went on with Tuhiwai Smith's list to invoke representing, gendering, envisioning, restoring, returning, naming, protecting, creating, discovering, and sharing, and asked: "So, shall we try to do something like that today?"

Each session was taped by a videographer, transcribed, and indexed for deposit in the Duke libraries, and excerpts of the sessions have been made available online through the SNCC Digital Gateway for both the 2016 and 2018 sessions.

## Who We Are and How We Fit In

We, Danita Mason-Hogans and Wesley Hogan, are both Gen X bridge organizers who came of age in campaigns to build Black Studies programs and to organize against South African apartheid. In 2013, we saw a new generation of activists coming into political activity in the wake of the murder of Trayvon Martin (Bates, 2018). We knew how much we had learned in the 1990s ourselves from 1960s activists and how, at that time, media outlets had tried to pit us against our elders, Gen X versus Baby Boomers, highlighting our disagreements rather than our continuities and solidarity. We thought we could be useful in bringing together young activists in the 2010s and the elders we'd learned from, to empower their mutual engagement and respect for one another without forcing our goals on any of them.

Initially, we wanted to create spaces and a platform for engagement, then step back to support and observe. Our first joint effort was a 2015 Voting Rights conference (https://vimeo.com/271129248), under the umbrella of the SLP-Duke partnership. Mason-Hogans was project director, bringing together one hundred youth activists with 150 Civil Rights-Black Power veterans for four days in September 2015 in Durham, North Carolina. With Mason-Hogans as project manager and Hogan as principal investigator, we worked hard with Geri Augusto, SLP, and civil rights scholars Emilye Crosby and Hasan Jeffries to bring forward the COH model in service to sharing "informational wealth" across generations of organizers and cultural workers.

SLP chair Courtland Cox noted that: "Our youth have to have the benefit of our information, if not experiences, so they have a head start as they continue their struggle in America." He called this project a "critical transfer of *informational wealth*." The term, developed by Cox, stuck. SNCC activist Joyce Ladner rejoined: "If nothing else will save the most vulnerable of this generation, then informational wealth may be used to do so." The SNCC Digital Gateway provides one model for how universities and social movements might partner on an egalitarian basis to identify, archive, and disseminate the lessons learned inside social movements. The concept of informational wealth was an important asset in this partnership.

The SLP's modified COH method created a model, which others might wish to replicate, of how to think about social change happening at the grassroots and how it can be documented in a way that upholds the values of mutual respect and reciprocity. Instead of seeing political movements the way the media does, as spontaneous eruptions involving marches, conflicts with authority, and then a sudden leap forward, people participating in this work learned and shared important lessons about how they might participate in similar local democratic practices as a part of their day-to-day lives. It furthered the insight of Eleanor Roosevelt that somehow, we must be able to show people that democracy is not about words but actions. We tried to view the collection and preservation of civil rights history through a social justice lens. We were aware that who tells the story, and from whose perspective that history is told, is at least as important as the evidence base. We were aware of the power of historical knowledge to inspire and inform future generations of activists. Further, since we were studying a social justice movement, it was important that we employed practices that were consistent with social justice as we collected the history, such as equal input and fair permission forms.

**Process-Oriented Work**

We were consistently aware of how we moved to consciously **facilitate, rather than drive,** the content of these sessions. Vital to this process, Hogan notes, is the powerful way Mason-Hogans interacted with every COH participant. From the moment she first contacted them to the time she dropped them off at the airport, Mason-Hogans lived a freedom movement ethos, not the sterile ethos so common in academic settings. Her family came to the sessions and greeted people. She asked and knew about participants' families. She made sure people had the equipment, food, and accommodations they needed. In a thousand small and meaningful ways, she showed people that they, not just their memories, matter. We self-consciously tried to come up with practical ways to escape sterile academic environments through a deliberative process of selecting project team members. Selecting Mason-Hogans as a community-based intellectual and educational activist rooted outside the university was important. Several of our student researchers were also local activists from North Carolina Central University, an HBCU (Historically Black Colleges and Universities) less than two miles from Duke. We selected a filmmaking collective for the 2018 sessions, Free Southern Media. We had to jump through legal and bureaucratic hurdles to create this team and this type of collaboration — the university makes it much easier to work with people only within it. We're trying to be transparent about the work it takes to make this happen, as it has been essential to the process to have this diversity of perspectives on the team.

What resulted from this type of collaboration, a transparent and intentionally inclusive process, was a collection of new historical information that deepens the larger narrative of the U.S. Civil Rights Movement. It has also provided an opportunity to offer clarity and correction to the popular narrative of **how** the freedom movement occurred and who drove it forward.

### A Model Mason-Hogans Took to Chapel Hill

*Mason-Hogans, while serving as project director, simultaneously continued her longtime work with the town of Chapel Hill, North Carolina. As a member of the mayor's Historic Civil Rights Commemorations Task Force, she recommended that the city adopt the approach to historical memory developed within the COH work. The Chapel Hill civil rights task force subsequently developed a partnership with the local library, local school system, university historians, and local activists to develop a timeline of civil rights history for Chapel Hill. What resulted was a discovery of local history that had not been previously explored or understood because of decades of mistrust in the way the history had been previously recorded, collected, and documented. The next section is in Mason-Hogans' voice, as she recounts how Chapel Hill adopted this methodology.*

In order for SNCC, Dr. King, or any other national figure or movement to become successful, there had to have been a local community whose citizens were ready to confront the realities of racism and embrace the change of the era. What we found were five common threads that sparked the U.S. Civil Rights Movement throughout the country on national *and* local levels. They were:

- The murder of Emmett Till
- Poverty and a lack of attention to basic needs of the community
- Terror and a systemic disenfranchisement of citizenry
- The actions of the Greensboro Four
- The power of and determination of young activists

We therefore attempted to use what we had learned through the COH process as a model framework for helping local communities to document and share the parallel local history of the Civil Rights Movement beginning in Chapel Hill.

The igniters of the Civil Rights Movement in Chapel Hill were long dissatisfied with the way their history had been told and understood, and they did not have the essential trust in the university system necessary to garner a full depiction of what happened in the local community during the freedom movement. Much of the existing research about the movement in Chapel Hill, like so many other cities and towns in the United States, was centered around the University of North Carolina-Chapel Hill (UNC)'s role in the Civil Rights Movement. The narrative about the native Black community's part was regulated to a single spontaneous event that propelled the university students into civil rights action.

We contacted Mayor Pam Hemminger with the town of Chapel Hill and informed her about the process that we developed at Duke, and she formed a Civil Rights Task Force to document civil rights history (https://chapelhillhistory.org/civil-rights/).

What resulted through the intentionally equal and collaborative process of the COH was a treasure trove of local history that had not been previously explored or understood. The partners included the local library, university-based civil rights historians, the local school system, and policy makers in the town. This was all done with the local movement veterans at the center of the interactions, while making a special effort to solicit local community memories paired with primary source material.

Because of the relationships that we cultivated with the local members of the movement and scholar activists, we were able to counter the popular narrative and replace it with first-hand accounts and primary source material that corrected the historical record. The Civil Rights Movement in Chapel Hill actually began as a youth movement that was a well-thought-out plan devised and executed by high school students at Chapel Hill's all-Black Lincoln High School.

The unexpected gift of this collaboration was an opportunity to collectively reflect on this important part of Chapel Hill history, which resulted in a town timeline, historical website (https://chapelhillhistory.org/), a new university archive, k-12 materials, town and community initiatives based on the history, a documentary (Chapel Hill History, 2018), an historical marker (Chapin, 2019), a national library association presentation on the process, and several local and trending national news stories (e.g., Inge, 2019) about the events.

Other cities and towns in North Carolina, including Durham, Raleigh, and Greensboro, have shown a strong interest in bringing the COH model to their communities and learning new ways of documenting history and cultural work. We are looking into ways to expand the model in a resourceful way.

In any social justice movement, many people who are involved typically feel unheard and disrespected by larger societal institutions. They often feel that their opinions and voices do not matter or that their reasons for participating in struggle are distorted. Since academic institutions are a part of a greater power structure, these perceptions hold true when collecting and documenting history in grassroots communities as well. Critical oral history offers a useful tool to employ a true collaborative process that upends the traditional unequal approach to building historical archives of civil and cultural work. The process provides an opportunity to open the floodgates of trust which, inevitably, leads to more accurate information and a greater understanding of societal evolution and mutual understanding. As one of our partners in Brazil said after seeing a presentation on the method, "This takes the idea of 'popular education' [a concept developed by Brazilian Paulo Freire] and applies it to building community archives."

More information on the project is available online (https://snccdigital.org/resources/lessons-learned/). We welcome any feedback or pushback, and hope people will share their experiences of building similar cultural archives with us at Danita.Mason-hogans@duke.edu, Geri_augusto@brown.edu, wesley.hogan@duke.edu.


**Note: Major Participants in Building the SNCC Digital Gateway**

The major participants in building the SNCC Digital Gateway include three institutions (SLP, CDS, DUL). From the SLP, Geri Augusto, Charlie Cobb, Courtland Cox, Bruce Hartford, Jennifer Lawson, Judy Richardson; from the Duke Center for Documentary Studies, Bill Chafe, Wesley Hogan, Lynn McKnight, Tim Tyson; from the Duke University Libraries, John Gartrell, Naomi Nelson, Will Sexton, Molly Bragg. Outside scholars central to the team were Emilye Crosby (SUNY-Geneseo) and Hasan Kwame Jeffries (Ohio State). SDG's Project Manager Karlyn Forner and Project Coordinator Kaley Deal pulled everyone and everything together. The Student Project Team included: Amina Bility, Aaron Colston, Colby Johnson, Meaghan Kachadoorian, Eliza Meredith, Alexandria Miller, Annie Piotrowski, David Romine, Sarah Scriven, Kristina Williams, and Kelsey Zavelo; SUNY Geneseo Interns: Hannah Embry, Jen Galvao, Tom Garrity, Jenna Lawson, Grace McGinnis, Lauren Plevy, and Tanairi Taylor; and Project Interns: Emily Abbott, Charmaine Bonner, Kenneth Campbell, Todd Christensen, and Ajamu Amiri Dillahunt. Teaching for Change's executive Director Deborah Menkart and Danita Mason-Hogans of the Center for Documentary Studies also participated in indispensable ways in the work of the SDG.

## References

Bates, K.G. (2018, July 31). A Look Back at Trayvon Martin's Death, and the Movement It Inspired. Code Sw!tch. *NPR.* https://www.npr.org/sections/codeswitch/2018/07/31/631897758/a-look-back-at-trayvon-martins-death-and-the-movement-it-inspired

Chapel Hill History (2018, December 7). Opening Our Future: The Chapel Hill Nine Story [Video]. YouTube. https://www.youtube.com/watch?v=F8UNQtFmg14

Chapin, J. (2019, March 1). Refused a Place at the Counter, Chapel Hill 9 to Get Marker on Franklin Street. https://www.newsobserver.com/news/local/counties/orange-county/article227003404.html          and https://www.newsobserver.com/news/local/counties/orange-county/article227003404.html/video-embed

Inge, L. (2019, February 28). Honoring the Chapel Hill 9. Morning Edition. *NPR.* https://www.npr.org/2019/02/28/698863817/honoring-the-chapel-hill-9

**About the Authors**

Geri Augusto has known SNCC activists from her teenage years, and later worked with a number of them in Washington, D.C. and in Tanzania, and for the last thirteen years has taught and led research at Brown University within International and Public Affairs and Africana Studies. A Watson Faculty Fellow, Augusto is currently part of Watson's Brazil Initiative, and also serves on the working group for Brown's new Native American and Indigenous Studies (NAIS) program. Augusto earned her BA in economics from Howard University, MPA from Harvard Kennedy School and Ed.D. from George Washington University. The primary focus of her scholarly work centers on how knowledge gets created and practiced in contexts where there is human difference without equality. As a member of the SLP, she has been centrally involved in the SLP-Duke partnership since 2013. For more information, visit https://watson.brown.edu/people/faculty-fellows/augusto.

Wesley Hogan is Research Professor at the Franklin Humanities Institute and History at Duke University. She writes and teaches the history of youth social movements, human rights, documentary, and oral history. Her most recent book, *On the Freedom Side*, draws a portrait of young people organizing in the spirit of Ella Baker since 1960. In July 2021, a book she and Paul Ortiz have co-edited was released, *People Power: History, Organizing, and Larry Goodwyn's Democratic Vision in the Twenty-First Century*. Between 2003-2013, she taught at Virginia State University, where she worked with the Algebra Project and the Young People's Project. From 2013-2021, she served as Director of the Center for Documentary Studies. She co-facilitates a partnership between the SNCC Legacy Project and Duke, The SNCC Digital Gateway, whose purpose is to bring the grassroots stories of the civil rights movement to a much wider public through a web portal, K12 initiative, and set of critical oral histories.

Danita Mason-Hogans is a community-based historian from Chapel Hill, North Carolina. She is a curriculum specialist with a theater arts background and has been an education activist for thirty years. She is employed with the Center for Documentary Studies where she serves as program manager for the Critical Oral Histories Component. Her current projects involve working with veteran civil rights activists on the national and local level in order to document their experiences and transform them into K-12 civil rights curricula. She works with school systems, universities, activists, and historians to document local and national history from the "inside out" and from the "bottom up."

# SECTION 4

GRASSROOTS LEADERSHIP &
CULTURAL ACTIVISTS

# CHAPTER 15
# THE SONG I DIDN'T PLAY

JOHN FLYNN

## INTRODUCTION

By Susan J. Erenrich

This chapter features another long-time troubadour of conscience — John Flynn. John has been singing for social justice for close to four decades.

John is a recipient of the 2019 National Association of Criminal Defense Lawyers Champion of Justice Humanitarian Award. And in 2018 he won the Phil Ochs Award in recognition of his music and activism for social and political change.

I first met John at a Phil Ochs Song Night many moons ago and later booked him to perform at the May 11, 2013, Mother's Day Concert Against Gun Violence at the Peoples' Voice Cafe in New York City. The show was a benefit for the Children's Defense Fund. John had written a salient song titled *You Can't Tell*, following the Sandy Hook Elementary School massacre that took place in Newtown, Connecticut on December 14, 2012. Having heard the compelling tune (https://youtu.be/Bb-J67d6gSs), I knew John had to be part of the evening's lineup.

In this chapter , *The Song I Didn't Play,* John shines a light on another cause he has devoted time and energy to since 2005 — helping incarcerated and returning citizens to successfully transition from prison to freedom. It is an exemplary model for cultural movers and shakers who want to lend their voices to the ongoing battle for human rights. John's strong belief in mutuality and his egalitarian spirit is an archetype for those who want to lead horizontally and collaboratively.

I hope readers are inspired by John's piece. He demonstrates how an individual can truly make a difference and how, if you have "a willingness to be changed by each person you encounter" and you "allow yourself to be impacted and affected," this can have a "slow but always powerful effect on all involved."

## THE SONG I DIDN'T PLAY

By John Flynn

Last year, I got to perform a special concert in a part of a state prison where the men were kept in "administrative segregation," which means apart from all the other offenders. Although I normally accompany myself on guitar when I sing, during this particular performance it was actually a song that I *didn't* play that seemed to have the biggest impact on all who attended my show.

Since I've been a singer-songwriter by trade, most folks, upon hearing about the inordinate amount of time I spend in prisons these days, assume I'm engaged in some kind of creative writing or arts-centered project with inmates. But most of the time I leave my guitar at home. This concert was a rare exception. I was grateful to the warden for the opportunity to provide something different for these men who, for reasons dealing with lengthy, high-profile trials resulting from a prison riot and the killing of a corrections officer here in Delaware in 2017, did not have access to many of the normal therapeutic, educational, or recreational outlets that most offenders enjoy. This was a big deal for my guys. And for me.

Along with my music career, I'm the executive director of New Beginnings-Next Step, Inc. (http://newbeginnings-nextstep.org/) (NBNS), a non-profit that helps incarcerated and returning citizens to successfully transition from prison to freedom. We do this primarily by running weekly peer support groups inside and outside of a growing number of Delaware prisons. Since my early years with New Beginnings (the part of our organization that works within the prison), when I unexpectedly found myself as the program's sole volunteer, our mission and footprint have expanded significantly, and we are now supported by a growing and passionate cadre of volunteers as well as a diverse and talented board of directors. It's been a life-changing ride that has gradually caused an aging folksinger to cut back on his touring because he's found an audience deeply hungry for a different kind of song.

I'd actually been volunteering at the prison for years before anybody on the staff even suspected that I *was* a musician. Back in 2008, the Philadelphia Phillies asked me to sing the national anthem at one of the National League Championship games held at Citizens Bank Park, and the warden's secretary happened to see my picture in the local paper the following day. An invitation to perform at the prison ensued and has led to repeated concert appearances for inmates here in Delaware.

As a performer who worked primarily on the national folk circuit, my incarcerated audiences were rarely familiar with me or the kind of music I played. But the fact that my songs attempted to distill the lessons I'd learned in my years of prison work into some relevant and resonant truth seemed to win over even the most skeptical listeners. By far the biggest of these lessons had to do with mutuality. These men were — I'd come to know again and again — just like me.

The biggest misconception many of us have when we start working with the marginalized is that they are different from us in some fundamental way. This difference, we might reason, would help explain their situations. If so, then what is required is to identify the cause of this difference and help "fix" it. This approach initially seemed completely logical to me. After all, I wasn't in prison. Therefore, I must be doing *something* right, something that the folks who were locked up could learn to do as well. So, the job, as I initially understood it, was to assist someone in identifying some missing component (e.g., life skill, emotional management tool, sobriety-maintenance strategy), help the individual in question acquire and employ said component(s), and then, stand back and watch the inevitable success that would follow. After all, big jobs need big tool kits, and many of the men I'd meet had never even been exposed — let alone learned — to employ some of the approaches to problems we regularly talked about in New Beginnings.

Knowledge is power. Or at least it can be. So, equipping our guys with new tools as they left prison was very exciting. And, initially, there were lots of enthusiastic and promising starts. Guys were getting jobs, finding places to live, paying off fines, meeting all the requirements of their probation. They were, in short, checking off all the little boxes that represented successful re-entry, accomplishing all the things we'd talked about while they were locked up. But, too often, their early successes were short-lived. At some point something would invariably go wrong.

It seemed that no matter how much our guys prepared themselves for the difficult challenges that we all knew awaited them, life would always intervene in some unexpected way. A loved one would die, a spouse would leave, a job would be lost. One of a thousand different things would seem to come out of nowhere. This created a moment of extreme vulnerability when access to all the shiny new tools acquired in prison — as well as the desire to use them — seemed to vanish entirely. Sometimes this crisis lasted only for the briefest of moments, but often that moment would be all that was required to send the individual back to jail. In that period of unexpected duress, the returning citizen would often default to a kind of "survival" mode and return to old patterns of thinking and behaving. Quite colorfully, our guys compared this often-temporary surrender to coming down with the flu. They called it getting "a case of the f**k its."

What was required, it seemed, was to find some way of inoculating our guys against this devastating malady. We needed to help them build resilience, enough that a person could be knocked down by life, not just once, but repeatedly (for we all are!) and find a way to keep getting back up and pushing forward. To, in fact, *believe* there was a reason *to* keep pushing forward. And back then, that vaccine simply wasn't something I knew how to provide.

Despite this frustrating and disappointing realization, there's some truth to the old adage that a big part of success is just "showing up." Especially when you keep doing it. Although it seemed that much of the information I was trying to impart in prison each week was of limited value, I was gradually beginning to understand that the fact that I was there "imparting away" was critically important. My role as a volunteer created a context that allowed me to develop ongoing relationships with men I would otherwise never know. But these relationships had strict sets of boundaries. Some were set by the prison. Some, by the men themselves.

As a volunteer for the Department of Corrections (DOC), I'm prohibited from any communication with offenders outside my New Beginnings sessions. No personal visits, no phone calls, no letters, no social media contact are allowed. So, the ninety minutes we'd spend together on Tuesday mornings and Thursday evenings was it until a few of my guys and I had an idea. Facing re-entry, several offenders asked if we could continue our weekly meetings outside of prison when they got home. This we did. The payoff for this decision was as large as it was unexpected. One of our successful returning citizen members speaks to the power of this new continuity and sense of deep relationship in this video https://youtu.be/woi0d3_ealM on YouTube.

It turned out, apart from their intrinsic value, our new outside support groups for returning citizens were freighted with unanticipated symbolic meaning that soon changed the entire dynamic of our groups *inside* the prison. The fact that our interest in our guys didn't merely extend to the end of our cinderblock classroom or surrounding prison walls, that we were willing to be an ongoing part of their lives when they went home, resonated with those still serving their sentences like nothing else ever had. Men who seemed reticent to put their faith in much of anything began to believe in me and (by this time) my other New Beginnings volunteers. The men began to open up and invest more of themselves in our discussions, to make themselves more transparent and more vulnerable. The volunteers, in turn, responded by sharing more deeply from our own life experiences.

For example, one of my new volunteers had lost a son to a drug overdose. I'll never forget the effect her willingness to share such a deeply personal and painful experience had on all those present in the prison's multi-purpose room that evening. Nor will I forget the tenderness and profound respect with which our men listened and (in their way) ministered to her. This represented a powerful new kind of mutuality. We weren't there trying to "fix" them anymore. We were all now partnering in something exciting and fresh. And we were helping *each other*.

The truth is that we are *all* missing a piece or two. We have all been, at some level, and at some time, damaged. And, for me, this realization, and resultant toppling of the lofty though invisible pedestal on which I'd unconsciously perched for so long, allowed me to understand and act in new ways. For a performer, of course, this pedestal is called a stage. But more on climbing down from that later….

Yes, the men I met were truly just like me. For a myriad of reasons, they had faced almost unendurable challenges that made my personal struggles seem almost inconsequential. They bore burdens that I frankly couldn't imagine carrying, but their hearts and spirits, their capacity for love and goodness, were no different than mine. As I began to see this, the realization changed me profoundly. I continue to go into prison and work with some of those whom our society views as utterly disposable, not to change the ones I meet, but to continue to be changed *by* them. A willingness to be changed by each person you encounter, to allow yourself to be impacted and affected, has a sometimes slow but always powerful effect on all involved. It engenders trust and builds relationship. Physical presence is essential in this process. Over the years, I've encountered the healing effects of presence repeatedly, and not just in prisons.

One dramatic illustration of the power of presence came to me while I was in Oakland, California attending a folk music convention some years back. (If you've never been to a folk music convention, simply imagine yourself in an overpriced hotel with 300 banjo players.) During an early afternoon walk a few blocks from my hotel, I encountered a man asking for spare change. I offered to buy him something to eat at a nearby Burger King and, since I hadn't had lunch, when we went in, I ordered for two. When the younger man, whose name was Larry but who liked to be called "L," received his tray of cheeseburgers, large fries, and extra-large coffee, I invited him to join me in a booth by the window. We spent a very pleasant half hour together and had a fascinating conversation in which L told me a great deal about his life. When we'd finished our lunch, L thanked me earnestly and, to my surprise, pronounced me the "nicest person" he'd ever met on the streets of Oakland. When I protested that I'd only spent a few dollars on his lunch and that I was certain he'd met many more generous people than I, L responded in a soft voice, "John, I've met a lot of people that gave me more money, but I never met anyone who wanted to *eat* with me." This simple statement stayed with me and actually inspired a song I'd later write called, "Don't Just Do Something (Stand There)."

You can view a performance at https://youtu.be/-MqXuaAKt-k. The lyrics are:

*Don't Just Do Something (Stand There)*

It's what we do, ain't it?

If it looks worn paint it

If something's broke mend it

When it's bent, un-bend it

But when a heart's breaking

Or someone's soul's shaking

And your bag of tricks is

Clean out of quick fixes

CHORUS:

Don't just do something

Don't just do something

Don't just do something

Stand there…

Don't quote from renowned sages

Or Sunday school pages

Paths of least resistance

Will keep at a distance

The challenge of seeing

The whole human being

In all their fierce beauty

And your profound duty (chorus)

BRIDGE:

In the still and screaming silence

With the illness and violence

Where the cosmic joke is on us

Tears and laughter keep us honest

Whether it's deep sadness

Or borderline madness

Do not disrespect it

Or look for the exit

Stand in the breach, brother

Stand with one another

Your presence, sweet sister

Can heal and minister (chorus)

The word gravity comes from the root "gravitas," which means weightiness. And just as large objects have observable fields that affect each other's paths, human presence has its own kind of invisible sway, especially in "heavy" situations. Although most of our current NBNS members tend to do very well when they get home (our recidivism rate is close to 15% compared to the state average of 77%), those in recovery have by far the greatest challenges. In NBNS we've had our share of victories but also our fair share of devastating heartbreaks. Several men I'd grown very close to never seemed to find the peace they sought in this world. And, even for the luckier ones, it can sometimes take more than one agonizing try at a clean and sober path to get it right. One of these men was Michael (not his real name), a man I met when he was locked up, who confided in me that his deepest fear was that he would continue to return to, and eventually die in, prison. After making a great start when he came home, Michael overdosed on cocaine that had been laced with fentanyl. After a month in the hospital, he came out of a medically induced coma to find that both of his legs had been amputated above the knee.

Before visiting Michael, I called New Beginnings founder, Franciscan Friar, Brother David Schlatter, O.F.M. Brother David had recruited me as a volunteer before being transferred to Silver Spring, Maryland where he was to become a chaplain at the Walter Reed Medical Center. Knowing that his new work was now exposing him to the kind of profound injury Michael had experienced, I asked Brother David for advice to prepare myself for my hospital visit. After all, what could I do or say that would be of any use in this situation? I knew enough to avoid offering Michael platitudes or clichés but knowing what not to do is seldom enough.

David was simple and straightforward. He told me that when I entered his hospital room, I should be sure to physically position myself as close to Michael's wounds as possible. "And don't stand above him," David warned, "Get down to eye-level." (Again... mutuality!) David explained that our — often unconscious — impulse is to put as much distance between ourselves and this type of distress as possible. He strenuously warned me against this. "We are called to accompany each other," he told me. "And sometimes that means walking right up next to the flames." I did as Brother David advised and, upon entering his room, pulled my chair right up to the middle of Michael's hospital bed, positioning myself only inches away from his bandages. Although I was mostly at a loss for words (and confessed it) the place where I chose to sit told Michael what he needed to know. Within a short time, he and I were actually finding a way to talk deeply and even — occasionally — laugh together. (We also indulged in some rather profane language as I recall.) I hope and believe my visits with Michael during those early days of his recuperation were, at least in some small way, helpful to him. If they were, it was simple presence, not words, that made them so.

Physical presence requires context. I can say, "I love my neighbor," but if I rarely see my neighbor, what does this actually mean? Is my compassion just a feeling I try to nurture, or am I called on to seek out regular occasions of contact in which this declaration can be manifested? In other words, can this love be made "real"? New Beginnings-Next Step creates these occasions and these realities.

The New Beginnings part of our work takes place with offenders during incarceration, and the Next Step portion commences after offenders are released. Along with the weekly support groups, during the first year out of prison, Next Step also provides returning citizens with weekly transitional assistance in the form of bus passes and grocery store gift cards. Most of this has — so far — been paid for through the generous contributions of folks who follow and support my musical endeavors. Upon release from prison, our returning citizens are also given special New Beginnings-Next Step backpacks, a tradition which originated when we realized that many of our members start out deeply housing insecure — couch surfing at best and homeless at worst — and their luggage usually consisted of a plastic trash bag. Our guys always seem so proud to receive these backpacks, and these days, the merchandise table at my concerts always features an open one to receive financial donations.

The transitional assistance we provide plays a huge part in what we do, but our main work is based on the sense of hope we try to instill. As the re-entry portion of our mission evolved, I began to observe that the resilience, which guys once seemed to lack, was now evidencing itself. Our guys were doing better, and for longer and longer periods of time. And I believe this was a direct by-product of this new sense of community. And this hope.

The importance of resilience and its connection to hope were originally articulated for me by Father Greg Boyle, the founder of Homeboy Industries out in Los Angeles, and author of the bestseller, *Tattoos on the Heart.* Homeboy is the largest and most successful gang intervention organization in the world. As Father G puts it, an educated or employed homie might reoffend, but a "healed" homie will not. This healing is slowly born of the tenderness and "radical kinship" that make Homeboy such a special place. I've seen the amazing power of these things in Delaware.

Many of the men NBNS works with have experienced the worst things life can throw at a human being. They've been physically and emotionally abused. They've been beaten, shot, or stabbed. They've lost loved ones, overdosed, been locked up — sometimes for decades. Since these men cannot be scared, they've long ago grown completely indifferent to threat. But, because it is often something to which they've never been exposed, they have almost no immunity to hope. Hope is a tangible thing in NBNS and, once encountered in regular doses, is often a key to a radical reexamination of life's prior assumptions, choices, and trajectories. This hope is derived from the recognition of the awakened sense of potential and worth that comes from community, from connection, from relationship.

When human beings are willing to forgo snap judgements and look long and deeply at each other, they come to discover unsuspected beauty and the potential for true goodness. In my experience, there is almost no exception to this. And, when someone else begins to see goodness and beauty in you, you — sometimes very slowly — begin to recognize it in yourself. The result is a truer understanding of self and self-worth. This process is very much like looking into a new and powerful kind of mirror. And NBNS facilitators are charged with being exactly these kinds of mirrors.

Along with mirroring, New Beginnings-Next Step employs active listening as one of the most basic and powerful expressions of human respect. True respect is in short supply in prison, a place that — by its very nature — deprives the individual of a measure of dignity. Offenders spend an inordinate amount of time and energy trying to make up for this by fashioning personas that inspire fear. They view respect as a prize in a zero-sum game, where it must be gained at the expense of another. The realization that they can simultaneously receive and bestow this precious commodity through the power of their own attention is often a profoundly empowering revelation.

A newly discovered sense of self-worth and dignity, along with the growing connection to a community of hope, gradually allows NBNS members to examine devastating and often foundational wounds that have often unconsciously influenced the course of their lives. In the protective settings of our groups, these wounds can be carefully revealed, acknowledged, and even sacralized. Spirituality in which all faith traditions are welcomed and honored plays an important part in our work. Finding spiritual meaning and even value in your journey, no matter how unfair, difficult, or painful it has been, can help transcend the ultimately corrosive bonds of mere victimhood. The self-loathing and bitterness that accompanies these wounds often gives way to a realization that an offender's most painful experiences and secrets, once confronted and shared, lose much of their long-held power. In this way, these wounds can often become sources of deep wisdom and profound empathy.

I once wrote a song called "Kintsugi," (https://youtu.be/XoC5QSkb-eg) about an ancient Japanese art form that repairs broken pottery by using the dust of precious metal in the adhesive. Rather than giving in to the impulse to camouflage a restoration effort by seamlessly reattaching the shards, Kintsugi celebrates the brokenness as the repaired item quite literally becomes a work of art. The new piece exposes the fractures and, now veined with silver or gold, transcends its original form becoming something truly unique and exquisite. New Beginnings-Next Step members regularly share from their own pain and brokenness in order to help others. Courage is the artisan and compassion the precious metal that allows for this living form of Kintsugi. And all of this happens within the context of the community, the sense of kinship that NBNS strives to create and embody.

The prison environment is not always accepting of those who have grown weary of "the game" and its requisite attitudes and postures of menacing indifference. To speak in the general population in an unguarded way about your own deep wounds can open an offender to contempt, derision, or worse. The New Beginnings community provides a safe place and culture within the prison walls for men to explore courageous new ways of understanding, without cynicism, judgment, or exploitation. Even so, this vulnerability comes with some risks.

I've seen New Beginnings members take some amazing chances, putting themselves and their closely guarded reputations of street-style toughness at risk in order to help others who were — only days or weeks before — almost total strangers. I've seen tears of compassion fall from eyes that have seen too much pain, too much despair, too much hopelessness. I've been taught the meaning of the word gratitude by a shy young man who would, within a few weeks, be released and murdered in a drive-by shooting. I've offered the eulogy at the casket of another gentle soul who — just months out of prison and proudly wearing the new uniform I'd purchased for him — was gunned down for dice winnings on his way to catch the bus to his second full-time job. I've seen a man, who was only months from being set free, risk serious injury as well as the certainty of being known as a coward (often the most dangerous thing you can be called in prison) by allowing himself to be beaten by two other inmates while offering no physical retaliation. He did this to avoid any potential lengthening of his sentence, which would cause him to break a promise he'd made to his eight-year-old daughter. (He'd told her that he wouldn't miss another one of her birthday parties, and he didn't.) I've been honored by the trust of men who have known abandonment and betrayal from so early an age that they had learned to try to avert crushing disappointment by deliberately sabotaging any real opportunities for success. And I've learned about resiliency from men who have consistently refused to give up on the chances to author wonderful and previously unimagined new chapters of their lives, although almost everyone they'd ever known had already closed the covers on those books. People don't believe me when I tell them that some of my spiritual advisors are serving time, but it's true.

How NBNS works is simple. We take turns. We talk to each other. And we listen to each other. No one is the teacher. No one is the student. We're all just people. Which brings me back to my little concert.

Although I'd done my share of prison concerts in the past, this was the only audience I had ever performed for that had had shackles removed from their arms and legs before they entered the venue. There'd been no advance word of the show, so the sight of my guitar case brought a lot of smiles to the men in orange jumpsuits as they filed onto the metal benches in front of me.

One aging offender in attendance had been telling me for months that he'd been a guitar player in his youth. He sported the beard and shaggy hair of a rocker (I can't throw stones here…) and knew that I earned my living as a musician. He had always seemed to enjoy my stories of the road, especially the ones about working legends like Arlo, Kris, and Willie. The "Old Rocker" approached me as I was undoing the latches of my guitar case.

His eyes lit up as he spoke, and it seemed to me that he was excited just to be in the presence of the instrument itself. He began to speak in an animated, almost breathless way, about a time long ago when he got to see Willie Nelson's guitar in person, describing the storied autographs on its face and the famous chasm that Willie's flat pick had worn in its iconic spruce top. The growing excitement with which he recounted this description marked — for me — a big change in this man, who had always been one of the most reticent and standoffish members of our group.

I cracked the lid on my guitar case, and suddenly the Old Rocker stopped talking. His eyes widened when he saw my battle-scarred old Martin D-28 bearing its own pick-gouged hole, as well as the sharpie-inscribed signatures of folks I've performed with over the years — including Willie's. I drew the guitar from the case and handed it to him. His eyes darted back and forth as he whispered, "Are you sure?" I *wasn't* actually because this particular tier operated with enhanced security protocols. But at that very moment, something higher than a simple regard for the strictures of the Department of Corrections seemed to be moving in me. "Sure," I said. "It's not a holy relic." With something akin to reverence, the Old Rocker extended his right knee and cradled my forty-year-old dreadnaught on his thigh. He thumbed a G chord and a broad smile beamed from a face that wasn't recently practiced in that particular expression. I winked at him and intoned in my best baritone the words ... "I hear the train a comin'."

The Old Rocker's eyes widened again. He tentatively ventured another chord. I responded with, "It's rollin' round the bend." At this point I more than half expected a correctional officer to intervene. But they kept their places. (Again, something higher...)

The Old Rocker's expression turned to unrestrained joy as we launched into an impromptu version of Johnny Cash's "Folsom Prison Blues." Laughter and cheers of recognition erupted from the audience. As I sang the world's most famous line of iconic badass-ery — "I shot a man in Reno just to watch him die" — the room exploded in applause.

The Old Rocker was lost in exultation — his eyes closed, his eyebrows arched, savoring the song, the approval of the crowd, the long-missed but oh-so familiar vibration of a good guitar ringing out against his rib cage. The prison walls melted away as he strummed. Soon we were rolling through open country in a fancy dining car as rich folks smoked big cigars. To prolong the feeling of freedom, I fished a harmonica out of my case and blew a short instrumental before finally singing ...

"Well, if they freed me from this prison

If that railroad train was mine

I bet I'd move it on a little

farther down the line ..."

When we reached the words, "I'd let that lonesome whistle," everyone — and I mean *everyone* — in the room sang... "blow my blues away."

The cheering was ecstatic. More than once I heard someone say, "Damn, he really *can* play! I thought he was always bullsh*tting." The Old Rocker handed me back my guitar and, although I couldn't hear his voice over the applause, I clearly saw his mouth say the words

"Thank you." As he took his seat for my concert, he became the notably sheepish recipient of vigorous rounds of backslapping. The man sitting next to him looked at me and laughed, saying, "He's *high* right now. I've never seen him high before. But he's definitely high right now." The Old Rocker must have needed to catch his breath a bit because he grinned at me and, in a voice loud just enough to hear, said the words, "Breathe ... Just ... breathe."

In a very real way, this story embodies what New Beginnings-Next Step is all about. The joyful and, I believe, healing energy of the few short minutes I've recounted didn't come from the performance of yet another painfully earnest folk singer or the (very fine... trust me on this!) songs he'd composed. It came from mutuality and from relationship. It came from stepping down from a pedestal and simply being there. Face to face and at eye level. Nothing else could have had the same redemptive force. The rest of my little concert went great. The men were incredibly enthusiastic. The Old Rocker's smile never left his face for an instant and every song I sang received his personal standing ovation. But the best song by far was the one I didn't play.

## About the Author

John Flynn is an American singer-songwriter and activist known for his powerful music and tireless efforts on behalf of the lost and the lonely, the shackled and scarred. His career has embodied an authentic troubadour odyssey that moved legendary folk DJ Gene Shay to call Flynn "the most quintessential folk singer in my life," and Deana McCloud, Executive Director of the Woody Guthrie Center in Tulsa, Oklahoma to write, "John Flynn is the real deal. His work follows in the footsteps of Woody Guthrie, Pete Seeger, Kris Kristofferson, and other social justice troubadours as he speaks the truth and gives a voice to society's disenfranchised. His work fills your heart and opens your eyes as he continues to walk the walk of a true advocate for equality, justice, and peace."

Kristofferson himself has called John one of his favorite country artists, singing on several of Flynn's albums and writing that John's "work in prisons, rehabs, and half-way houses is distilled into the truth and the beauty of heartfelt and heartwarming slices of life".

In 2005 Arlo Guthrie invited John to join musical legends like Willie Nelson and Ramblin' Jack Elliott on the historic "Train to New Orleans" tour following Hurricane Katrina.

Flynn's many years of volunteer work in Delaware's Howard R. Young Correctional Institution led him to create and serve as the Executive Director of a non-profit called New Beginnings-Next Step which helps incarcerated and returning citizens avoid recidivism after prison.

In 2019 Flynn, along with Stevie Wonder, was a co-recipient of the National Association of Criminal Defense Lawyers Champion of Justice/ Humanitarian Award. And the National Board of Directors of the Vietnam Veterans of America has honored John by requesting he write and perform a new song at the official ceremony marking Vietnam Veterans Recognition Day in Washington, DC on March 29, 2022.

# CHAPTER 16
# ROQUE DALTON: REVOLUTIONARY POET OF EL SALVADOR

RANDAL JOY THOMPSON

## INTRODUCTION

By Susan J. Erenrich

This chapter features Randal Joy Thompson, an ILA BLB editor and author. Randal retired after 28 years as a Commissioned U.S. Foreign Service Officer and continues to work in international development, helping to improve systems around the globe that impact civil society. While working in conflict and post-conflict countries, she became interested in how artists and their art have led to positive social transformation. For example, while she was in Bosnia, she became intrigued by the story of the "Cellist of Sarajevo." The musician, who played his instrument in bombed out buildings, helped to strengthen the will of Sarajevans to withstand the siege and offered a glimmer of hope for the future. Her chapter on Vedran Smailovíc is published in *Grassroots Leadership & the Arts for Social Change*.

Now she has turned her attention to Roque Dalton, a revolutionary poet from El Salvador, who was executed on May 10, 1975. For readers not familiar with Dalton, Randal shares a rich account of his life, his political work, and his art. He was executed for his activism a few days before his 40th birthday. Throughout the chapter, she explores the way his art spoke to her while she lived in El Salvador — educating her about the historical currents in the country and influencing her development work there.

Roque Dalton is just one example of an artist who created so dangerously that it cost him his life. He is not alone. Quite often, the consequences of leading from the bottom-up carries a high price. Sometimes the results are imprisonment, censorship, torture, and death, as illustrated in Randal's piece. Nevertheless, artists continue to take these risks. A special thanks to Randal for shining the light on this important and timely subject.

## ROQUE DALTON: REVOLUTIONARY POET OF EL SALVADOR

By Randal Joy Thompson

Note: For more details on Roque Dalton's life, see *Small Hours of the Night: Selected Poems of Roque Dalton*, edited by H. St. Martin.

Moving to a new country is always like entering through a maze of preconceived notions, stereotypes, initial impressions, and old memories. This was true when I came to El Salvador to work in 2017. Violence was the engraved image of El Salvador in my mind coming from memories of the long civil war and talk of the gangs. Indeed, several colleagues offered their condolences and asked me if I was looking forward to having armed guards protect my every move. Soon after arriving in El Salvador as an international development professional devoted to ensuring that foreign aid had a positive impact, I became entranced with a murdered revolutionary poet, Roque Dalton, as one of the grassroots leaders who gave his life for the cause of justice and equality in a country that has been, and still is, characterized by a culture of violence and repression. Little did I know at the time, that Roque, a true grassroots leader, would be my guide to understanding the country, its complex history, and its continued undercurrent of tensions between the haves and the have nots. His leadership would influence my own and his story would come to resonate with my experiences as I navigated through the streams of contradictions that characterize El Salvador.

Roque Dalton lived and died for the revolution, for the hope that El Salvador would become an egalitarian country where the poor and marginalized would have opportunity and live in dignity. His poems tell of love, of death, of politics, of his forlorn country, and often speak through the voices of his oppressors. He believed that poetry could catalyze change by exposing the corrupt ruling elite and revealing the plight of those struggling to survive. Poetic language, to him, works to engage readers on an affective level such that they identify with the perspective of the poet and join with him or her to lead the social change process, which can be non-violent or revolutionary. He believed that poetry should include more ideas than words (Leisch, 2013) and his art was influenced by French New Wave cinema and filmmakers such as Chabrol and Truffaut as seen in his application of their use of montage, the succession of uninterrupted images.

Ironically, he died at the hands of fellow revolutionaries, proving that many revolutions result only in the substitution of one form of oppressive government with another. Even today, Roque continues to lead people through his poems, his histories, and his life. His words speak to the hearts and hopes of all those living in the grassroots of a society that refuses to allow them opportunities and the chance to advance. Although he was murdered in 1975, his words continue to encourage people in their struggle for social justice while his poems and the music that many of them have been set to continue to ring the sounds of hope. By reading his poems and listening to the ones put to music, Roque has taken me on a voyage to the hearts of El Salvador.

Roque lived a revolutionary life supporting the poor and marginalized, expressing their plight and the brutality of the government through his poems. As an exile, he lived in Mexico, Cuba, and Prague (in what was then Czechoslovakia) and was imprisoned on several occasions when he returned to El Salvador. While in Cuba, he joined the *Casa de las Américas*, a gathering place, publishing house, and information center for many exiled leftist Latin American writers. He also worked for Radio Havana where he announced that since the history of Latin America was one of violence, poetry had to be full of violent material because only revolutionary violence could end the violence of the region (Leisch, 2013). In 1969, he won the Poetry Prize *Casa de las Americas* for his book *Taberna y otros lugares* (Tavern and Other Places), which he had written in Prague shortly before the end of the Prague Spring in 1968 (Atwood, n.d.). He dedicated his prize to all those "who pay in advance the high price of the future happiness of our people" (Leisch, 2013). During this time, he wrote his poem OAS (named for the Organization of American States) claiming that the military dictators of Nicaragua (Somoza), Paraguay (Stroessner), Honduras (López Arellano), and Haiti (Duvalier) were presidents of El Salvador along with the Salvadoran military dictator Fidel Sánchez Hernández. Furthermore, the poem adds that the President of the United States was even more president of El Salvador than Hernández (Prashad, 2019). As I read and thought about this poem, I understood the negative view of Salvadorans toward the United States' imperialism and recognized that as an American I could not be an authoritarian leader if I wanted to be accepted. My leadership style would need to be transformational, horizontal, and participative.

My life in El Salvador contrasted sharply with my initial mental image of the country. Living in a luxury apartment on the 20th floor overlooking the forest and the mountains, lounging on my huge terrace, and easily walking to three ultra-modern shopping malls in a row next to my apartment complex did not jibe with images of violence. Walking a mile to and from work every day and lunching in one of many international restaurants near my office, I only saw beautiful, lush grass and nice houses. I only heard about gangs, about poverty, about suffering. I only caught glimpses of that distant reality as I greeted the armed guards along my route and was reminded that, for a lot of people, we lived in a city under potential siege. It was Roque who led me through the seemingly invisible reality of El Salvador.

Through his poetry and nonfiction books, Roque first taught me the violent history of El Salvador. Understanding that history helped me lead with compassion and with the understanding that many of my staff and their parents and grandparents had experienced terrible violence in their lives. Roque's biography of peasant-revolutionary *Miguel Mármol* (Dalton, 1972), immortalized and etched forever in history the 1932 Salvadoran peasant uprising which, when put down, resulted in the virtual annihilation of Indigenous peoples in the western part of El Salvador and solidified the totalitarian military government in the country. Through reading his history, I came to understand why Indigenous peoples were invisible in El Salvador and why the tiny remaining groups, about 10% of the total population, existed only on the fringes of the country. I understood why, when our team conducted our gender and social inclusion analysis for the United States Agency for International Development (USAID), we needed to interview and highlight those lost peoples and make the government aware that they deserved education and social services too.

Roque drew, and his work continues to draw, attention to some of the most atrocious historical events in El Salvador so that the public will remember them and keep fighting against the injustices that they represent. Roque's poem, "The Sure Hand of God," helped me understand the totalitarian military government that led El Salvador from the massacre of the Indigenous people in 1932 until the civil war that began in 1979. The poem speaks through the voice of the servant of ex-president Maximiliano Hernández Martínez, who led the massacre of 30,000 peasants "piled high as a volcano" (St Martin, 1996, p. 108) in 1932 when he was a general and retells how, after many years of faithful service, he murdered Martínez after Martínez spat on him.

The servant recollects his master as a general and as president and applauds his machismo and his cunning while decrying his barbarity. He talks of retribution and claims that God will never forgive them and reminds the reader that there are others still living in El Salvador who are worse than Martínez and who continue to commit atrocities. Shocked at himself for murdering a president who, like all presidents, is forever bathed in gold, the servant characterizes his act as "touching a tiger's balls" (St Martin, 1996, p. 110) and admits that things were heating up in El Salvador and that communism would not die.

That so-called "communism" led to the uprising in 1979 against the military regime by the peasants and also by many highly educated professionals and intellectuals. Roque's poem helped me to understand the schism that exists post-civil war in the current government between the Arena political party, comprised of the conservative elite, and the Farabundo Martí National Liberation Front (FMLN) political party, comprised of former-guerrillas and other leftists. Being aware of this schism helped me understand the different political views of my team and made me realize I needed to always find a common ground in the way I led them.

In the documentary *Roque Dalton, Fusilemos la Noche!* (Leisch, 2013), random Salvadorans carry around life-size cardboard cutouts of Roque and ask people on the streets of San Salvador to read his poems. One of the poems, "Poema de Amor," tells of the *guanacos*, the poor "eternally undocumented" peasants, "the saddest sad people in the world," who provide labor throughout Central America and the downtrodden, desperate prostitutes that service them (Dalton & Silver, 2020). In the film, one man in the street comments that all Salvadorans are "undocumented." A woman explains that Roque was one of the few leaders in El Salvador with morals and compassion for the people. A jailed compatriot of Roque recounts his murder by fellow guerrillas as the resolution of a power play and false allegations. Fellow radical writers tell stories of how Roque challenged entrenched political powers and dressed as a woman to insult the corrupt system. His wife remembers their wedding night and when they were arrested and falsely accused of treason.

"Poema de Amor" has become a soulful song sung to a typical Salvadoran tune (Xmotursax, 2012). I listen to the song often as I drive through the countryside and reflect on the long suffering of the campesinos, first persecuted by the government and now by the gangs. I love the fact that the youth are so energetic and hopeful of a future in which they can realize their dreams, but I hate the fact that the family structure has been torn apart by war and forced migrations, leaving many youths vulnerable to assimilation by the gangs.

Roque recognized that he was only one voice battling against a powerful system, just as I recognize that I am just a small fish in a big pond trying, in a small way, to build an egalitarian society. In his poem, "The Social Being Determines Social Conscience," for example, Roque mixes revolution with love as he recognizes that he is just a "hack in the smallest Communist Party in the world" who will try to carry out revolution without thousands killed and who notices "the hole left in his chest" by his country (St. Martin, 1996, p. 142; Sotoski, 2008). He continues, "Latin America is a gorgeous anaconda thrashing its teeth with its tail" (St. Martin, 1996, p. 143; Sotoski, 2008), and he reflects on his life and how he ended up a revolutionary as he battles between his political conscience and the desire to make love to the woman in the poem. He concludes that "the social being plays ping pong with one's conscience especially in winter" (St. Martin, 1996, p. 145; Sotoski, 2008).

I can personally relate to Roque's split focus, although I am certainly not a revolutionary. Life requires us to make constant choices between managing and living our own lives and continuing the challenges of social change. It is an impossible task to be a full-time "revolutionary" or to work full time to help change a society whose structures and powers have been built over decades, if not centuries.

Similarly, Roque's poem "Like You" reveals that, just like us, he "love[s] love, life, the sweet smell of things...." His "blood boils up" like everyone's and he "laugh[s] through eyes that have known the buds of tears." He concludes the poem by affirming: "I believe the world is beautiful and that poetry like bread is for everyone. And that my veins don't end in me but in the unanimous blood of those who struggle for life, love, little things, landscape and bread, the poetry of everyone" (Poets.org, n.d.).

Roque's poems speak of the love-hate relationship he had with El Salvador. In his poem, "In a Fit of Anger," he concludes that El Salvador does not exist "except as my deformed shadow, a word coined by my enemy" and that, as an expatriate, his country becomes "ex-patria" (St. Martin, 1996, p. 103). Roque cries "dismembered country," in his poem "The National Soul." "You slip into my hours like a poisoned pill.... Who are you crawling with masters like a bitch scratching herself on the trees she pisses on?" (St. Martin, 1996, p. 104). Sometimes I feel the same way. On the one hand, I love Salvadorans but on the other, I despise the system that oppresses them. After interviewing many women and LGBTQ+ leaders, I felt so much respect for them, but I hated what they called "the social imaginary," which has justified the violence against them and accounted for the increase in femicides and in the torture and murder of transgender persons. The refrain from Roque's poem "El Salvador Will Be

Beautiful" comes to mind: "The problem is that today El Salvador has a thousand incentives and a hundred thousand inequalities, cancers, castoffs, dandruff, filth, sores, fractures, weak knees and offensive breath."

Today, the dead are still clamoring for justice in El Salvador as the perpetrators of the massacres during the totalitarian rule of the military and the civil war have never been held accountable for their crimes against humanity. In "The Warriors Resting Place" those who died trying to gain justice are getting restless. They are asking questions from the grave and are ironic and sarcastic because they realize that they are now the majority, that they now outnumber the living (India, 2018). Many past leaders have denied that these massacres occurred, even as the few remaining survivors account in vivid detail what transpired. In 2018, the courts agreed to re-open the case of the massacre of 1000 civilians in Mozote in order to finally bring the perpetrators to justice, but as of this writing the case has not finished and the National Assembly is debating extending the Amnesty Law, which relieve all perpetrators of guilt and punishment.

President Najib Bukele has argued not to extend the Amnesty Law but to bring perpetrators to justice whether they were in the army or in the guerrilla groups. Both committed atrocities. Many non-governmental organizations, women's, and LGBTQ+ groups, along with international organizations such as the United Nations, are actively trying to change the legal system so that victims of violence can receive justice. Bukele, somewhat of a young renegade, won the election with over 50% of the votes. As of June 2019, he has implemented a new kind of blended administration that includes former guerrillas as well as wealthy businessmen intent on ending corruption and impunity and ensuring that the justice system works as it should. He has established an international organization to try corruption cases and has established new governmental ministries to actively improve the lives of the poor. Although U.S. President Trump stopped foreign aid to El Salvador because of the migrations, Bukele reestablished relations with the United States seeking investment not "free aid."

I visited Catholic University in San Salvador, the location of the slaughter by the military of six Jesuit priests who spoke out for the poor during the civil war. When I visited the museum that houses their bloody clothes and the photos of them blood splattered and spread eagle, naked on the grass, I thought of the Jesuit Saint Oscar Romero and of Roque and how they also died for those whose voices have not yet been heard.

Just as there has never been justice for Saint Romero or the six Jesuit priests whose murderers remained in power in El Salvador, there has never been justice for Roque. Roque's two living sons have pursued justice for their father's murder throughout the decades (Renderos, 2010) and in 2018 a court ruled that "the country's prosecuting office had failed to investigate the kidnapping and murder of Dalton" and that the case could be reopened (TeleSur, 2018). As of this writing, its outcome is still pending.

As the beginning lines of Roque's poem "El Salvador Will Be" state, "El Salvador will be a beautiful and without exception, a dignified country when the working class and the people of the countryside enrich it, bathe, powder and groom it, when they cure the historical hangover and add enough to it by a hundred fold to reconstitute it and start it moving along" (Socialist Resurgence, 2019). Let us hope that the time has finally come for a significant change. Roque lived and died for change, but he was ahead of his time. His hope remains in his poems as they continue to work on the conscience of Salvadorans and on foreigners living here like me, who will not give up trying to make a difference. As famed Salvadoran writer Claribel Alegria wrote, Roque kept trying despite having a "contradictory, dialectical love-hate relationship with his country – El Salvador – both in and out of exile and illustrating his profound conviction that the poet can and must in his life as well as in his work, serve as the finely-honed scalpel of change, both in word and deed, when he lives in a profoundly unjust, stagnant society…. Roque achieved a seamless unity between his two callings, revolutionary and poet…. His personal ethics and aesthetics, forged in the incandescent reality of El Salvador, produced a human being whose personal life and poetry were of a single piece" (St. Martin, 1996, p. xv).

As Roque's fellow-revolutionary and dear friend, Ernesto Cardenal, concluded, "Roque Dalton's commitment to the revolution was like a marriage contract. He was married to the revolution. It was his destiny to not only sing it but also to give his life for the revolution" (St. Martin, 1996, p.xiii). And, as Roque wrote in his poem "Small Hours of the Night," "when you know I'm dead, don't say my name....don't say my name, don't say my name, when you know I'm dead, don't say my name" (St Martin, 1996, p. 47). I, for one, find it difficult not to say his name and hope that he will rise from the grave to lead the still needed revolution. His life and his work have impacted me in a profound way, and I will forever remember the journey that Roque, revolutionary poet, led me on in El Salvador.

## References

Atwood, R. (n.d.). Looking for Trouble - The Life and Poems of Roque Dalton. *Latino Life.* https://www.latinolife.co.uk/articles/looking-trouble-%E2%80%93-life-and-poems-roque-dalton

Dalton, R. (1972) *Miguel Mármol*. Curbstone Books.

Dalton, R. & Silver, K. (2020, November 15). Love Poem and Response. *The Massachusetts Review.* https://www.massreview.org/node/9335

India, S. (2018, September 15). *Poems of Our Times: Roque Dalton* [Video file]. YouTube. https://www.youtube.com/watch?v=dvFJGH_WAoo

Leisch, T. (Director). (2013, May 10). *Roque Dalton, Fusilemos la Noche!* [Roque Dalton, Let's Shoot the Night!] [Film]. Witcraft Szenario (Production Company). Icarus Films & LATcinema. https://vimeo.com/423108146

Poets.org (n.d.) Like You (J. Hirschman, Trans.). https://poets.org/poem/you-1

Prashad, V. (2019, February 22). The President of the United States Is More the President of My Country Than the President of My Country. Inter Press Service News Agency. http://www.ipsnews.net/2019/02/president-united-states-president-country-president-country/

Renderos, A. (2010). El Salvador, in Celebrating Roque Dalton, Confronted by a Bitter Past. *Los Angeles Times.* http://articles.latimes.com/2010/may/25/world/la-fg-salvador-poet-20100525

St. Martin, H. (Ed.). (1996). *Small Hours of the Night: Selected Poems of Roque Dalton.* Curbstone Press.

Socialist Resurgence. (2019, December 19). Roque Dalton: 'El Salvador Will Be.' https://socialistresurgence.org/2019/12/19/roque-dalton-el-salvador-will-be/

Sotoski. (2008, May 21). *Roque Dalton - El Ser Social Determina la Conciencia Social* [Video file]. YouTube. https://www.youtube.com/watch?v=dTRGys6uXdM

TeleSur. (2018, July 17). Murder Case of Salvadoran Poet Roque Dalton's Reopened. https://www.telesurenglish.net/news/Reopening-the-Case-of-Salvadorean-Poet-Roque-Daltons-Murder-20180717-0028.html

Xmotursax. (2012, October 23). *Poema de Amor (Roque Dalton 1935-1975) El Salvador Compatriotas* (HD Limpio) [Video file]. YouTube https://www.youtube.com/watch?v=ek6Qu24ej8A

**About the Author**

Randal Joy Thompson has been living and working in the developing world for many decades, leading changes that hopefully will benefit the so-called poor and marginalized peoples of the world. While working in conflict and post-conflict countries, she became interested in how artists and their art serve as one of the most effective ways to lead positive social transformation. In Bosnia, she became entranced by the story of the "Cellist of Sarajevo" who played his cello in bombed out buildings and served to strengthen the will of Sarajevans to withstand the siege and maintain their cosmopolitanism. She wrote the cellist's story in the volume *Grassroots Leadership & the Arts for Social Change*, edited by Susan J. Erenrich and Jon Wergin. She continues to explore the lives of artists who have played similar roles as grassroots leaders and believes that art can direct the most lasting changes because it enlightens our hearts and souls. She edited along with Devin Singh and Kathleen Curran the 2021ILA BLB publication *Reimagining Leadership on the Commons: Shifting the Paradigm for a More Ethical, Equitable, and Just Society*; wrote the 2019 book *Proleptic Leadership on the Commons; Ushering in a New Global Order*; and edited, along with Julia Storberg-Walker, the 2018 ILA BLB publication *Leadership and Power in International Development: Navigating the Intersections of Gender, Culture, Context, and Sustainability*, which won the 2019 R. Wayne Pace HRD Book of the Year Award.

# CHAPTER 17

# THE CHILEAN MURALIST BRIGADE AND BEYOND: CULTURAL ACTIVISTS OVERFLOWING BOUNDARIES THROUGH VISUAL ART

FRANCISCO LETELIER

## INTRODUCTION

By SUSAN J. Erenrich

This chapter features my dear friend and Grassroots Leadership & the Arts for Social Change author, Francisco Letelier. I first met Francisco in 2016. He was painting a mural in the Katzen Arts Center at American University to mark the 40th anniversary of the assassination of his father, Orlando Letelier, and his father's colleague, Ronni Karpen Moffett.

For readers not familiar with Orlando's story, he was a Chilean economist who served as an ambassador to the United States during Salvador Allende's presidency. Orlando and his family went into exile after the September 11,1973, coup. They came to Washington, D.C., where Orlando was a Senior Fellow at the Institute for Policy Studies.

On September 21, 1976, a bomb was planted in Orlando's automobile while he slept. It exploded on Embassy Row near Sheridan Circle in Washington, D.C. Orlando's legs were severed, killing him instantly (Freed, 1980). At the time of the blast, Ronni Karpen Moffitt, a junior staffer at the Institute, died along with Orlando. Her husband Michael was injured but survived. Francisco, who was seventeen at the time of his father's murder, continued in the spirit of his father, pouring his energy into art and activism.

Francisco's chapter is accompanied by an episode of my radio show, *Wasn't That A Time*, which originally aired on September 28, 2018. The broadcast marked the 45th anniversary of Victor Jara's death. Victor was a Chilean singer-songwriter, poet, theatre director, and political activist. He was tortured and killed during the coup that brought dictator Augusto Pinochet to power on September 11, 1973. Nine former Chilean soldiers were finally convicted in July 2018 for Victor's murder. Francisco wrote a tribute that was incorporated into the show.

I hope readers and listeners are inspired by Francisco's piece and the companion Victor Jara Tribute. They illustrate how impactful and powerful grassroots leadership and the arts for social change can be to make this world a better place to live.

**Listen**

*Wasn't That A Time - Episode 89: Remembering Chilean Singer Songwriter Victor Jara (1932-1973)*

This episode marked the 45th anniversary of Victor Jara's death. Victor was a Chilean singer-songwriter, poet, theatre director, and political activist. He was tortured and killed during the coup that brought dictator Augusto Pinochet to power on September 11, 1973. Nine former Chilean soldiers were convicted in July of 2018 for Victor's murder. Listeners will hear songs performed by Arlo Guthrie, Holly Near, Magpie, Phil Ochs, Victor Jara, and Colleen Kattau. Remembrances penned by Holly Near, Joyce Horman, Sonny Ochs, and Francisco Letelier will be read throughout the program.

https://www.mixcloud.com/WasntThatATime/wasnt-that-a-time-episode-89-remembering-chilean-singer-songwriter-victor-jara-1932-1973/

## Reference

Freed, D. (with Landis, F.). (1980). *Death in Washington: The Murder of Orlando Letelier.* Lawrence Hill.

# THE CHILEAN MURALIST BRIGADE AND BEYOND: CULTURAL ACTIVISTS OVERFLOWING BOUNDARIES THROUGH VISUAL ART

By Francisco Letelier

*Chapter 17 Image 1.* Brigada Orlando Letelier, Washington, D.C., 1977. Photo Courtesy, Brigada Orlando Letelier.

In June 2018, I was invited to lecture at the MSSA, Museo de la Solidaridad Salvador Allende (Salvador Allende Solidarity Museum), in Santiago Chile concerning the murals and other cultural actions by the Brigada Orlando Letelier 1977-1987, a Chilean muralist brigade created in exile in the United States.

The Museum was first created in 1971 when Salvador Allende and his Popular Unity government promoted the idea of creating the "Solidarity Museum," an art museum for the people of Chile established through donations by prominent artists and institutions throughout the Americas and Europe. After the coup of 1973, the project became known as International Museum of Resistance Salvador Allende as many more international and Chilean artists added works to museum holdings in response to the brutal actions of the Pinochet dictatorship.

In the United States, as Chilean exiles, the Brigada Orlando Letelier (BOL) painted solidarity murals that incorporated marginalized voices ignored in U.S. histories as we engaged in solidarity work. Increasingly we identified with larger struggles for social justice within the United States. Our work, and that of the large international networks of artists that were formed in exile, was created within a context that no longer emphasized artists that had commercial success or were represented in mainstream institutions and galleries. Instead, we imagined new institutions, work methods, and patronage relationships as we focused on work made by artists that resisted the economic relationships that had led to the loss of democracy and the rise of the military dictatorship in Chile.

Characterized as a muralist brigade, the brigade did not, in actuality, limit its work to murals. Our work crossed boundaries of media and discipline, audience, and venue. Our intention was to insert cultural ideas into larger conversations as we disseminated information about ongoing events in Chile. Our work emphasized human rights and social justice even as it responded to other events and initiatives. The Brigade stopped functioning as a collective in 1987, but these experiences and ideas have continued to inform my ongoing work as a muralist, artist, and cultural activist in the United States and elsewhere.

My practice reflects an immersion in the cultural exchange and solidarity that I view as essential components of resistance and exile. One result is that my "nation" and identity have ever widening borders that continue to reformulate concepts of identity and belonging.

One of the effects of exile is that it postpones institutional evolution and processes. In 1971, donations from a more narrowly defined art world were considered a primary way of creating a "peoples" art museum. The inherent contradiction between academic and "popular" art was never fully addressed in the short-lived Allende government and our ability to do so was further truncated by the psychological and cultural weight of exile. Although Chile returned to an imperfect democracy in 2000, our re-creation of cultural and social institutions has often re-created the nepotism, elitism, and, at times, shortsighted vision of the arts that was more prevalent in the early 1970s.

After almost 20 years, post-dictatorship Chile, along with the rest of the world, has changed enormously. Mural art has also changed. On streets crowded by murals, graffiti, and street art, it is hard for many to distinguish between them. On any street you may find art that aims for participatory and collective expression as well as work that is more individual or created primarily for financial gain. Despite what may seem a new day for public expression, there are few places that so unerringly return to "business as usual" as the art world. The phenomena of global art stars such as Banksy, Shepard Fairey, and Chilean muralist INTI further complicate matters with strident social messaging that nevertheless creates new elites and often continues to leave the public in the role of passive observer and consumer. A great illustration of this business-as-usual dynamic was the recent shredding of Banksy's *Girl With Balloon* painting at auction — an act that may have been trying to make an anti-capitalist statement with regards to the sale of the piece but which simultaneously, ultimately, increased the value of the art for the buyer.

My invitation to the MSSA came as part of the ambitious exhibit *Past Disquiet* curated by Kristine Khouri and Rasha Salti. The exhibit examined the international networks of artists created in the 70s and 80s during a time when many were in exile and preparing for a new "art order" that would reflect our lives and political struggles. Citizens and exiles of places such as Nicaragua, Palestine, and Chile imagined institutions that would be able to contend with our contemporary histories and our changing concepts concerning cultural expression and the arts.

As I planned to talk about experiences in the United States, Palestine, and elsewhere, I invited the participation of artist colleague Carlos Lizama in order for the talk to be contextualized within Chile as well. Lizama and I worked together on the mural *Mujer del Bosque* in the working class El Bosque district of Santiago in 2007. Our lecture at the museum was unusual, as Carlos is precisely the kind of artist that has been underrepresented at the MSSA. His work in Santiago deals with cultural memory and pays tribute to individuals who lost their lives during the dictatorship. In his introductory statement, Lizama said, "I am above and before all else a *poblador*." Poblador is the term for a person who lives in a shanty town or working-class settlement.

It may seem strange to imagine that after 20 years the MSSA does not regularly feature artists from the social fabric that Salvador Allende and his supporters so firmly believed in and from whom they hoped to harvest talent and vision. Our popular songs, poetry, and literature have long reflected aspirations for a more equal society, and these convictions were further galvanized during the years of military dictatorship. Yet Chilean institutions exist in an international space ruled by market economies led by neoliberal policies. It is a challenge of a high order to manage a collection of fine art considered valuable and important by scholars and institutions, who themselves may participate in mechanisms that perpetuate a world economic order that habitually silences alternative cultures and modes of expression. It is a tricky task for the new generation of critics and writers on art to work within institutions and the media in a coherent manner.

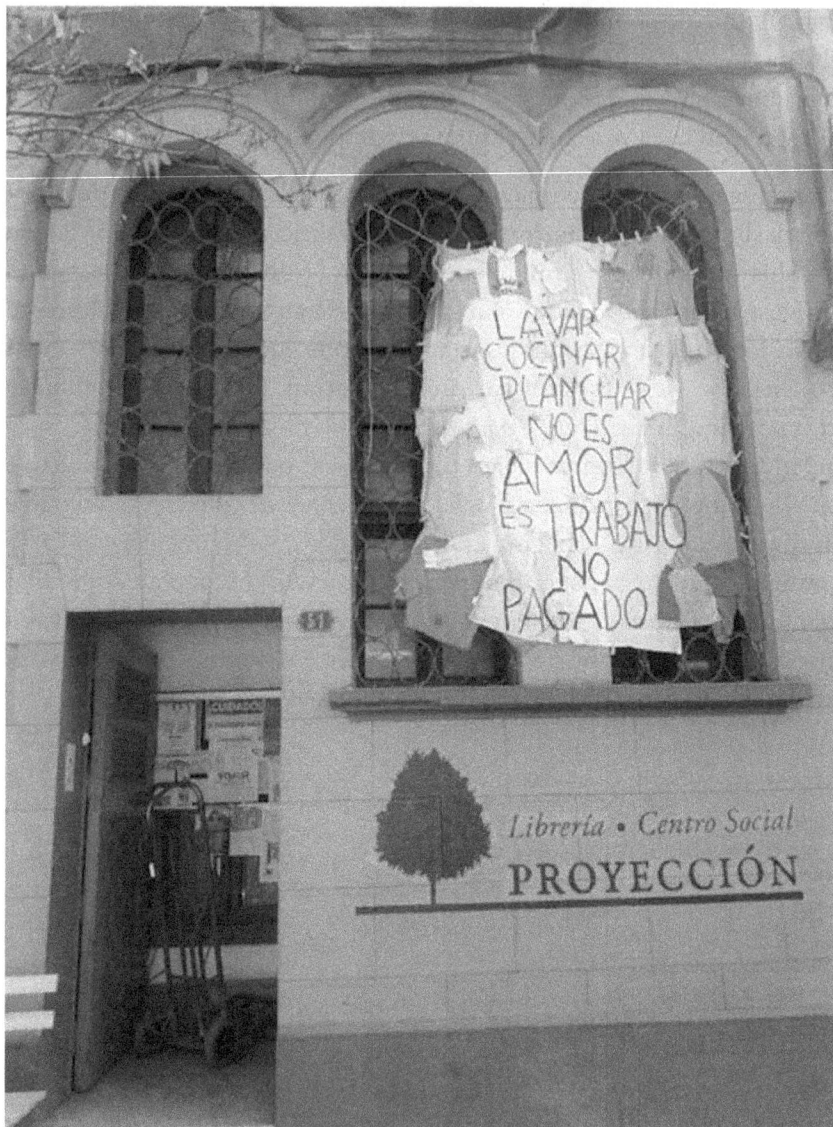

*Chapter 17 Image 2.* Photo Credit: Francisco Letelier.

Sociologist and arts writer Javiera Manzi moderated our talk at the museum and proved adept at navigating the contexts and conditions confronting artists in Chile as well as throughout the world. Manzi is co-author with Nicole Cristi of *Resistencia Gráfica. Dictadura en Chile: APJ – Tallersol*. The book examines the political posters created during the dictatorship with a special eye on the collectives that created graphic images in universities, labor syndicates, cultural centers, political organizations, and the barricades, but have now largely disappeared. Manzi represents a new generation of curatorial and critical activity in Chile. In the days after our talk at the Museum, Manzi and her colleagues invited me to visit the Proyección collective in Santiago. Created by young students in 2010 in response to the lack of cultural spaces that could readily respond to social realities, Manzi is a founding member.

Online, Proyección is called a bookstore, and it certainly is that. After making your way up the winding steps of a downtown brownstone in the University district, you find yourself in a well-lit and astonishingly eclectic bookstore where visitors are welcome to pull up a chair or use a study area or conference room. Upstairs, a few members of the collective share a living space. What became clear during my visit is that just as murals became a calling card for the Brigada Orlando Letelier — as we also engaged in the creation of events, exhibits exchange, posters, and publications — Proyección and its members and community are involved in an overlapping array of social justice, academic, and political activities. The place is a cultural center and meeting place that flows through the well-stocked bookstore. Proyección is an excellent model for cultural work based on collective models of participation, and like the Brigada once did in exile, it aims to reach many through a wide array of activities.

This kind of work is vital at a time when information sources are suspect, and news is fabricated. It is crucial to discern differences in modes of creation and intention. The difference between a place that sells books for profit and a place that has books on shelves so that we may be radically informed is an important one. When we see a new work of art in a public space, it can help to ask: Who did this? Why did it get made? Where is the patronage? Where is the livelihood? Where is the sustainability?

In answer to those who feel limited by these guidelines, I must agree that art must overflow boundaries and permit unbridled and abstract expressions. Art must certainly avoid orthodoxy and allow for the unlimited output of human imagination. Perhaps difficult conversations that engage the public and encourage participation should remain few and far between, but to be curious is always valid, whether the work is playful, frivolous, serious, Artx, or #metoo.

Our future as artists depends on the themes and ideas the art world and its institutions are willing to take on. When moral and ethical attitudes and issues of race, colonialism, and gender are bypassed, trivialized, or mocked, you can be sure that the public is being asked to shut up, listen, and buy. The potential and possibility of creative expression is, of course, much larger than a monetary transaction. When artists, art, and the public act as social agents, we have the ability to influence and promote change. Sometimes we advance, but today we are living historic moments where our already challenged spaces of freedom, culture, and communication are threatened.

In both the United States and Chile, we have recently confronted huge threats to institutions, laws, democratic principles, and freedoms many have taken for granted. In 2017, a Charlottesville, VA, gathering of White nationalists and supremacists turned into a tragic weekend when a rally-goer roared his car into a crowd of counter demonstrators and others. According to witnesses, 19 were injured when James Alex Fields, Jr. drove into one crowd and reversed into another. Heather Heyer, 32, was killed. When commenting on events, President Donald Trump claimed both sides were to blame, failing to denounce the Virginia White supremacists and their Nazi allies.

In Chile, during a massive July 2018 march for women's reproductive rights and the right for free and safe abortions, three marchers were stabbed on the streets of Santiago with knives by opponents. In carefully orchestrated statements the anti-abortionist president and government spokespersons called for tolerance, even when people think differently, casting those who march for women's rights as an aberrant but constitutionally protected minority.

Francisco Estévez, director of Chile's Museo de la Memoria y los Derechos Humanos, (Museum of Memory and Human Rights) understands the institution's role in fulfilling a public responsibility (as mandated by the Chilean Truth and Reconciliation Commission) to guarantee "Never Again." The renowned institution fulfills a vital need and moral imperative for the nation and its citizens scarred by Augusto Pinochet's violent regime where concentration camps, mass killings, and torture of the civilian population became ubiquitous.

Yet earlier in 2018, Chilean President, conservative Sebastián Piñera, appointed a Minister of Culture, Mauricio Rojas, who, in 2015, had stated that the museum was, "a montage which purpose, undoubtedly achieved, is to shock the spectator, leave him astonished, to prevent him from reasoning," and that the museum represents a "shameless and liar use of a national tragedy that touched so many of us so hard and directly" (teleSUR, 2018). In a 2016 interview he reiterated his belief that the Museo de la Memoria was a "museum on the left-wing, to tell a false version of the history of Chile" (teleSUR, 2018).

*Chapter 17 Image 3*. Photo Credit: Francisco Letelier.

Massive public outcry, protests, and a demonstration by the country's artists led to the resignation of Rojas less than a week after his appointment. President Piñera had the acuity to distance himself from his failed appointee, however he's currently pursuing a project to create a Museum of Democracy that, in many ways, seems to underscore efforts to create a new equivalency where respect for human rights and the application of law to criminal acts committed during the dictatorship are optional. As in Charlottesville and elsewhere in the U.S., the ideological frameworks of a resurgent right in Chile carry the possibility of a return to social conflicts and challenges many felt had been left behind.

It is at these pivotal moments when independent organizations and associations are most needed and when art can play a critical and wise role. Yet, we must be careful to avoid resurrecting cultural frameworks of elites and be wary of being led by the same forces that put Donald Trump on TV and made him a well-known national figure prior to the U.S. presidential election. We live in moments when we must question the past, question leadership, and continue to question ourselves about models of activity and resistance.

Since my visit to Chile in June 2018, I have continued to be inspired by the role of Proyección, Javiera Manzi, and her collaborators. It has been many years since the Pinochet dictatorship, and even as we grapple with long overdue processes towards justice for its victims, it is helpful to focus on the Chile of today and how many are responding towards ideological trends and the effects of neoliberal policies that perpetuate social injustice and inequality. In this respect and others, both Chileans and citizens of the United States inhabit nations with similar goals and struggles.

**Learn more about Proyección:**

https://youtu.be/Bpuw3OY7svE

https://youtu.be/xY9ZNbFzOaM (Feminist marches and occupation of University Campus)

https://youtu.be/O4dxVfgdW-k (Collective banner painting for demonstration)

## Reference

teleSUR. (2018, August 12). Chile Culture Minister Under Fire for Criticizing Memory Museum. https://www.telesurenglish.net/news/Chile-Culture-Minister-Under-Fire-For-Criticizing-Memory-Museum-20180812-0006.html

## About the Author

Chilean artist Francisco Letelier creates art that crosses disciplines and cultures. His work blends history with contemporary experiences with an emphasis on the social circumstances that affect individuals and communities. Integrating narratives that explore cultural memory and identity, his projects offer opportunities for cultural exchange and education. Known for both his words and images, Letelier's perceptive writing and spoken word unite with his legacy of creating powerful experiences in the visual arts. Involved in projects throughout the Americas, Europe, India, and the West Bank of Palestine, his interdisciplinary collaborations integrate a variety of media and facilitate collective and participatory activities. Letelier received a Grammy nomination for his work on musician Jackson Browne's *World in Motion* release. In 2009 Letelier received the LA Artcore award for contributions to Southern California culture. SPARC (Social and Public Art Resource Center) awarded him the Siquieros Muralist Award in 2012. Letelier's mural installation, "Todas Las Manos," created at American University in Washington, D.C. in 2016 was dedicated by Chilean President Michelle Bachelet. Based in Venice, California, the artist's Los Angeles murals include the soaring monumental ceramic tile murals, El Sol and La Luna (The Sun and The Moon) that adorn the Westlake/Macarthur Park Metro Station in Los Angeles. The works carry on the legacy of the Chilean mural tradition and serve as a symbol for the diversity of Los Angeles. Learn more at: http://www.Letelierart.blogspot.com.

# CHAPTER 18

# ARTIST AS ACTIVIST: LOOKING AT SELECTED WORKS BY SWOON AND TOMÁS SARACENO

## ANU M. MITRA

## INTRODUCTION

By Susan J. Erenrich

In this chapter, penned by Anu M. Mitra, a chapter author in our *Grassroots Leadership & the Arts for Social Change* book, Anu compares and contrasts the art of two cultural activists — Swoon (née Caledonia Dance Curry) and Tomás Saraceno. She sheds light on how they "engage, provoke, incite, agitate, and, in the end, they build jobs in communities, invoke respect among diverse groups of people, and nurture harmony in the natural order of things." Furthermore, Anu believes Swoon's and Saraceno's artmaking is "synonymous with creating a better world in measurable ways, involving all of us together, or as many as are needed to get the raft to float or the flying machine to soar in the air."

I hope readers enjoy this portion of the book.

# ARTIST AS ACTIVIST: LOOKING AT SELECTED WORKS BY SWOON AND TOMÁS SARACENO

By Anu M. Mitra

W.E.B. Du Bois famously advised the curious seeker of knowledge to: "Begin with art, because art tries to take us outside ourselves. It is a matter of trying to create an atmosphere and context, so conversation can flow back and forth and we can be influenced by each other" (Dechow, 2015). It is in the interest of maintaining this simple flow of give-and-take, this easy exchange of mutuality and empathy that artists like Swoon and Tomás Saraceno reach out to their worldwide audiences. They engage, provoke, incite, agitate, and, in the end, they build jobs in communities, invoke respect among diverse groups of people, and nurture harmony in the natural order of things. Their ability to perform, enact, engage, create, and catalyze speaks to their roles as artist/ social entrepreneur/activist/leader. For them, artmaking is synonymous with creating a better world in measurable ways, involving all of us together, or as many as are needed to get the raft to float or the flying machine to soar in the air. In the name of art that speaks of a larger purpose, Swoon and Saraceno both breathe vitality into a series of actions that bring "theory into being" (MacKenzie, 2007; Callon, 2007).

In this essay, I share insights on the work of the street artist/activist Swoon and the architect/scientist turned artist/futurist Tomás Saraceno. It may be useful first to synthesize the commonalities between these two artists.

- Both Swoon and Saraceno are meticulous students of the arts and sciences, insatiably obsessed with how to compost waste on a raft that journeys over great distances or how to track the rhythmic movements of spiders who are systematically exposed to inter-species interactions.

- Both artists are involved in practices that are carefully choreographed to jumpstart honest, ethical practices in a community.
- Both have a single-minded focus on making communities thriving organisms of creativity and innovation.
- Both are singularly dedicated to making the world a better place by seeking solutions that lie beyond theoretical platitudes. Swoon and Saraceno are instrumental in bringing ideas into intentional action to enact radical change in society.
- Both are in search of a harmonious world where human beings can resist the hierarchical constructs of color, race, gender, and socioeconomics and contribute their expertise for the improvement of the world.
- Both artists have demonstrably moved out of the confines of what an artist does to a larger definition of the impact that an artist can have.
- Both are committed to bringing significant change in the structure of how things work on a communal as well as a planetary scale. As informed leaders, Swoon and Saraceno thus serve as willing ambassadors of social action, engagement, and exchange.

Ultimately, both Swoon and Saraceno are optimistic about the human condition, and it is in the stories of specific individuals or events in community that their art finds full meaning. Where Swoon is grounded in the unique needs of a specific, local community, Saraceno is moved by visions of utopia and futuristic, sustainable metaverses that can one day become part of our physical reality. Where Swoon wants to upend social and local practices in the name of responsible action, Saraceno aims his sights on global public policy where big ideas such as ecological and climate justice are addressed for the good of the planet.

I stumbled upon Swoon and Saraceno as a docent at the Contemporary Arts Center in Cincinnati (CAC), Ohio, where I have worked for over two decades. The 50 docents at the CAC come from vastly different backgrounds. We are reproductive lawyers, frontline healthcare workers, educators, corporate executives, artists, stay-at-home parents, musicians, and chefs. We bring our unique lenses into the ways in which we see and interpret contemporary art — the art of the moment. CAC docents are hands-on students fully committed to a community-based model of learning. While the curator of a particular show is the acknowledged content expert, no one person can know and interpret the complexities of contemporary life as fully as each one of us can, together. With a sharp HB (hard black) No 2 graphite pencil in hand, we accompany the expert, and often the artist, through the galleries every time a show comes to town. Pre-COVID, approximately 10-12 new exhibitions opened at the sprawling museum each year, which was designed by architect Zaha Hadid at the corner of Sixth and Walnut in downtown Cincinnati. Each time, docents, curators, and the education head made meaning together. At times, we aided in the process of installing art and writing wall copy or an education guide. Sometimes we spoke to the press on behalf of the CAC. Whatever the case, we worked in community, talking through ideas, seeing, thinking, and feeling the art until we were able to come to terms with it.

Over the years, I have been greatly influenced by the art I have seen at the CAC. I remember the smell of poverty evoked by the sculptural pieces of Titus Kaphar. Doh Ho Suh's architectural ingenuity in keeping our environment minimalistic but creatively overlayed made me ponder the ways in which we can hide and conceal spaces (even within ourselves) that we don't want to share with the world. And there are many others who have left an unforgettable mark on me.

It was with this open slate quality of a beginner's mind that I came to the art of Tomás Saraceno in 2016-17 and Swoon in 2017-18. I had not known either of their work and had but slim encounters with their names prior to my experience. But their art took me for a complete loop when the cavernous doors of the elevator stopped on CAC's 5th floor Cincinnati location, opening to a vast ocean of experience that lay before me. Swoon's *Thalassa* rose in raw emotion from the ocean floor, at once her best friend, Naima, and a sea goddess with seaweed as clothes, crab claw horns, and an oar in hand. Who was this 21st century goddess in this gigantic sculptural piece that took up the height of a floor and a half? Why did Thalassa demonstrate her powers in these unambiguous ways? What had she overcome? What was she reclaiming? The overlapping of biography and mythology led to many unanswered questions, yet I couldn't stop thinking of the artist's belief in the power of her own voice.

In most of her recent projects, Swoon (a word that suggests an out-of-body experience) ventures into larger, more outward-facing encounters between herself and community. In my analysis of some of her ongoing projects, I explore the intent of Swoon's social action projects which seamlessly bring together responsible action with acts of the imagination.

Similar impulses guide the work of Tomás Saraceno, an Argentinian futurist who now lives and works in Berlin. Where Swoon creates around the theme of water and floating cities (she spent her early years in Florida, near the ocean), Tomás Saraceno imagines communities that live up in the air but are tethered to the earth. Questions that he asks include: How do we respect the resources of the earth by using what we need and not what we want? How do we live in communities even as we float in the air? Is it possible to be independent without being interdependent? I was fascinated with Saraceno's *Solar Bell* which is a part of the cloud cityscapes that are under construction. *Solar Bell* soared above the cathedral-like lobby of CAC and was awe-inspiring as a model for the 450-meter-tall structure that it was conceptualized to become. Web-like in the way in which it was tethered in space without floating away, *Solar Bell* claimed independence even as it was grounded in interdependence.

So strong was my desire to understand Saraceno's work that in October 2016, I made a pilgrimage to his Berlin studio. A massive, industrial, multi-story complex in the outskirts of Berlin, Saraceno's studio is organized like a Renaissance workshop. Dozens of trained artists, biologists, engineers, materials experts, arachnologists, and craftspeople are employed in the facility, adding their expert knowledge to Saraceno's multidisciplinary projects. Most magnetizing were his double floors of exotic, sometimes, near-extinct, spider species collected and carefully reared from all over the world. Research scientists and arachnologists in white lab coats track the spiders' every move, controlling the temperature and lighting of this enormous housing complex that supports Saraceno's spider population. Monthly musical salons held by violinists, cellists, and flautists are conducted and Saraceno's research notes show that in the days following each concert, the complexity of the spiders' web making seems to become more involved and interesting. These web-making designs are subsequently simulated in Saraceno's tethering of his floating cities.

I witnessed Saraceno's unassuming presence in almost every floor of his workshop complex. I saw how he married art with technology — with systems that provide a sounder ecology and designs that speak of an inner, fantasy world. The boyish Saraceno spoke to us of the natural world being our best teachers and the importance of slowing down and being in its natural rhythm. He spoke of spiders providing in their web design the original template of the universe, and how, because these spiders were virtually blind, they could only communicate through vibrations. He shared how each spider was intentional in their actions and how their reverberations influenced and affected other spiders. Saraceno saw how spiders lived their lives not in "linear platforms" but as fantastical storytellers, weaving a web of complex narrative lines. As young mechanical engineers and artists labored together, I witnessed a single-minded ambition to preserve and sustain our planet before it is too late. An element of lightheartedness also prevailed — as young, amused faces huddled in patient forbearance of the group of Americans who had come to watch them at work. I saw them joyful and alive in how they were practicing their craft. One could tell that Saraceno was bringing together interdependence and independence. He was combining their unique strengths to create a lighter footprint. Ultimately, I saw how Saraceno's art, like Swoon's, was designed to make the world sustainable, creative, and inclusive of all humanity (T. Saraceno, studio visit and conversation with the artist, October 19, 2016).

### Swoon (b. 1977, American)

According to her website, the street artist Swoon, born Caledonia Dance Curry in 1977, works primarily with drawing, printmaking, site-specific installations, street interventions, and performance and community-based projects (Swoon, n.d.). Since 2010, her work has become increasingly political in motivation, with Swoon blurring the line between artist and activist. "The walls of cities should be a public sounding board, a sort of visual commons," (as cited in Carlsson & Louie, 2010) Swoon emphasizes, thus underscoring the notion that, as an artist, she is more interested in becoming a part of the world that she creates. By bringing her art into actual practice that improves the lives of many others, Swoon rewrites the manifesto on the social conventions of artmaking and art viewing. She proposes that artmaking is best viewed "as sites of inquiry between the artist, artwork, viewer and setting" (as cited in Jagiello, 2017).

In this section, I highlight three of Swoon's large-scale collaborative projects that continue to live beyond her direct involvement. These three undertakings involve a wide spectrum of communal talent and include artists, educators, musicians, farmers, architects, and scientists who promote sustainable ways of living and working in site-specific communities. Projects are conceptualized with an eye toward their functional and aesthetic nature. Evolving over eleven years in three different locations in the United States, Europe, and the Caribbean, Swoon worked with communities in situ. Exemplifying the philosophy of Brazilian educator Paulo Freire, she gives broad definition to communal needs by creating practical and artistic solutions to projects that affect a significant number of people. From being an individualist-centered do-it-yourself (DIY) project, Swoon's projects become do-it-together (DIT) ones. In this way, she contests the idea of the artist as solitary genius and, instead, creates a platform where all types of influences come together in honest engagement and improvement. Swoon's ideology and practice is echoed in the Paulo Freirean dictum to engage all people in their common uplift: "The important thing is to help men (and nations) help themselves, to place them in consciously critical confrontation with their problems, to make them the agents of their own recuperation. In contrast, assistencialism robs men of a human necessity—responsibility…. Responsibility cannot be acquired intellectually, but only through experience. Assistencialism offers no responsibility, no opportunity to make decision, but only gestures and attitudes which encourage passivity" (Freire, 1974, p.13).

*Chapter 18 Image 1.* Rafts. Photo Credit: Tod Seelie. Photo Courtesy, Swoon.

Swoon resists any passive subservience of the community in all her projects. Everyone has a voice which factors into how a project becomes actually manifested. In one project, she gathered an eclectic crew of diverse community talent (Jeff Stark and John Rinaldi were especially key at the inception of the project) to build a series of rafts that served as "swimming cities" that were as "much performative armadas as sociological experiments" (Bullock, 2015). She explained, "I wanted to build a floating microcosm of all that I held dear…. I wanted to live on a honeycomb of junk rafts, grow food, compost our waste, build our own motors that run on grease and learn how to live in a different way than the systems we know now" (as cited in Bullock, 2015). Pioneering a 21st century version of a life lived simply but cooperatively rather than competitively, Swoon spreads her message through a variety of media which invites communal engagement through an active farm-to-table culture. *Miss Rockaway Armada* evolved into 110 feet of "junk raft" that floated 800 miles over the Mississippi River; the *Swimming Cities of Switchback Sea* was a collection of seven rafts that floated down the Hudson River, whose waters switch direction twice a day; and *Swimming Cities of Serenissima* floated across the Adriatic from Koper, Slovenia, to Venice, Italy, crashing the Venice Biennale and overcoming police warnings in order to sail down the city's Grand Canal. Her installations are meticulously planned with precise scale models for the rafts, which are officially registered as water-worthy rafts ensured by architects and engineers. As models that elicit curiosity, wonder, and post-urban possibility, she comments of the project, "I could feel...we were changing lives in some modest but stubbornly glimmering way" (as cited in Bullock, 2015).

*Chapter 18 Image 2.* Konbit Shelter Project. Photo Credit: Bryan Welch. Photo Courtesy, Swoon.

In Cormiers, Haiti, Swoon interconnected art with human rights and civic revitalization by comixing interdisciplinary talent with communal needs. Swoon worked with architect Nader Khalili's pre-engineered humanitarian designs, which were then woven into the plans of her own engineers. Khalili designed his Super Adobe construction method utilizing local materials to create earthquake resistant structures. Like

Khalili, Swoon was inspired to "empower the world's poor and refugees to build homes using the earth under their feet" by building earthquake-resistant housing (Cal Earth, n.d.).

The Konbit Shelter Project followed Haiti's devastating 2010 earthquake, where a quarter of a million lives were lost. CAC's Education Notes defines Konbit as "a traditional form of cooperative labor in Haiti where the able-bodied people ...help one another prepare the fields. It is a time of solidarity in the face of adversity" (Contemporary Arts Center, Cincinnati, 2017). With the help of Haitian farmers and artists, Swoon's team set up a triage, addressing the immediate needs of providing shelter to the displaced. Although Swoon's project began in 2010 as a quick response to the earthquake, it has since evolved into a long-term commitment for herself and others. Indeed, this is a typical trajectory for her ideas. Following the devasting August 2021 earthquake in Les Cayes, Haiti, it will be important to see how Swoon's Konbit Shelter Project is scaled to Les Cayes, where early reports indicate that more than 2500 are presumed dead (Haiti Earthquake Death Toll, 2021). In her work, Swoon relies on donations from well-wishers and the sale of her work. "I think of money as a verb," she said, "because you have it and it has to go out in the world to do things" (as cited in Ryzik, 2014). Other artists who pulled together around the projects, donated art to fundraising auctions as well.

JR, the French artist and TED prize winner, is impressed by her ethos. "The fact that she does it the way she does, and just struggles her own way" allows her "complete freedom" as an artist (as cited in Ryzik, 2014). "She has always managed to have some social impact with her work and at the same time stay an artist, not an activist... That's very rare" (as cited in Ryzik, 2014). I would argue that by centering the artist in a critically urgent social issue, Swoon's art does make a case for the useful reconfiguration of action steps. By being a form of social commentary, Swoon's art effectively provides real outcomes in the colorful Super Adobe earthquake resistant structures that become the homes of displaced Haitians. And in this way, perhaps, she fits the roles of both artist and activist.

*Chapter 18 Image 3.* The Music Box. Photo Credit: Bryan Welch. Photo Courtesy, Swoon.

In New Orleans, Swoon helped create The Music Box — a series of small shotgun houses that provide easy access to their contents. Each house is designed as a musical instrument that references New Orleans' cultural heritage in music and architecture. She was invited to this project in 2010 by New Orleans' Airlift, "whose mission is to inspire wonder and connect communities through the creation of experimental public artworks" (Contemporary Arts Center, Cincinnati, 2017). Working closely with artists Delaney Martin, Jay Pennington, and Taylor Lee Shepherd, "this vision expanded to become a fully-fledged musical architecture for New Orleans," (The Heliotrope Foundation, n.d.) visited by thousands of people in the first year of the project alone.

Swoon went to work on her "performative installation" utilizing the remains of an 18th century Creole cottage that did not survive Hurricane Katrina intact (Osborn, 2012). Swoon's inspirations for this installation were the band Tiny Music, "who employ their surroundings as noise-making instruments," (Contemporary Arts Center, Cincinnati, 2017) as well as the big band sound of New Orleans' brass band parades. With her collaborators she, "re-imagined the timeworn cottage as a musical house with built-in instruments" (Contemporary Arts Center, Cincinnati, 2017) that could be played by the expert and novice alike. Musical instruments were "embedded in the floors, ceilings, walls, and staircases. This radical reinvention of the musical instrument and the musical stage hosted performances throughout 2011-12 with collaborations between musicians and composers from all over New Orleans and the globe." (The Heliotrope Foundation, n.d.). The Music Box continues as a source of hands-on learning and has, since 2016, evolved into an entire village, with multiple Music Boxes that people of all ages can experience.

In each of these projects, Swoon served as the hub and spokes of a wheel, advancing human rights, social justice, and civic revitalization. She used art as a catalyst to connect a community and its citizens and to bring attention to important social causes, all premised on the idea of belonging and connection. In this way, Swoon invites people into a form of critical conversation of their needs and desires beyond the limits of Freire's "assistentialism."

### Tomás Saraceno (b. 1973, Argentinian)

Tomás Saraceno is an Argentinian futurist, scientist, and artist who was inspired by his biologist mother. In one of his earliest memories, in his grandparents' home in Miramar, Argentina, when he was six or seven, "he watched dust illuminated by a ray of light through parted curtains. A camera obscura of the street appeared through a hole in the curtain, making the world outside appear on the wall, upside down" (Bradley, 2018). In another piece of nostalgia, he remembers his family home in Italy, "in a centuries-old house whose attic was filled with spiders: "Were the spiders living in my house or was I living in the spider's house?" he queried (Bradley, 2018).

These early fascinations led Saraceno to explore the mysteries of the sciences while noting the artistry that goes into the creation of natural phenomena. Saraceno attended the International Space Studies Program at NASA; studied art and architecture in Buenos Aires and Frankfort am Main; and went on to amass many awards including the

Calder Prize in 2009. He is known for his collaborations with scientists and has worked with MIT students to create some of his work. He has shown in international solo and group exhibitions at Palais de Tokyo, Paris (2015 and 2018) and the Metropolitan Museum of Art, New York (2012), among others. He has broken six world records for creating a human lifting device that operates by wind and solar energy without the benefit of fossil fuels. Naturally inclined as an interdisciplinarian, Saraceno is often associated with unorthodox thinkers who exploded the artificial boundaries of disciplines to find common solutions to planetary problems. Rebecca Lamarche-Vadel, curator of Saraceno's Palais de Tokyo show in Paris, said: "He's a great artist, comparable to Marcel Duchamp or even Leonardo da Vinci, who always thought outside and combined disciplines" (as cited in Bradley, 2018). Saraceno has remained both academic and creative in his approach to global, planetary problems. He is deeply committed to the emergence of multiple solutions and is flagrantly interdisciplinary in his approach to large-scale issues and problems.

In his work, Saraceno seems to utilize precepts from design thinking to explore what Tim Brown calls the "T-shaped" form of knowledge curation. The vertical of the T-form signifies depth of knowledge, as demonstrated by the content expertise of the scientists that he surrounds himself with, who are mostly schooled in engineering, physics, chemistry, aeronautics, and material sciences. The horizontal table-top of the T, according to Brown, constitutes the generalist application of this deep knowledge, usually done by those trained in interdisciplinary studies or who have a propensity to breach boundaries in search of viable, real-life applications (Brown, 2009, pp. 27-32).

As an artist, Saraceno studies the nature of materials to explore how they work in space and densities, and how alternative cities can be built in the air that provide easy access to earth. His desire is to save the planet from overpopulation and over-consumption by creating alternative communities that may become habitable. In the creation of this community, Saraceno works with "inflatable and airborne biospheres with the morphology of soap bubbles, spider webs, neural networks, or cloud formations, which are speculative models for alternate ways of living" (ARTS Center for Art, Science & Technology at MIT, n.d.). He cultivates and studies spiders from all over the world, in situ; he analyzes their web-making activity and explores the mechanism that bind together the fragile threads of a single web. This serves as an experiment for how he binds, in perfect adhesion, his floating spheres. Saraceno uses spider silk to "work with his interest in the natural world and arachnology… his work is described as visual geography, where interconnectedness is demonstrated on both macro and micro levels." (Contemporary Arts Center, Cincinnati, 2016). He strengthens the capability of the vast hordes of spiders that take up entire floors of his Berlin studio. Routine interspecies salons are staged between virtuosos and spiders which are documented with rigorous lab notes. The web-making practices of the spider population following these salons show enhanced complexity and tensile strength.

Saraceno's flying machines are inspired by Alexander Graham Bell and designed as "a tetrahedron-shaped kite…to maximize surface area and minimize weight…with the goal to carry man into flight" (Contemporary Arts Center, Cincinnati, 2016). Saraceno updates this framework with "contemporary technologies and materials." In *Solar Bell*, he creates a prototype of a "much larger and inhabitable platform-kite and the possibility for a flying kite plaza, fully lifted by the power of wind alone" ( Contemporary Arts Center, Cincinnati, 2016). Many of his pieces, like *Solar Bell*, are part of his larger *Cloud City* series, where Saraceno "imagines cities floating above the clouds which are powered entirely by renewable human, social, and environmental ecologies" (Contemporary Arts Center, Cincinnati, 2016). Saraceno emphasizes that the model for Solar Bell is "the diamond lattice of molecular bonding — diamond being the Greek word for 'unbreakable' — and that these systems are formed in nature: in the physics, mathematics, and chemistry of carbon and graphite" (Contemporary Arts Center, Cincinnati, 2016). In his art-making practice, Saraceno looks for ways in which to re-think and re-configure his environment. He works in the space of collaborative inquiry, formulating and conceptualizing and planning his projects which are situated firmly among his teams of experts. His approach is steeped in the knowledge of materials and their properties; yet he brings into focus the sense of wonder and abandon that are specific to the art-making process.

In summary, Saraceno's floating, portable, alternative environments address humanity's real and immediate problems like overcrowding and scarcity of resources. His work "defies traditional notions of space, time, gravity, consciousness and perception .... and each work is an invitation to conceive of alternative ways of knowing, feeling, and interacting with others" (Alonso, 2015). Tomás Saraceno's immersive installations conjure a scenario in which humanity ceases to negatively impact our planet's fossil-fuel resources, and instead becomes airborne in minimalistic, sustainable, and collective environments.

Stepping beyond the framework of artist, entrepreneur, leader, and/or activist, both Swoon and Saraceno take on the challenge of pushing the limits of human ingenuity and innovation. As a result, they are seen as leaders, activists, artists, and entrepreneurs with a mission. Their leadership lies in asking and responding to simple questions. In the case of Saraceno, the questions are: "If you couldn't live on earth, where would you want to live? What would we need to live there?" In the case of Swoon, the questions are: "What social issues are of urgent interest to you? How could you use art to address them?" (Contemporary Arts Center, Cincinnati, 2016; Contemporary Arts Center, Cincinnati, 2017).

## Resources

To learn more about Swoon, please visit: https://swoonstudio.org/

To learn more about Tomás Saraceno, please visit: https://studiotomassaraceno.org/

FRESH TALK: How do we build to better? | Liz Ogbu & Swoon in Conversation from the National Museum of Women in the Arts https://youtu.be/sF9JO9j-CVs

Swoon's Konbit Shelter - Art in the Streets - MOCAtv Ep. 7 from The Museum of Contemporary Art https://youtu.be/7YBbK-XAHYw

Swoon's Musical Architecture for New Orleans from artnet. https://youtu.be/HQDAg7rEULA

Tomás Saraceno: Building "future flying cities" with spiders from San Francisco Museum of Modern Art. https://youtu.be/rjVDyxTXGAg

Would you live in a floating city in the sky? from TED2017. https://www.ted.com/talks/tomas_saraceno_would_you_live_in_a_floating_city_in_the_sky

## References

Alonso, Rodrigo. (2015). Wall Didactic at the Contemporary Arts Center, Cincinnati, Ohio.

ARTS Center for Art, Science & Technology at MIT. (n.d.). Tomás Saraceno. https://arts.mit.edu/cast/symposia/seeing-sounding-sensing/participants/tomas-saraceno/

Bradley, K. (2018, October 19). With Spiders and Space Dust, Tomás Saraceno Takes Off. *The New York Times*. https://www.nytimes.com/2018/10/19/arts/design/tomas-saraceno-palais-de-tokyo.html

Brown, Tim. (2009) *Change by Design: How Design Thinking Transforms Organizations and Inspires Innovation.* Harper Collins, pp. 27-32.

Bullock, L.K. (2015). *Moral Vandals: Street Artists in the Service of Change* [Unpublished doctoral dissertation]. University of California, San Diego. https://escholarship.org/content/qt9d29x870/qt9d29x870_noSplash_2df9d1f9e9f0993494cabdcec59e7785.pdf

Cal Earth. (n.d.). Our Founder. https://www.calearth.org/our-founder

Callon, M. 2007. What Does It Mean to Say That Economics Is Performative? In D. MacKenzie, F. Muniesa, & L. Siu (Eds.), *Do Economists Make Markets? On the Performativity of Economics.* Princeton University Press.

Carlsson, B., & Louie, H. (2011). Street Art Cookbook: A Guide to Techniques and Materials. Dokument Press.

Contemporary Arts Center, Cincinnati. (2016, June 18). Education Notes for Docents, on Saraceno [Unpublished document].

Contemporary Arts Center, Cincinnati. (2017, September 22). Education Notes for Docents, on Swoon [Unpublished document].

Dechow, S.L. (2015, September 2). "Begin With Art." *The Listening*. http://welcometothelistening.org/blog/2015/8/26/begin-with-art

Freire, Paulo. (1974). *Education for Critical Consciousness*. Bloomsbury Academic Press.

Haiti Earthquake Death Toll Rises to 2,200. (2021, August 22). *USA Today*. https://www.usatoday.com/story/news/nation/2021/08/22/haiti-earthquake-2021-death-toll-rises-over-2-200/8235246002/

The Heliotrop Foundation. (n.d.). In 2011, New Orleans Airlift invited Caledonia Curry to create a sculpture in a condemned shotgun house in the Bywater. [Images Attached] [Album Description]. Facebook. https://www.facebook.com/HeliotropeFND/photos/?tab=album&album_id=417166375117110

Jagiello, Jolanta. (2017). *Performance, Exhibitions, and Performativity*, AoMO Conference 2018 didactic.

MacKenzie, D. 2007. Is Economics Performative? Option Theory and the Construction of Derivatives Markets. In D. MacKenzie, F. Muniesa, & L. Siu (Eds.), *Do Economists Make Markets?: On the Performativity of Economics*: 54-86. Princeton University Press.

Osborn, K. (2012, January 25). In the Music Box, New Orleans Residents Hear Hope. All Things Considered. *NPR*. https://www.npr.org/2012/01/25/145845744/in-the-music-box-new-orleans-residents-hear-hope

Ryzik, M. (2014, August 6). A Cultural Leap: Life of Wonderment. *The New York Times*. https://www.nytimes.com/2014/08/10/arts/design/swoon-blurs-the-line-between-art-and-activism.html

Swoon (n.d.) About Swoon. https://swoonstudio.org/about

## About the Author

Anu M. Mitra, PhD, is faculty in the Ph.D. in Interdisciplinary Studies Program at Union Institute & University. She is also the facilitator of the Museum Studies and Design Thinking Certificate programs at Union. She has taught at the University of Rochester, Yale University, Sichuan University, and Antioch College in Yellow Springs, Ohio. She has won multiple teaching and research awards including the Gopman Excellence in Research Award at Union Institute and the Greater Cincinnati Consortium of Colleges' Celebration of Teaching Award in 2011, 2018, and 2021.

From 2019-24, she has been selected as a Fulbright specialist with plans to serve in Trinidad/Tobago. Her research centers around arts-based learning spaces, pedagogy, and practices; Design Thinking; Visual Culture; Art History and Interpretation; Museum Studies; Social Justice Theory and Practice; Literature; and Writing. She has co-edited eleven books on arts-based practices and authored numerous articles in peer-reviewed journals. She is increasingly interested in the relationship between visual practices and public memory.

Her intensive training in museum studies and art history/interpretation continues as a docent at the Cincinnati Art Museum and the Contemporary Arts Center. She is also a board member at the Cincinnati Art Museum; the Ohio Advisory Board of the National Museum for Women in the Arts; and the Institute for Social Justice at the Union Institute & University.

Anu is the proud parent, along with her husband, of three adult children and one Siberian Husky. In her spare time, she loves to wander museums, read memoirs, watch films, and travel wherever the road will take her.

# SECTION 5

GRASSROOTS LEADERSHIP,
PARTICIPATORY DEMOCRACY, &
THE ROLE OF THE ARTS IN
SOCIAL MOVEMENTS

# CHAPTER 19

# ZILPHIA HORTON: THE SINGING HEART OF THE HIGHLANDER FOLK SCHOOL

## CANDIE CARAWAN

### INTRODUCTION

By SUSAN J. Erenrich

This chapter features my dear friend Candie Carawan. She has written about an influential, relatively unknown figure in American history, Zilphia Horton. Zilphia, an accomplished instrumentalist and vocalist, was "The Singing Heart of the Highlander Folk School."

For those not familiar with Highlander, it was launched in Monteagle, Tennessee, in 1932 by Myles Horton and Don West. It is a place where "average citizens can pool their knowledge, learn from history, sociology, and seek solutions to their social problems" (Dunson, 1965, p. 28). Cultural expression has been a salient component of the school's curriculum since its earliest days when Zilphia joined the staff in 1935.

Known as Zilphia Mae Johnson, prior to her marriage to Myles Horton on 6 March 1935, she incorporated the arts into every facet of the Highlander program. The daughter of an Arkansas mine owner and a graduate of the College of the Ozarks, she was determined "to use her musical and dramatic abilities in some field of radical activity" (Glen, 1996, p. 43). Highlander was the perfect venue.

Zilphia died in 1956. Prior to her passing, she amassed 1,300 songs from unions, progressive organizations, traditional Appalachian culture, and the South (Dunson, 1965). This chapter honors Zilphia, a woman who truly believed in horizontal leadership, and who left an indelible impression on the cultural activists who tried to fill her shoes. I hope you enjoy Candie Carawan's piece, which draws heavily on interviews with Zilphia's sister, Ermon Faye Duschenes, and former Highlander staff member, Ralph Tefferteller. A companion Zilphia Horton tribute accompanies this chapter from the 31 March 2017 *Wasn't That A Time* radio broadcast.

## Listen

*Wasn't That A Time - Episode 12: A Tribute To Zilphia Horton*

https://www.mixcloud.com/WasntThatATime/wasnt-that-a-time-episode-12/

## References

Dunson, J. (1965). *Freedom in the Air: Song Movements of the Sixties.* International Publishers.

Glen, J. (1996). *Highlander: No Ordinary School.* University of Tennessee Press.

## ZILPHIA HORTON: THE SINGING HEART OF THE HIGHLANDER FOLK SCHOOL

By Candie Carawan

Zilphia Horton is perhaps best known for her role in shaping and passing on the historic anthem of the U.S. Civil Rights Movement, "We Shall Overcome." The song came to Highlander in 1947 with striking food and tobacco workers from Charleston, South Carolina. As a staff member, Zilphia always asked what songs people knew and what songs were being used in their campaigns back home. When she heard "I Will Overcome" with its new words of "we will organize" and "the Lord will see us through," she knew it was a song with meaning for communities all across the South. She adapted it to her accordion and sang it at union meetings and community gatherings, and at Highlander workshops. It became a kind of theme song at Highlander throughout the labor movement period of the 1940s and 1950s.

From its earliest days, Highlander Folk School was a place that nurtured cultural expression as well as educating for change. Founders Myles Horton and Don West had each been impressed by the strong role that cultural expression served in the Danish Folk School movement. As people struggled to solve difficult problems in their communities, they tapped into sources of self and community worth. Myles knew that he would need skilled staff members to draw upon the cultural strengths in Southern communities.

Zilphia Mae Johnson was a talented and well-trained musician and singer. The child of an Arkansas mine owner, she graduated from the College of the Ozarks and went off to teach high school music and Spanish in Sallisaw, Oklahoma. She came back to her hometown of Paris, Arkansas, and began to join young people at the home of Claude Williams, a local Presbyterian minister.

Her sister Ermon Fay Duschenes remembers:

Claude was a very interesting person. A lot of the young people gathered at his house, just to be sociable and to talk about ideas. Zilphia did some singing there, but not much. It was more to talk about what kind of a world we live in. In 1935 she left home and went to Highlander. Claude Williams got her interested in going. Zilphia went to Highlander after an argument with my father over smoking. I guess it was really a matter of one will against another.

She was married to Myles less than a year after she got there. She was probably twenty-seven or twenty-eight (March 1935). She was doing music there and giving some interesting life to the kitchen and to the food. She was doing singing and using the piano. She had to develop a repertoire once she got there. She did not know the folk songs when she came. She started collecting in the mountains in Tennessee, and then when she came back to Arkansas to finish her degree in choral music, she went into the mountains there and collected (E. F. Duschenes, personal communication as cited in Carawan, n.d.).

Ralph Tefferteller was another early Highlander staff member. Growing up in East Tennessee, he was familiar with traditions of dance and play party games, pie suppers, and ice cream socials. He left the mountains to study at Union Theological Seminary and found that people in the North wanted to learn about his Southern heritage. He made it a point to relearn the traditional dances and put them to good use at Highlander. He explained that there was a twofold approach to singing at Highlander:

Highlander was an interesting mix of "conservers" and new ideas: The mix of traditional songs and music, which were to be found in the lives of the Cumberland mountain people, with the new struggle songs, which were evolving out of the sharecropper experiences in West Tennessee, the eastern part of Arkansas, and other areas in the Southeast as the sharecroppers attempted to form unions, organize, and seek better economic and social concessions from the owners. They turned to the old traditional tunes in order to construct their parodies, and to use the familiar for voices of hope and protest and determination. People in poor, rural areas came together for singing in the rural churches, so this was a familiar art form for them, and made it possible for them to use it effectively when it came to the need to carry new and strong messages to each other and to the outside world.

I would say the cultural program was sort of co-leadered, during the short time I was there (1934-38), between Zilphia and myself. I headed the outreach part of the community work in recreation, and I was the dance instructor in residence. Zilphia was really the musically talented person and had this great ability to get others involved in music. Of course, the singing became deeply embedded in all of the work at Highlander through the years. She came with the technical training; I came with some of the spirit and very little formal training. I just had a deep love and appreciation for people, how they lived, sang, and used music in their lives, whether at the work site, in the fields, or in the factories.

The cultural work evolved from the people we were working with. We picked up on the opportunities of the moment — the patterns of topical interest growing out of the experiences of people who came. After all, Highlander was a place where you threw what you had into the pot, as it were. You brought yourself; you brought the sum of your experiences; and along with these, came the different modes of life — from the factory, the field, and the farm. Those experiences, by the mid-1930s, had already generated some of the great struggle music in the Southeast part of the country.

It was also during this time that there were disturbances occurring in mills and factories in the lowland — especially around Chattanooga. Someone could call up and say, "Hey, we've got a strike on, and I need help. Come on down!" Many a morning I can remember getting in the old rickety station wagon — some half dozen of us — and making the run from Monteagle down to the picket line to reinvigorate tired folk and let them know they had friends who would put themselves out and stand to help a flagging spirit.

This was one of the functions of a place like Highlander. It meant that there were informed, finely honed human-service skills in the Highlander community that could be summoned in time of crisis.

Whenever there was trouble, there was usually a way in which Highlander could make a contribution.

One vital aspect of that contribution and that spirit is that of music. When people like Zilphia would get songs going on the picket lines, you could feel people's spirits rising. Or in workshops — if ever there was a person who could invigorate and move a group of adults with musical participation, she was the prime example of an artist at work. The walls of the old building at Highlander rang with the songs of people during those years, and with the music, which she generated and was always encouraging individuals to create in their own way and to bring as contributions to the sessions that were held.

She knew, and would use, anything that seemed to suit the occasion — popular music of the late '20s and early '30s, Broadway tunes, old tunes. I'll never forget how effectively she used the song "Brother, Can You Spare a Dime?" in little playlets to arouse the emotions of either working people or people to who [sic] she was trying to give some appreciation of what the life of the unemployed worker was like.

It was just a joy to be a part of it with her and to sit in any group and to see how they would respond. She had an infectious type of presentation that enveloped you and drew you in. You weren't on the outside as a spectator — you became wholeheartedly involved with the moment. And that was singing either one of the traditional labor songs, which spoke of the struggle of years past and had an application to today, or a new song that had been brought in by a participant in one of the workshops, which was then ingested and became a part of the collective material and would eventually appear in print as part of a little songbook. "No More Moanin'" for example, was literally put together right there in the kitchen at Highlander. People coming from wherever — factories, sharecropper country — brought a little of their lifestyles with them to workshops, and ways they had learned to communicate with each other, and singing was one of those ways.

The old songs became vehicles for carrying new messages and singing became a unifying force. And because of those deep-rooted traditions of singing in churches and homes, it was very natural that singing should develop in the Southeastern part of the country as a natural adjunct to the struggle to overcome inhuman situations and to deal with them in song. Preachers and workers all had this sort of experience, whether they were Blacks or Whites (R. Tefferteller, personal communication as cited in Carawan, n.d.).

Many songs, which later became anthems in the Southern labor movement, were first used to draw people together at Highlander. Zilphia used songs to educate people too. She knew songs that spoke of struggles all around the world and included them in workshops and in Highlander songbooks. She thought it important that people involved in a local struggle realize that many others in distant places faced similar issues and had organized to resist oppression.

Zilphia traveled to the communities of workshop participants, as did other staff members. She sang on countless picket lines and in union meetings, and she helped spread the repertoire of labor songs. She also mimeographed the words to songs and left them in communities after she had been there or passed them out at Highlander meetings.

Theater and creating skits and plays was another important cultural activity at Highlander. Zilphia developed the theater program and spent a period of time in New York studying with the New Theater League. Returning to her work at Highlander, she helped workshop participants build plays with music out of their own struggles. Often, they took the plays to union meetings and labor conferences. Those that were well received were then mimeographed and made available to labor groups around the country.

Mary Lawrence was on the Highlander staff in the 1930s doing educational work with unions. In 1945, she published *Education Unlimited: A Handbook on Union Education in the South* and made keen observations about cultural work:

> At Highlander, during the regular six-weeks' terms one of the most exciting courses has been dramatics taught by Zilphia Horton. Of course, the students turn up their noses in disdain when they first come. They all have preconceived opinions of dramatics, and they

aren't very flattering. But when they find that no learning of lines or putting on dull plays is involved, just living out their own experiences, they fall for it like a ton of bricks.

One of the most amazing experiences we have in the class is watching the suspicious expression on their faces turn to one of hilarity and excitement as they let off steam acting out a picket line. They just outsmart each other in a hurry trying to improve that improvisation of a picket line. Yet they soon learn that a bunch of heads is a whole lot better than one. Each one is then asked to pick out a union problem to present to the group and is allowed to pick the actors he wants from the audience. They go into the hall for a short ten minutes, and after much gleeful shouting they come back and present the problem. Then the audience suggests ways of making it go over better. The result is that the class is putting on full length plays, completely improvised, on some vital problem of the day before the month is over. Often, we take these plays to union meetings, and we always give one on Saturday night to our guests. One of the best was "South of the Ballot," a play about the poll tax.

Because of the isolation of the school, planned recreation and entertainment by the students is essential. The students are usually amazed to discover what wonderful times they can plan for themselves by themselves. The final night is always a big night. Several weeks ahead, the Entertainment Committee works on arrangements for the big night. Our main hall is turned into some kind of a cabaret, the motif varying from year to year according to the tastes of the students. The hall has to be completely redecorated, and our only tool is the ingenuity of the students. The other big job is lining up the entertainment in the style of a floor show. Working out the details for this program, the students realize what a wealth of talent there is among a group of amateurs. It gives them an idea of what could be done in their own locals by utilizing the talents of the group (as cited in Glen, 1996, pp. 81-82).

Another early staffer, an Antioch work student, Lanie Melamed, adds to the description of the banquet:

The skits were always political action skits. They always had a political message. They were performed at the banquet at the end of a session. Two days before the banquet there was always time in the afternoons left for preparation for the banquet.

The banquet was the culmination of the term, and it became a kind of ritual, because every term would have it. Remember, it's a residential setting. The intensity of the total experience of living together and working together — mostly the living and the meals and just sharing so much of yourself beyond your cognitive or your intellectual self-created the kinds of connections between people that are nothing short of magic. And the staff knew that, or had learned that, so the room was transformed.

The tables were put around all the sides of the room. There was a decoration committee that went out into the woods and got boughs and plants and flowers for every table. There was a program that was put together, and the menu was very, very special. Then there was a master of ceremonies that was appointed, and there were speeches, and there were little rolled diplomas with little ribbons around them given out, and there was singing. Wow. And that last night, singing — because the closure, the whole idea of leaving was added to the emotionality of the event, and then there were the skits. Oftentimes outsiders came; big shots from the unions would come down to the banquet.

Then the people made testimonials. That was always the time for my tears.

Some of the most eloquent things were said. People would talk about what the school meant to them and what they had learned. That's the juice of all this kind of work. In one week's time, we see people change their perspectives — on themselves, their self-esteem, their ability — and also a lot of this preparation and learning was for the purpose of going out there on the front lines and doing a better job organizing, getting the fertilizer co-op started or whatever. You needed a lot of juice to be geared up, prepared, because you were going to be more alone once you were out there (L. Melamed, personal communication as cited in Carawan, n.d.).

Lanie also described the influence that Zilphia had on her personally:

She was very genuine when she was working. She came alive. When she was leading singing, it was a total blending of herself with the music, with the people, and it never bombed. There was a magic when she picked up the accordion, and she just had a vibrancy and an aliveness in her voice and in her face that just made you sing. Made you want to sing. She, of all the people who were at Highlander, was the one I connected with. I guess I wanted to be that kind of a leader too — a person who was so congruent with what she believed, and her skill in being able to connect with people.

It seemed like the school was a living embodiment of what she believed. It didn't seem like she was pushing herself to be part of it. Later in my life I did what Zilphia did. I was always interested in what she did, and later I was perfecting myself in the field of music and dance and people (L. Melamed, personal communication as cited in Carawan, n.d.).

Zilphia's younger sister Ermon Fay Duschenes came to work at Highlander too in the early 1940s, glad for a chance to spend time with her big sister. She described a bleak time at Highlander during the war years. "The unions were turning away from the school and Zilphia wasn't invited as much to go and sing for the unions" (E.F. Duschenes, personal communication as cited in Carawan, n.d.).

Joie Willimetz also talks of those times and tells how the staff went from around twenty people to three while she was there. She says of Zilphia, how sad it was that she did not live to participate in the Civil Rights Movement of the 1960s. Zilphia died in 1956. The '60s would see a new resurgence of energy in the country and at Highlander. The role of music would incredibly stimulate the music of the movement.

Ermon Fay Duschenes remembers: "I was there when 'We Shall Overcome' came to Highlander. Zilphia and I went into the library with these ladies from Charleston and started singing it and making up verses to go with it. Zilphia adapted 'We Shall Overcome' to the accordion and carried it around the South and the country to countless gatherings of people working and hoping for change" (E.F. Duschenes, personal communication as cited in Carawan, n.d.).

Zilphia was at the heart of the cultural work at Highlander for twenty years. Duschenes has summed up her importance to the school:

> Zilphia and Myles really acted like a team, but they performed quite different functions. Myles provoked people and got them thinking. And Zilphia welcomed people. You have to have both things. You need someone to form an atmosphere and take an interest in the individual. Zilphia had a lot of energy, and she was lively and curious, and people reacted to her as a genuine person. She was an ear. She was a mother to people. She was fun. Zilphia had lots of ideas, and she was very capable. She gave you a sense of life, and of loving life. She encouraged any and everybody to do something creative.

> The women at Highlander did the traditional things and then they did the educational work too. Zilphia got tired sometimes and discouraged. When the school was attacked, she got discouraged.

> The music, the cultural work, was the juice. The music by itself is not important. But the music used as part of the work, with its content, is very important (E.F. Duschenes, personal communication as cited in Carawan, n.d).

In Zilphia Horton's own words:

> Singing, poetry, literature — all these things that we think make life richer — are like the water lilies. What determines how beautiful that water lily is and how strong it is, is the rich mud at the bottom of that pond. And that's the way I think about songs that we sing. To me, what people stand for represents the roots in the mud at the bottom of the lake. There has to be some central core that holds people together

before anything worthwhile comes out in the way of culture. I don't care if people do have one nationality, if they have one religion; there is something else that is essential before they can sing, and that is that they believe in something (Horton, n.d.).

## References

Lawrence, M. (1945). *Education Unlimited: A Handbook on Union Education in the South*. Highlander Folk School.

Carawan, C. (n.d.). Zilphia Horton: A Profile. [Unpublished manuscript]. Highlander Research and Education Center.

Glen, J. (1996). *Highlander: No Ordinary School*. University of Tennessee Press.

Horton, Zilphia. (n.d.). Unpublished papers and recordings. Highlander Research and Education Center (formerly Highlander Folk School) records, 1917-2005. Wisconsin Historical Society archives at the University of Wisconsin-Madison Libraries. https://search.library.wisc.edu/catalog/999465347602121

## About the Author

Candie Carawan has been based at the Highlander Center in Tennessee for more than fifty years. She worked alongside her husband Guy as a cultural worker in the South, ushering in many of the important movements for social change. Together they performed nationally and internationally. They produced four books and more than a dozen documentary albums reflecting traditional cultures of Deep South, African American, and Appalachian communities and the adoption of these cultures into social movements. They have also recorded 12 albums of their own music. Guy is best known for spreading the song, "We Shall Overcome" throughout the South in the early 1960s. He played guitar, banjo, and hammered dulcimer. Sadly, Guy passed away on 2 May 2015. Candie has continued her important journey. She is also an artist and potter.

CHAPTER 20

# THE MISSISSIPPI FREEDOM DEMOCRATIC PARTY: A BOTTOM-UP LEADERSHIP MODEL

MIKE MILLER

## INTRODUCTION

By Susan J. Erenrich

In this chapter, my good friend, Mike Miller, writes about an important juncture in U.S. history that has served as a model for bottom-up leadership for more than half a century. Picture this:

The year was 1964. Mississippi was the poorest state in the USA. Close to half the population was African American, but fewer than 5% were registered to vote. Most African Americans who managed to register were concentrated in Jackson or along the Gulf Coast (Mississippi Freedom Democratic Party, n.d.). During this time period, African Americans were subjected to beatings, arrests, cross-burnings, shootings, bombings, lynchings, and assassinations for trying to exercise their inalienable rights, including the right to the ballot.

On February 9, 1964, during a Council of Federated Organizations (COFO) meeting, Bob Moses (Robert Parris Moses), one of the early Student Nonviolent Coordinating Committee organizers in the state, proposed a sophisticated new strategy to combat their disenfranchisement. They would create a new party, the Mississippi

Freedom Democratic Party, otherwise known as the MFDP, and challenge the existing Democratic Party in Mississippi to represent the state at the party convention later that year (MFDP Challenge to the Democratic Convention, n.d.). The MFDP was open to all regardless of if they were officially registered to vote. Everyone who joined could participate in the party and its actions and decision making. At the same time, efforts to register African Americans using the official state process continued, as did the state's efforts to deny African Americans the vote. Although their challenge was not accepted, many, such as noted civil rights leader John Lewis, cite the event as a turning point in the fight for civil rights.

In the months leading up to the convention, human and civil rights movement organizers had engaged disenfranchised communities in an exciting voter registration campaign, culminating in a state-wide convention on August 6th at the Masonic Temple on Lynch Street in Jackson, Mississippi. Eight hundred elected delegates and one thousand enthusiastic supporters were on the scene. As Howard Zinn described the gathering: "It was a beautifully-organized, crowded, singing assembly of laborers, farmers, housewives, from the farthest corners of Mississippi, and made the political process seem healthy for the first time in the state's history. It was probably as close to a grass roots political convention as this country has ever seen" (Zinn, 1964/2013).

Just like the Industrial Workers of the World (IWW), and many other movements, the Civil Rights Movement was a singing movement. Julian Bond, who served as the Student Nonviolent Coordinating Committee's Communication Director in 1964, penned the following liner notes for *The Long Walk to Freedom Reunion Concert* CD that I produced in 1997. Julian had served as the Master of Ceremonies during a live event that had taken place approximately one year earlier at the Holton Arms School in Bethesda, Maryland. The historic gathering was captured, recorded, and shared with the public. Bond (1997) writes:

Almost everyone in the Civil Rights Movement of the 1960s sang. Not all were singers, but everyone sang. We sang in churches at mass meetings, on picket lines, in jails and prisons, and even when we were off duty — in Freedom Houses, in roadhouses and after-hours bars, in hamburger stands, and in our cars. Some sang alone, but most in groups of three or more — frequently gospel and spirituals from the church, popular songs from the radio and always, the Freedom Songs that came from each of these sources.

The Movement taught us the Freedom Songs; some we wrote ourselves, and in turn, the Freedom Songs made the Movement.

The Movement was, above all, a singing movement, not at all unusual for a movement that was made by Southern Black people.

Like all Southerners, Black Southerners are storytellers, and these songs told stories. They told of people bound in jail and of determined eyes kept on a distant and elusive prize, and of people holding on. Some sang of the Movement's dark side — murder and mayhem. Some were meant to evoke laughter. Some literally rocked the church. All were meant to instill courage and stiffen determination. In their descriptions, these songs served as musical newspapers, reporting the day's events to an evening crowd.

Some served as inspirational hymns. Their song leaders were Movement cheerleaders, summoning spirit and celebrating victories small and large. And they allowed a fearful and frightened people, squeezed together in a tiny church encircled by hostile policemen or walking slowly toward a county courthouse surrounded by dead Confederate statues and live Confederate sympathizers, to overcome fear and fright. You can often say in song words you can't — or shouldn't — say in speech, and these songs give permission for bold thought, which give sanction to bold action.

It has been almost 40 years since I first heard "We Shall Overcome" or "I'm Gonna Sit at the Welcome Table" or "Ain't Gonna Let Nobody Turn Me 'Round." But when the people we used to call the band of brothers and sisters and the circle of trust get together—and get together we continually do—we cannot gather without song. Song meant everything to us then. Songs and singing bound us together in shared experience, as chains could never have done. Voices raised together in struggle mean everything to me—to us—then and still mean everything now.

As you listen, you'll find you can't resist—open your ears, mouth, and heart, throw your head back, close your eyes, and SING!

In this chapter, we are going to take another walk down memory lane and learn from these noteworthy movers and shakers who blazed trails for the rest of us. I hope you enjoy Mike Miller's piece along with the *Wasn't That A Time: Stories & Songs That Moved The Nation* radio broadcast that accompanies this chapter.

### Listen

*Wasn't That A Time Episode 2: The 1964 MFDP Challenge*

Enjoy this special Inauguration Day program as we look back at another turbulent time in American electoral politics.

https://www.mixcloud.com/WasntThatATime/wasnt-that-a-time-episode-2-the-1964-mfdp-challenge/

### References

Bond, J. (1997). *The Long Walk to Freedom Reunion Concert* [CD liner notes]. Revolt In! Records.

MFDP Challenge to the Democratic Convention. (n.d.). Civil Rights Movement Archive. http://www.crmvet.org/info/mfdp_atlantic.pdf

Mississippi Freedom Democratic Party (MFDP) Founded (April). (n.d.). Civil Rights Movement Archive. http://www.crmvet.org/tim/timhis64.htm#1964mfdp

Zinn, H. (1964/2013). *SNCC: The New Abolitionists - A Detailed History of the Student Nonviolent Coordinating Committee.* Haymarket Books

# THE MISSISSIPPI FREEDOM DEMOCRATIC PARTY: A BOTTOM-UP LEADERSHIP MODEL

By Mike Miller

From mid-1962 to the end of 1966, I was a field secretary for the Student Nonviolent Coordinating Committee (SNCC) ("Snick" was its shorthand name). During the summer and early fall of 1963, a year before the big Mississippi Summer Project, I was in Greenwood and, for a shorter period of time, in Hattiesburg, Mississippi.

SNCC was about building people power so that it could take political power. I was part of the Freedom Vote, in which Black Mississippians demonstrated by voting in a "parallel election," 83,000 strong, that they wanted to vote — a Constitutional right systematically denied them. That vote laid the basis for the Mississippi Freedom Democratic Party (MFDP), the vehicle created by a joint effort of the state NAACP, Congress on Racial Equality (CORE), Southern Christian Leadership Conference (SCLC), and SNCC to put voting rights and racial justice on the national agenda of the Democratic Party by dramatically challenging its national convention to refuse seating the racist "regulars" as delegates, and then, in early 1965, at the opening of Congress, to challenge the House of Representatives to refuse seating the "elected" racists. Both challenges were rejected.

SNCC also tried to organize economic power: The Mississippi Freedom Labor Union (MFLU) organized plantation tractor drivers and others, and it took over an abandoned military base in the Delta as part of its protest against firing and eviction. There was also the Poor People's Project (PPP), a vehicle through which local craftspeople marketed their products to sympathetic buyers in the north. Later, Movement veterans assisted local Black farmers in their efforts to win seats on Department of Agriculture local boards that determined crop allotments.

Underlying the alphabet soup was what we knew as "The Movement," the energy, ideas, and people who held it all together. It was a singing movement: spirituals with freedom movement lyrics and songs newly created for The Movement by its singers and song writers to lift and hold high spirits. In SNCC itself, a number of full-time workers with musical gifts began singing and creating music together. They became The Freedom Singers. They sang across the country to raise funds for The Movement, and they sang in the intense week-long SNCC staff meetings, moments of deep division among us, to bring our focus back to the larger struggle in which we were engaged and to remind us that we were sisters and brothers in that struggle. Those early Freedom Singers included Bernice Johnson Reagon, who went on to organize Sweet Honey In The Rock and become an internationally recognized cultural worker.

It was a theater movement: initially in skits whose Black characters were fearful uninvolved local residents, a SNCC organizer, a "local person" active in The Movement, and a White plantation "boss man" and/or sheriff. Under the direction of SNCC organizer John O'Neal, these characters, all local people playing the roles, acted out overcoming fear and standing up to The Man. Lines were improvised around a core script. These skits were the highlight of mass meetings. Based on them, John built the Free Southern Theater.

Most of my time on the SNCC staff was spent as its representative in the San Francisco Bay Area: fundraising, recruiting volunteers, putting pressure on the Justice Department to enforce the law and Congress to pass better laws, and educating Northerners about what was going on in the South. Our office published what became a national monthly newspaper, *The Movement*, in whose pages, articles reported on and analyzed Deep South civil rights/Black power struggles, organizing California farm workers, anti-urban renewal fights, and much more. In 1965, in its pages I wrote, "The Mississippi Freedom Democratic Party: 'Race Has Kept Us Both in Poverty'." I revisited the subject in "The Mississippi Freedom Democratic Party: 50 Years Later a Time for Evaluation," published in *Social Policy* in 2014.

This is an update on the update. In it, *in italics to distinguish them*, are excerpts from the 1965 article to give a flavor of those times.

**Excerpt From 1965 Article**

*To Rally Against Fear*

*Beginning in 1961, Negro citizens increasingly sought to register to vote. For SNCC, two basic problems had to be faced. First, the overwhelming fear based on the experience of beatings, killings, home bombings, evictions and firings that confront Negroes who seek their constitutional rights in the State; second, more subtle, and more difficult to work with, was the feeling shared by many Negroes in the State that politics wasn't their business. The phrase commonly used was, "politics is white folks business"... For two years, first one at a time, then in tens, then in hundreds, Negroes went to county courthouses seeking to register to vote. In some cases, they were not even allowed to fill out the application form that precedes registration. In most cases, they were told they failed to successfully complete the application. Two questions were generally used to flunk the applicant: (1) interpret the following section (chosen from 383 sections of the Mississippi State Constitution) of the Constitution; (2) interpret the duties and obligations of citizenship under a constitutional form of government. Whether the applicant passed or failed was determined by the registrar of voters, usually a member of the White Citizens Council.*

## A PARALLEL POLITICAL FORCE

*The Mississippi Freedom Democratic Party was a logical extension of the concept of freedom votes and freedom candidates. That the new Party be a Democratic Party was a matter of some discussion in the State. Following the November 1963 freedom election success, another state-wide meeting of civil rights activists in Mississippi, held April 2, 1964, discussed the future.*

*Their decision was to create a parallel Democratic Party -- one that would, in every respect, comply with the rules and regulations set down by the Mississippi State Constitution for the conduct of political parties, and that would be Democratic because it was in the Democratic Party that significant decisions about the lives of the people in the State were made. However, the MFDP was independent in the sense that it owed no patronage or appointments to the National or State Party. This double character of the Freedom Democratic Party, at once inside and outside the system, is a major source of its national strength and the fear that it later caused the "pros" of the National Democratic Party.*

*Underlying the Atlantic City Convention challenge were three basic considerations. A special MFDP report named them as "(1) the long history of systematic and studied exclusion of Negro citizens from equal participation in the political processes of the state ... ; (2) the conclusive demonstration by the Mississippi Democratic Party of its lack of loyalty to the National Democratic Party in the past ... ; (3) the intransigent and fanatical determination of the State's political power structure to maintain the status-quo, ..." At its founding meeting, the MFDP stated, "We are not allowed to function effectively in Mississippi's traditional Democratic Party; therefore, we must find another way to align ourselves with the National Democratic Party." So that such an alignment could be established, the MFDP began organizing meetings throughout the State to send delegates to the Atlantic City Democratic Convention. ...*

### ROCKING THE BOAT FROM THE BOTTOM

*The Congressional Challenge is based simply on the idea that the Congressmen of Mississippi have been illegally elected and should, therefore, not sit in the House of Representatives. On the opening day of Congress, acting in close contact with the MFDP, but using a different legal basis for the Challenge, Congressman William Fitz Ryan of New York introduced a "Fairness Resolution" which stated that in all due fairness to the challenging MFDP candidates and in recognition of the discriminatory practices of the Mississippi Democrats, the Mississippi Congressional delegation should not be seated and the contestants, Mrs. Fannie Lou Hamer, Mrs. Victoria Gray, and Mrs. Annie Devine, should be given floor privileges through the session of the House so that should their challenge be successful, and should they later be named Congresswomen, they would have the opportunity of knowing the history of the session of Congress.*

*Again the Freedom Democrats stirred the nation -- and rocked the political boat. Working through ad hoc committees in many Congressional districts, through Friends of SNCC groups, CORE chapters, some NAACP branches, ACLU and ADA chapters, and other organizations, the FDP was able to build a movement that led, finally, to 150 votes in support of the Challenge. While the final result is impressive, it was not enough to win. Equally impressive was the way in which the' coalition backing the challenge was built. Many of the national organizations that were to finally back the FDP's challenge only did so after they began to receive pressure from their own members at home. The final January 4th grouping that was around FDP was built from the bottom up, beginning first with maverick chapters, branches, and locals of national organizations that only after questions from below began to move.*

### After Defeats

The convention and congressional defeats expressed the power of the Dixiecrats — Southern racist Democrats whose political roots were in the Confederacy — in both the Democratic Party, where the South provided necessary votes for presidential candidate victories and were sometimes necessary for a presidential candidate's nomination to run, and in Congress, where seniority rules made them chairmen of key committees in both the House and Senate. In those days, liberals in the North pursued a "realignment" strategy to get Northern liberal Republicans (they then existed) to join the Democratic Party, and Southern racist Democrats to join the Republican Party. Their idea was that there then would be a clear election choice for voters between liberals and conservatives. It was, however, Republican presidential candidate Richard Nixon's "Southern strategy" that implemented at least part of the realignment: the massive switch by southern white Democrat politicians and voters from their historic party to the Republican Party.

MFDP returned to Mississippi and campaigned for the national Democratic Party ticket. Despite its loyalty to the Democrats, the newly elected President Johnson began funneling poverty program funds into the state through organizations that were integrated into the national party structure. As voting became safer in the state after the passage of the 1965 Voting Rights Act, the campaign to create an alternative to the MFDP grew as well; the Mississippi Democratic Conference (MDC) was its name. By the 1968 national convention, a new delegate body represented the state — most of it neither MFDP nor segregationist "Regulars." These were the "Loyalists," a quarter of whose delegates were MFDP.

A more visionary Democratic Party leadership might have changed the direction of the nation if it had seated the MFDP at the party convention instead of making a take-it-or-leave-it offer of two seats at large as honorary delegates and if it had refused to seat the Dixiecrat racists in Congress. In so doing, it would have declared unequivocal war on the old guard Dixiecrats. Having crossed that Rubicon, the Democrats might have gone on to pass serious full employment legislation. Other things might have followed to move the party in a more liberal direction. Instead, "Moderation" (and the Vietnam War) triumphed.

But my interest is less in what the Democrats might, or should, have done. My interest lies more in what "we" could have done to more effectively pursue the goals of political, social, cultural, and economic liberation. In what follows, I pose questions. Some of my answers are confident; others are tentative. The questions SNCC faced then remain and face us today if we are going to figure out how to turn the country (and world) around.

### Should COFO have launched MFDP, or was there a better way to break the wall of Mississippi racism and achieve real power?

The emphasis on the right to vote led inevitably to questions: "Who would we vote for, if we could vote?" "Do we want to be part of the regular Mississippi Democratic Party?" "Why not form our own party?"

Was SNCC's work too skewed toward electoral politics? Even given the electoral emphasis, could political power be achieved in a form other than a political party? I will return to this question below.

There is a deeper set of questions related to the timing of electorally focused action. Had we then known what we were soon to learn, we might have wanted greater depth of organization throughout the Black population of the state before directly engaging in politics.

In Holmes County, SNCC/MFDP left a strong legacy. An independent Black politics emerged within the framework of the Democratic Party as early as 1965/66. SNCC's on-the-ground organizing presence in Holmes paved the way for what MFDP accomplished there. Holmes County had the largest percentage of independent Black farmers in the Delta. Because of its rolling hills, there were no vast plantations that carried on a de facto slavery long after slavery had been made unconstitutional. The community SNCC had to work with was, therefore, an easier one to organize for independence. Indeed, the Black farmers were already organizing themselves before SNCC even arrived. But Holmes was the exception to the rule.

As the next five years unfolded, it turned out that SNCC built the road and the MFDP car that initially drove on it, but someone else's car completed the drive. In the four-seater, MFDP had only a single back seat. With the passage of the 1965 Voting Rights Act, and the presence in the state of Federal "examiners" to register people to vote, a whole new set of players entered the electoral arena. The more cautious people, including most of the church leadership and many of the people in the pews, now became engaged in voting. They were the base for the reformed Democrats who received support from the national Democratic Party by various means including Poverty Program patronage. In this new Mississippi Democratic Party constellation, the one that represented Mississippi at the 1968 Democratic National Convention, MFDP people had one quarter of the seats. Others occupied the remaining seats.

There was a complication for SNCC. For the most part, SNCC's organizing bypassed the churches. Pastors who became involved were a distinct minority of the Black clergy. Historically, the three major leadership groups in the Mississippi Black community were teachers, preachers, and independent Black business — farmers and professional people. SNCC focused on the 80+% of the Black population who were day laborers, domestics, sharecroppers, tenant farmers, the unemployed, those on welfare, and other low-income people and mavericks from the leadership groups for whom civil rights included addressing poverty. It was, in effect, dealing with both class and race in its organizing work. Race, of course, was a unifying factor. But dealing with class meant also raising economic issues and the question of "qualifications" — i.e., overcoming the deference toward one's "betters" often found in a setting like Mississippi. SNCC lacked the tools to fully overcome this organizing challenge. But the challenge was made more difficult by the immediate focus on electoral politics.

### Should MFDP have accepted the two-seat "compromise"?

There was a time when I hardly entertained the question. Indeed, I was probably quite arrogant about it. All SNCC people at the time thought the offer was insulting at best. But over the years, I've had second thoughts. I come to the same conclusion — the offer wasn't enough. But I have some additional observations.

It is important to note that "compromise" isn't what was going on. President Lyndon Johnson said we're offering two seats and Aaron Henry and Rev. Edwin King are the people who will occupy them. This was a unilateral dictate, not the result of a negotiation. What if MFDP had said, "the number of seats is negotiable, but our delegation is going to name who fills them."

At the time, SNCC juxtaposed its "moral" position to the "pragmatic" politics of wheeling and dealing. But that's what politics is: wheeling and dealing. Indeed, when there is a rough equality among the parties, there's nothing the matter with wheeling and dealing when properly understood. Different groups have different interests and points of view. Politics is the means by which they make agreements so that we can all live together. That entails compromise. Nothing wrong with that. The alternative is war. Compromise becomes wrong when there are vast economic inequalities that distort the negotiating process or when there are whole groups of people excluded because of their race, religion, gender, economic status, or some other characteristic of their identity.

Having decided to play in the electoral arena, there are rules by which that game is played. To change those rules required power that the SNCC/MFDP alliance did not have. Lacking that power, the criteria for making the decision should not have been an abstract moral one, but an organizational one. Namely, will accepting a compromise contribute more than a rejection to strengthening our work so that we can more effectively pursue our moral ends? That remains a very good question. What the evidence points to is that it was Johnson, not the MFDP, that was unwilling to negotiate. For example, a compromise that divided the seating equally between the racists and the integrationists (MFDP invited White participation in it) would have been unacceptable to the regulars; they would have walked out.

### After the Convention

### Excerpt From 1965 Article

### *THE MFDP: BELONGS TO ITSELF*

*Just as the FDP raises fundamental questions and issues, so does it also function in a way that is frightening to the manners of polite society. The FDP is genuinely a party of the grass-roots people in Mississippi. They participate in and run the Party. Sharecroppers and domestics, laborers and unemployed, they make up and control the destiny of their Party. Because this kind of participation has become so alien to American political thinking (the Town Meeting was alright then, but after all ... ), many Doubting Thomases have questioned its existence. Generally, they advance a conspiracy theory regarding the FDP. It is, they say, manipulated from someplace else - - most frequently it is alleged that SNCC manipulates the FDP. And the more SNCC staff pulls out of Mississippi to begin work in other places where the movement has not yet begun to take hold, the more sinister is SNCC's control over the MFDP.*

*The two qualities of MFDP – its rank and file participation and its ability and desire to raise basic issues and questions - - are related. It is, after all, those who are hungry. ill-housed and ill-clothed, those who are denied the right to vote and who are beaten and abused by local police who are most likely to raise questions of poverty and civil rights. And because they have nothing to lose, having nothing to begin with, they are also least likely to "sell out". Thus, their participation in and control of the MFDP is intrinsic to its ability to remain a voice of honesty, dealing with central issues, refusing to substitute rhetorical gains for substantive victories. And it is here, in this area, that the day-to-day politics of the MFDP is fought out. For some time, it was argued that the Mississippi movement ought to be guided by a national Board of Directors that would include representatives of the major liberal and civil rights organizations in the Country. It was always SNCC's position – and others came to share it -- that such an idea was a direct violation of the spirit of "one man, one-vote." SNCC workers took the position that people who lived and worked in the State of Mississippi would have to be the ones who made the decisions. This did not mean that everyone had to automatically accept these decisions; it did, however, mean that control of decision making would have to be in the hands of the people of the State.*

*This decision has now been accepted -- in part because it is a reality, and, in part because some have come to see the merit of the view.*

*There tends to be a correlation between social status in the Negro community and the militancy advocated for the movement and the issues to be raised. The moderates tend to be the people with more status in the community -- whether this be the status of money or education or position. The moderates also tend to be the traditional leaders (or non-leaders) of the community, and this relates to the whole question of qualifications and who can participate in politics. There is now a new leadership in the State, built around people like Mrs. Hamer. Some of the people of status in the Negro community have joined with this new leadership in raising basic questions. Most have not.*

*The issue is particularly painful as the voting bill nears passage. Even on its face, the bill has serious inadequacies. In particular, it offers no protection against economic harassment against Negroes who seek to vote, nor is it clear why this bill will be any more forcefully executed than the many good laws already on the books. It is clear, however, that some Negroes are going to register to vote - - and that this number may, in some cases, be a key bloc vote able to carry primary elections or even general elections one way or the other. So basic questions are raised. Will Negroes continue to support the MFDP and its present positions?*

*Will Negroes support white "moderates" when they run against blatant racists? ...*

*Whatever the future for MFDP, it constitutes, in the eyes of many, the most exciting political event of the post World War II era. Whether the MFDP will be able to maintain itself as a movement of the poor or whether it is only the first in the development of new movements at the grass roots level that are soon to join in the development of a program that addresses' itself to the basic problems of the society can only, at this point, be a question.*

MFDP became a target for the national leadership of the Democratic Party who sought, with whatever means were at their disposal, to bypass MFDP's principal leadership. State NAACP Chair Aaron Henry abandoned MFDP and became a key figure in the emerging new Democratic Party formation within Mississippi. Unfortunately, the remaining MFDP leadership lacked the depth of base at home to force the Democrat Party establishment to deal with it as the voice of Black Mississippians. Lawrence Guyot, Victoria Jackson Gray (Adams), and Annie Devine continued working in movement politics, but after 1968 Fannie Lou Hamer withdrew to her home in Ruleville where she started the Freedom Farm Cooperative and otherwise engaged in local non-electoral work. Guyot, a brilliant tactician, did the best that could be done by a leader who didn't have many resources at his disposal. Too often, deference to more middle-class leadership combined with patronage combined with doubts about SNCC's militant rhetoric provided openings at the base to the new political configuration that MFDP leaders could not overcome. They thus had to find a path between cooptation and isolation. They couldn't find it because by this time it didn't exist. Though they were part of the 1968 delegation that was seated, they were a distinct minority, and their fortunes as a statewide party (there remained pockets of strength in some counties) declined precipitously afterward.

The SNCC/MFDP legacy remains in the state, expressed in the 2013 election of Jackson's mayor, Chokwe Lumumba — who tragically died in February 2014 before he could put his agenda for reform in place. In 2017, that victory was repeated with the election of his son, Chokwe Antar Lumumba, Jr., who promised that his city would become "the most radical on the planet." He described himself as a "Fannie Lou

Hamer Democrat." It is also expressed in the persistence of various local organizations and organizing that carry on the SNCC tradition.

**Question: What lessons are there for today when we think about the relationship between community organizing and electoral politics?**

In those days, SNCC people, myself included, thought that we organized while Martin Luther King, Jr.'s Southern Christian Leadership Conference (SCLC) mobilized. It is an important distinction. Indeed, it continues to play itself out in the multiple revolutions taking place around the world — Egypt being the clearest recent example of a direct-action mobilization, and Syriza in Greece being an example of an electoral one.

Our formulation of the issue was too one-dimensional. We ignored the fact that SCLC often mobilized through deeply rooted local organizations, namely through the Black churches. As I heard former Mississippian Rev. Dr. Amos C. Brown say, "The Black church is the only institution we own lock, stock and barrel." While SNCC organized many church people, particularly the women of the churches, and while pastors were often pushed from within by their own members to endorse SNCC's work, most of these pastors were never wholeheartedly in "The Movement." When an alternative opened, they moved toward it — and often took most of their congregation with them.

SNCC, on the other hand, was deeply influenced by Ella Baker, who was suspicious of the kind of strong leadership exercised by most Black pastors. She had a lifetime of experience in dealing with it. As she put it, "strong people don't need strong leaders." She saw organization as key to developing strong people. But building strong organization outside the framework of the Black church proved to be a difficult proposition. Indeed, often the strong people around whom Baker imagined organization being built were, themselves, reluctant to see others develop. Amzie Moore, one of the Delta's most courageous Black strong people and one of Bob Moses' first contacts in the state, was himself rather controlling within his own turf in Bolivar County.

The organizing versus mobilizing discussion doesn't go away. But framing it simply in these terms is a mistake: It is not simply mobilization versus organization. Rather, the questions should be: Is organization the vehicle through which mobilization takes place? Is organization built or strengthened during a period of mobilization? What kind of organization are we talking about to begin with?

Sometimes mobilizations are close to spontaneous: An outrage takes place and thousands of people express their anger by taking to the streets. For example, see the film *Detroit* for a portrayal of race riot/insurrection pre-Martin Luther King, Jr.'s assassination, or take the Watts Rebellion in Los Angeles in 1965. Sometimes a relatively small activist or cadre organization mobilizes large numbers of people in response to a crisis; when the mobilization is over, the same relatively small organization remains — with possibly a few additional recruits.

There is an additional combination of organizing and mobilizing, and it is not alien to the American experience. The organization of industrial workers in the 1930s is the best example. In city after city across the United States, the Congress of Industrial Organizations (CIO) built strong union locals in the context of dramatic mobilizations of workers and confrontations with their employers. These locals, and the internationals of which they were a part, reached deeply into the lives of their members, and extended that reach to their families and the communities in which they lived — making an impact on politics and community life. The best of them pursued a program of "Black and White, unite and fight" and implemented it.

In Chicago's Back of the Yards Neighborhood Council (BYNC), with Saul Alinsky and Joe Meegan the principal organizers, a mass-based community organization brought the packinghouse workers union together with Catholic parishes and other neighborhood groups to create the people power to force the "Big Six" meat packing companies to recognize the union and negotiate a contract with it. They also won a number of additional important benefits for its neighborhood from the city's political machine.

## A Different Strategy for These Times?

Two propositions:

- Political parties tend to be run by politicians who have a deep interest in controlling them. Thus, "member-run political parties" tend to be a contradiction in terms. International experience in democracies confirms this.
- Politicians tend to have an interest in moving up to higher offices. Thus, they have in mind two constituencies — the one that elected them and the one that they hope will elect them. Further, their eyes are focused not only on voters but on who will pay for election campaigns.

What if COFO, instead of sponsoring a new political party, had sponsored a new statewide, non-partisan, dues-paying membership-based, multi-issue organization with chapters in cities, towns, and rural areas throughout the state? What if this organization had demanded that the Democratic Party refuse seats to the "regulars" but had not demanded seats for itself, leaving to politicians the formation of a statewide party *that it would hold accountable* — in the same way that today money power holds both Republicans and Democrats accountable? What if this new organization adopted a platform, widely publicized it, informed the electorate where candidates for office stood on that platform, then registered and turned out voters in a coming election? And, after the election, what if this people power organization continued to hold elected officials accountable to implement their election campaign promises?

What if, in addition to its electoral activities, there was a strategically balanced program that included:

- Direct negotiations backed up with "Main Street" boycotts with local employers (over hiring and respectful service issues) and with local governments (over police treatment, city services — black topping roads, street lights, drainage, etc., — voter registration, public accommodations, and school desegregation)?
- Self-help and mutual aid done through buying clubs, producer and consumer cooperatives, support groups of various kinds, and other means that, on their face, appear more conservative because they don't involve direct confrontation with the powers that be?
- Workplace organization with the possibility of national and international boycotts to place pressure on producers of products bearing a "made in Mississippi" label?
- Large delegations lobbying politicians on issues of concern and letting the electorate know how the politicians are responding with an eye toward creating good and/or bad records for them come the next election? And the same kind of lobbying in relation to various governmental agencies whose programs are supposed to serve the people but don't?
- Continuous internal cultural, educational, and social programs that create and deepen a small "d" democratic life in the people power organization?

I think it is in these directions that today's people power builders need to look. If they fail to do so, they risk the fate of SNCC/MFDP — creating roads and vehicles to ride on them that don't reach their liberation destination because, before they can, someone else takes them over.

## About the Author

Mike Miller was a leader in the pre-1960s birth of the student movement at University of California Berkeley, a Student Nonviolent Coordinating Committee field secretary from 1962-end of 1966, and director of a Saul Alinsky community organizing project. As Director of ORGANIZE Training Center, he has initiated organizing projects, led organizing workshops, mentored organizers, and consulted widely in the field. He taught community organizing at University of California Berkeley, University of Wisconsin/Milwaukee, San Francisco State and Stanford, among other universities. His books include *The People Fight Back: Building a Tenant Union*; *A Community Organizer's Tale: People and Power in San Francisco*; *People Power: The Community Organizing Tradition of Saul Alinsky (Aaron Schutz, co-editor)*; and *Community Organizing: A Brief Introduction*; as well as numerous articles on labor and community organizing, politics, and related fields. For more information visit http://www.organizetrainingcenter.org.

# CHAPTER 21

# RACE AGAINST TIME: A REPORTER REOPENS THE UNSOLVED MURDER CASES OF THE CIVIL RIGHTS ERA

JERRY MITCHELL

## INTRODUCTION

By Susan J. Erenrich

This chapter is written by award-winning journalist Jerry Mitchell. Through investigative reporting and the art of storytelling, Jerry has been leading through example since 1986. In his book, *Race Against Time: A Reporter Reopens the Unsolved Murder Cases of the Civil Rights Era*, Jerry documents his decades-long pursuit of justice, helping to solve some of the most heinous murders of the civil rights era in the United States. Despite a multitude of roadblocks, Jerry persevered in his work, which contributed to convictions in several unsolved murders perpetrated by members of the Ku Klux Klan.

Jerry graciously agreed to share a shortened version of his narrative for this volume to illustrate how a little courage and determination by a single individual can lead to change. **It is important to warn readers upfront that the subject matter is horrific and much of the language recapped in the interviews Jerry conducted is offensive.** No matter how distasteful the speech may be, however, grassroots leaders should listen. We will never be able to combat this type of hostility, if we don't understand what is in the hearts and minds of the haters. Even Jerry, knowledgeable as he is, was deeply shocked by some of what he heard.

This is not the first time that an author has tried to capture what is in the soul of a killer Klansman. On June 28, 1963, shortly after the assassination of Medgar Evers, acclaimed Mississippi writer Eudora Welty penned a fictional story for the *New Yorker* titled, "Where Is the Voice Coming From" (https://www.newyorker.com/magazine/1963/ 07/06/where-is-the-voice-coming-from). When commenting on the piece, Welty said: "I wrote from the interior…that world of hate that I felt I had grown up with and I felt I could speak as someone who knew it" (as quoted in Pollack and Marrs, 2001, pp. 10–11).

I first met Jerry around 1992. At the time, Jerry was a long-time reporter for *The Clarion-Ledger* in Jackson, Mississippi and I was editing a book titled, *Freedom Is a Constant Struggle: An Anthology of the Mississippi Civil Rights Movement, which was reissued in 2021.* Jerry unabashedly handed over Horace Doyle Barnette's November 24, 1964, FBI (Federal Bureau of Investigation) confession regarding Barnette's involvement in the Mississippi Burning killings for inclusion in the book.

In his 1992 introduction to the document, Jerry writes: "Consider this fact: more than 3,449 Black Americans lost their lives in lynchings in the U.S. in the century following the Civil War" (as quoted in Erenrich, 1999, p.344). We now know that number is vastly underreported. In the latest report issued in 2020 by the Equal Justice Initiative (EJI), *Reconstruction in America,* however, the organization has documented 6,500 racial terror lynchings in this country between 1865 and 1950. Thousands more Black people have been murdered by White mob lynchings whose deaths may never be discovered. Jerry concluded his introduction by stating the following: "What this nation needs is its own Nuremberg-like trials to see that those who killed with impunity are finally punished. What the South needs is a chance at redemption to purge the past that has long plagued its present" (as quoted in Erenrich, 1999, p. 345).

Thirty national awards later, including a 2009 MacArthur Fellow "Genius Grant," Jerry is still at it. He no longer works for the *Clarion-Ledger*. Instead, he founded the Mississippi Center for Investigative Reporting, a nonprofit that allows him to continue his work exposing injustices as well as growing a new generation of investigative reporters.

I hope readers are both disturbed and inspired by Jerry's article and that his urgent message sparks a deeper conversation about this somber topic.

## References

Erenrich, S. (1999). *Freedom Is a Constant Struggle: An Anthology of the Mississippi Civil Rights Movement*. Black Belt Press.

Equal Justice Initiative. (2020). *Reconstruction in America: Racial Violence After the Civil War, 1865-1876*. https://eji.org/report/reconstruction-in-america/

Mississippi Center for Investigative Reporting. https://www.mississippicir.org/

Mitchell, J. (2020). *Race Against Time: A Reporter Reopens the Unsolved Murder Cases of the Civil Rights Era*. Simon & Schuster.

Pollack, H. and Marrs, S. (2001). *Eudora Welty & Politics: Did the Writer Crusade*. Louisiana State University Press.

## RACE AGAINST TIME: A REPORTER REOPENS THE UNSOLVED MURDER CASES OF THE CIVIL RIGHTS ERA

By Jerry Mitchell

I am a muckraker.

I know. I know. It's not fashionable to be a muckraker anymore. Or at least that's what I've been told.

Plenty of people misunderstand what muckraking is. They think it's the press capturing celebrities in compromising positions with cell phone texts, photos, and videos. Or they think it's reporters obsessed with smearing politicians.

Muckraking is much different and was best summed up by the late American journalist Finley Peter Dunne who quipped that journalism's role was to "comfort the afflicted and afflict the comfortable." It's a philosophy sadly lacking in this age of social media, where notoriety and fame are hardly distinguishable and where one person's pain represents the possibility of another reality TV series.

For much of my journalism career, I have felt like a dinosaur, hopelessly out of step with the times. Lately, however, I sense that I'm not alone. I sense that journalists of a new generation are waking up and wondering how they, too, can use the tools of muckraking to effect change in a society sorely in need of change.

———

I don't know if you're like me, but if somebody tells me I can't have something, I want it a million times worse. Mississippi had a segregationist spy agency, which had collected spy files on more than 10,000 people and 250 groups it deemed "subversive, militant, or revolutionary." The governor himself headed that spy cabal in hopes of heading off any attempt by the federal government or others to desegregate, amassing more than 132,000 pages of records. That was a number I could hardly wrap my head around. When I found out that the Mississippi Legislature had sealed all those records for 50 years, my first thought was — there must be something in those records.

A tip from a fellow reporter at *The Clarion-Ledger*, where I worked, led me to a federal court file that contained a sealed spy report accidentally made public. The story on the file led me to longtime civil rights activist Ken Lawrence, who explained that he had to sign an agreement with a federal judge to keep quiet about the contents of the Sovereignty Commission that he had seen. I pressed him anyway.

"I regard the state law sealing these files as unconstitutional, but I don't want to go to jail," he said. "And that's what Judge Barbour [William H. Barbour, Jr.] will do if I tell you what's inside these files."

"But don't you think everybody should know what the commission did?"

"Listen, I want these files opened more than you do. Don't you understand? I want everyone to know every despicable thing that this commission did. I want the people responsible to be punished."

"Responsible for what?"

He chuckled. "Nice try, Jerry."

I tried a different tack. Instead of asking for specific details, I asked for a hint of what was contained in the files.

"What do *you* think is connected in the files?" he asked.

"I don't know."

"Take a guess."

"The state committed more theft?"

"No, no, worse than that."

"I don't know."

"C'mon, what's the worst crime imaginable?"

"Murder."

Silence followed, the most deafening I have heard.

Moments later, he spoke. "Now do you understand?"

————

I began to develop other sources, which eventually led me to a cache of 2,400 pages of these spy files. They showed that at the same time the state was prosecuting Byron De La Beckwith for Medgar Evers' murder, the spy agency was secretly assisting Byron De La Beckwith's defense, trying to get him acquitted.

My story ran October 1, 1989. At the time, the odds were more than a million to one against the case being reopened. There was no transcript, no murder weapon, no other evidence.

But Myrlie Evers [Medgar's widow] believed, and she prayed, and some amazing things happened. Not long after that, Jackson police were cleaning out a closet and found a box containing crime scene photos of Medgar Evers' murder, including the fingerprint of Beckwith, lifted from the murder weapon. A few months later, Myrlie Evers shared with me her copy of the old trial transcript. A few months after that, the prosecutor found the murder weapon in his father-in-law's closet.

It didn't take much reading to learn that two all-White juries had failed to agree on a verdict for Beckwith in 1964. It didn't take much more reading to learn that, by all appearances, he had gotten away with murder.

Old newspaper stories and magazine articles portrayed him as the lone, obsessed assassin, determined to kill the NAACP's number one man in Mississippi. The case against Beckwith had certainly been convincing. His high-powered rifle had been found near the murder scene, complete with his fingerprint. Witnesses placed his white Valiant, with his law enforcement–like whip antenna, near the scene. Two taxi drivers testified that he had asked directions to the NAACP leader's home a few days earlier. When FBI agents arrested him, they found a circled cut around his right eye, and Beckwith admitted it had come from firing his rifle. If all that weren't enough, his words provided a motive. "The NAACP, under the direction of its leadership," he wrote in a letter to the *Jackson Daily News*, "is doing a first-class job of getting itself in a position to be exterminated!" (as quoted in Mitchell, 2020, p. 53).

In his defense, Beckwith offered an alibi. Two policemen testified he was more than ninety miles away, in Greenwood, a half hour from the time Medgar Evers was killed in Jackson. Beckwith maintained his .30-06 Enfield rifle had been stolen days earlier. Prosecutors weren't helped by the fact that Ross Barnett, who had served as Mississippi's governor until days before the first trial began, attended the trial and showed his support, shaking hands with Beckwith.

Jurors deadlocked 7–5 in favor of finding him not guilty. At his second trial, jurors deadlocked again, this time even closer to acquittal. After that, prosecutors dropped the case, and Beckwith returned home to the Mississippi Delta a hero.

When I telephoned him, I brought up the Sovereignty Commission, which he praised as a "good and wholesome" organization. "I was very disturbed with those who brought it to the close." Back in 1956, he had unsuccessfully applied to work for the commission. He assured the governor then that he was an "expert with a pistol, good with a rifle, and fair with a shot gun [sic]," vowing to "tear the mask from the face of the NAACP and forever rid this fair land of the DISEASE OF INTEGRATION!"

He talked about his two murder trials for "killing that [N-word]. Every once in a while, I see his picture in the paper. He is a high yellow, a very light-skinned [N-word]. His brother is as black as soot. There's no true bloodline. They're just mongrels. God hates mongrels. To adulterate is to mix blood. It's forbidden in scripture and forbidden in society."

The longer he talked, the more racism he spewed. Part of me wanted to argue back, but the other part of me, the journalist, knew that the best thing I could do would be to keep him talking.

"So, who killed Medgar Evers?" I asked.

"I don't know who killed him, and I don't care."

I asked him if he felt any sympathy toward the family.

"I feel about as much compassion for the Medgar Evers family as a [N-word] getting run over by a streetcar in Chicago." He cackled. "Do they still have streetcars in Chicago?"

His laugh seemed to hang in the air as the conversation ended. What kind of man cracks a joke like that, finding joy in the grief of a family? A man named Byron De La Beckwith.

———

Nothing attracted me to the idea of another conversation with the man I considered a racist killer, but I knew if I didn't, the case would remain stuck, and he would remain free, just as he had been for the past quarter century. I also knew I'd get the most out of him if I went to chat with him in person.

As I snaked up the winding road to his home in Signal Mountain, Tennessee, my stereo blared the Beatles' song *Everybody's Got Something to Hide*....

As I turned onto Albion Way, I figured out I had the right address when the number matched the one written on my notepad. I knew I had the right address when I saw the David Duke bumper sticker and the Confederate battle flag flapping in the wind.

Over the next six hours, Beckwith spewed a torrent of warped and hateful views. He said that any opponent of the White Christian way of life should be punished "quietly, secretly, and mysteriously. The Klan must once again become a submarine and stop acting like a tank." As he described his version of Christianity, it was utterly alien — a place where only faithful White people could be saved, where those of African descent are no more than soulless animals, and where those of Jewish descent are the literal offspring of Satan. He told me that all those stories I had heard in Sunday school were lies. He clasped a black leather Bible in his hand, opening the book to make a point with his jagged finger. "[N-word]s are beasts. It says so in here in the book of Adam."

He explained he was part of the Christian Identity Movement, flipping over to the book of Genesis and reading aloud about the Garden of Eden. "It says here, 'There was no man to till the soil.' The word 'man' in Hebrew is 'adam,' which literally means 'blood in the face.' Now, blood in the face means when you blush. Now you ain't never seen a [N-word] or a Jew blush. We all know that the White race is the only one that can blush."

The more he talked, the more I felt I had stumbled upon a backwoods preacher before the snake-handling part of the service began. He said our White ancestors were the true children of God, that Jesus was a "Hebrew," and that "anyone who calls Jesus a Jew is blaspheming." He mentioned the Caucasus Mountains. "That's why we're called Caucasians," he whispered, as if sharing a centuries-old secret.

The veins in his neck jutted out. He went on an antisemitic rant, claiming Jews possessed satanic powers, and that one day, the "true Israelites" would destroy these Jews.

When I asked him about being charged with murdering Medgar Evers, he instead suggested the real killer was Lee Harvey Oswald. I figured he would deflect, but I almost laughed out loud at the absurdity of his answer.

Instead, he talked of his own later conviction in 1975. He had been caught with a time bomb made up of six sticks of dynamite. In his car, New Orleans police found a map marked all the way to the home of Jewish leader A. I. Botnick, who headed the regional office for the Anti- Defamation League. This time, a jury convicted Beckwith. He insisted to me that he had been set up, saying that he had traveled to New Orleans to appraise china his grandmother received as a gift from Jefferson Davis's widow. He blamed his conviction on the "little Jewish prosecutor" and the "[N-word] women" on the jury.

He talked of his home state of Mississippi and bragged about it having more churches per capita than any other state. "That's a fact — till the [N-word]s started having all those holy roller meetings and NAACP meetings in those churches. Then they began to burn down." He paused. "You know, [N-word]s are careless with matches."

He cackled, his voice echoing through the house. He was his own perfect audience. I felt overwhelmed, stunned that such a person could exist, let alone that he could be celebrated — and worse — protected by those in power.

Outside the window, the sun had already slipped behind the redbud trees and darkness had begun to cover the mountain. I mentioned it was time to go, and his wife slid a turkey sandwich inside my briefcase.

He grabbed a flashlight, opened the door, and stepped outside. "Let me walk you to your car."

"That isn't necessary."

He walked ahead of me anyway, his flashlight slicing through the gloom. When I opened the driver's door on my Honda and moved to step in, he blocked my way. He glared at me, shadows covering his face.

"God will bless you if you write positive things about White Caucasian Christians. If you write negative things about White Caucasian Christians, God will punish you."

He paused, then locked eyes. "If God does not punish you directly, several individuals will do it for him."

He stepped aside, and I closed the door.

I was glad to have something, even just a pane of glass, between him and me.

I couldn't start the engine fast enough. As I drove down the street, I never looked back. I pressed the gas and sped down the mountain, hoping to make it out of town before the darkness closed in around me.

———

Just before he was arrested for murdering Medgar Evers, Beckwith made clear what he thought: "I'm willing to lay my life down to rid evil from this country. I'm willing to kill the evil in this country that would push me out."

On October 3, 1990, I learned of at least one person he considered evil. After losing his extradition battle, he was now forced to appear in a Mississippi courtroom. Upon entering, in handcuffs, he spotted me and exclaimed, "Speak of the devil!"

After appeals and court delays, Beckwith finally went on trial in January 1994. Jury selection led to nearly two weeks of testimony, and the jury began to deliberate as a huge storm hit Jackson. The next morning, the jury returned to the courtroom with their verdict: guilty.

In that moment, Myrlie Evers would later tell me, she felt all the hate rushing out the pores of her body. She and her daughter held hands and wept. Darrell let out a whoop, and a few in the audience said, "Yeah, yeah."

Beckwith sat still in his Confederate gray suit while his family burst into tears. His wife sobbed.

The judge pounded his gavel. "Order in the court."

As the courtroom grew silent, I heard waves of joy cascading down the hall until they reached a foyer full of people, Black and White. The crowd erupted in cheers, and I felt a chill because the impossible had suddenly become possible.

When I finally stepped outside the courtroom, I noticed that the rain had stopped. I felt lighter, relieved of the burden I had not realized I had been carrying for the past five years. It was over. It was really over. Byron De La Beckwith had been convicted of murdering Medgar Evers.

———

The new charge in Medgar Evers' murder brought hope to more than one hundred families. They had seen their mothers, fathers, sisters, and brothers die at the hands of hate — gunned down, drowned, burned, and blown up. The trail of civil rights cold cases stretched beyond Mississippi and beyond the South to much of the rest of the nation.

Many of these families had been calling for justice long before a grand jury indicted Byron De La Beckwith in December 1990, but his charge gave them the leverage they felt they needed to prod authorities into reopening these cases.

Months after Beckwith's indictment, a man named Dennis Dahmer (pronounced "DAY-mer") telephoned me. As a child, he dreamed of becoming a doctor, but after his father's murder, he felt lost, struggling in the classroom. When he saw his mother weep over his grades, he rallied. He became a salesman with a Fortune 500 corporation and later started his own business, selling bioresearch laboratory equipment. But for him, the defining day of his life remained January 10, 1966 — the day the KKK attacked his family. If not for the courage of his father, Vernon Sr., who died defending them, he said, Klansmen "probably would have killed us all."

His mother, Ellie Dahmer, wept as she told me about her husband, Vernon Dahmer, a farmer and NAACP leader dedicated to voting rights. The Klan hated him for that and attacked him and his family the night of January 10, 1966. They firebombed the house and fired their guns inside. Vernon Dahmer woke up, grabbed his shotgun, ran to the front of the house, and returned fire so that his wife and children could escape safely out a back window.

But the blaze seared his lungs. After he and the family were taken to the hospital, she said he had to breathe from an oxygen tank because of the damage to his lungs.

"I thought he was getting better," she told me.

She choked with emotion, her lips quivering. "I guess you see what you want."

At the time of the attack, Vernon Dahmer had four sons in the armed forces. They had defended their nation — only to return home and find that none of their countrymen were defending them.

A few weeks after the funeral, his voter registration card arrived. He had spent his whole life fighting for the right of all Americans to vote but never had been able to cast a ballot himself.

The man who ordered the killing was Sam Bowers. He headed the White Knights of the Ku Klux Klan in Mississippi — the most violent Klan organization in the United States, responsible for at least 10 killings. He had been tried but never convicted in the killing.

The district attorney agreed to look at the case, only to get cold feet. I had almost given up on the case when a mystery man called me in 1997. Turned out he overheard Bowers give the orders to kill Vernon Dahmer. The case was reopened.

The key witness against Bowers had been Billy Roy Pitts, who had been involved in the killing, dropped his gun, got caught, turned state's evidence, and pleaded guilty to murder. In 1998, I discovered he had never served a single day of his life sentence in Mississippi.

But I had no idea where he was. I knew of one website that didn't require a city or state, so I typed in his name. The website gave me his name, address in Denham Springs, Louisiana, and his phone number.

The first 20 minutes of the conversation went like this: "How'd you find me? How'd you find me?"

"The Internet."

"The Internet? I've got an unlisted phone number."

As a result of my story, authorities issued a warrant for his arrest. He didn't like that. In fact, he ran. While he was on the run, he mailed me an audiocassette: "Jerry, I just want you to know you've ruined my life. But I promised you that if I talked to anybody, I'd talk to you."

And he proceeded to tell me all about his involvement in killing Vernon Dahmer, all of his involvement in this other Klan violence. A few days later, he turned himself in to authorities, and this led to the arrests of Sam Bowers and his right-hand man, Deavours Nix, who headed the Klan Bureau of Investigation.

At his bond hearing, his family pushed him into the courtroom in a wheelchair. The seventy-two-year-old man held a green tank as he breathed oxygen, something he told the judge he had to do all the time. He said radiation treatments had burned up his lungs — a choice of words that could only make me think of Vernon Dahmer. Nix also told the judge he was confined to a wheelchair. The judge said he did not usually release criminal defendants without bond, but he would make an exception in this case because of Nix's poor health.

Eleven days later, I telephoned Nix. I wanted to learn more about the man, and I found him surprisingly forthcoming. He talked about golf and then the White Knights. He confirmed belonging to the KKK — something few Klansmen ever did. Then he talked again of golf, boasting about his plan to hit the greens. "I'm going to be down at the first tee at Bear Creek Golf Club at eight thirty in the morning."

Here was a man too sick to go to jail, or even post bond, because he was bound to a wheelchair, breathing oxygen. Now he was going to play golf?

The next morning, a *Clarion-Ledger* photographer snapped pictures of Nix whacking his ball down the fairway of the 6,832-yard course. He carried his oxygen tank in the back of the golf cart.

My story ran with pictures in the next day's newspaper, and after seeing them, the judge had Nix jailed. "If you're well enough to play golf," the judge barked, "you're well enough to post bond."

———

Members of the Vernon Dahmer family took the witness stand to share with jurors what happened that night. Ellie Dahmer testified that she woke at about 2 a.m. to a stuck car horn, hearing bullets pelting the house and realizing that their home was on fire. Dennis Dahmer recalled a wall of fire outside his bedroom and choked back tears as he described seeing the family grocery store, where his great-aunt lived, engulfed in flames.

The testimony of Bettie Dahmer, only ten at the time, captivated jurors as she recounted fleeing from the flames as they seared her skin. After the family escaped to a nearby barn, she said, "My father was sitting there on a bale of hay with the skin hanging off of his arms, but he never complained the whole time he was there. The only thing he was concerned about was us ... He wanted to know we were all right."

She held out her arms, covered with pink scars, and her fingers, still gnarled from the blaze. That night, she had rolled on the cold ground, trying to stem the throbbing pain.

In cross-examination, Buckley sought to prove that his client was nowhere near the crime. "Miz Dahmer," he said, "you, of course, didn't see anything that happened that night."

"I saw my house burn," she shot back, hot tears streaming down her face. "I saw the skin hanging off my daddy's arms. I saw that."

Buckley suggested she and her family wanted to strike back in anger.

"No, Mr. Buckley. I just want my daddy to have the same justice that everybody else in America can have. That's all I want."

———

Billy Roy Pitts and other Klan witnesses recalled Bowers giving the orders to kill Dahmer. Pitts said he guarded a Klansman who took his pocketknife, jabbed holes in one jug, and used a forked stick with a rag as a fuse. The firebomb smashed through the Dahmers' living room window. Pitts crouched on the corner of the house, his quick-draw holster on his hip, ready to pull out his .22-caliber Magnum and kill anyone who came. No one did, but before Pitts left, "I heard a man's voice. Sounded like someone in distress."

Cathy Dunn, the ex-wife of one of Bowers's best Klan leaders, recalled Bowers visiting their home days later. Dressed neatly in a white suit with a red tie, the Klan leader strode in, clutching a folded-up newspaper that contained a headline and story about the killing of Dahmer. When he unfolded the paper for the Dunns, he pointed to the headline and smiled. "Did you see what a good job my boys did?"

The testimony seemed to send a chill through the courtroom, the cold reality of a Klan leader beaming over his bloodshed. After Cathy Dunn left the witness stand, she told me that her then-husband, Burris, bragged about jobs the White Knights carried out, including bombings, cross burnings, and other violence. Just as terrorists have cells, she told me, "The Klan had groups that would go and pick up somebody, kill them, and bury their body."

She said her husband, Bowers, and other Klansmen regularly listened to tapes of the sermons of Christian Identity preacher Wesley Swift, whose racist teachings included that Adam and Eve were White, that non-Whites have no souls, and that Jews were the offspring of Satan. Before 1967 ended, the White Knights began bombing Jewish homes and synagogues.

After several hours of deliberations, the jury convicted Bowers, who was sentenced to life in prison like Beckwith. The Dahmer family wept, and as they existed the courthouse, the crowd outside applauded them. "Oh, this is a happy moment for us," Ellie Dahmer said, surrounded by her children. "It is a moment we have been waiting for for about thirty years."

The more tears she wiped away, the more followed. "These are tears of joy. I am shedding them for Vernon because I know he is looking at us today."

Back home, the family gathered on the front lawn beneath the shade of the towering oaks. Friends drove by. They honked their horns and yelled out in victory. The joy of justice had finally come.

———

The last thing I expected in 1999 was an invitation to interview a Klansman who happened to be one of the last living suspects in the 1963 Birmingham church bombing that killed four girls, Addie Mae Collins, Denise McNair, Carole Robertson, and Cynthia Wesley, who were in the girls' bathroom in the basement of the Sixteenth Street Baptist Church, getting ready for the youth service after a Sunday school lesson titled, "A Love That Forgives." When the clock struck 10:22 a.m., a bomb hidden beneath the church's outside stairs exploded, killing them and injuring dozens of others.

That Klansman was Bobby Cherry. I took him and his wife to eat barbecue in Gun Barrel City, Texas. Rib bones stacked up, and Cherry licked remnants of sauce from his fingers. "Before I die, I want my name cleared. I didn't have nothing to do with that bombing."

Back at his home, the tall man with the bulbous nose and the wavy gray hair said he joined the Klan in 1957 because "I didn't like the communistic way things were going." Soon after, his chapter of the KKK joined with several other chapters to form the United Klans of America, Alabama's equivalent of the White Knights, led by Imperial Wizard Robert Shelton. "We figured if we all got together, we'd have a stronger voters' league." Cherry worked as a security guard for the KKK, guarding both Shelton and Alabama governor George Wallace, who "called all the shots." He said he quit the group a year before the bombing, but acknowledged he continued to keep company with these Klansmen. Then he began to rail against the FBI, saying they started harassing him after the 1963 church bombing.

"Tell me about it," I replied.

"The day before that, I was up there at Snow's Modern Sign Company," just a few blocks from the Sixteenth Street Baptist Church. While inside the company, he said he ran a silk machine to make Confederate battle flags and signs for White protesters outside an all-White Birmingham school "to keep their kids from going to integrated schools."

That night, he said, about six men walked inside Modern Sign Company, including Bob Chambliss and Thomas Blanton. In 1977, Chambliss had been convicted of making the bomb that killed the girls. Blanton was the other still living suspect.

Cherry said he left the sign shop that night at a quarter till ten, because he was heading home to watch live Studio Wrestling on local TV. This was part of his Saturday routine, he said. He also mentioned another reason for heading home that night — doctors had recently diagnosed his wife with cancer — in 1961, or maybe 1962 — giving her six months to live. "They sent her home to die four or five times, but she straightened back up. She lived till March 1968."

Cherry said that on the night before the bombing, a friend of the family, Flora Thomas, came over to help take care of his wife. He handed me her 1980 sworn statement in which she said Cherry "was at home at 10 o'clock Saturday night because he never missed wrestling on TV. I stayed up most of the night due to sickness in the family. Bobby never left the house."

When I asked Cherry about an FBI report that said he was seen hours before the bombing, planting a bomb outside the church, he shot back that it was a lie. "Shit, I was home before wrestling. I always made sure I was home for wrestling."

The next morning, he said he woke up about nine and returned to the Modern Sign Company. "I went up there to get them signs. That's when I found out about the bombing. I left [at] about fifteen to ten to go up there." Cherry said the bomb exploded before he ever got to the sign shop. He saw a "fire wagon go down there," and when he arrived he could hear "the sirens all settling down." When the owner of the sign shop, Merle Snow, returned, Snow told them people outside the church were saying "some of these White folks done blowed the church up down yonder and the Ku Klux done it."

Cherry told me he passed two lie detector tests for the FBI but failed a third because the technician bumped the needle. He shared a copy of the test, in which he was asked, "Have you ever been present when a bombing was planned?" The polygraph examiner concluded Cherry showed "evidence of deception." The examiner reported that Cherry showed a "strong reaction" to the question: "On Friday night, was Tommy Blanton with you making a bomb?" Cherry also reacted to the question, "Did you bomb the Sixteenth Street Baptist Church?"

Back at *The Clarion-Ledger*, our librarian obtained copies of television schedules that showed it was impossible for Cherry to have been watching televised wrestling that night because there was no wrestling to watch.

When I telephoned Cherry back to ask him about these schedules that poked holes in his alibi, he replied, "Son of a bitch, something's wrong. Wrestling was on."

At trial, prosecutors introduced the television logs to show there was no wrestling, and a jury convicted Cherry, who was given four life sentences. One for each of the girls.

————

Once again, I was told I couldn't have something, and once again, I wanted it more than ever. It turned out that Imperial Wizard Sam Bowers, who never gave interviews, gave an interview with the Mississippi Department of Archives and History. Unfortunately, it was sealed.

Over time, I developed sources, who let me read a copy of that interview in which the Klan leader talked about their 1964 killings of three civil rights workers, James Chaney, Andy Goodman, and Mickey Schwerner. Bowers, who had ordered the killings, referred to himself as "a criminal and a lunatic," justifying lynchings and killings as ways of preserving the Southern way of life: "Citizens not only have a right but a duty to preserve their culture."

"By taking someone's life, though?" he was asked.

"If that person wants to put his life on the line in order to destroy that culture, yes."

Just as I'd been hoping, Bowers didn't hold back on the subject of the Mississippi Burning case. He said he threw his might into frustrating the investigation and said authorities "could have gotten me for obstruction of justice." When the jury convicted him, he said he felt no anger. "I was quite delighted to be convicted and have the main instigator of the entire affair walk out of the courtroom a free man. Everybody — including the trial judge and the prosecutors and everybody else — knows that that happened."

The imperial wizard's words banged around in my brain. Bowers was taunting the federal authorities, bragging that "the main instigator" in the killings of the three civil rights workers had walked free. Who was he talking about? Edgar Ray Killen, also known as "Preacher" Killen.

When I reached him by telephone, he had no trouble talking and no worries that the case would ever be resurrected. He seemed comfortable talking now, so I brought up Bowers' statement. I read what the KKK leader said about the "main instigator" walking away a free man, asking Killen what he thought.

Killen hesitated and then spoke. "I don't know what main instigator he's talking about." He insisted he didn't even know Bowers until they met at the 1967 trial. Testimony from the trial told a different story — that Killen had received orders from Bowers to kill Schwerner.

When it came time for Killen's defense, his lawyer had put witnesses on the stand who insisted the preacher had spent his night at the funeral home, where there were two wakes, including one for a young child. I wondered if his alibi might trip him up all these years later, just as it had Bobby Cherry.

"Now, I understand you had an alibi," I said.

He launched into a description of being at the funeral home that night. "It wasn't a setup alibi. It was something unplanned," he said. "Country folks, if we set up, we'd set up with family."

Nothing like a Klansman to explain the right way to set up an alibi.

All the same, I was grateful that he was eager to talk. So, I asked Killen a question I had been waiting to ask, about how he saw things decades later: "What do you think should happen to the people who killed these three men?"

He paused and answered, "I'm not going to say they were wrong."

He continued. "I don't believe in murder. I believe in self-defense."

It sounded like a line he had been repeating to himself for years.

———

Months later, I invited him and his wife to a downhome restaurant that served all-you-can-eat catfish, hush puppies, french fries, slaw, and sweet tea for just $8.95. After parking my Honda, Edgar Ray Killen greeted me, wearing his cowboy hat.

I sipped water from a red plastic glass while Killen devoured catfish like the room was on fire. The waitress served him four whole fish before whisking away the bones.

I asked him about District Attorney Ken Turner possibly reopening the case.

Killen shook his head. "Turner really doesn't have a lot of evidence. That's what's been his reluctance."

He denied belonging to the KKK, but that didn't surprise me. Few Klansmen admit that. "I would even say I was for" the Klan, he said, wiping his mouth with his napkin, "if I had control."

*If he had control?*

He leaned forward, tilting his hat. "Say I did have a Klan, and something blew up twenty miles away." He shook his head. "Even if I knew nothing about it, I'd be blamed."

His main complaint about the Klan, it seemed, was that one couldn't be an open member without dealing with the hassle of suspicious authorities all the time. I hadn't heard that one before.

He denied testimony at the 1967 trial that identified him as telling Klansmen in spring 1964 that Mickey Schwerner's killing had already been approved by Imperial Wizard Sam Bowers.

The preacher said he had no motive for killing the three civil rights workers. It wasn't until later, he explained, that he learned Schwerner and Andy Goodman "were both communists."

Killen insisted Martin Luther King Jr. was a communist, too. After King's assassination, FBI agents knocked on Killen's door, wanting to know his whereabouts on April 4, 1968. "They asked me to make a statement, and I told them the only statement I'd make was in front of twelve of my peers."

He told me he did have an alibi for King's killing. But he said that if he had shared it at the time, agents would have harassed the person vouching for him. Even so, days later Killen couldn't resist picking up the business card the FBI agent had left. The preacher dialed the number, and when the agent answered, Killen asked who killed King.

"Why do you want to know?" the agent asked. "Man," Killen replied, "I want to shake his hand."

After paying the bill and tip, I waved goodbye to Killen and his wife. I headed toward my Honda, and I had already unlocked the door when I noticed Killen heading toward me.

I waited, expecting him to speak. Instead, he strolled past me and stepped behind my car. I saw his eyes darting in a straight line, realizing too late that he had just read my license plate number.

In a flash, I knew what this meant. He could contact the clerk's office in Jackson, get my address, and pay me a personal visit. Or more likely, send his friends.

On my long drive back to Jackson, all I could think about was what a terrible mistake I had made.

On June 21, 2005 — the exact anniversary of the killings — a jury convicted Preacher Killen, who was sentenced to 60 years in prison, where he died.

Unfortunately, the same hate that led the Klan to kill has never gone away. In 2015, Dylann Roof walked into an African American church in Charleston, South Carolina, and opened fire, killing nine people. Two years later, a man entered a synagogue in Pittsburgh and killed 11. And in 2019, a Texas man traveled all the way to El Paso. There, he killed 23 people and injured 23 others, writing in a manifesto that he had to stop the "Hispanic invasion." In 2020, videos captured the killings of Black Americans by police and others.

Before people hate, they fear, and when they fear, they dehumanize, just as a Wisconsin police officer did when he pumped seven bullets into the back of Jacob Blake, leaving him paralyzed. For more than a century, politicians have preyed on Mississippians' fears, castigating "outsiders" and "invaders" as the ones attacking us, seeking to destroy "our way of life." Now other politicians across the U.S. are borrowing from that playbook.

We have reached a moment of reckoning, much like what the nation experienced in 1955 in the wake of Emmett Till's murder, when thousands of people of color took to the streets in city after city. Many White Americans have joined the latest protests, and Black Lives Matter has transformed from a simple slogan into a cause that has reached from Madrid to Mississippi. In the small town of Starkville, Mississippi more than 2,000 people, mostly White, marched in a Black Lives Matter protest.

We keep repeating history because we have failed to learn our history. Many students in the U.S. are still being taught that the Civil War was fought strictly over states' rights, ignoring documents such as Mississippi's Articles of Secession, which declared, "Our position is thoroughly identified with the institution of slavery."

It is time that we welcome a true account of our painful past so that we can move toward an honest present and a vibrant future. It is time that we move to change what needs to be changed so that Americans of all colors can be treated equally under the law — the cause for which Medgar Evers and so many others died.

It is time.

## About the Author

The stories of investigative reporter Jerry Mitchell have helped put four Klansmen and a serial killer behind bars. His stories have also helped free two people from death row, exposed injustices and corruption, prompting investigations and reforms as well as the firings of boards and officials. He is a Pulitzer Prize finalist, a longtime member of Investigative Reporters & Editors, and a winner of more than 30 other national awards, including a $500,000 MacArthur "genius" grant.

His memoir for Simon & Schuster, *Race Against Time*, details how some of the nation's most notorious murders came to be punished decades later. *The New York Times* made it an Editors' Pick, and NPR selected it a Best Book of the Year.

After working for three decades for the statewide *Clarion-Ledger*, Mitchell left in 2019 and founded the Mississippi Center for Investigative Reporting, a nonprofit that exposes injustices, investigates cold cases, gives voice to the voiceless and raises up the next generation of investigative reporters.

# CHAPTER 22

# THE FORM AND PRESSURE OF THE TIME: ARTISTRY AND ACTIVISM IN THE 1980S

DAVID EDELMAN

## INTRODUCTION

By Susan J. Erenrich

David Edelman's piece, "The Form and Pressure of the Time: Artistry and Activism in the 1980s" is a personal narrative about coming of age during the AIDS crisis. It is an intimate portrait of what it was like to be young, gay, and on the front lines of cultural activism during a scary, turbulent time in America.

Previously, David penned a chapter for the book, *Grassroots Leadership & the Arts for Social Change* (part of the International Leadership Association's Building Leadership Bridges series) titled, "Acting Up & Fighting Back: How New York's Artistic Community Responded To AIDS." Unlike that article, which explores the intersectionality of movements of participatory democracy and the arts in the United States from a historic perspective, in this chapter, David shares his personal story. It's an honest, thoughtful walk down memory lane.

Be sure to read to the end for David's top ten pedagogical insights — based on his story — which have guided his teaching of graduate arts management students over the years.

## THE FORM AND PRESSURE OF THE TIME: ARTISTRY AND ACTIVISM IN THE 1980S

By David Edelman

"You're on earth. There's no cure for that." - Samuel Beckett

I've been a professor and the director of the Performing Arts Leadership and Management Program at Shenandoah University in Winchester, Virginia for the past ten years, and I, like most other people I suppose, look back on my life and wonder how I got here. It's not a nostalgic act for me and it does not kindle fond memories of the good ole days. For me, it's a pedagogical question. For though I teach leadership and management, I have no training in either. I have an undergraduate degree in drama and a master's degree in acting; I never studied leadership theory, organizational management, accounting and finance, arts marketing, or non-profit fundraising. And yet, I teach all of these subjects to graduate students seeking a career in arts management. Ten years ago, I had precious little teaching experience, I wasn't published, and I didn't have a Ph.D. Why on earth would a distinguished academic institution hire me to run one of its programs? I think the university took a risk on me because they saw potential, but I'm not quite sure that even they, at the time, fully understood why they decided to hire me.

In his book, *Start With Why*, author Simon Sinek uses the story of the Wright Brothers to illustrate his thinking on leadership. The brothers were uneducated, unfunded, and unknown when they began their search for a vehicle that would propel people into the sky. Others were also competing to be the first, and most of them were educated engineers, backed by wealthy sponsors with the attention of the press on their trials and tribulations. But despite their competitors' advantages, it was the Wright Brothers, working out of their bicycle shop in Dayton, Ohio, self-funded and unknown, who succeeded. I love this story because within it I see a bit of myself; the autodidact whose experience, perseverance, and passion propels him forward through life's discoveries toward an unknowable future.

In hindsight, I have come to understand that my path was not all chance and luck. I now believe that the opportunities I seized over the course of my thirty years as an artist and arts leader not only provided me with important experience, but also helped to shape my principles and values and taught me how to learn — about myself, about others, about politics with both a small and large "P," and about the ways of the world.

Are these lessons learned of interest to others? Can they help leadership educators better understand how to assimilate and cohere life experience into a pedagogical approach? Or is it just hubris to think that my story might have relevance to others? After all, who am I? Just an average person with some good skills and talents who learned from experience and made the most of life's opportunities and challenges. I'll let you be the judge. Here's my story.

In the spring of 1981, I completed my MFA in acting from Rutgers University and moved into a rather nasty studio apartment on the Upper West Side of New York City (NYC) to pursue my career on the stage. Ronald Reagan was six months into his presidency, the city was just barely emerging from the economic crisis of the previous decade, and Jerry Falwell's Moral Majority was ascendant. The gloom was palpable.

I was 24, living in the big city, and ready to take my place in the world of the theatre. My five-floor walk-up building at Columbus Avenue and 105th Street was home to one of the most unusual slices of NYC life that I ever experienced. I was on the fourth floor. Above me lived a madam who ran her working girls from the apartment. Silk embroidered pillows, lampshades with fringe, and the smell of frangipani. The latter was essential to cover up the ever-present odor from her gaggle of Pekinese dogs who were fed boiled chicken and crapped on newspapers that covered the floors. Across the hall lived a 40-something, gay Black man who spoke Yiddish quite well on account of his long years as a gardener for a wealthy Jewish family. The one and only time my parents visited me in New York, he greeted them from the landing above, wearing a bright-red Japanese peignoir, with a "Yoo-hoo! Hello, David's *mishpacha* [Yiddish for family]." I remember that my mom's and dad's faces had the same look as the audience in *The Producers* watching *Springtime for Hitler*. (I inject a healthy dose of Yiddish words into my classroom, to the point that I am sure there are former students in China who *kvetch* about having to *schlepp*).

Below me lived a very handsome drug addict who periodically caused a melee in his apartment, usually around 3 a.m. Despite the screaming, crashing, and pounding that sounded like there was some serious whooping going on, it was him and him alone. None of us in the building could figure out how his solo pummeling was able to sound like a saloon brawl. Below him was a very nice, young, single mother who I would often see at the laundromat next door. I noticed that she added ammonia to her wash and when I asked her what the value was, she replied, "Kills the lice." For me, a nice, suburban Jewish boy, these good people — and they were good — were revelatory. I should have written a play.

My life was fairly typical of a young performer starting out in New York's theatre world. Lots of auditions and a few small parts. In 1982, I was cast in my first New York show, a lovely production of a play based on the Jewish legend of the Golem that played at La Mama ETC in the East Village. Later that year, I got my Equity card performing in an adaptation of a Eugene Ionesco play called *Victims of Duty* at The Colonnades Theatre Lab on Lafayette Street. The title was apt, and the *New York Times* called this black comedy "almost stupefyingly humorless" (Gussow, 1982). Fortunately, the review barely mentioned me, and I avoided the ignominy of a pan by one of the great theatre critics. For all the auditioning I did, I had little to show for it. The early 80s were a dreadful time for the theatre in New York City; Broadway grosses for those years were abysmal, and there was a depressing pall over the entire theatre community. While working at the Colonnades Theatre, I auditioned for a play reading presented by the Threshold Theatre, a company that specialized in the translation and presentation of socio-political plays from Eastern Europe, then under the thumb of the Soviets and their censors. The directors of the company took a shine to me, and I became a regular, appearing in numerous staged readings of newly translated plays and, when there was a bit of money, an off- or off-off-Broadway production. I liked the people and the political nature of the work, and I was a member of the company until 1987. But these were not paying gigs and a living had to be made.

I had tried my hand at waiting tables while in graduate school but only lasted a couple of weeks. I really didn't suffer fools well in those days, which is not a good character trait if you are in customer service. But once out of school, I landed a part-time job as the coordinator of the New Jersey State Teen Arts Festival. This provided enough of an income to pay the rent and eke out a living – barely. At some point in 1983, I was introduced to Gerald Chapman, who was running the Young Playwrights Festival out of the Dramatists Guild of America offices. (Gerald and I became great friends in the 1980s. He was a talented director, program leader, and a founder of the gay theatre movement in London in the 1970s. He died of AIDS in 1987). Gerald had started a young playwright's program in the UK at the Royal Court Theatre, and he was tapped by Broadway legend Stephen Sondheim to set up a similar program in the United States. Gerald encouraged me to replicate the program in New Jersey, and to feed the winning plays to the national festival in New York. Because of my statewide Teen Arts Festival contacts, I was able to launch the program in 1984 with funding that I had secured from the New Jersey State Council on the Arts. From the beginning, it was a success, and I created a plan for New Jersey's professional regional theatres to host the annual NJ Young Playwrights Festival on a rotating basis. Between my work with the Teen Arts Festival and Young Playwrights, I was learning the nuts and bolts of program development, organizational management, and fundraising.

In December of 1984, a group of gay men and women purchased a former high school on West 13th Street in Greenwich Village as a first home for the city's LGBT community. In short order, the New York City Lesbian and Gay Community Services Center became a hub of activism, hosting a never-ending stream of meetings by newly emerging LGBT political and social organizations and opening up the center to all kinds of cultural programs such as exhibits, lectures, and performances. A few months after the center opened to the public, I saw a notice for auditions for a new play to be performed in the center's auditorium in the spring of 1985 and I decided to try out. I was cast as Mercutio in *My Romeo*, a gay version of Shakespeare's *Romeo and Juliet*, the first theatre performance in the new center and one of its first cultural events. In accepting the role, I crossed a personal Rubicon, overcoming my fear of a public spotlight directed on me as a gay man.

*Chapter 22 Image 1.* Audition Headshot of the Author

I had recently split up with my first partner of three years and felt at sea. He was a social worker who specialized in working with gay youth who had been thrown out of their homes, and he was an early volunteer with the Anti-Violence Project. Harvey Milk and Mayor George Moscone had been assassinated in San Francisco in 1978 and the LGBT community became more radicalized as a result. As the community became more out, visible, and organized, brutal attacks on gay men and lesbian women became more frequent. Two of the most horrifying were the beating of two gay teens in New York City in 1979, which resulted in the death of one boy, and the drive-by murder of gay men in front of the Ramrod bar in the Chelsea neighborhood, which killed two and wounded six. (These crimes were committed in a time well before our current age of Sandy Hook Elementary School, Pulse Nightclub, Parkland High School, the Route 91 Harvest Music Festival, and The Tree of Life Synagogue; I fear we have become inured to such violence.)

The Anti-Violence Project was formed in 1980 to demand police and community protection and to provide services to those who were the victims of attack. My ex became an ardent activist because of this violence against the LGBT community; I was more focused on my career and making enough money for us to afford our recently acquired apartment in Brooklyn's Park Slope neighborhood. But I couldn't ignore all that he shared with me about his work and all that was happening around me. And so, my anger began to rise.

Rehearsals at the center, in the early spring of 1985, were an exhilarating experience. People of all stripes were coming and going and the joy of having a place of our own was palpable. Scores of groups, large and small, were gathering at the center, and the bulletin boards were plastered with hand-made signs announcing events, protests, and meetings. I was busy with the production of *My Romeo*, which ended its short run on May 12, 1985, but once it was over, I felt the need to connect with all of the fervent activity that I was witnessing. At some point that summer, I went to see Larry Kramer's play *The Normal Heart*, which was running off-Broadway at Joe Papp's Public Theatre. The play was emotionally devastating, but also inspiring, and I decided to volunteer for the Gay Men's Health Crisis (GMHC).

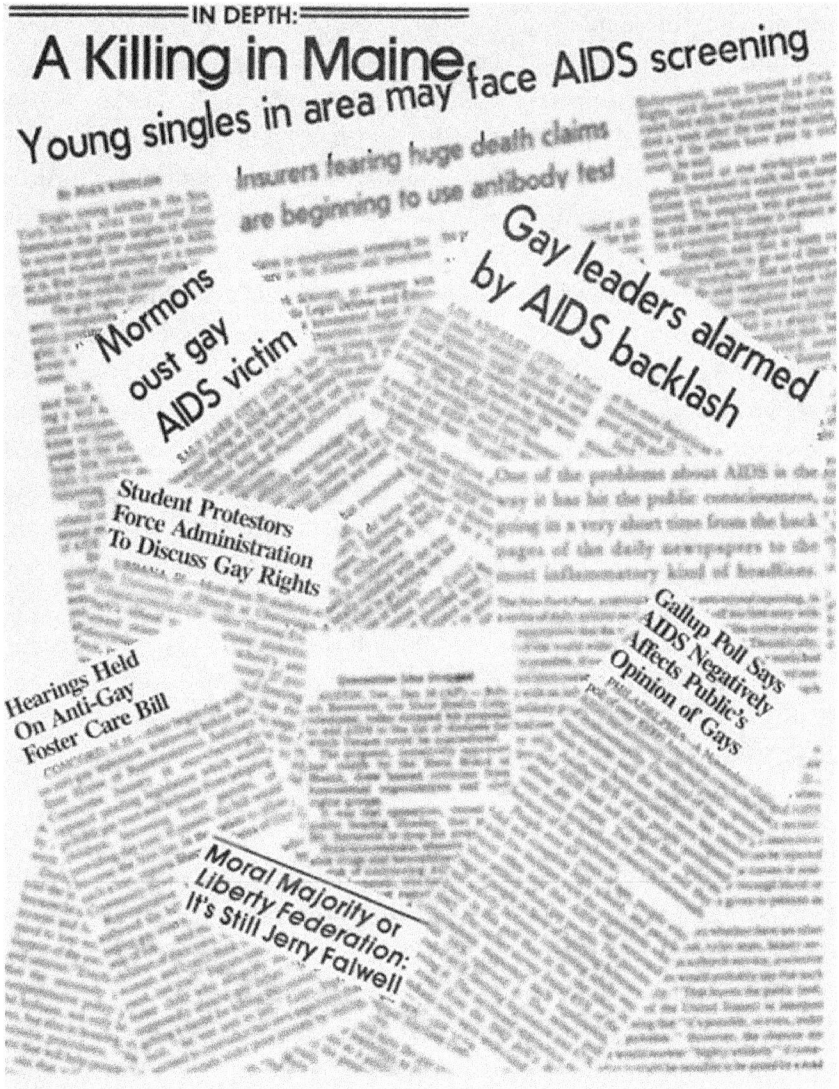

*Chapter 22 Image 2.* AIDS-Related headlines. Clippings from author's personal collection.

The first news article about Gay Related Immunodeficiency Disorder (soon to be renamed Acquired Immune Deficiency Syndrome or AIDS) was in the *New York Times* on July 3, 1981, under the headline "Rare Cancer Seen in 41 Homosexuals" (Altman, 1981). That was the summer I moved to New York City. Over the next several years, as the disease turned into an epidemic, the panic grew. Members of the LGBT community were rightfully terrified, as we witnessed the devastation caused by opportunistic infections and the horrible deaths of our friends and lovers. Shortly after the first reports of AIDS, screenwriter Larry Kramer and a group of his friends – many of whom were writers and artists – formed the Gay Men's Health Crisis (GMHC) to raise money for research, to provide care to the increasing number of gay men who were sick and dying, and to provide safe sex education to the entire gay community. GMHC was just three years old in 1985, but the AIDS crisis was rapidly expanding. The number of sick and dying was overwhelming the health care system and the need for education and prevention was acute. I volunteered to do "street" outreach and had two assignments: working in the heart of gay Greenwich Village at the corner of Seventh Avenue South and Christopher Street and working in the bath houses. Both assignments had me handing out safe sex literature, condoms, and bleach kits (for needle sterilization). As innocuous as it sounds, this volunteer job was a difficult experience for me. The baths, in particular, were a controversial political issue for both the gay community and for the city. Bath houses were hugely popular among gay men as a place to meet and find sex partners. But they were more than this. Bette Midler got her start singing in the Continental Baths on New York's Upper West Side in the early 70s, accompanied on the piano by a very young Barry Manilow. St. Mark's Bath, where I volunteered, was clean, shiny, and newly renovated (it opened as a Turkish bath in 1906) with a restaurant and a spacious area for sitting and chatting. The clientele was upscale, too — students from NYU, artists and performers, and suburban married men on the downlow. In some ways it functioned as much as a club for meeting friends as a vast cruising parlor. By the mid-80s, the baths had become a hot political issue as the AIDS epidemic spread.

I was welcomed by the St. Mark's management whenever I showed up for my shift with boxes of literature and free condoms. The Everard Baths, my other assignment, was quite different. There had been a tragic and deadly fire there in 1977 and only a portion of the building had been rebuilt. It seemed dingy and dirty to me, and I saw far too many young men who looked dissipated, many with track marks on their arms. My efforts to educate and save lives were often met with scorn and derision from the customers, as if it was me who was ruining the party, even as they helped themselves to the free condoms. I found myself on the front line of the debates about safe sex, public health, and gay rights and I was rather unprepared for the emotional toll this took on me. I lasted about nine months as a street outreach volunteer.

Protest the VICIOUS
remarks of William F. Buckley
(tattooing people with AIDS and
people who are HTLV III positive)

Call The National Review
office: 679 — 7330

Call the N.Y. TIMES:
556 — 1234

*Chapter 22 Image 3.* Flyer advertising protest. From author's personal collection.

At some point during the fall of 1985, I wandered into a room at the center where perhaps a dozen people had come together to discuss how to combat media portrayals of gay men and lesbian women and the biased reporting on the LGBT community, particularly reporting surrounding the AIDS crisis. For the public at large, who relied on the press for their information, what they read and heard about AIDS and gays was hysteria and fearmongering. U.S. Representative William Dannemeyer of California proposed locking away AIDS victims in a modern-day version of a leper colony (Lindgreen, 1986). Columnist William F. Buckley, Jr. suggested, in a *New York Times* editorial, that any gay man detected with AIDS should be tattooed on his buttocks to warn off potential sex-partners (Buckley, 1986). Funeral homes refused to take the bodies of men who had died of AIDS. Insurance companies were denying coverage to gay men. Gay men, already stigmatized by their sexuality, now faced the double whammy of AIDS stigmatization. In 1985, when the first test for HIV antibodies was approved by the Food and Drug Administration, I went to a hospital to get tested. The nurse who drew my blood was so nervous that her hands shook and she fumbled with the needle, nicking my vein and causing me to bleed. And then she started to sob. She was terrified. I started to cry too; I realized that she was afraid of me. I had never felt this before, and I was stunned by both of our reactions. The two of us were a mess.

All of the gains that the LGBT community had experienced since the 1969 Stonewall Rebellion were at risk of undoing by the public reaction to AIDS — and we knew it. Journalist Andy Humm, writing in the *New York City News*, said, "For all of us who were worried that the conservative backlash in this country would bring about unnamed terrible things, the future is now" (Dunlap, 2016). So, when I walked into that meeting in the LGBT community center in 1985 and heard this group of men and women talking about the crisis situation our community was facing and what to do about it, I felt the need to take a seat and enter the conversation.

**STOP**

**THE**

**LIES**

# PROTEST THE N.Y. POST

**FIGHT**

**AIDS!**

**NOT**

**GAYS!**

As Gays & Lesbians, we are facing an unprecedented attack on our lives. The *New York Post* whips up hysteria and defames us in a manner that no self-respecting community should have to bear.

Join us in expressing our outrage at the homophobic, racist, sexist, editorial policy of the *New York Post*. In memory of our loved ones whose voices have been silenced, and for the love of ourselves, we must say enough is enough.

## D E M O N S T R A T E

SUNDAY, DECEMBER 1, 1985 2PM

The *New York Post* Headquarters

210 South Street

Take the IRT or IND to Fulton Street in Manhattan, or F train to East Broadway

The *Post* is a rag! Bring Rags to the Rally!

Every time the *Post* offends you, call their

City Desk line and complain, 212-815-8500

Sponsored by the Gay and Lesbian

Anti-Defamation League,

Box 809, 263A 19th Street, New York, NY 10011.

*Chapter 22 Image 4.* Flyer advertising demonstration. From author's personal collection.

This group named itself the Gay and Lesbian Anti-Defamation League and officially formed in November of 1985. (The Anti-Defamation League of B'nai Brith threatened legal action for use of the name and so in 1986 the organization was re-named The Gay and Lesbian Alliance Against Defamation (GLAAD), and it is known today as one of the LGBT community's most successful and far-reaching civil rights organizations). Its immediate object of protest was *The New York Post*, whose bigoted and inflammatory style of journalism under its new owner, Rupert Murdoch, had earned it the scorn of the LGBT community. As the *Columbia Journalism Review* stated in 1980, the "*New York Post* is no longer merely a journalistic problem. It is a social problem – a force for evil" (*Columbia Journalism Review*, 1980). Fed up with the *Post's* lies and distortions, the word was put out to demonstrate in front of the *Post* building in lower Manhattan on December 1, 1985. To our amazement, a crowd of 1,000 people showed up waving rags, reflecting our opinion of the newspaper, and holding signs that read "Fight AIDS, Not Gays" and "Close the Post, Not the Baths." We were noisy, raucous, and mad. Speakers included the late Vito Russo, author of the *Celluloid Closet* and a leading activist in the LGBT community. (I was recently watching the documentary *Vito* and I fairly leapt out of my recliner when I saw my young self, front and center, in a snippet of video of the demonstration). The *Post* did not respond to any of the group's demands for an end to its malicious journalism nor did it offer an apology to the LGBT community, as demanded, but it did scale back the inflammatory rhetoric after the protest. It was the first signal to the media that maligning the LGBT community had its consequences.

GAY AND LESBIAN ALLIANCE AGAINST DEFAMATION
Box 809
263A West 19th Street
New York, New York   10011

December 14, 1985

Dear Friends,

The Gay and Lesbian Alliance Against Defamation was formed in November
to spearhead action against the ever increasing defamation of our community.
Judging from the enormous response at our November 14 Town Meeting and at the
December 1 demonstration against the New York Post, our community is ripe
for action.

To that end, we are coordinating an elaborate phone tree that will enable us to
reach a large number of people in a very short time.  In the event of blatant
homophobia, the tree will be activated and a suggested collective response
will be passed along.  The community may be asked to flood a TV station with
protest calls, to blitz a newspaper with letters to the editor, or to spread the
word about a demonstration.  Our ability to act quickly and as a united community
will increase our effectiveness many fold.  To be united, we don't have to
agree on everything.  We just have to agree that we will no longer allow ourselves
to be defamed.

As a start, we are reaching out to a vast array of Lesbian and Gay organizations
that have proliferated over the last decade.  Please share our plans with your
membership and ask those interested in being a part of the tree to contact us.
Ideally, we would like to have one member of each group act as liaison/captain
of his/her branch of the tree.  Each person will receive one call and make three.

David Edelman, a member of this committee and New Jersey resident, would be happy
to talk with your organization to explain how to join in the action.  Feel free
to contact him at 201-653-5907.  Help us beat back the backlash!

As one family,

Sincerely,

Hal Offen
Co-chairperson
Swift and Terrible Retribution Committee
Gay and Lesbian Alliance Against Defamation

*Chapter 22 Image 5.* Letter. From author's personal collection.

The protest and its immediate aftermath were empowering and
exhilarating, and I was in for a pound. I volunteered to be a member of
the Swift and Terrible Retribution Committee (what a great name!),
which organized media events and protests, and the Phone Tree
Committee, which summoned volunteers to demonstrations and calls
for action. A proposal for a nationwide campaign was created and

adopted, called Challenge Bigotry, whose purpose was "to affect the way straight America perceives gay Americans," and it divided the work into two phases. "In Phase 1, the campaign is an organizing and fundraising tool aimed primarily at gay Americans; in Phase II, the campaign is a print media campaign aimed foremost at larger society" (Kuropat, 1986). It was a simple and brilliant strategy that soon catapulted GLAAD to the top of the LGBT community in both fundraising and social action.

DEMONSTRATE

ON

FRIDAY, DECEMBER 13<sup>th</sup>.

12 NOON AT

| CITY HALL |

TO PROTEST NEW YORK STATE'S

BIGOTED SEX REGULATIONS

FRIDAY IS THE LAST DAY PUBLIC COMMENT

ON THE STATE HEALTH DEPARTMENT'S

REGULATIONS -- AND THE CITY'S ENFORCEMENT

OF THEM-- CAN BE MADE. VOCALLY

REGISTER YOUR COMMENTS ON

YOUR LUNCH HOUR!

*Chapter 22 Image 6.* Flyer advertising demonstration. From author's personal collection.

Soon after the *NY Post* demonstration, GLAAD launched a series of protests in NYC, including demonstrations on December 13, 1985, at City Hall against the New York State Health Department's misguided safe sex guidelines and against The Right to Life Party, that demonstrated against New York's newly founded Gay Film Festival.

Our phone tree summoned 300 counter-protestors to demonstrate against their dozen or so. On March 18, 1986, GLAAD sponsored a large rally in City Hall Park to support New York City's stalled Gay Rights Bill and the rally helped push the bill over the top – City Council approved the bill on March 20th (Purnick, 1986).

In addition to attending the protests and rallies, I launched into a flurry of letter writing to the editors of magazines and newspapers to criticize those who slandered and attacked us and to praise those who wrote fair and accurate reporting. I also decided to set up the first state chapter of GLAAD in New Jersey (I had moved to Hoboken in late 1985), and so I began speaking at events organized by other New Jersey gay organizations to spread the GLAAD message. While the state chapter never materialized and GLAAD abandoned its idea to form state and regional chapters, it was my first foray as a leader in the cause. Gregory Kolovakos, chair of GLAAD's steering committee, was Literature Director of the New York State Council on the Arts, a member of the Executive Committee of The Nation Institute, and a noted translator of Latin American literature. We became great friends over the course of the winter of 1986 and exchanged letters about life, art, and protest. (Another great personal loss for me. Gregory died of AIDS in 1990). His letter to me of March 11, 1986, is a window into the work of protest and its emotional toll: "My day began at 7 a.m. with a live interview (a debate really) with the lawyer from the archdiocese on the *Alan Colmes Show* (WABC radio). Pain in the ass, but I think I demolished the good lawyer. Today should be devastating in its hatred and venom (as was yesterday's *POST* editorial and essay by Ray Kerrison), and I find myself strangely close to tears a lot. I'm immensely sad, and I can't shake it."

No one should doubt the psychic toll that LGBT and AIDS activism took on its leaders. This was hard work, demanding work, and we did, indeed, cry… a lot.

As I was immersing myself in the gay activist movement, I was also moving forward with my career, although not quite in the way that I expected. I spent the winter of 1986 as an artist-teacher in residence at an elementary school in Newark, under a grant from the New Jersey

State Council on the Arts, and as the newly installed volunteer executive director of Threshold Theatre Company, which was seeking to move beyond a series of one-off readings and performances to a more organized subscription-based company. At the same time, I was planning, organizing, and, in some cases, conducting playwriting workshops for high school students all over the state of New Jersey as well as planning for the adjudication and performance of the winning plays. In the first two years of the Young Playwrights Festival, the winning student one-acts were performed at Rutgers University and then at George Street Playhouse in New Brunswick. In 1986, the third year, the host was The Whole Theatre in Montclair, and I came to the attention of its artistic director, Olympia Dukakis. She was impressed by my entrepreneurial skills, my ability to raise money, and by my passion for both the theatre and my LGBT activism. She hired me as the theatre's development director in 1986 and it marked a turning point for me. Up until then, I had thought my life in the theatre would be as an actor on the stage. But the offer of a full-time position as an arts manager with a real salary, health benefits, and job security meant I would have to give up my dream. It caused me no small amount of trepidation and anxiety. But, as with so many of the events of my life up until then, I somehow understood the need to grab on to opportunities when they arose, and so I did with Whole Theatre.

# TOP COURT OKs GAY SEX BAN

## Rally at Sheridan Sq. Tonight at 7p.m. July 1st

*Chapter 22 Image 7.* Flyer advertising rally. From author's personal collection.

In 1986, I was juggling my new job as an arts administrator, performing in a Threshold Theatre play off-Broadway, and continuing my work in LGBT activism. It was a very busy year. The biggest protest event in GLAAD's first year occurred on June 30, 1986, in response to the Supreme Court's ruling to uphold Georgia's ban on sodomy (Bowers v. Hardwick), which criminalized gay sex between consenting adults. The anger about the court's decision was intense and the call went out the same day to gather at 7:00 pm in Sheridan Square, the heart of gay Greenwich Village. At least a thousand people showed up and the protest turned into civil disobedience when the enormous crowd sat down in the middle of Seventh Avenue and closed the street (Blair, 1986). An a-frame ladder was set up for speakers, who addressed the crowd with a megaphone, but the speakers were not matching the energy and anger of the crowd. Gregory Kolovakos pulled me aside, told me to get up on the ladder, and give the crowd some red meat. He knew I was an actor and had heard me speak with passion and force. I grabbed the megaphone and spoke impromptu, telling the thousands of protestors that if (Attorney General) Ed Meese stuck his nose in my bedroom I would slam the door on it. The crowd went wild, and I reinvigorated a rally that was starting to slip away from the organizers. The event made national news and established GLAAD as a force to be reckoned with.

One outcome of the rally was a call for a Fourth of July protest march through lower Manhattan's Battery Park. A small group of several hundred demonstrators showed up for the rally and the march. I was one of the rally speakers, telling our small but boisterous group that "We are here today in our rage and in our defiance to say that no law, no government, no power on earth can take away our dignity and pride.... It's time to put our minds and muscle into a nationwide effort to end the bigotry and the violence against gay men and lesbians." But it was clear from the outset that this would be a different experience from the Sheridan Square sit-down protest. On June 30 we were among friends in the heart of New York's gay neighborhood. The July 4th march wound its way through a park packed with tourists and straight families out on a gorgeous Friday afternoon to celebrate the holiday. They looked at us with a combination of surprise and contempt, and the police, who were there in force since the march had been advertised days in advance, looked on us menacingly. Our anxiety about the onlookers and the police grew as we marched. When we arrived at the west side of Battery Park, we were met by a phalanx of police in riot gear and wooden police barricades blocked the path in front of us. There was a quick meeting of the organizers, who had to decide if we confront the police and get arrested or back down. We decided to back down since we were surrounded by both police and a hostile crowd and there were no media present to report on the confrontation and arrests. It would have been a painful confrontation resulting in no tangible gain. That was the last time we backed down.

Within a year, GLAAD had emerged as a leading LGBT civil rights organization. It sponsored a letter published in the *National Law Review,* signed by over 250 law school faculty and deans, protesting the Supreme Court's decision in Bower's v. Hardwick; created a weekly, short radio broadcast called *Naming Names* to call out prominent bigots and their media enablers; and met with Max Frankel, Executive Editor of *The New York Times*, to push (successfully) for an increase in positive reporting of issues important to the gay community.

But my time as a New York gay activist was coming to an end. I was now living and working in New Jersey, and I began to shift my focus closer to home. In late 1985, I fell in with a group of gay men and lesbians in Hoboken who had formed an organization — more social than political — to serve the needs of the city's LGBT population, this despite the fact that most gay men and lesbians who had moved to Hoboken to save on rent were much more oriented to New York City than to New Jersey. Our Hoboken group was small — we met in members' apartments — but we nonetheless qualified for membership in the New Jersey Lesbian and Gay Coalition (NJLGC), the state's leading LGBT organization that brought together scores of smaller groups under one umbrella. My reputation trying to organize a New Jersey chapter of GLAAD had preceded me and, at the end of 1985, I was elected president of the NJLGC. My two years as a leader of the statewide organization focused on two initiatives: 1) to secure funding for a statewide AIDS education and outreach program targeting gay men; and 2) the passage of a state anti-discrimination bill. Our efforts to secure funding for AIDS education were very successful, particularly from New Jersey's robust pharmaceutical industry, who was feeling the heat about the slow pace in developing treatments for HIV/AIDS. Our education campaign, called "Frisky, Not Risky" tried to put some fun back into sex while at the same time helping to save lives. On the political front, we had been successfully meeting with members of Governor Tom Kean's administration, members of the state legislature, and other statewide leaders, and we were making the case for the extension of state civil rights protections to the LGBT community. I wrote to Tom Kean in June of 1986, citing all of the previous un-answered letters that NJLGC had written to him, and I suggested that "the concrete concerns of lesbians and gay men in New Jersey receive the serious and careful attention of your Office" (D. Edelman, letter to Gov. Tom Kean, June 27, 1986). The time seemed right and, shortly after sending the letter, I met with the governor's chief of staff to nail down a commitment to support a gay rights bill for

New Jersey. But the promise of support was wishy-washy, and it took another five years and a Democratic governor before New Jersey amended its law against discrimination to include sexual orientation.

Working at Whole Theatre in 1987-89 was a heady time. I found myself in a leadership role within the state's arts community, was elected to two terms as president of the board of the New Jersey Theatre Group, and was a founding board member of ArtPride, a statewide arts advocacy organization. The quality of Whole Theatre productions was first-rate, and Olympia was able to pull in some of the most talented people working in the theatre. But all of that was about to become eclipsed by two extraordinary events. Olympia appeared on Broadway in 1986 in the play, *Social Security*, with Ron Silver, Marlo Thomas, and Joanna Gleason. The play was directed by Mike Nichols, who then cast her in the film *Moonstruck* with Cher and Nicholas Cage. *Moonstruck* was released in December of 1987, the same year that Olympia's cousin, Massachusetts Governor Mike Dukakis, ran for the Democratic nomination for President of the United States. In April of 1988, Olympia won the Academy Award for Best Supporting Actress and Mike won the New York primary, which put him over the top for the Democratic nomination. It was a dizzying whirl of high-profile activity, and I played my part. Olympia had no personal staff at the time, so I and another senior staff member of the theatre were her escorts, drivers, personal shoppers, and hand holders through all of the hurly burly of the campaigns for the Academy Award and for president. I had a vision of being appointed cultural attaché in the U.S. Embassy in London or Paris.

In the end, Mike lost the presidential race to George H.W. Bush, and we all went back to the business of running Whole Theatre. But it was not the same. The finances of the theatre were shaky, Olympia was often away filming new movie projects, we had a misguided consultant whom Olympia trusted to make big decisions, and the board was full of high-sounding talk but little else. I became increasingly anxious about the finances and indignant about bad decision-making and so, in 1989, Olympia and I parted ways. I was hired by George Street Playhouse in New Brunswick, New Jersey as managing director and stayed for three seasons until young women on the staff and in the community put their complaints about sexual harassment on the part of the producing director in writing. I was enraged and brought the complaints to the board of directors, demanding an investigation. I basically told the board it was either him or me and when they gave him a slap on the wrist, I quit. (Six years later he was caught again when a young actress reported him to Actors' Equity Association and the scandal became public. This time the board fired him. In hindsight, I should have done more to oust him and protect other young women, but it was a different time, and I had such a bad taste in my mouth from the board's inaction, that I just wanted to get away).

I decamped for Delaware where I was hired as managing director at the Delaware Theatre Company and where my personal activism achieved a level of maturity that truly blossomed. I served as president of the board of AIDS Delaware; was appointed to the state's Human Relations Commission; negotiated the agreement to create a $21 million Delaware Arts Stabilization Fund; developed an urban infra-structure enhancement program for the theatre's neighborhood on the Christina River waterfront; and served on the boards of Sister Cities, The Delaware College of Art and Design, the Wilmington Riverfront Business Improvement District, and the Wilmington Arts Commission. At the Delaware Theatre Company, I led the creation of an award-winning theatre education program serving mentally challenged children, youth at risk of academic failure, single teenaged mothers, adjudicated and incarcerated youth, and chronically ill children. I had become a confident leader and was sought after by other community leaders for my expertise, my level-headed thinking, and my ability to communicate with ease and to great effect.

I left Delaware Theatre Company after the founding artistic director resigned and his successor was in place for a full season. It was the right time to leave, and I headed for new challenges in Columbus, Ohio and then back to New York City, where I served as Executive Director of the New York City Gay Men's Chorus. I thought it would be a dream job, but it turned out otherwise. I had never run a membership arts organization before and I discovered that, in this case, it was like trying to lead a small gay country. The drama was way over the top. In 2009, after 27 years of leadership in the arts and in the civic life of my various communities, I decided to apply all that I had lived and learned to teaching young people and I was lucky enough to be hired by Shenandoah University's Conservatory to lead its arts management program. I've been with the Conservatory since 2009 and have served in leadership roles on the boards of academic associations, founded a journal in the field of arts management, and been an active conference presenter.

But most of all, I love teaching. It took me three years to figure out how to teach, to develop my curriculum, and to learn the ways of higher education. It felt like all of my life's work — professional as well as volunteer — had led me to this point and I relished the opportunity to share what I've learned over the years with my graduate arts management students.

My story, in a nutshell. The point of sharing this with you? Aside from the glimpse it provides into our recent past, I think it helps to illustrate why I hold certain views about the teaching of management.

1. I am a coach as much as a teacher. I treat my students the same way I treated my young employees, giving them good learning tools, encouraging them to fail — since we all know that we learn from our mistakes — and providing guidance rather than tutelage.

2. Self-discovery is the road to learning. I often ask students the question, "what would you do under these circumstances?" It's the same question that artists ask themselves as they endeavor to create.

3. Get to know the world. It sounds simplistic, but so many of todays' students understand precious little of the world around them and that's a serious liability. We don't create art in a vacuum. Our arts organizations exist within and are tied to community, and that community has become the world in our globally connected age.

4. Embrace personal risk. You won't avoid pain and suffering by being risk averse, so you might as well push the envelope. Besides, it's better to suffer when you are young than when you are old. At my age, suffering is superfluous.

5. Care about people. This is how you engender trust, build relationships, and become an agent of change.

6. Do not settle for mediocrity. If you are going to lead, it better be for something worthwhile. It's okay if your first job is with an organization that produces tepid work. Learn the ropes, gain some experience, but then you must move on to something better.

7. Artistic creation is social justice. That's a two-pronged idea. First, recognize that all art worth its salt explores what it means to be human in the world and, as is too often the case, how the world attempts to de-humanize us. Second, create the circumstances by which art is made accessible to everyone. As arts leaders and managers, we have an obligation to support artists and arts organizations that seek to make a difference and to give all people the opportunity to share in this great gift.

8. Be critical. Cultivate doubt, spend time in reflection, learn to craft an argument, and dare to be wrong.

9. Allow your emotions to serve a higher purpose. We all get angry, frustrated, and resentful from time to time. Don't allow these feelings to highjack your judgment; keep your eye on the prize.

10. Think about thinking. Gain understanding about how your heart and mind work, and how they work together. Undertake a practice of mindfulness.

I could go on with lessons learned but I think 10 is enough. As you can see, readings, lectures, discussions, assignments, rubrics, assessments, and all the other hallmarks of the classroom are missing from my list. It's not that these aren't valuable and important, but rather they are merely tools that can be used or tossed, as needs be, in the service of creating a platform in which students explore their values, principles, and experience; learn and fail; and, hopefully, gain wisdom. In this way, I hope that my students are truly able to learn from my experiences.

And if you, the reader, learned anything from my experiences, I am truly delighted.

## References

Altman, L. (1981, July 3). Rare Cancer Seen in 41 Homosexuals. *New York Times*. https://www.nytimes.com/1981/07/03/us/rare-cancer-seen-in-41-homosexuals.html

Blair, W. (1986, July 3). City's Homosexuals Protest High Court Sodomy Ruling. *The New York Times*. https://www.nytimes.com/1986/07/03/nyregion/city-s-homosexuals-protest-high-court-sodomy-ruling.html

Buckley, W.F., Jr. (1986, March 18). Crucial Steps in Combating the Aids Epidemic; Identify All the Carriers. *New York Times*. http://movies2.nytimes.com/books/00/07/16/specials/buckley-aids.html

Columbia Journalism Review. (1980, Jan/Feb). Comment - Doing the Devil's Dirty Work. *Columbia Journalism Review*, 18(5), 22-23.

Dunlap, D. (2016, June 15). New York's Own Anti-Gay Massacre, Now Barely Remembered. *New York Times*. https://www.nytimes.com/2016/06/16/nyregion/new-yorks-own-anti-gay-massacre-now-barely-remembered-orlando.html

Gussow, M. (1982, July 30). Theatre: Ionesco Mystery. *The New York Times*. https://www.nytimes.com/1982/07/30/theater/theater-ionesco-mystery.html

Kuropat, R. (1986). *Challenge Bigotry: A Two-Part Proposal for Gay Community Organizing and Positive Message Advertising*. New York: The Gay and Lesbian Alliance Against Defamation.

Lindgren, K. (1986, July 6). Enter on Stag Right: Crusader Dannemeyer, Defender of His Faith. *Los Angeles Times*. https://www.latimes.com/archives/la-xpm-1986-07-06-me-23093-story.html

Purnick, J. (1986, March 21). Homosexual Rights Bill Is Passed by City Council in 21-14 Vote. *The New York Times*. https://www.nytimes.com/1986/03/21/nyregion/homosexual-rights-bill-is-passed-by-city-council-in-21-to-14-vote.html

**About the Author**

David Edelman is Professor of Arts Management and Director of the Performing Arts Leadership and Management Program at Shenandoah Conservatory. He is the founder and editor emeritus of The American Journal of Arts Management. Prior to joining the Conservatory faculty, he was Executive Director of Big Apple Performing Arts in New York City. Prof. Edelman has served as the Executive Director of the Contemporary American Theatre Company in Columbus, Ohio, Managing Director of Delaware Theatre Company, Managing Director of George Street Playhouse in New Jersey, and Associate Producer at the late Olympia Dukakis' Whole Theatre in New Jersey. He has served as President of the NJ Theatre Alliance and sat on the Boards of ArtPride, NJ's arts advocacy organization, the Association of Arts Administration Educators and Social Theory, Politics and the Arts. He was a founding member of the Arts Consortium of Delaware and the Riverfront Wilmington Business Improvement District. He also served on the boards of Sister Cities of Wilmington, the Wilmington Arts Leaders Roundtable, Brandywine Valley Cultural Tourism Planning Committee, AIDS Delaware, the Wilmington Metropolitan Area Planning Commission, and the Ohio Department of Education's Arts Standards Advisory Committee. Prof. Edelman received his undergraduate degree from Washington University in St. Louis and earned his MFA from Rutgers University's Mason Gross School of the Arts.

# SECTION 6

PEOPLE POWER, COMMUNITY
BUILDING, & THE ARTS FOR
SOCIAL CHANGE

# CHAPTER 23
# STARTING LOCAL, RIPPLING OUT – HULL-HOUSE, YOUTH POETRY, AND A MUSICAL

KRISTIN LEMS

## INTRODUCTION

By Susan J. Erenrich

This chapter features an article penned by long-time troubadour of conscience Kristin Lems. I first met Kristin in 1980 at an anti-nuclear conference at Kent State University. Her song, *I Wasn't Surprised*, dedicated to the two fatally wounded victims of the May 15, 1970, killings at Jackson State College — Phillip Lafayette Gibbs and James Earl Green — sent shivers up my spine. It was the first time anyone had composed a song honoring the Mississippi martyrs, who died at the hands of the state on that college campus. I became an enthusiastic devotee.

Shortly thereafter, I learned about Kristin's other musical contributions highlighting the battle for the Equal Rights Amendment, women and human rights, safe energy, peace, racial equality, and other pressing matters. Her commitment to causes she believes in has never dwindled.

In this chapter, Kristin delves into her family's history with Jane Addams, the founder of Hull-House and the first American woman to win the Nobel Peace Prize. Moved by the role Addams played in her family's survival in the late 1800s, Kristin recently wrote a musical titled *Saint Jane and the Wicked Wicks* that explores the relationship between her great grandmother, Nellie Wicks, and Addams. In the second half of the article, she ties Chicago's Louder Than A Bomb poetry slam to these deep traditions of art and social justice in the region.

I hope readers are heartened by Kristin's piece. It is both a glimpse into the past and a look at how art can, in the present, bring people together for social change.

## STARTING LOCAL, RIPPLING OUT – HULL-HOUSE, YOUTH POETRY, AND A MUSICAL

By Kristin Lems

My family history — my mother's side of it, anyway — is intertwined with many social conditions in 19<sup>th</sup> century Chicago. My mother's family was formed in Chicago in the 1880s when her great grandmother, a teenager from upstate New York, ran away with a dashing older man, a "carnie" who assembled and tore down carnival rides. Once they settled in Chicago, he worked as a laborer, putting up scaffolds to support the walls of new buildings. He soon became a ruthless alcoholic, beating and maiming all of their five children. Their first daughter, my great grandmother Nellie Wicks, was taken back to New York by her grandmother, who saw the mistreatment of her daughter's children and wanted to "rescue" at least one of them, but Nellie was forced to return to Chicago when her grandmother died unexpectedly of a stroke.

According to family lore, Nellie had only been back in Chicago for a short time when her mother went into labor in their tiny apartment, and her drunken father began to savagely beat the laboring woman. That fateful night, in March 1890, Nellie ran across the street and banged on the door of the only building with light in the windows, begging for help. Providentially, the door was opened by Jane Addams. The building was America's first settlement house, Hull-House, which had opened just a few months earlier (see Knight, 2005, p.463 for detailed evidence). Addams, Ellen Gates Starr, and Julia Lathrop called for a doctor, hurried across the street, and drove Nellie's father away, saving both mother and newborn. This dramatic night began a 30-year relationship between Jane Addams and my great grandmother Nellie, and it has reverberated to me across five generations.

Jane Addams' relationship with Nellie likely saved Nellie's own children as well, one of whom was my grandmother, Edna. Nellie raised 11 children, mostly on her own, and if you think women's wages are unfair now, you'd be shocked at the pathetic wages women received for their grueling work in the late 1890s and early 1900s. Hull-House opened the Mary Crane Day Nursery in 1908, and Nellie took Edna and her two younger siblings there every morning so that Nellie could work in a large industrial laundry ten hours a day, six days a week. Like other single mothers abandoned by their husbands, Nellie considered the nursery a godsend. Laundry jobs were dangerous, exhausting, and low-paid. Nellie's arms were scalded, and her legs were burned from heavy bedsheets she lifted, plunged, and removed from vats of boiling water.

Likely, her one comfort was knowing that her three small children were clean, safe, and fed. Nellie was lucky that her children were able to be accepted at Mary Crane Day Nursery. Many single working women had nowhere to take the children, and some were so terrified that their children might rush into the street and be crushed by a horse or a car that they tied their children's legs to the stairwells of their tenement buildings. While women workers in the industry began to successfully organize into unions, founding the International Ladies' Garment Workers Union in 1900, it remained a hazardous occupation as horribly illustrated by the Triangle Shirtwaist Factory fire in New York City, which killed so many women in 1911.

Jane Addams and the other well-educated women residents and volunteers at Hull-House were a lifeline for the girls and women in the area, many of whom were immigrants. Hull-House offered a wide variety of free classes, clubs, discussion groups, meeting rooms, a dining hall, an urban garden with fresh vegetables, and it supported the women's reform organization working to create public baths in Chicago, the first of which was built near the house (Williams, 2005). Always thinking of children's health and welfare, the activists of Hull-House opened the "first model playground in America" in 1894 (McArthur, 1975), a novel concept addressing children's needs in the overcrowded streetscape. Donations by philanthropists and by educated women casting off the Victorian lives that had restrained them allowed Hull-House to continue to grow into a complex of buildings that nearly occupied a full city block. Additionally, Louise DeKoven Bowen, a Hull-House trustee, purchased and endowed Hull-House with a 72-acre property in Waukegan, Illinois so that urban children could have a summer getaway from the polluted, teeming city. Staff at the day nursery believed in fresh air, and children in the nursery were often taken to the roof of the building to listen to stories, even during the cold months when they were bundled into seasonal coats and jackets.

My great grandmother Nellie's generation was born too early to realize the benefit of Social Security. Nellie, always desperate for money, modeled "pregnancy corsets" as a living model in a downtown department store window. We've always wondered if this job resulted in two of her younger daughters being born with severe disabilities, including the daughter she named Jane Addams in homage to her friend. The only government support Nellie received for the two girls, who were not able to live on their own, was a miniscule stipend for the blind from the state because one of them was legally blind.

My grandmother Edna, Nellie's second child, was fortunate. She met and married a bright young man, who ran a candy store she frequented, and he studied to become a dentist. This brought them both into the relatively new middle class. My grandfather Paul bought a house for himself and his wife and child while also providing continuing support for his mother-in-law Nellie and her two disabled daughters. My grandmother, who had spent her early years going door to door selling handmade menstrual pads and aprons made by her mother, was now freed from work. It was meaningful that Edna did not need to have a job in order for the family to pay the bills. Unlike her father, her husband reliably provided for their family.

Regardless of their new level of comfort, my grandmother spent her adult life volunteering nearly every day of the week in an orphanage and Brailling books for the blind. Edna gave more than 50 years of steadfast volunteer service and won many accolades. My grandparents also sponsored foster children with whom they exchanged correspondence and for whom they provided tuition and gifts. Rather than buying more expensive items or taking luxurious vacations, Edna plowed all of her free time into volunteer work. Moreover, when my dentist grandfather retired, he immediately began to volunteer as a literacy tutor and did this for another decade.

When I was young, their volunteerism didn't make that much sense to me, but now, I understand and admire it. My grandparents, who professed no religious affiliation, were devotees of the "Church of Jane Addams" – or perhaps better said, the Church of Social and Civic Engagement. They were not alone. Jane Addams herself once wrote, "...for many people without church affiliations the vague humanitarianism the settlement represented was the nearest approach they would find to an expression of their religious sentiments" (as cited in Davis, 1973, p. 105).

The women and men of Hull-House, in the 1890s and in the decades beyond, became effective agents of social change both inside and outside government. Florence Kelley, an early and influential resident, helped establish mandatory factory inspections, universal public education for children, and lower mandatory hours for working women; she also spearheaded one of the first, comprehensive studies of a neighborhood, *The Hull-House Maps and Papers* (Crowell, 1895; Knight, 2010). Julia Lathrop, one of the three women who helped chase away the drunken abuser that night in 1890, helped set up children's rights organizations, including the first juvenile court. Jane Addams herself was a founding member of the American Civil Liberties Union (ACLU, n.d.) and the National Association for the Advancement of Colored People (Michaels, 2017), and she founded the Woman's Peace Party, which evolved into the Women's International League for Peace and Freedom, serving as its first president (Jane Addams Peace Association, n.d.). Astonishingly, she was appointed a garbage inspector for the Nineteenth ward in the 1890's. The overflowing garbage — including rotting carcasses of horses, piles of trash swarming with rats, and sewers overflowing with fetid sewage water — were a hazard to community health, and, when Addams and her colleagues could not get Alderman Johnny Powers to take action, they mobilized and got Addams appointed (Elshtain, 2002, p.170).

## Central Role of the Arts

Hull-House always positioned the arts in a central role. The arts provided not only access to beauty and a release from daily cares, but also a public way to honor renowned European artists and the art of immigrants and working people. Hull-House's Butler Art Gallery hosted more than 300 visitors per day by 1893 (Knight, 2005). There were free weekly Sunday afternoon concerts; a music school offering piano, voice, and dance lessons; a theatre company; and several choruses. Hull-House offered woodworking and pottery classes in addition to numerous book clubs and philosophy clubs. Another innovation was the Hull-House Labor Museum, opened in 1900, for which Addams hired older skilled artisans, most of them women immigrants, to demonstrate their expertise in textiles, woodworking, and pottery (Davis, 1973, p. 129). The Museum was an attempt to counter increasing mass production and machine production and showcase the importance of fine craftmanship as well as pass along those skills to second and third generation immigrants (Hull-House Labor Museum, n.d.). Hull-House had plays, festivals, and numerous social clubs for boys and girls that engaged thousands of children in recreational and cultural activities. In this way, Jane Addams and the women of Hull-House abided by the words of the famous poem by James Oppenheim (later made into a song by several composers): "Hearts starve as well as bodies; give us bread, but give us roses" (Oppenheim, 1911).

## Writing a Musical

When my grandmother Edna gave birth to my mother Carol in 1924, Jane Addams knitted her a sweater. A sweet picture was taken of my mother in that sweater, and it's a good thing the photo was taken because not long afterward, curious toddler Carol tried to "trim" the edge with scissors and destroyed the whole thing. In 1934, shortly before she died, Addams also gave Great Grandmother Nellie a signed photograph of her, which is now my prized possession. Jane Addams' role in my family, her activism, love of reading and the arts, and the two photographs would already be enough reason to write a musical play about her. After all, I have written, recorded, and published many songs, often about women's history and rights, so this would be a logical thing to do.

*Chapter 23 Image 1.* Author's grandmother Edna and mother Carol in a sweater that Jane Addams knitted for her. Photo Courtesy, Kristin Lems.

*Chapter 23 Image 2.* Jane Addams, autographed and given to the author's great grandmother Nellie. Photo Courtesy, Kristin Lems

However, when my mother casually mentioned to me in 2015 that there was a big box of additional materials sitting in her closet, sent to her by her cousin in 2009, the project suddenly became a lot more compelling — and urgent. My grandmother's older sister, Florence, had written a history about the family's life during the 1890s and 1900s. It included many vivid, firsthand descriptions of her visits to

Hull-House and conversations with Jane Addams. The manuscript detailed the books that Jane Addams gave Florence at every holiday and also confirmed that Jane had supported Nellie financially through several crises. This never-published history, in fact two drafts of it, were sitting in that box, and my mom and I read through them hungrily. Here was a unique primary source about what it was like to grow up in the squalor and the vitality of the Nineteenth Ward at the turn of the previous century. It was truly a stunning find.

At the time, I was also contending with the slow decline of my mother, who was already in her nineties and having trouble living on her own. In the last two years of dear mother's life, which concluded in summer 2019, I completed a draft of a musical about these extraordinary women and events called *Saint Jane and the Wicked Wicks*. Happily, my mother attended two readings of it, one only four days before she passed away. Her approval was what I hoped for most, and I had her blessing that the "story must be told" – and told by me!

Encompassing 15 years in the life of Hull-House and the early life of my great grandmother, Nellie Wicks, *Saint Jane and the Wicked Wicks* opens with Nellie's original encounter with Jane Addams on that dramatic night in 1890 and continues through 1905, when Nellie married for the third time, and Jane set her up in a new home in Englewood. During this time period, the World's Columbian Exposition also took place in Chicago in 1893, and the musical includes the day that Nellie and her brother take a day off work to attend the fair, courtesy of Jane Addams. *Saint Jane and the Wicked Wicks* has 13 scenes and 15 original songs and is directed by renowned director Douglas Post and performed by a cast of nine professional actors/singers. Despite the pandemic and all of its setbacks, it is now available online as an audio musical play (Lems, 2021) and can be enjoyed for free (https://youtu.be/eLVj5waLTf8) or for a voluntary donation (https://www.saintjaneplay.com/).

My involvement in the arts in Chicago is not only rooted in the history of my family and of Hull-House, it also includes another influential Chicago initiative: Louder Than A Bomb, an international poetry slam that was renamed the Rooted & Radical Youth Poetry Festival in 2021.

Louder Than A Bomb originated in Chicago at the turn of the millennium and has now spread to many sites across the country and around the world. I published an article about Louder Than A Bomb (Lems, 2020) in a previous issue of the International Leadership Association's *Interface* newsletter, and the remainder of this article incorporates most of that essay along with edits and updates.

*Chapter 23 Image 3.* Louder Than A Bomb Poetry Festival. Photo Credit, Kristin Lems.

## Louder Than A Bomb: A Powerful Brew

In March of 2020 the Louder Than A Bomb Poetry Festival took place around Chicago, offering five weeks of youth poetry performances at assorted venues throughout the city. Billed as "the largest youth poetry festival in the world," these electrifying slam competitions, featuring all original work by high school and college-aged poets, have included as many as 130 teams from around the city and suburbs. The youth prepare for the event over many months, in both solo and group numbers, usually under the guidance of a school coach or club sponsor. Because of COVID-19, the semifinals and finals for the 2020 LTAB festival occurred by means of YouTube live streams. In 2021, the festival renamed itself the Rooted & Radical Youth Poetry Festival and was fully virtual, broadcasting a 1-hour show on the 18$^{th}$ of June (https://youtu.be/-jQS-o-CSLk).

LTAB was legendary, having been the subject of a celebrated award-winning documentary which tracked the progress of several contestants as they prepared their performances in 2008 (Jacobs & Siskel, 2011). The festival has won numerous grants and engages in many partnerships adding new forms and formats each year such as school residencies for students at the junior high school level, a Latinx-themed competition "Louder Than A Bomba," rapper-led training in emceeing through a weekly "Emcee Wreckshop," and a free weekly writer's salon for queer and questioning youth called "Queeriositiy." Like Hull-House, Louder Than A Bomb/Rooted & Radical has deep roots in Chicago culture. Below I describe the Chicago origins, evolution, and impact of the festival and its parent organization Young Chicago Authors.

### Chicago Origins

At least three strands have nourished the roots of Louder Than A Bomb/Rooted & Radical. The first is improvisational comedy. The Second City comedy club, which emerged in the Old Town neighborhood of Chicago in the 1960s, featured a new kind of comedy — comedy on the stage, with humor created on the spot. Second City showcased (and continues to showcase) irreverent, uproarious, truth-telling sketches about current events in an immersive, interactive format. The format consists of a small team of multitalented actors who use impersonations, voices, costumes, and props on stage, along with bits of music or musical parodies, sight gags, and even dancing.

An evening at Second City consists of two acts. The first consists of pre-written short scenes, and for the second, the cast solicits words and topics to create sketches right on the spot. Half the fun is watching the actors grapple with improbable words and topics, as the audience tries to stump them — and somehow, never does. Also in the second half, a couple of audience members are dragged up on stage as "extras" for scenes in which they are drafted for a role. The audience roars in approval, and a good time is had by all.

The Second City format spawned not only many spinoffs, including comedy clubs, sketch comedy, improv classes, and competitive Improv Olympics, but the hit television series *Saturday Night Live* (SNL). Many of America's great comedians and talk show hosts trained at Second City, including Tina Fey, Steve Carell, Stephen Colbert, Amy Poehler, and Seth Meyers. Even Trevor Noah's *Late Show* on Comedy Central can be considered a variation of the topical comedy genre started at The Second City.

The second strand of Louder Than A Bomb/Rooted & Radical's Chicago roots comes from the Uptown Poetry Slam, which has been held at the Green Mill Tavern every Sunday evening since 1986 (Kogan, 2011; Smith, n.d.). This homey, un-gentrified jazz club attracts aspiring poets who want to try moving a crowd with their words. Performers arrive by six on Sunday evening to sign up for a spot, and a small house band provides continuity between performers. Three judges are randomly selected from the audience, and the "purse" is a grand prize of $10. This counter to pretentious literary events is open to all. The term "poetry slam" originated with the Green Mill's emcee Marc Smith, who said in a *Chicago Tribune* interview on the Slam's 20th anniversary, "I was being interviewed by some reporter and asked what these things were called and I had just been watching a baseball game and I was thinking ... slam, grand slam ... Poetry slam" (as quoted in Kogan, 2011).

The third and probably most consequential strand of Louder Than A Bomb/Rooted & Radical's Chicago roots is hip hop and rap culture, which is popular and influential in the city, especially among urban youth of color. Black, Latinx and other youth of color create and perform in many venues and are central participants in LTAB. Although hip hop and rap did not originate in Chicago, they certainly thrive here. World-renowned hip hop and rap artists who have grown up and built their careers in Chicago include Common, Twista, Kanye West, and multiple Grammy-winner Chance the Rapper.

It's easy to see the intertwined roots of these three converging in Louder Than A Bomb/Rooted & Radical. The Louder Than A Bomb/Rooted & Radical format consists of a small team that performs individually and in combination, similar to the cast of Second City. The idea of oral poetry slams in small performance spaces is an offshoot of the poetry slams at the Green Mill. Hip hop and rap provide the models for the self-expression and social activism that inform the work of the Louder Than A Bomb/Rooted & Radical artists.

*Chapter 23 Image 4.* Louder Than A Bomb Poetry Festival. Photo Credit: Kristin Lems.

### My Involvement With the Festival

I had the pleasure of serving as a judge for one round of the Louder Than A Bomb tournaments for three successive years prior to the pandemic. Judges were chosen through a simple online application at the Young Chicago Authors website where we declared that we had no conflict of interest and an abiding interest in youth poetry. Judges sat in the front row of the performance space, were given a small erasable whiteboard and marker, and were instructed to write a score from 1-10 (with 10 being a "perfect" score and one decimal point allowed) immediately after each performance.

The performances I witnessed were short, passionate, original, and often featured themes of fighting injustice and finding resilience. The pieces were heartfelt, sometimes heartbreaking, and always inspiring. During the performances, audiences were allowed to show approval only by quietly snapping their fingers. No verbal feedback was permitted. This created a respectful atmosphere and professional vibe. At the end, the scorekeeper announced the top scoring team, and the crowd was allowed to cheer and applaud. All the teams exchanged hugs, compliments, and fist bumps, as camaraderie and mutual respect seemed to fill the room. All of us lucky enough to be in the Louder Than A Bomb audience not only heard and saw outstanding artistic talent and skill, but we also experienced something like "group therapy" as gifted young people disclosed their vulnerabilities and struggles through poetry in an intimate environment. It was a privilege to be there.

With the reimagining of the festival from Louder Than A Bomb to Rooted & Radical, the organization has also changed up the system for scoring and judging the performances. Many coaches felt that the scoring system was "commodifying students' pain" by "asking students to share, sometimes, the hardest thing they've ever lived through, in front of an audience," and then "giving it a score" (as quoted in Moore, 2021).

*Chapter 23 Image 5.* Louder Than A Bomb Poetry Festival. Photo Credit: Kristin Lems.

Both Hull-House and Louder Than A Bomb/Rooted & Radical have had a huge impact on Chicago and beyond. Jane Addams and Hull-House effectively launched the fields of social work, urban studies, and created a clarion call to civic engagement. Louder Than A Bomb/Rooted & Radical's winning combination of performance poetry, writing skill development, and grassroots community activism has given rise to a whole generation of young people ready and able to speak their truths. These creative ways to involve communities are both cutting edge and timeless. The ripples of Jane Addams and her band of merry women extend far and wide — my new musical is one such ripple in the water — and Louder Than A Bomb/Rooted & Radical reverberates around the city and around the country. Songs and stories that illuminate the struggles of the past, combined with today's stirring young poets, are sure to make more waves for many years to come.

## Resources

To learn more about Hull-House and Jane Addams visit https://www.hullhousemuseum.org/

To learn more about the Young Chicago Authors and the Rooted & Radical festival, visit https://youngchicagoauthors.org/

## References

ACLU. (n.d.). Jane Addams. Women Who Put Women's Rights on the ACLU Agenda. https://www.aclu.org/other/women-who-put-womens-rights-aclu-agenda

Crowell, T.Y. (1895). *Hull-House Maps and Papers: A Presentation of Nationalities and Wages in a Congested District of Chicago, Together With Comments and Essays on Problems Growing out of the Social Conditions.* https://openlibrary.org/books/OL14013937M/Hull-House_maps_and_papers

Davis, A.F. (1973). *American Heroine: The Life and Legend of Jane Addams.* Oxford University Press.

Elshtain, J.B. (2002). Jane Addams and the Dream of American Democracy. Basic Books.

Hull-House Labor Museum. (n.d.). Jane Addams Digital Edition. https://digital.janeaddams.ramapo.edu/items/show/134

Jacobs, G. & Siskel, J. (2011). Louder Than A Bomb. http://www.louderthanabombfilm.com/

Jane Addams Peace Association. (n.d.). Jane Addams and Social Justice. https://www.janeaddamschildrensbookaward.org/about/jane-addams-and-social-justice/

Kogan, R. (2011, July 15). Marc Smith Celebrates 20 Years of Poetry Slams. *The Chicago Tribune.* https://www.chicagotribune.com/entertainment/ct-xpm-2011-07-15-ct-ae-0717-kogan-sidewalks-20110716-story.html

Knight, L.W. (2005). *Citizen: Jane Addams and the Struggle for Democracy.* The University of Chicago Press.

Knight, L. (2010). *Jane Addams: Spirit in Action.* Norton.

Lems, K. (2021). *Saint Jane and the Wicked Wicks.* www.SaintJanePlay.com.

Lems, K. (2020, April). Louder Than A Bomb: Poetry Slams and Community Activism Create a Powerful Brew. Grassroots Leadership & Arts for Social Change Corner, Susan J. Erenrich Ed. *Interface Newsletter.* International Leadership Association. https://intersections.ilamembers.org/member-benefit-access/interface/grassroots-leadership/louder-than-a-bomb-by-kristin-lems

McArthur, B. (1975). The Chicago Playground Movement: A Neglected Feature of Social Justice. *Social Service Review,* 49(3), 376–395. http://www.jstor.org/stable/30015251

Michaels, D. (2017). Jane Addams. National Women's History Museum. https://www.womenshistory.org/education-resources/biographies/jane-addams

Moore, T. (2021, July 21). A Silence Louder Than Words. *Chicago Reader.* https://chicagoreader.com/news-politics/a-silence-louder-than-words/

Oppenheim, J. (1911 December). Bread and Roses. *The American Magazine.* https://jwa.org/media/bread-and-roses-poem

Smith, M.K. (n.d.). Marc Kelly Smith. http://www.marckellysmith.net/about.html

Williams, M. T. (2005). Baths, Public. *The Electronic Encyclopedia of Chicago.* Chicago Historical Society. http://www.encyclopedia.chicagohistory.org/pages/119.html

## About the Author

Performing songwriter and folksinger Kristin Lems has been active in the movements for civil rights, peace, and safe energy over 4 decades. She founded the National Women's Music Festival in Champaign-Urbana Illinois in 1974 and has enlivened countless events, especially for women's rights, with her wit and warmth. The New Yorker calls her "a charmer in the most literal and least artificial sense of the word." Kristin has released 8 albums of mostly original songs on her own label, Carolsdatter Productions, named for her mother, Carol Lems-Dworkin. Her topical songs about women's rights are included in two Smithsonian/Folkways collections and many publications. She is also a professor with an extensive catalog of publications, mostly about literacy and language learning. Her first full length musical, Saint Jane and the Wicked Wicks, based on the true relationship between the young Jane Addams and Kristin's great grandmother, Nellie Wicks, was written, directed, and produced during the COVID-19 pandemic. It can be enjoyed in its entirety at: Saint Jane and the Wicked Wicks - full show (https://youtu.be/eLVj5waLTf8). She looks forward to a stage production of the show. Contact: kristinlems@yahoo.com.

# CHAPTER 24
# HENRY STREET, THE ARTS FOR SOCIAL CHANGE, & OTHER PROJECTS

## NAIMA PREVOTS

## INTRODUCTION

By Susan J. Erenrich

In the fall of 1983, I met the author of this chapter, Naima Prevots. She was the chair of American University's Dance Program, and I was a budding graduate student. During our time together, we discussed my three-week intensive workshop with the Wallflower Order Dance Collective. The experience was fresh on my mind because in the summer of 1982, I had gone to Cambridge, Massachusetts to study with the politically oriented company. The adventure was transformational, and it literally changed my life.

For readers unfamiliar with the horizontally led women's dance troupe, it was founded in Eugene, Oregon, in the 1970s. Themes during the early years were feminist in nature. As the collective matured, its attention shifted to topics of global significance such as South Africa, Chile, and Central America. Through dance, theatre, music, sign language, and the martial arts, the Wallflower Order powerfully delivered their message to everyone who crossed their path.

Following three weeks of technique, Wallflower repertory, and choreography, the Cambridge community was invited to a celebratory benefit performance. It was a sold-out crowd. Proceeds from the evening were donated to women of war-torn El Salvador and women in prison. I had found my calling, which led me to Naima Prevots, first as a mentor, and then a lifelong friend.

In the midst of my first semester at American University, Naima introduced me to Chester Wolensky, who performed with the Limón Dance Company from 1956 – 1962. Chester was the visiting artist that term. He took me under his wing and helped me choreograph *Hay Una Mujer Desaparecida* for the fall concert. It was the tenth anniversary of the U.S. backed military coup in Chile — the other September 11th of 1973, decades before the fall of the twin towers in New York City.

The three musicians on stage, April Powers and Steve and Peter Jones, originally sang *Hay Una Mujer Desaparecida*, written by Holly Near, for the annual Orlando Letelier / Ronni Karpen Moffett remembrance. See chapter 17 by Letelier's son, Francisco, for further details of Letelier's assassination on September 21, 1976, on Embassy Row in Washington, D.C.

For four nights, *Hay Una Mujer Desaparecida* was introduced to full houses. The spectators did not know how to react. Should they clap? There was always apprehension. As the political climate changed in Chile, so did the end of the dance as I resurrected it during subsequent anniversaries.

Dancing for social change is not a new phenomenon. It didn't start with the formation of the Wallflower Order Dance Collective, and it certainly didn't end with the troupe. Naima reminds us in her guest column that this art form has always been an integral part of the long trajectory of cultural activism.

I hope readers are enlightened by Naima's piece. It accentuates how this misunderstood and under appreciated art form is a universal language that can be used as a force for good.

# HENRY STREET, THE ARTS FOR SOCIAL CHANGE, & OTHER PROJECTS

By Naima Prevots

For the past three years, Susie has been asking me to write something for the guest column of "The Grassroots Leadership and the Arts for Social Change Corner." I have read the columns with excitement, and I am consistently impressed with the vitality, importance, and imagination of those writing about the programs artists and activists have developed. I did not see my past work in the arena of social change as being directly related to what was featured, and so I declined. But somehow, in the last weeks, it occurred to me that maybe the past has some meaning for the future and that what I did in the 1950s-90s could raise questions, initiate discussion, and be of interest.

In looking back, the environment was different when I started to get involved in the 1950s. I do not remember people talking about "grassroots" in conjunction with "the arts for social change." I don't remember artists in the trenches, building theatres, dance groups, galleries in and for communities, and working on specific issues. The WPA (Works Progress Administration) government/arts programs of the1930s had been eliminated by 1943. When the NEA (National Endowment for the Arts) and NEH (National Endowment for the Humanities) were created in 1965, and the government once again got involved, this changed the landscape and helped foster what we have now. My first experience with "social change" was my 1955 job at the summer camp operated by the Henry Street Settlement House.

The concept of a settlement house was first developed in the UK in the 1880s. Social reformers took over existing physical facilities in poverty-stricken urban areas. They would live in these buildings and create programs for educating and helping immigrants and others. The idea of "settling" in a place and establishing programs that would change the lives of those who had very little soon came to America. The first American settlement houses were established in the mid-to-late 1880s and included the Neighborhood Guild in New York City and Hull-House in Chicago (see chapter 23). In 1893, the Henry Street Settlement House was created on New York's Lower East Side by Lillian Wald, who came from a wealthy German Jewish family. She received her nursing degree in 1891, and she made the decision to devote herself to helping the "poor and needy."

By 1893, she had "settled in" and lived in a tenement near the families she was serving in the Henry Street area. In 1895, the banker and philanthropist, Jacob Schiff, purchased the property at 265 Henry Street, and this became Wald's housing and headquarters. She created many programs to help and serve her families, including classes in English, literature, history, disease prevention and health maintenance, and also in a variety of arts. By the late 1920s, the settlement house movement had peaked, but at one point there were more than 400 settlement houses in the United States, largely in the Northeast and Midwest. Henry Street Settlement House became well known for its programs in dance, theatre, and music. It housed the Neighborhood Playhouse, created in 1915, which became a showcase and experimental laboratory for dance and theatre. In 1927, the Henry Street Music School was created for classes and performances at all levels, including the training and showcasing of young professionals and classes with important composers and performers.

I remember there were about 100 boys/young men who had been given the opportunity in 1955 to be at the Henry Street Settlement House camp. They were ages thirteen to sixteen, and most were recent immigrants from Puerto Rico. There were also campers from Asian, African American, and White families. Lillian Wald, from the very beginning, mandated racial inclusion, and in 1909, she was involved in the founding of the NAACP. The goal was to give these campers experiences that would provide a positive and encouraging environment and help increase their future opportunities. I had just graduated from college and was happy to have a job at the camp as a drama and dance counselor. I worked with the boys at the camp in small groups, trying to help them imagine, think, share, and learn while giving them tools for their return to the city, to school, to overcrowded and small apartments.

Each of my groups met every day, and I struggled to reach out to them and make our sessions productive and interesting. We talked about their families, their lives, their hopes and dreams, the disturbances in their lives, their siblings, and histories. I would go back to my cabin each day and try to write these stories up. When I felt we were ready, I would create scripts that they could read and rehearse and also change and improvise. When we were ready, we presented these and received feedback. There were times when I shifted gears and took heroic stories and wrote these up for them to work on, discuss, and ultimately present to us all. I wanted them to work together to create, and I wanted them to understand their past and work for a better future. Was I using the arts as social change? That term was not used in my situation then, but I believe our work together was helping them reimagine their place in the world. As I look back, this was an effort to use the arts as social change, to help these students feel more confident, to better understand themselves and others, and to feel hope for the future.

Another opportunity arose more than ten years later, when I got involved in a new government initiative to improve children's lives through participation in the arts. In 1965, the Elementary and Secondary Education Act was passed in the United States — an unprecedented move by the government to improve public school education. One of the projects created was the CAREL (Central Atlantic Education Laboratory) Arts and Humanities Curriculum Development Program for Young Children. There were five components — dance, theatre, music, literature, and visual arts — and the goal was to make these integral to learning in the classroom. This would enable children ages three to eight to explore and understand the world in ways that would make them more capable of achieving personal and academic fulfillment. From 1968-69, I worked with a colleague, Dr. Geraldine Dimondstein, in CAREL'S dance component. We worked with fifteen teachers in Washington, D.C., Maryland, and Virginia, from preschool through third grade, representing the inner city and suburbia, with children and teachers of many different backgrounds and ethnicities.

We met with classroom teachers in three consecutive and eight bi-weekly workshops, which lasted two hours each time. The workshop content was based on participants solving movement problems focused on the basic concepts of dance, time, space, force. Every workshop was devoted to a single concept. As an example, one workshop was focused on the concept of force. Teachers explored movement qualities: percussive, sustained, vibratory, swinging. They were asked to solve the problem of creating a study based on the specific quality of an inanimate object and individual solutions brought out a roll of scotch tape, a pencil sharpener, waves in the ocean, an egg beater. Working in groups, three teachers created a "sewing machine dance," three variations on aspects of a campfire, and a complex "oil drill dance" with several moving parts.

Teachers were observed every week in their classrooms, and there were individual consultations, weekly reports, and evaluations. In one first grade class I observed a "Solar System Dance," which the students had created based on their study of spatial patterns and their trip to a museum. In another class, the study of movement qualities produced several "weather report dances." Four children told of storms and rough seas, and another group danced about sandstorms and winds in the desert. Teachers worked with the boys and girls in the classroom, and some 400 children were involved in the CAREL project.

As a working mom, I would sometimes take my six-year-old daughter with me. When I recently shared with her that I was writing about CAREL, she told me: "Mom, I remember going to schools with you. It was fun. I remember getting a cupcake while children were dancing!" In the last few weeks of the project, we hired three young professional movie men and shot 6000 feet of film, which I then edited down to 500 feet. *Children Dance* is the name of the film we produced, and for many years it was available from the Extension Media Center in Berkeley. In January 1971, an article on CAREL was published in *Dance Magazine*, and recently the curriculum we wrote was made available on DELRdi, the data base of the National Dance Education Organization.

It is my belief that our work with CAREL showed teachers how to utilize dance to make learning accessible, interesting, and productive for all children whether they were children who typically learned concepts easily or who usually had more difficulty. By making dance part of the classroom experience, teachers changed the attitudes of students who were often left behind while those students who usually succeeded found new imaginative possibilities in learning and doing. We did not use the phrase "arts and social change," but as I look back, this was clearly an integral part of what we were doing.

In 1967, I began my forty-year career as a professor at American University. In finishing these reflections, I will share two efforts at passing on the baton of involvement. The first was with the great African American choreographer/teacher/performer Pearl Primus, and the second was a HUD (Housing and Urban Development) program. In 1992, American University and Howard University (a historically Black university) were awarded a grant from the Lila Wallace-Reader's Digest Arts Partners Program (coordinated by the Association of Performing Arts Presenters, now known as The Association of Performing Arts Professionals) to have Pearl Primus in residence and bring the two different communities and audiences together. Primus was in residence from September through December. She auditioned students from both schools and prepared them, in classes and rehearsals, for two performances: one at Howard University and one at the John F. Kennedy Center for the Performing Arts (Kennedy Center). The performances in December consisted of reconstructions of older works including *Invocation, Prayer of Thanksgiving; The Negro Speaks of Rivers; The Wedding; The Griot; Caribbean Vignettes*; and a new work *"Dance to Save Lives."*

Pearl Primus (1919-1994) is one of the giants of American dance and an important artist who influenced many in their understanding and appreciation of African dance and culture. She was born in Trinidad and came to New York with her parents when she was two years old. In 1940, she graduated from Hunter College as a "pre-med" student with a biology major. Her plan was to enroll in medical school and work in a science laboratory to earn money, but racial discrimination made it impossible for her to get work. Primus took a series of odd jobs instead, and one was as wardrobe assistant in a New Deal project: The National Youth Administration's production, "America Dances." When there was need for a substitute dancer, Primus stepped in. Not only did she love doing this, she was very good. By 1941, she was immersed in classes at the New Dance Group, whose motto was "dance is a weapon of the class struggle."

In 1943, she made her debut as choreographer and performer at the 92nd Street Y in New York City, which has long been a center for the arts. Included in that concert were two works that exemplified her involvement with both African American life and African dance and culture. "A Man Has Just Been Lynched" was set to the poem "Strange Fruit" and became one of her signature works. Created when lynchings were commonplace, the dance showed the anguish and cruelty of these horrors. Another dance on the program was "African Ceremonial," which was one of many choreographies she created exploring African dance and culture. As the recipient of many fellowships, she was able to travel to Africa to conduct research, and she also travelled to the South to learn more about African American life in the United States. In 1978, she finished her PhD in anthropology at New York University (NYU). She taught in many colleges and universities and continued her concert work until her death.

For the American University students who auditioned and participated, the experience exposed them to new worlds of movement and culture. The Howard University students may have had some background, but the depth of understanding provided by Primus was beyond anything they had known. Rehearsals were intense and involved questions, conversations, and sometimes lectures on various components of African life and dance as well as discussions of life in America for African Americans. Sometimes the differences in the two groups were clear and strong, but fortunately, often all came together in this joint venture.

One of the students recalled: "For a little bit we really broke down barriers.... Whatever things we came in with, whatever walls, brick by brick we were taking them down." It was very clear to me that for most of the American University students who participated, the experience of working closely with African American peers was very new. Furthermore, going to the Howard campus for rehearsals and experiencing a very different campus was sometimes startling. For many in the audience at each performance, exposure to the work of a great African American artist and pioneer was a revelation. This was probably particularly true of the Kennedy Center audience. The project was not always easy and there were tensions, but those involved remember a unique experience.

The last project I want to share is the grant I received from HUD (Housing and Urban Development) in 1996 to develop after school dance activities in Anacostia in Washington, D.C., which was a significantly underserved area with a largely African American population. I asked two of my American University graduate dance students to teach and direct dance classes over a period of several months. Recently, I was in touch with one of them, Barry Blumenfeld. He is active in dance education in a variety of ways, as he is an Adjunct Professor at NYU and teaches at New York's 92nd Street Y. He is also the Director of Dance at a Friends School in New York where he created the school's K-12 dance program. Every student at the school is involved in classes, and there are special activities for those with strong interests. In 2019, he was recognized by the National Dance Education Organization with the Outstanding Leadership Award for his many initiatives in the field of dance education. His participation in the HUD program provided him with new experiences. He emailed me as follows: "From my vantage point now, I can see how unaware I was of the community's culture and what it meant being a White person there. It was definitely a good experience for me and helped me develop as an educator" (B. Blumenfeld, personal communication, October 8, 2020).

The other graduate student involved in the HUD project was Brooke Kidd, who created the non-profit World Dance Focus, which supports two facilities in Maryland — one in Mt. Rainer and the other one in Suitland. She established Joe's Movement Emporium in 1995, and the web page, at the time of this writing, notes that this is a "community that stands for justice" and is a "cultural hub that acts as a catalyst for creative and economic opportunity for all." Brooke was already leaning in the direction of working in underserved communities, when I applied for the HUD grant, and it gave her more experience and reinforced her interest in going in this direction. In 1991, Brooke received her undergraduate degree from American University in International Relations and was very active in the dance program where she took classes, was involved in performances, and did an honors final project. She received her MA in Dance Education in 1998, and was already developing her important arts center in Mt. Rainer, which the website (pre-pandemic) noted serves more than 70,000 visitors annually.

It is my hope that reflections on these past projects will generate questions and memories from others. What other projects existed from the 1950s through the turn of the century? How were they generated, who were the constituents, and how were they evaluated? How do they compare with what is happening today and did they influence current activities and initiatives? These are some of the issues that perhaps can be generated by my memories of past efforts.

### Resources

HenryStSettlement. (2018, June 22). Baptism of Fire - The House on Henry Street [video]. YouTube. https://youtu.be/0dcP2b5_8dg

James, A. (2012, December 24). Luncheon Honoring Pearl Primus @ Howard U. 1192.m4v [video]. YouTube. https://youtu.be/KX6GGZhvTdE

### About the Author

Naima Prevots has worked in the arts and education worlds in many capacities including as a dance critic, administrator, teacher, choreographer, performer, educator, writer, historian, and panelist. In 1952, as a sophomore at Brandeis University, she was chosen as one of two students to perform with Merce Cunningham at the school's first Creative Arts Festival. This prompted a return to New York, a transfer to Brooklyn College, and study with Martha Graham, José Limón, Hanya Holm, and Alwin Nikolais. Study with Marie Marchowsky, a former Graham dancer, led to membership in her company and performances at Henry Street Settlement House Playhouse. This was followed by study at Juilliard, work as a dance and drama specialist in schools and in the New York Recreation Department, and then a year working in Israel with immigrant children. Upon returning to the United States, she completed her Master's at the University of Wisconsin after which she moved to Washington, D.C. In D.C., she co-founded a dance company that pioneered concerts in K-12 schools, taught at Norwood School as a dance specialist, and performed with Pola Nirenska's company.

The years at American University (AU), from 1967 to her retirement in 2003, involved new directions: advocacy in Arts Education; leadership and involvement in boards and arts agencies; consulting in Israel for the Ministry of Education; and six Fulbright Fellowships to Australia, Belgium, the Netherlands, Portugal, and Germany. The European Fulbright awards involved an EU project in the arts and humanities and the development of a Master's at the Hochschule in Cologne. From 1971-1981, she created an intensive summer program at AU that involved residencies of companies and artists including Twyla Tharp, Erick Hawkins, Murray Louis, Laura Dean, Paul Taylor, and José Limón. Originally hired at AU in the Physical Education department, she helped create the university's Department of Performing Arts. In 1974, appointed full professor, she served as Director of Dance and later as Chair of the Department. AU's dance graduate program became one of the largest graduate programs in the College of Arts and Sciences. Over the years, she served on numerous boards and panels including the U.S. Department of Education; National Endowment for the Arts, National Endowment for the Humanities, D.C. Commission on the Arts and Humanities, Fulbright Association, Congress on Research in Dance, and National Dance Education Association. During the years at American University, she chaired several international conferences, including three for the Fulbright

Association. She recently consulted for the development of a Master's program at a college in Israel.

During the 1980s, Naima began to turn more to writing: books, articles, criticism, reviews. Her books all involved research into material that had not been explored in depth. They are: Dancing in the Sun; Hollywood Choreographers, 1915-1937; American Pageantry: A Movement for Art and Democracy; Dance for Export: Cultural Diplomacy and the Cold War. Her articles, book reviews, and criticism have been widely published in journals and newspapers as well as online. Currently she teaches online for the National Dance Education Organization where the new course she created focuses on Black, Women's, and Indigenous Voices in contemporary choreography. She is the recipient of many awards from American University and from various other organizations. Her most recent award was the 2019: Lifetime Achievement Award from the National Dance Education Organization (view her acceptance speech at https://www.ndeo.org/content.aspx?page_id=22&club_id=893257&module_id=355040). She was particularly thrilled that her now 17-year-old twin boy grandchildren were there in Miami when she gave her acceptance speech, and they took out their iPhones and filmed her... !!!

# CHAPTER 25
# THE PEOPLES' VOICE CAFE IN NEW YORK CITY
## STEPHEN SUFFET

## INTRODUCTION

By Susan J. Erenrich

This chapter spotlights the Peoples' Voice Cafe (PVC) (https://www.peoplesvoicecafe.org/) and is written by my longtime PVC compatriot — Steve Suffet.

For folks not familiar with the Cafe, it is an all-volunteer collective that has produced praiseworthy performances for New York City for almost 40 years. Every Saturday night from September through May, the Cafe provides a platform for the artistic expression of a wide variety of humanitarian matters and concerns.

The Cafe was originally a response to the changing political landscape of the 1970s. Artists involved in social change initiatives or community and movement building campaigns were experiencing an adverse reaction to their message. Many troubadours were unable to obtain paying engagements unless they changed or softened their rhetoric. Others had to find alternative ways to convey their sentiments. Topical singer-songwriters (who had been sidelined or who had been forced to find substitute employment) and performing artists from the New

York City area engaged in a number of conversations and, along with Pete Seeger, decided to take a stand. Judy Gorman, a singer-songwriter who was leading the charge, held the first meeting in her Manhattan apartment. A collective was constituted, and the balladeers searched for an appropriate space. Peoples' Voice Cafe was born.

As a member of the PVC booking committee since 2004, and a producer of many shows throughout my tenure, I am thrilled to feature this chapter for readers interested in horizontally led groups and institutions and the podcast that accompanies it.

As you're reading the chapter, please keep in mind that it was originally written prior to the COVID-19 global pandemic, which has been extremely challenging for performance venues like the Peoples' Voice Cafe. Still, the cafe carries on, even as the pandemic has exacerbated the challenges Steve identifies below.

### Listen

*Wasn't That A Time - Episode 86: The Peoples' Voice Cafe Celebrating Its 40th Season*

This episode salutes the Peoples' Voice Cafe. Folks will hear songs performed by The Ray Korona Band, Judy Gorman, Pete Seeger, The Kennedys, Carolyn Hester, Reggie Harris, Magpie, Kristin Lems, Colleen Kattau, and Rod MacDonald.

https://www.mixcloud.com/WasntThatATime/wasnt-that-a-time-episode-86-the-peoples-voice-cafe-celebrating-its-40th-season/

# THE PEOPLES' VOICE CAFE IN NEW YORK CITY

By Steve Suffet

If you ever find yourself in Manhattan on a Saturday night between mid-September and mid-May, and you are looking for performing artists who have something important to say and the voice with which to say it, then the Peoples' Voice Cafe is the place to be — as it has been for nearly 40 years.

Just don't let our name fool you, because if you are looking for a cafe in the usual sense of the word, you will not find one. Although coffee, tea, juice, and home-baked goodies are available for purchase immediately before each show and during intermission, the Peoples' Voice Cafe is not a small restaurant. We have no menus and no wait staff. Seating is often theater style, meaning in rows, rather than cafe style around small tables. That is because the Peoples' Voice Cafe is a volunteer run, collectively governed, politically progressive listening room. The music or other entertainment is not in the background while people dine and drink with their friends. It is, instead, the focus of the Peoples' Voice Cafe — the very reason for our existence.

*Chapter 25 Image 1.* Performer at the Peoples' Voice Cafe. Photo Courtesy, Steve Suffet.

Although the dozen or so people who first organized the Peoples' Voice Cafe resided throughout the New York metropolitan area, they all agreed that the Cafe should be located in the borough of Manhattan, and they found space available in Saint Joseph's Roman Catholic Church on Sixth Avenue at Washington Place in Greenwich Village. Since we first opened our doors on November 3, 1979, the Peoples' Voice Cafe has had to move half a dozen times, but we've always stayed within Manhattan. For the past ten years we have been located on the lower level of Community Church of New York, a venerable Unitarian-Universalist edifice on East 35th Street, just west of Park Avenue in Midtown. Ten years is the longest time period we have been in one place, and we hope to remain at Community Church for the foreseeable future. They have been a good landlord, and in many ways their mission is congruent with our own. [Note: Since this chapter was written, the Peoples' Voice Cafe moved back to Greenwich Village and, as of December 2021, resides at the Judson Memorial Church Assembly Hall at 239 Thompson Street.]

**What Do We Mean by Volunteer Run, Collectively Governed?**

From the beginning, the Peoples' Voice Cafe has been run by volunteers. While volunteers can get reimbursed for actual expenses they have paid out of their own pockets, no one gets paid for doing the many jobs that must be done. These include, among other things, booking the talent, publicizing the shows, handling the banking and bookkeeping, negotiating with the landlord, purchasing insurance, maintaining the mailing lists and other records, taking care of and operating the sound system, preparing and selling the snacks, making the announcements, introducing the acts, and helping the artists sell their merchandise.

Taken as a group, the currently active volunteers constitute the PVC Collective. As of this writing, the PVC Collective meets as a whole at least once, and usually twice, a year — although in the earliest days of the Peoples' Voice Cafe it met more frequently. Operating by consensus whenever possible, the PVC Collective is and always has been the ultimate governing body of the Peoples' Voice Cafe, but in practice its responsibility has been to set the general direction of the organization rather than supervise the specific operations. For example, the PVC Collective does not tell our volunteer programming committee which specific artist to book. It has, however, decided that the Peoples' Voice Cafe should present more performers of color, more openly LGBTQ performers, and more performers under thirty-five years of age, so the programming committee has followed up by making a conscious effort to book such artists.

The question of, "Who, exactly, is a member of the PVC Collective?" had for many years been a difficult one to answer. Would someone, for example, become a member by volunteering only once or twice during a season? Would someone be a member if he or she volunteers nearly every week but chooses not to attend any meetings?

For the first thirty-five years of our existence, an inner core of exceptionally active volunteers who assumed the leadership usually answered such questions. They decided when and where to hold meetings of the PVC Collective and whom to invite. In a very real sense, they became a "Collective within the Collective" without ever calling themselves that. Over time, of course, the membership of both the inner core and the larger PVC Collective continuously changed. Existing members lost interest, became less active, moved away, developed health problems, or in some cases died. Meanwhile, new members joined. There was, however, no formal mechanism for becoming a member of either the PVC Collective or its inner core. Some might say: "It just happened."

That all changed on May 16, 2014, when, after several years of discussion within the PVC Collective, the Peoples' Voice Cafe finally became a nonprofit corporation under the laws of New York State. Under our corporate bylaws, we have a board of directors that invites volunteers to become members of the PVC Collective. If they accept, they become members for three years, after which time their memberships expire and they have to be invited again. In turn, the members of the PVC Collective elect the PVC Board of Directors. That election takes place annually at a meeting of the PVC Collective. In this manner, we now have a clearly defined PVC Collective, as well as a leadership that is also clearly defined and that the PVC Collective has formally chosen.

I will examine the role of the PVC Board of Directors and its relationship to the PVC Collective farther down. But I first want to look at several other important issues.

*Chapter 25 Image 2.* Performer at the Peoples' Voice Cafe. Photo Courtesy, Steve Suffet.

## What About Peoples' Voice Cafe Membership?

In addition to the PVC Collective, the Peoples' Voice Cafe used to have actual members — people who paid annual dues to join. Being a member meant that you received periodic mailings, usually monthly except during the three-month summer hiatus, from the Peoples' Voice Cafe. It also meant that you were asked to make a smaller contribution for admission than nonmembers were asked to make. For example, during our 2013-2014 season we asked members to contribute $10 for admission, while nonmembers were asked to contribute $18. We say "contribute" because we had, and still have, a "no one turned away for lack of money" door policy.

Being a member, however, did not confer any voting rights, and the PVC Collective continued to be a self-selecting body rather than an elected one. Since incorporation in 2014, what had been called Peoples' Voice Cafe members are now known as Peoples' Voice Cafe subscribers, a much more accurate term. They still receive certain benefits, but as before, they do not have voting rights.

## What Is a Politically Progressive Listening Room?

When we say that the Peoples' Voice Cafe is a politically progressive listening room, we do not mean that we are affiliated with any particular political party or organization. We are not. Furthermore, our tax-exempt status under Section 501(c)(3) of the U.S. Internal Revenue Code prohibits us from supporting or opposing any specific candidates for public office, so we are not political in terms of electoral politics. Do not expect us to host a concert for such-and-such candidate. Even if we were allowed to do so, that is not who we are.

What we do, and have done from the beginning, is to present performing artists whose material directly relates to issues of peace, freedom, human rights, environmental protection, and social justice. Among these have been some very well-known artists including Pete Seeger, Odetta, Si Kahn, Kim and Reggie Harris, and Holly Near. But we have also presented many lesser known, enormously talented artists, such as Jean Rohe, Lindsey Wilson, and Joshua Garcia.

Our definition of politically progressive, however, is much broader than simply relating to the particular issues I previously mentioned. For example, we provide a venue for what we consider to be authentic voices of underrepresented cultures. This could mean presenting a Hawaiian music and dance night where the performers are from traditional Hawaiian society, either by birth or by adoption. Or it could mean presenting Appalachian music performed by people who are really from Appalachia or Ladino-Sephardic music performed by people who actually come from Ladino-Sephardic backgrounds.

In addition, politically progressive means offering a venue for union-based or community-based choruses or choirs. Over the years, these have included the New York City Labor Chorus; the Solidarity Singers, a union-based chorus from New Jersey; Voices of Shalom, a vocal ensemble from the African American Hebrew tradition; Lavender

Light, a mostly African American LGBTQ Gospel choir; the SAGE Singers, a chorus of LGBTQ seniors; and the Raging Grannies, a chorus of older women who write and sing political parodies.

For us, politically progressive also encompasses artists who "break the mold," so to speak, by defying the usual expectations and conventions of who should be performing what. For example, the Peoples' Voice Cafe has presented the Johnson Girls, an all-female quartet that sings sea chanteys, a genre that is overwhelmingly dominated by male groups. As far as we know, there have only been three all-female sea chantey groups worldwide, and the Johnson Girls are the only ones still in existence. In a similar vein, the Peoples' Voice Cafe has presented both Hubby Jenkins and Norris Bennett, two African American musicians who perform old-time country music, a genre that many people mistakenly believe to be exclusively White. We have also presented Pamela Jean Agaloos, a Philippine American woman whose repertoire comprises many traditional Celtic songs, including several that she sings in Irish or Scots Gaelic.

*Chapter 25 Image 3.* Performer at the Peoples' Voice Cafe. Photo Courtesy, Steve Suffet.

## A Question of Genre

Let me state right now that the commercial music industry would classify most of what Peoples' Voice Cafe presents as contemporary folk music or contemporary acoustic music, whatever those labels mean. We will accept that, but with the understanding that we are not entirely a folk music venue. In any given season, our program of approximately thirty to thirty-two shows might also include hip-hop, jazz, world beat music, poetry, storytelling, and dance. We have even put on theater from time to time, and in our very first season the Peoples' Voice Cafe presented a one-act play co-written and directed by Eve Ensler. That was in 1979, seventeen years before her well-known play *The Vagina Monologues* debuted.

## Division of Labor

From the very beginning, it was apparent that some Peoples' Voice Cafe volunteers possessed more skills, experience, and interest in certain areas than did other volunteers. For example, not everyone was equally adept at baking goodies, designing leaflets, keeping books, or operating a sound system, nor was everyone interested in becoming adept in each of those areas. This led almost immediately to a division of labor within the PVC Collective that still exists today.

A small working committee, often comprised of just one person, has generally emerged to handle each of the tasks required to keep the Peoples' Voice Cafe going. These committees and their leaders have usually been informally chosen or self-selected, often with the PVC Collective later giving its approval. Sometimes, however, the PVC Collective takes no formal action, and the committee continues to function as long as the PVC Collective does not object. For example, the PVC Collective has not, to my knowledge, ever taken action to formally approve our volunteer bakers.

As new tasks developed, such as creating and maintaining a Peoples' Voice Cafe presence on the Internet, volunteers have stepped forward to assume responsibility. Deciding upon overall policy, nevertheless, has always remained in the hands of the PVC Collective. That body, for example, authorized the creation of a Peoples' Voice Cafe website, accepted a volunteer's offer to serve as webmaster, accepted another volunteer's offer to help optimize the website's search engine visibility, and approved using a web-based service for maintaining the Peoples' Voice Cafe's email list.

Most of the time, the Peoples' Voice Cafe has welcomed any volunteer who is ready, willing, and able to work. If particular skills are required, then a Volunteer Coordinator assesses the volunteer's skill level and provides or arranges for training if necessary. One exception has been for the volunteers who operate the sound system. In that case, a Technical Director assesses their skills and provides or arranges for any necessary training. We also now have a Program Director to coordinate the activities of the volunteers who develop programs, book artists, and produce shows.

To summarize what is stated above, the PVC Collective, as a body, is responsible for setting the general direction of the Peoples' Voice Cafe as an organization. The specific operations, however, are left to the volunteers, either acting as individuals or in committees, sometimes with the guidance of the Volunteer Coordinator or the Technical Director.

*Chapter 25 Image 4.* Baked goods for sale at the Peoples' Voice Cafe. Photo Courtesy, Steve Suffet.

## Limits of Collective Governance

Whether the members of the PVC Collective knew it or not, the Peoples' Voice Cafe functioned for nearly thirty-five years as an unincorporated association under the laws of New York State. Without going into all the legal details, that status made it very difficult for the Peoples' Voice Cafe to obtain tax exemption under Section 501(c)(3) of the United States Internal Revenue Code. It was also nearly impossible for the Peoples' Voice Cafe to receive grants or solicit large donations. Being an unincorporated association also meant that members of the PVC Collective, and possibly members of the Peoples' Voice Cafe itself, could be held personally responsible for the Peoples' Voice Cafe's debts and liabilities. Fortunately, that never became an issue, but prior to incorporation, the potential for serious consequences existed.

Being an unincorporated association proved sufficient for more than three decades. What changed, in a nutshell, were finances. From the beginning, the Peoples' Voice Cafe shared the gate receipts with the performers who got to keep sixty percent. The remaining forty percent went to pay for PVC's ongoing expenses such as rent, insurance, publicity, equipment, and supplies. Membership dues, food sales, the sale of donated items, and small individual contributions also helped to cover those expenses, and in time, the Peoples' Voice Cafe built up some modest cash reserves.

About five years ago that began to change as our expenses went up while our income either grew too slowly to keep pace, remained the same, or declined. It became apparent that in order for the Peoples' Voice Cafe to survive in the long term, we would need to do more vigorous fundraising, which included applying for grants and soliciting large donations. Before that could happen, obtaining 501(c)(3) tax-exempt status was a must, and the easiest and most reliable route to do so was by first forming a nonprofit corporation. The PVC Collective agreed, and as mentioned above, the Peoples' Voice Cafe became a nonprofit corporation on May 16, 2014. We quickly filed for tax-exempt status, which the Internal Revenue Service granted us on January 2, 2015, retroactive to our date of incorporation.

### The Role of the PVC Board of Directors

Incorporation brought with it several mandates regarding governance. New York State requires nonprofits to have a Board of Directors that meets at least once a year and keeps official minutes of its meetings. We are also required to elect officers, have written bylaws, and adopt a formal conflict of interest policy. In addition, before we could solicit donations, we needed to register with the Charities Bureau of the Office of the New York State Attorney General. On the federal level, the IRS requires us to file a Form 990 tax return annually, even though we owe no taxes.

These mandates mean, in effect, that the Peoples' Voice Cafe now has a dual system of governance. There is still the PVC Collective that meets in person, usually twice a year, and otherwise communicates online through a Google group. It is still the body that determines general policy. For example, at a recent meeting on November 28, 2017, the

PVC Collective decided by consensus that the admission contribution requested from students and youth would be lowered to $12, the same amount requested from PVC subscribers, rather than the $20 currently requested from the general public.

As mentioned earlier, the PVC Collective elects the PVC Board of Directors once a year, and there are certain responsibilities that fall entirely to the PVC Board of Directors. Among these are:

- Electing officers, which currently include President, Secretary, and Treasurer.
- Inviting volunteers to become members of the PVC Collective.
- Approving the disbursement of funds.
- Approving the annual rental agreement with Community Church.
- Assuring compliance with federal, state, and local laws.

These are essentially administrative responsibilities rather than matters of policymaking. To carry them out, the PVC Board of Directors usually meets in person two to three times a year, but otherwise remains in close contact by email, phone, and the occasional informal meeting before or after shows. By assuming these important administrative responsibilities, the PVC Board of Directors has allowed the PVC Collective to focus more of its attention on the overall direction of the Peoples' Voice Cafe. As a result, meetings of the PVC Collective have become shorter, more productive, and less contentious.

Regardless of this dual system of governance, the actual running of the Peoples' Voice Cafe remains unchanged. It is left to the volunteers, either acting as individuals or in small working committees, the same as it was when we presented our very first show in 1979. To say that we are volunteer run and collectively governed is still accurate, even if we have to add an asterisk to account for the Board of Directors and other mandates of incorporation.

*Chapter 25 Image 5.* Performer at the Peoples' Voice Cafe. Photo Courtesy, Steve Suffet.

## New Challenges Facing the Peoples' Voice Cafe

Organizations evolve over time, and the Peoples' Voice Cafe is no exception. The social, political, cultural, and economic environment has changed since 1979, and unless the Peoples' Voice Cafe can adapt to those changes, we will go the way of the woolly mammoth and the saber-toothed tiger.

Yet learning how to adapt brings with it new challenges. Here are two in particular that the Peoples' Voice Cafe faces.

The first challenge is attracting and holding an audience. Filling seats in New York City on a Saturday night has never been easy. In addition to competing with other live music venues, the Peoples' Voice Cafe is up against Broadway and off-Broadway theater, comedy clubs, movies, and almost every other kind of entertainment you can imagine. Since the mid-2010s, however, the situation has grown even more daunting. For reasons that are murky, the average size of our weekly audience has been declining, and many of our longtime subscribers are no longer attending as frequently as they once did.

If we could present a so-called "big name artist," such as Holly Near, every week, we would have no problem, but that is an impossible task. Anyway, that is not what the Peoples' Voice Cafe is all about. We need to find room in our program for performers like Dilson Hernandez, Lizzie Hershon, Lois Morton, and Dian Killian. "Who are they?" you might ask. Our response would be: "They are artists who have something important to say and the voice with which to say it. Even though you might never have heard of them, and even though you might be unfamiliar with their genre, please come anyway and bring your friends. You will not be disappointed. The Peoples' Voice Cafe does not book schlock."

Sometimes this approach works, but sometimes it fails. The sad fact is, we have occasionally presented some truly wonderful shows to paying audiences of fewer than twenty people. Fortunately, only a few nights are like that every season, but they are occurring more frequently than they once did. Sometimes we can blame the weather, but a little rain or an inch of snow does not cause the New York City theaters and movie houses to shut down. Regardless of the weather, and regardless of what else is going on in town on a given Saturday night, we need to figure out how to bring in new audiences while holding onto our old ones. That is, perhaps, the biggest challenge the Peoples' Voice Cafe faces.

Our second challenge is keeping ourselves financially solvent. This is closely related to the issue of attracting and building an audience. If we could find a way to increase our paying audience by an average of just fifteen people per show, our shortfall would disappear. Without that increase, we have to find ways to bridge the budgetary gap.

For the coming 2018-2019 season, we have found ourselves three grants and several donors. There are also several artists who will return some or all of their share of the gate receipts to the Peoples' Voice Cafe. We are not in any immediate danger. Beyond May 2019, though, our future is uncertain. Two of the three grants cannot be renewed and relying on large donations from a handful of people is always risky. Furthermore, while amateurs and semi-pros might be able to give up some of their earnings, full-time working musicians cannot. One strategy we are trying, is to find people who will each make a small monthly, sustaining contribution through PayPal or a credit card. But so far, we have had only limited success.

Will the Peoples' Voice Cafe be able to meet these dual challenges and survive as a volunteer run, collectively governed (with an asterisk), politically progressive listening room? Or, for that matter, will it even survive at all? There is no way to predict with any certainty what will happen. Nevertheless, the model has worked well enough for the Peoples' Voice Cafe to get through thirty-nine seasons. I remain cautiously optimistic about its future.

## About the Author

Stephen L. Suffet is a retired educator who worked thirty-eight years for the New York City public school system. He has been a member of the Peoples' Voice Cafe (PVC) Collective since 2002, and he currently serves on the organization's Board of Directors and as its Program Director. Sources for this article include documents in the Peoples' Voice Cafe files, Suffet's conversations with current and former members of the PVC Collective, and his own first-hand knowledge. In his spare time, he occasionally performs as a folksinger under the name Steve Suffet.

CHAPTER 26

# "THERE AND BACK AGAIN" — AN AUDIOVISUAL JOURNEY INTO ROADWORK, 1978-2018

AMY HOROWITZ

## INTRODUCTION

By Susan J. Erenrich

This chapter features an article penned by Amy Horowitz. I formally met Amy on July 7, 2018, at the John F. Kennedy Center for the Performing Arts' Millennium Stage in Washington, D.C. She was at the venue to kick off the fortieth anniversary celebration of Roadwork and Sisterfire, which you'll learn about below. The event was part of the Smithsonian Folklife Festival. The purpose of the commemoration was to shine a light on the group that literally helped put women artists on the map in 1978.

For readers not familiar with Roadwork, the D.C.-based multiracial coalition was a groundbreaking enterprise. Women leaders, involved in social movements in the 1960s and 1970s, came together through the arts to work for a more diverse, inclusive, and tolerant society. Their intersectional activism across gender, race, class, and sexual orientation galvanized thousands, helped break down barriers, and created lasting transformational change.

Amy's chapter is accompanied by an episode of *Wasn't That A Time* that aired on March 8, 2019. The episode, which marked International Women's Day, featured some of the troubadours of conscience on the Roadwork roster. "International Women's Day is a time to reflect on progress made, to call for change and to celebrate acts of courage and determination by ordinary women who have played an extraordinary role in the history of their countries and communities." This chapter celebrates the courageous leadership and coalition building of Sisterfire and Roadwork organizers. They were exemplary trailblazers, so we are dedicating this space to them.

I hope readers and listeners are moved by Amy's piece and the companion *Wasn't That A Time* tribute. It is an important glance into a moment in time that transposed history from the bottom up.

**Listen**

*Wasn't That A Time Episode 107: Celebrate International Women's Day With Roadwork/Sisterfire Artists*

Songs performed by Sweet Honey In The Rock, Holly Near, Alix Dobkin, Odetta, Laura Nyro, Tracy Chapman, Ronnie Gilbert, and Cris Williamson will be played throughout the broadcast.

https://www.mixcloud.com/WasntThatATime/wasnt-that-a-time-episode-107-celebrate-international-womens-day-with-roadworksisterfire-artists/

## "THERE AND BACK AGAIN" AN AUDIOVISUAL JOURNEY INTO ROADWORK, 1978-2018

By Amy Horowitz

I have been asked to join you in virtual community to write about the Sisterfire celebration marking Roadwork's 40th anniversary that took place in July 2018 as part of the Smithsonian Folklife Festival. Since many may be new to Roadwork and Sisterfire, I see this audio/visual essay as a journey "There and Back Again," to quote the title of a song composed by the 2018 Sisterfire curator, Toshi Reagon (Reagon, 2011). In our real lives, time does not exist in chronologies — that is, we live simultaneously in past/present/future. So, I'll move between historical narratives, future aspirations, and the actual goings-on at the National Mall on July 8th at ... whatever you want to call it: Sisterfire reunion, celebration, ritual of passage, revival, to be determined.

In 1977, Roadwork was an idea brewing on the back porch of a Washington, D.C., row house. Many late nights were filled with heated discussion about what the organization would be. Was it possible to launch an organization based on the concept of coalition, of women working together, sharing power and responsibility across racial, cultural, and class lines to produce, promote, and discover women's culture as it exists on a global level? The concept of coalition was not new; however, most coalitions were formed by a coming together of various organizations working around issues where a common thread could be found. There were very few models for an organization that was in itself a coalition. The name "Roadwork" expressed the vision that was developing: the work of building roads for women artists and the search for our historical links to women's cultural contributions missing from history books and from White feminist herstories.

**The Spark of an Idea: Sisterfire 1982**

SISTERFIRE was one of the clearest manifestations of the principles of Roadwork. The festival grew to be a concentrated celebration of the booking, production, and coalition work that we carried out year-round. I can remember the spring of 1982: The Roadwork house at 1475 Harvard Street NW was buzzing with activity. The phones were ringing off the hook with producers checking in on national tour dates for Sweet Honey In The Rock, Cris Williamson, June Jordan, June Millington. Our high school intern (also drummer, bass player, songwriter, singer), Toshi Reagon, ran across the street to the All Souls Church copying machine. The weary wheatpasting crew had worked late, hit The Florida Avenue Grill for breakfast, and was still at work plastering the city with posters — in the 1980s we publicized events by pasting posters on actual walls instead of posting virtually on social media.

The Roadwork house was especially teeming with folks as we were about to produce a one-day fundraising event to offset the traumatic cuts to grassroots arts that were crushing us as Ronald Reagan's policies took hold. "Sisterfire" was the name that emerged as board members and staff sat around the dining room table at Bernice Johnson Reagon's Kennedy Street home. In addition to the Roadwork staff, Sistersparks — volunteers and tenants who traded hours for low rent while attending law school or working at progressive local organizations — filled the house. The backbone and heart of the forthcoming fundraiser, Sistersparks were people who resonated with the inclusive, urban, multiracial mission of the festival. Sweet Honey In The Rock, Holly Near, Cris Williamson, Alexis De Veaux, Michelle Parkerson, Women of the Calabash, and The Harp Band had volunteered to perform.

Listen to the words and sounds of Sisterfire online in this film by Victoria Eves at: https://vimeo.com/195868964.

*Chapter 26 Image 1.* In This "There and Back Again," Amy Horowitz (l) is on stage at Sisterfire with Dr. Shirley Childress Johnson (Of Blessed Memory) in Takoma Park, Maryland, 1982. Screen shot from film by Victoria Eves.

*Chapter 26 Image 2.* Sisterfire 2018 on the National Mall. Photo Credit, Ryan Whittermore.

**Genesis of Roadwork**

Bernice Johnson Reagon and I incorporated Roadwork, Inc. in 1978 to "put women's culture on the road" through tours, festivals, concerts, and workshops. This was a time, not unlike today, when activist-artists engaged in urgent responses to violations of human rights in Latin America and in Wilmington, North Carolina, the AIDS epidemic, nuclear madness, racism, and the ongoing war against women.

In the cauldron of local, national, international, multi-racial, cross-cultural issues, Roadwork wove together a coalition effort based on artistic collaboration among diverse communities. We saw ourselves as the children of the Black Southern Civil Rights Movement and the labor movements, and we were determined to be a visible force in the emerging women's and lesbian/gay rights movements, both of which were too often dismissed as irrelevant to larger social justice concerns.

Roadwork was born in a context of profound sexism. Misogyny in the music and entertainment industries severely limited women — especially women of color — promoters, recording engineers, and independent artists. Despite these obstacles, an underground women's culture of poets, visual artists, filmmakers, and musicians flourished from the 1970s into the 1990s, finding voice in coffeehouses, independently produced concerts, festivals, and protest rallies.

Women and feminist men formed record labels, organizations, and networks like Olivia Records, Redwood Records, the Women's Music Distribution Network, Seattle's Riot Grrl movement and grunge scene, and Boston's Rock Against Sexism. Underground festivals were born such as the Michigan Womyn's Music Festival, the West Coast Women's Music and Comedy Festival, the New England Women's Musical Retreat, and Roadwork's own Sisterfire Festival. Independent producers and distributors built alternative economic models that challenged the mainstream music business.

Roadwork emerged at a time when the United States was engaged in widespread, covert intelligence operations both domestically (in opposition to civil rights and anti-war movements) and globally (in places like El Salvador, Nicaragua, Honduras, Chile, and countries in the Middle East). Anita Bryant was campaigning against lesbian and gay rights across the country (1977-1980s); Jerry Falwell and the self-proclaimed Moral Majority were attacking women's rights, abortion access, and gay rights; California voters were facing a ballot initiative that would have banned openly gay people from teaching in schools (1978); and a conservative Supreme Court was rolling back civil rights gains.

The idea that culture could be a strategy of resistance lay at the heart of Roadwork's mission. Through concerts that brought activists and artists into collaboration, Roadwork inspired tens of thousands of people to generate social change in reactionary times. Roadwork trained a generation of organizers, producers, and women leaders to recognize that domestic politics in the United States are integrally tied to struggles for justice globally. Roadwork mobilized diverse audiences and built lasting coalitions across the lines of race, gender, sexual orientation, and economic class.

Roadwork's guiding principles, articles of incorporation, and by-laws derived from a Coalition Statement that Dr. Reagon and I wrote in 1977 to serve as the principles of engagement for a recording project between Holly Near's White-women-run company, Redwood Records, and the Black women singers of Sweet Honey In The Rock. The recording project and a West Coast tour that I booked with Holly's support laid the groundwork, or "Roadwork", for the organizational principles that we developed in D.C.

By August 1978, Konda Mason had joined me on the back porch and together we booked Sweet Honey In The Rock, The Varied Voices of Black Women, June Jordan, Holly Near, Alive, and the Wallflower Order Dance Collective, and we produced concerts, including the first annual Sweet Honey In The Rock anniversary concert (their sixth anniversary). Over the next twenty years, we produced a dizzying number of local concerts and national/global tours for over thirty women artists and groups.

# SISTERFIRE
## STATEMEMENT OF PURPOSE

W̶E EXTEND to all of you a warm welcome to SISTERFIRE.

SISTERFIRE was conceived as a celebration...an acknowledgement of women as vital carriers of culture. This festival is a demonstration of commitment to social change and hope. Since its inception in 1982, SISTERFIRE has more than doubled in size, and now encompasses two days of activities. Such growth would not have been possible without the concerted effort of a broad spectrum of community workers. This multi-racial, multi-ethnic, cross-cultural display of women's talent, brought together by diverse facets of our community, is the material expression of Roadwork's philosophy.

We face many challenges in America today. Violence against people of color escalates; racism triumphs in the marketplace and in the courts; weapons of annihilation and death receive maximum funding, while our elected officials deny basic human rights by slashing programs benefitting ordinary workers, and people of few means; tolerance that breeds homophobia and the abridgement of civil rights is sanctioned by "national leaders"; police power and repressive legislation broaden, while our freedom to dissent and gain access to information is curtailed; militarism is now more than ever the posture of the day. Women often bear the brunt of this anti-human assault.

SISTERFIRE praises the cultural expression of women fighting in liberation movements around the world and here in the U.S. We praise women's work in the home, and the nurturing and love they have always given their families...their communities. SISTERFIRE is a salutation to all women, working people, minorities and the poor who stand fast against dehumanizing political and economic systems.

Culture, in its most valid form, expresses a mass or popular character. It cannot, must not be defined and perpetuated by an elite few for the benefit of a few. Culture must, of necessity, reflect and chart humanity's attempt to live in harmony with itself and nature. So it was with the songs, literature and art of the labor movement '30s and the civil rights movement '60s; so it is with the New Song Movement and the political formations born out of anti-colonial, anti-imperialist struggles; so it is with new concepts of religion leading to Liberation Theology; all of it popular cultural expression confronting and dealing with impediments to human progress.

Whether it is the weaving of fabric or the kneading of bread, whether through the intricacies of philosophical thought or the simplicity of a praise song, whether it is passing on language or retaining history, SISTERFIRE acclaims the contributions women have made to advancing our culture...people's culture.

This is a women's festival held in an urban environment, making it more accessible to everyone who wishes to attend. It is significant that we come together near Washington, D.C. We want to proclaim that women will not let this or any administration strip us of our rights or our humanity.

We acknowledge the hard work all of us, women and men, have contributed to this festival. We are building bridges between the women's movement and other movements for progressive social change. We are playing with fire, and we want nothing less from this event than to set loose the creative, fierce and awesome energies in all of you.

The Women of SISTERFIRE

*Chapter 26 Image 3.* Sisterfire Statement of Purpose. Courtesy, Roadwork.

*Chapter 26 Image 4.* Bernice Johnson Reagon, Amy Horowitz, and Toshi Seeger at the Clearwater Hudson River Revival 1970s. Photo Credit, Amy Horowitz.

─── COALITION STATEMENT ───

The Concept of Coalition
Between Sweet Honey In The Rock and Redwood Records

December 1977

The women of Sweet Honey in the Rock and Redwood Records consider our coming together for this recording project as a major effort in coalition politics. In our development of the project we have tried to form a political/conceptual base that offers respect for the concerns of Redwood and Sweet Honey, as well as some guidelines of how we work out areas where there may be conflict in our identities and responsibilities to ourselves and our communities. It is with much hope that we all approach this project. We see that the project may in fact serve as a model for ways in which women working in coalition can grow and broaden our boundaries as we identify points of unity, while still maintaining our individual political priorities.

For us, the idea of joining together in a coalition project means that we share from our political base enough common ground to warrant the union. At the same time, being in coalition means that there may be aspects of our political base that are not identical. It has been important to articulate our personal and political needs and priorities to each other. One of the primary responsibilities we share in building the coalition is constantly articulating and reviewing as we develop. It is only from this communication that we will keep close sense of what ground we mutually share, what ground is mutually supported but not necessarily shared, and what ground may present conflicts in identity and focus.

We believe that to be in a coalition means to come to the union with all that we have, to come to the union open and with full awareness that working together will result both in a concrete product and in the process that brings about the product. The issues that bring Sweet Honey in the Rock and Redwood Records together center on all of us sharing a responsibility to be articulate around social, political, and economic struggles. We are all committed to cultural work as a means of speaking to these struggles. We see this process as one of growth for all of us.

*Misha Cummings*

*Tandy F. Dixon*

*Evelyn M. Harris*

*Amy Horowitz*

*Patricia Johnson*

*Holly Near*

*Bernice Johnson Reagon*

*Betty J. Williams*

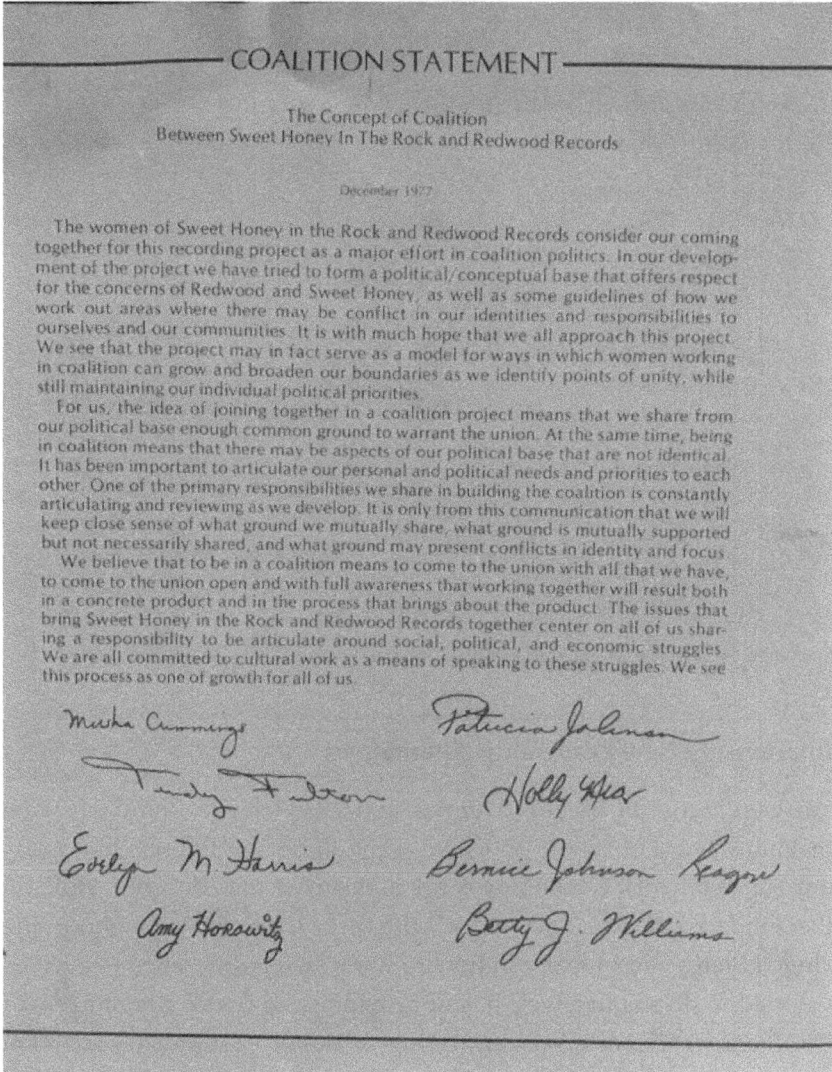

*Chapter 26 Image 5.* Coalition Statement: The Concept of Coalition Between Sweet Honey In The Rock and Redwood Records. Courtesy, Roadwork.

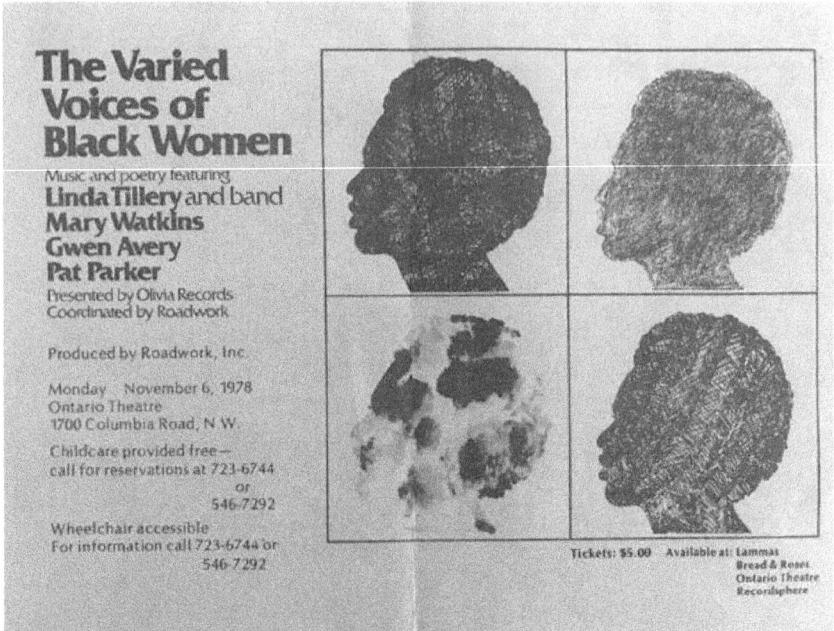

*Chapter 26 Image 6.* The Varied Voices of Black Women Flyer. Courtesy, Roadwork.

### Improvising New Leadership Alternatives

We were activists in our twenties and early thirties, and we were making the organization up as we went along. On the one hand was our concrete work of booking tours and producing concerts, while on the other hand was our work with organizations throughout the United States and globally in how to work across difference — even as we tried to do so ourselves — and providing support for organizers of D.C.-based marches. We were trying to build a multiracial coalition structure. For a leadership model, we sought guidance from Roadwork co-founder Bernice Johnson Reagon's work in the Southern Black Civil Rights Movement as a singer, activist, and organizer and we sought lessons from our own work in anti-war collectives, women's health centers, and women's and gay rights movements.

We were aligned with the developing network of mainly White lesbian women's music producers, distributors, bookstores, and festivals. We were also aligned with Black churches festivals, and feminist groups.

Together we were building an alternative music network. At the same time, we were also intent on overturning the music industry, invading it, and taking it over. We saw ourselves as grassroots movement builders, infiltrators, and rabble rousers. In fact, we were allergic to the idea of leadership. The leadership models we observed in corporate, government, and progressive left circles fell short. In policies and practices, sexism, classism, homophobia, and racism were rampant. This allergy to leadership was a point of pride at the time; now it prompts critical reflection. We also resisted the (mis)leading notion that building an organization is the work of one person or a small handful of people. This is rarely the case. The story that often remains untold is of the many people and the hundreds of thousands of hours that go into creating and sustaining a vision.

**Signposts**

We chose the name Roadwork because we felt that in order to put radical, and primarily women of color, artists on the road we would have to build the roads. We liberated an orange and black Roadwork sign from a nearby construction site and placed it on the front porch — a defiant symbol of the Roadwork ahead.

Other signposts were developing. The Black lesbian Combahee River Collective's pioneering work on race, gender, and sexual orientation was deeply instructive. Their challenge to the White feminist movement and their "open to all" position resonated with our evolving direction. Their stance about inclusion informed what we were hoping to build at Roadwork: "Although we are feminists and Lesbians, we feel solidarity with progressive Black men and do not advocate the fractionalization that white women who are separatists demand. Our situation as Black people necessitates that we have solidarity around the fact of race, which white women of course do not need to have with white men, unless it is their negative solidarity as racial oppressors. We struggle together with Black men against racism, while we also struggle with Black men about sexism," (Combahee River Collective, n.d.).

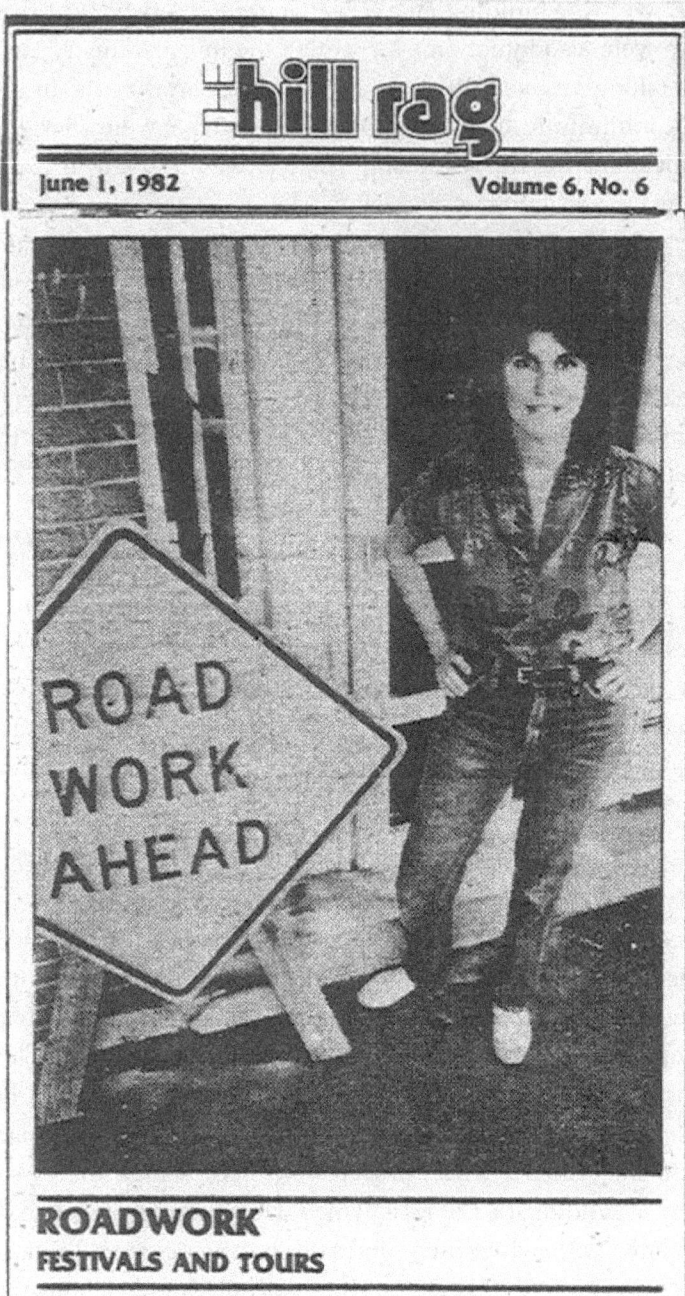

*Chapter 26 Image 7.* Amy Horowitz Stands Next to the "Road Work Ahead" Sign. Reproduced With Permission of *The Hill Rag*. Courtesy, Roadwork.

### The Power and Perils of Coalition

The reactionary response to the gains of the Civil Rights Movement and the women's movement led to the election of Ronald Reagan in November 1980. Four days later on November 8th, Dr. Bernice Johnson Reagon called out the need to build coalition when she introduced *Echo* at Roadwork's Sweet Honey In The Rock 7th Anniversary concert at All Souls Church in Washington, D.C. One of Roadwork's volunteers, a young Black woman housing activist named Yulanda Ward, had just been murdered and the election weighed heavy. Dr. Reagon's call, digitized and transcribed from that concert, reverberates today like an echo:

This next song, the words, were written by Assata Shakur. She says, "Everything we see, we have seen before." I mean, you can go around and be shocked about being in Washington, D.C., and be shocked about Yulanda Ward being killed, about sixteen children killed in Atlanta, and be shocked about the Klan gunning people down .... But this poem says, we know about this, and there's something we have to do, because we do know what it means for us. First, we've got to take what we know very seriously. It can get you killed, as we have seen. And the things we sing about, some of them are building things so that we stay together as human beings, other things are really about what we see happening to ourselves and to our community, and Black people in this country, and human beings in this country, and you know Reagan's been here before to Washington. You don't just live through it! You don't just coast through this decade! You don't get to sleep through! (Applause). If you are still here in 1990 and in the year 2000, it is going to be because you have been visible.... It is very important that all of us find some place to be and to organize with people who sort of have the same issues you have, so one day, if you disappear, someone will miss you if you're gone. (Applause). It is very much open season for Black people in this country. We can't just read about it, and about the FBI sent down to Atlanta to look for those children. There was a time when they lynched Black men in this country, and when you get them sort of young it does something to you, or it should. So, we hope that this gathering tonight is some kind of coming together. We sing about a lot of things because we feel a lot of things.

Dr. Reagon laid out coalition principles rooted in the historical institution building of Black organizers, in this case, Sojourner Truth, taking us beyond the moment to a fuller genesis history of movement building in this country: "It's like the tradition of Sojourner Truth, who could talk against slavery and for women's rights in the same breath without choking. And we must be on our case about our inability to stretch across issues — [about how we may] be correct in one position and [unconsciously] oppressive and bigoted in another. (Applause)." Listen to Echo at: https://youtu.be/IGCYcI_Om1I.

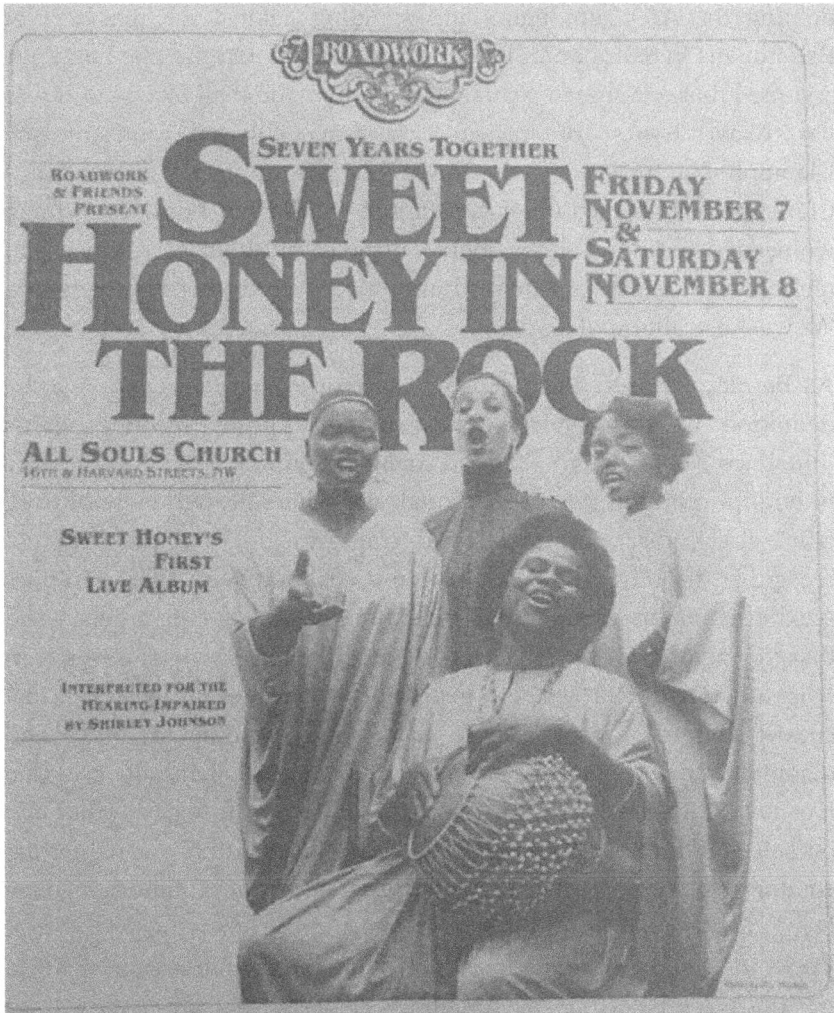

*Chapter 26 Image 8.* Sweet Honey In The Rock 7th anniversary Concert Flyer. Photo Credit, Sarna Marcus. Courtesy, Roadwork.

And there we were at Roadwork ... a small cohort of primarily women-loving-women learning how to work together — even as we built the physical concert and festival stages, came together across difference, and gathered across asymmetrical relationship to one another. There we were moving against homophobia in the left and in communities of faith, fighting racism in the White women's movement, challenging women's exclusion in the music industry, fighting the AIDS epidemic, and standing against the massacre of Palestinians in Sabra and Shatila refugee camps. On the one hand, we assumed that our shared sexual orientation made it all okay. But it was not okay. Issues of racism, classism, ableism, antisemitism, Islamophobia threatened to drown out the applause in All Souls Church. We hurt each other constantly; we did not know everything we needed to know, either about ourselves or about each other, and racism was not just "out there" but in the White women in Roadwork. We were a coalition of learners.

As Bernice Johnson Reagon later went on to write, coalition is by definition uncomfortable because it presupposes meeting across difference. That is why it is called coalition and not home. It is not easy to build a coalition because although we "share" experiences of hurt, pain, anger, disappointment, and transgression, we often do not recognize the hurt in others. Forming coalition with others implies seeking common ground while identifying issues of divergence and disagreement. These are what I have described in previous writings as "disputed territories" in both geopolitical and internal locations, that coexist within each of us. We each bring multiple identities and disputed inner territories to the coalition table. Being in coalition means that we need tools to survive the hurt we cause each other and ourselves. Dr. Reagon keenly observed that coalition means getting comfortable with the discomfort of disagreement and fighting against being surprised and disappointed in one another when the thorny stuff pricks us, whether it is the racism of White women, divergent political positions on Palestine, asymmetries of class, education gaps, and generational divides.

*Chapter 26 Image 9.* Dr. Bernice Johnson Reagon speaks about the importance of coalition at the West Coast Women's Festival. With Dr. Shirley Childress Johnson (Of Blessed Memory). Courtesy, Roadwork.

In summer of 1981, Dr. Reagon arrived at the West Coast Women's Music and Comedy Festival and took the stage shortly after an explosive incident. She delivered a stirring, improvised oratory on coalition that formed the basis of her canonical essay, *Coalition Politics: Turning the Century*, originally published by Kitchen Table: Women of Color Press, which was founded by Barbara Smith (who also co-founded the Combahee River Collective).

Her essay drew upon the West Coast Women's Festival incident, but in broader strokes, her understanding of coalition came from growing up Black in Albany, Georgia; organizing in the Student Nonviolent Coordinating Committee; demonstrating at Albany State and studying at Spelman; negotiating across difference at the Smithsonian; and working in The DC Black Repertory Theatre, Sweet Honey In The Rock, and Roadwork.

For the fledgling group at Roadwork, Reagon's thinking on coalition provided a backbone and a cautionary tale. Being in coalition didn't mean becoming best friends. On the one hand, Roadwork tried to operate as a tight-knit family — a brigade of wheatpasting freedom fighters that sought nothing less than the transformation of society. But what about self-transformation? The Roadwork coalition became an unsafe environment when we placed ourselves and our institutional structure above and outside the issues we were fighting externally. In this way the "personal is political" became a lip-service phrase rather than a clarion call and created a collision of intention and unrealistic expectation. Coalition is best approached as a place to do some good work with others with whom you may not completely agree. It is not a place to find an intimate friend circle where the expectation is deep resonance. It's complex. We argue with our friends and we argue in coalition — but the terms of engagement are different.

These realizations would later inform my academic work on disputed territory, the Israel-Palestine conflict, the asymmetries between European and Mizrahi Jews. What I began to see through Roadwork was that coming together and sharing music across difference did not erase difference or create symmetry out of asymmetry. In fact, the expectation that a shared moment on stage, or in an all-night wheatpasting foray, would erase difference is romantic and problematic. In fact, shared experience can mask issues of racism, homophobia, sexism, and class — creating an illusion that in the euphoria of communal harmony the issues are resolved. I began to ask whether collective encounters across difference are a dress rehearsal for overcoming asymmetry or something that masks the asymmetry? This is not to say that shared moments are illegitimate, but there should be no illusion that a song will bring peace. Looking back, I see how we stumbled over the asymmetries of our diversity: race, class, religion, gender, sexual orientation, urban/rural, north/south, east/west.

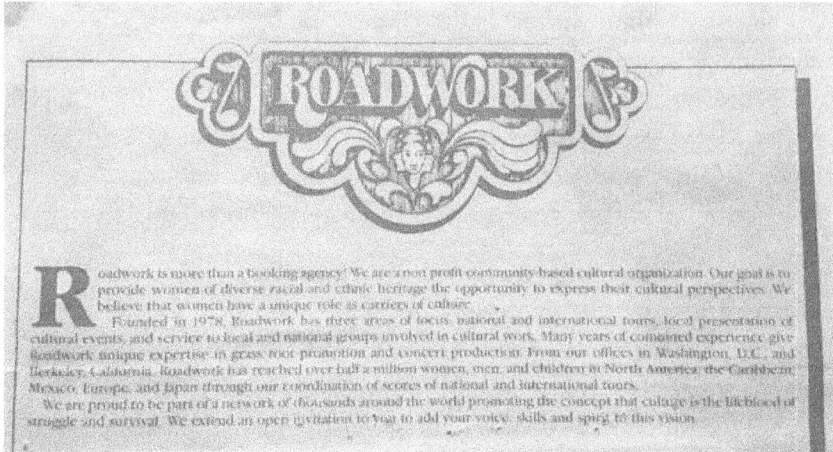

*Chapter 26 Image 10.* About Roadwork. Courtesy, Roadwork.

### Back to That Day in May 1982

We were busy trying to create a suitable location in the house for a reporter from none other than *The Washington Post* to interview us about Sisterfire. Furniture was sparse, though more plentiful than in 1979 when Smithsonian Festival co-founder Ralph Rinzler visited and sat on a floor pillow in his suit and tie. Fortunately, the reporter was Richard Harrington, who had previously written for the underground papers (Harrington, 1982).

### Roadwork During 1982-1994

Seeing ourselves in print in *The Washington Post* and, more importantly, the success of our first Sisterfire were organization-shifters for Roadwork. We created a Board of Directors — not just names for the IRS, but people who met and figured out a way forward. We gained more visibility, DC Arts Commission and Humanities Council awarded us grants, and Mayor Marion Barry proclaimed June 26, 1982, Sisterfire Day. Volunteers offered legal, graphic, and accounting expertise. We created committees for fundraising, artist friends, and direct mail. Grants came in from the National Endowment for the Arts and the United States Information Agency. Sisterfire grew from a one-day event in a Takoma Park field to two days with three stages at the Upper Marlboro Equestrian Center. Sisterfire presented Alice Walker, Tracy Chapman, Hazel Dickens, Elizabeth Cotten, and Ronnie Gilbert. Alicia Partnoy, Moving Star Hall Singers, Hala Deeb Jabour, and Sara Alexander shared stages with Sweet Honey, Holly Near, Cris Williamson and Alix Dobkin. And the audiences, marketplace vendors, and volunteers reflected this diversity.

And then, in 1987, a controversial incident changed everything. It is not surprising that the explosion that put Sisterfire into a twenty-year hibernation was a conflict in the marketplace between two White lesbian separatist vendors and two Black gay male Sisterspark volunteers. Much has been written about the volatility of gender and race in the marketplace. Still, it was difficult to remain academic during the explosion. When gay Black men/Sisterspark volunteers saw that a White woman-only space had been created in the marketplace, they reiterated the festival policy, that all spaces were open to all people. A confrontation ensued and we asked all four to leave the festival, but the outcry from White lesbian separatists (see their opinion piece and our response in the October 1987 issue of *off our backs*: daniels & fougere, 1987; and Roadwork Responds, 1987) resulted in reduced attendance in 1988 and 1989.

In 1989, Dr. Reagon invited me to write a chapter about my work with Sweet Honey and Roadwork for her edited book, *We Who Believe in Freedom, Sweet Honey in the Rock...Still on the Journey*. When I turned it in, she noted that I had left out Sisterfire and helped me craft a way to write about the end of the festival. We came up with the idea that Sisterfire was hibernating. "I like to think that Sisterfire is sleeping, in hibernation, gathering new strength and insights from the efforts of the first years. I like to think that she will wake up renewed again ... soon" (Horowitz, 1993, p. 194).

And hibernate Sisterfire did. Or so we thought!

Turns out that Sisterfire showed up at the Apollo Theater in 2015 when Toshi Reagon connected the young women producers of the *Women of the World Festival* with our work in D.C. In a story about the festival, *Newsweek* described Toshi as "a veteran of several female-focused festivals, including Sisterfire in the 1980s" (Anderson, 2015). And at Spelman College in Atlanta, it turned out, "SisterFire" is an open mic that encourages expression of all kinds, catering to women-identified, gender-nonconforming, and queer people. Roadwork's newest board member, Nicole Barden, attended the 2018 reunion at the Smithsonian thinking that it was in some way connected to her alma mater, and that was when she discovered the ancestry of Spelman's SisterFire.

I share these stories of other Sisterfire sightings because they are evidence of how important it is to "leave a trail" as Dr. Reagon encourages us to do. Leaving a trail is not for nostalgia but because there is something of value to pass on in the work that we did, in the successes that we celebrated, and in the mistakes that we made.

**Disputed Territory - Asymmetry**

As Paulo Freire (2018) writes in *Pedagogy of the Oppressed*: "Hopelessness is a form of silence, of denying the world and fleeing from it" (p. 91). Writing the Sisterfire section in the Sweet Honey anthology was a way of working against flight and denial. I took these lessons into my doctoral studies, where I put them to work in writing about Arab Jews in Israel and the discrimination *Mizrahim* experience. In the course of my studies, my Roadwork experience in building multiracial coalitions led to my understanding that disputed territories are more than geographical locations. Looking back on the idealism of our coalition statement, I questioned the simplified premise of an equal playing field, what Freire called "a horizontal relationship in which mutual trust between the dialoguers is the logical consequence" (p. 91). In what way could we have more directly articulated the unequal experiences that we embodied? As I researched Arab and European Israeli Jewish music, the unequal playing field became obvious. I wondered how it must have felt for women of color to enter into an idealistic paradigm that did not account for the White racist foundations of the society embedded in our own alternative experiment.

In most communication across difference, the dialoguers are asymmetrical partners. Looking at music in the asymmetrical context of Israel and Palestine, or back to the Roadwork days, are only two of many examples of how the aesthetics of art and culture are by definition political. For example, The West-Eastern Divan Orchestra founded by Israeli conductor/pianist Daniel Barenboim and Palestinian literary critic/pianist Edward Said comprises musicians from Israel and Islamic countries. Critics have asked whether, despite Barenboim's outspoken opposition to the Israeli occupation, the orchestra promotes coexistence rather than co-resistance, allowing musical dialogue to subvert solidarity aimed at ending occupation. In "Music as Social Medicine: Two Perspectives on the West-Eastern Divan Orchestra," David M. Washington and Devon G. Beecher (2010) note: "Watching the harmonious way the orchestra performs and interacts, one expects that the members would be more than musicians: perhaps an army of politically enlightened citizens bound to positively influence the future of the Middle East....They are not this; instead, they are fantastic musicians who are able to make fantastic music with people who otherwise and elsewhere would be their enemies. Their unity of musical feeling should not be seen as a metaphor for unity in the Middle East." (Watch their video https://vimeo.com/242210256 for a short introduction.)

Are the lessons learned from this courageous orchestra or during our multiracial coalition of the 1970s-1990s instructive in light of current attempts at coalition, say, in understanding the explosive issues that rocked the Women's March as women of color and Jewish women with White-skin privilege wrestled across race, White supremacy, Islamophobia and antisemitism? What will it take to build and sustain coalitions that can overtake the "deep history" of racial and economic injustice, greed, and hurt? Truthsayers like Nancy MacLean, who wrote *Democracy in Chains: The Deep History of the Radical Right's Stealth Plan for America*, remind us of the enormity of our task and the insidiousness of the 1% that rules and divides us.

*Chapter 26 Image 11.* Photo of Smithsonian Folklife Festival Ad in the Washington, D.C., Metro. Photo Credit, Amy Horowitz.

### How Did "Leaving a Trail" Lead Us to the National Mall?

How is it that Sisterfire, a festival initiated as a fundraiser in 1982 to offset Ronald Reagan's devastating cuts to grassroots arts, was transported from a modest field at Takoma Park Middle School in Maryland to the National Mall in Washington, D.C., 2018?

Dr. Reagon first posed the challenge that led to the reunion a decade ago. She said, "You've got to leave a trail about what Roadwork did — what we did, so that people can stumble across it." I think she meant a short essay! Five years later Roadwork board member Urvashi Vaid posed a similar challenge and "the trail" evolved into an oral history and documentary project. When our documentary director, Dr. Yvonne Welbon, considered joining the effort, her first thought was: "What about producing a reunion concert?" So, we gathered, wondering if the story of a multiracial coalition that put women's culture on the road in the 20th century might have lessons for the 21st.

Performing at the Smithsonian Folklife Festival seemed like a long shot, though it was historically fitting. In 1973, festival co-founder Ralph Rinzler invited Dr. Reagon to co-curate the festival's African Diaspora Program (1974-76). She went on to become the creator and director of the Smithsonian's Program in Black American Culture

(1977-1994). In 1979, Rinzler saved Roadwork from eviction by purchasing our rented row house on Harvard Street, and in 1983, he funded a live recording of Sisterfire performers that was released by Redwood Records. In the 1990s, I served as a festival curator and Acting and Assistant Director of Smithsonian Folkways. And before all this, in 1965, a twenty-three-year-old Bernice Reagon had recorded on Folkways.

Toshi Reagon, curator of this artistic Sisterfire reunion vision, embraced the Roadwork legacy and its potential resonance for younger artist-activists who may have never heard of the organization before. Their introduction to Sisterfire would be the rebirth of the experience itself. She wove a narrative that moved us beyond the traditional concert or festival format to an arts-based call to action — a round robin of intentionality. Fierce volunteers showed up like they always had — lawyers, activists, producers, and artist hospitality folks. Some were elders and had trained at Roadwork and some were experiencing Roadwork for the first time.

*Chapter 26 Image 12.* 2018 Sisterfire Audience in Front of the Washington Monument. Photo Credit, Ryan Whittermore.

## Building New Roads, Leaving New Trails

The sun is setting behind the Washington Monument as the two-day reunion draws to a close. All the artists, organizers, and participants are standing in congregation. Tonight, full-voiced, we sing together across race, generation, issue, ability, gender, religion, and sexual orientation. The songs fill our bodies, fill the National Mall and give us a beacon to a land that does not yet exist. The closing song at the festival is *Come and Go With Me to This Land.* Listen to it here https://youtu.be/G75CkYW_f7I from Reagon's 1965 Folkways LP.

I imagine where the 20-40-something artist-activists will take this experience as they join together with artists in their fifties, sixties, and seventies. Together they co-create and share a 2018 Sisterfire stage much as Toshi did with Elizabeth Cotten in 1983, like Moving Star Hall Singers co-created with Casselberry and Dupree in 1984, like June Jordan co-created with Tracy Chapman in 1987. I am thinking of the Sisterfire ancestors, Odetta, Ronnie Gilbert, Ampara Ochoa, June Jordan, Shirley Childress Johnson, Flora Molton, Elizabeth Cotten. It is not nostalgia — it is radical reverie.

*Chapter 26 Image 13.* Sisterfire "There and Back Again," Moment. Gwendolyn Hardwick and Alexis DeVeaux at Sisterfire 1982. Hardwick and Deveaux Performed at Sisterfire 2018. Photo Credit, Amy Horowitz.

*Chapter 26 Image 14.* Sisterfire 2018 on the Smithsonian Mall. Photo Credit, Ryan Whittermore.

What we saw as an ephemeral reunion to capture some footage for the oral history project has become, instead, a rebirth. In this way, Sisterfire lived up to her name and sparked herself out of hibernation and into service going forward. Roadwork has established a new and younger board leadership conjoined with elders from back in the day to rekindle aspects of Roadwork's mission that are relevant for these times. We realize that a multiracial coalition that centers women's culture in the service of justice is still relevant. Through the new leadership, Sisterfire Roadwork@40 and future projects do more than "leave a trail" for future generations of activists and artists — they are continuing the work of building new roads.

*Acknowledgements: This essay benefits from an essay co-authored with Urvashi Vaid, Roadwork Board member and inspiration behind the Oral History Project and from Roadwork Board Chair Jessie Washington. As I reflected on the history of Roadwork and Sisterfire, I was inspired to title the essay after Toshi Reagon's song, "There and Back Again" (Reagon, 2011) and used it with Toshi's permission.*

**Resources**

*The Sisterfires That Burned While Roadwork/Sisterfire Hibernated*

https://www.newsweek.com/women-world-festival-comes-harlem-340843

https://www.spelman.edu/academics/faculty/stories/stories/2017/05/11/bahati-kuumba

https://justseeds.org/product/sisterfire/

https://www.publishersweekly.com/978-0-06-055351-7

*Press on Sisterfire From 1980s*

https://www.washingtonpost.com/archive/lifestyle/1987/06/27/the-spread-of-sisterfire/11478341-f99f-4eb0-ab79-fb0bf36adc4a/?utm_term=.19d47ae88942

http://wearinggayhistory.com/exhibits/show/lesbiancapital/sisterfire

https://www.nytimes.com/1985/06/11/arts/sisterfire-festival.html

https://vimeo.com/195868964

*2018 Sisterfire Reunion*

https://festival.si.edu/2018/sisterfire

http://gomag.com/article/thousands-to-celebrate-roadworks-40th-anniversary-with-sisterfire-in-washington-d-c-on-july-7-and-8/

https://www.washingtoncitypaper.com/arts/music/blog/21012317/sisterfire-returns-for-smithsonian-folklife-festival

http://alexisdeveaux.com/sisterfire-2018-interview-with-alexis-deveaux/

https://festival.si.edu/blog/roadwork-poetry-and-change

https://festival.si.edu/blog/martha-redbone-drums-sisterfire

**References**

Anderson, S. (2015, June 8). Feminism at the Apollo: Women of the World Festival Debuts Stateside. *Newsweek*. https://www.newsweek.com/women-world-festival-comes-harlem-340843

Combahee River Collective. (n.d.). History: What We Believe https://combaheerivercollective.weebly.com/history.html

daniels, l. & fougere, m. (1987). Violence Against Lesbians at Sisterfire. *off our backs, 17*(9), 24-25. Retrieved from http://www.jstor.org/stable/25795904

Freire, P. (2018) *Pedagogy of the Oppressed (50th Anniversary Edition)*. Bloomsbury Publishing. Originally published in 1968 in Portuguese and translated by M. Ramos in 1970. https://bloomsbury.com/us/pedagogy-of-the-oppressed-9781501314131/. Learn more at: https://beautifultrouble.org/theory/pedagogy-of-the-oppressed/

Harrington, R. (1982, June 26). Laying the Roadwork for Sisterfire. *The Washington Post.* https://www.washingtonpost.com/archive/lifestyle/1982/06/26/laying-the-roadwork-for-sisterfire/9ca29813-da27-4071-b5b4-1516b4344a96/

Hollander, P. (2010, November 2). Israel's Eastward Beating Heart (Review). *Zeek.* http://zeek.forward.com/articles/117047/

Horowitz, A. (1993). Some Factors in the Equation. In B. J. Reagon (Ed.), *We Who Believe in Freedom, Sweet Honey in the Rock...Still on the Journey* (179-200). Anchor Books. https://amyhorowitz.org/wp-content/uploads/2018/06/Amy-Chapter-Some-Factors-in-the-Equation-in-Sweet-Honey-Book-.pdf

Horowitz, A. (1994). *Israeli Mediterranean Music: Cultural Boundaries and Disputed Territories* [Unpublished doctoral dissertation]. University of Pennsylvania.

Horowitz, A. (2010). *Mediterranean Israeli Music and the Politics of the Aesthetic.* Wayne State University Press. My Book

Horowitz, A. (2016). Next Year in Washington: The Jerusalem Program - Postponement and Rebirth. In O. Cadaval, S. Kim, & D. Baird N'Diaye, *Curatorial Conversations: Cultural Representation and the Smithsonian Folklife Festival.* University of Mississippi Press.

Kapchan, D. (1996). *Gender on the Market: Moroccan Women and the Revoicing of Tradition.* University of Pennsylvania Press. http://www.upenn.edu/pennpress/book/998.html

MacLean, N. (2017) *Democracy in Chains: The Deep History of the Radical Right's Stealth Plan for America.* Viking. Learn more at: https://www.nytimes.com/2017/08/15/books/review/democracy-in-chains-nancy-maclean.html

Reagon, B.J. (1983). Coalition Politics: Turning the Century. In B. Smith (ed.), *Home Girls: A Black Feminist Anthology* (356-368). Kitchen Table: Women of Color Press. https://womenwhatistobedone.files.wordpress.com/2013/09/1983-home-girls-coalition-politics-bernice-johnson-reagon.pdf

Reagon, T. (2011). "There and Back Again." *There and Back Again*. Music For Your Life.

Roadwork https://www.roadworkcenter.org/

Roadwork Responds... (1987). *off our backs*, 17(9), 26–26. http://www.jstor.org/stable/25795905

Smithsonian Folklife Festival: http://www.festival.si.edu/

Solnit, R. (2004). *Hope in the Dark: The Untold Story of People Power*. Canongate Books. https://www.brainpickings.org/2015/12/30/rebecca-solnit-hope-in-the-dark/

Sweet Honey In The Rock & Redwood Records. (1978). "Liner Notes." *B'lieve I'll Run On.... See What The End's Gonna Be*. Redwood Records - RR 3500.

Washington, D. & G Beecher, D. (2010). Music as Social Medicine: Two Perspectives on the West-Eastern Divan Orchestra. *New Directions for Youth Development*. 2010. 127-40. https://www.ncbi.nlm.nih.gov/pubmed/20391623

West-Eastern Divan Orchestra. (2017). West-Eastern Divan Orchestra Short Introduction [Video]. Vimeo. https://vimeo.com/242210256

## About the Author

Amy Horowitz straddles academia, social and racial justice arts, global Indigenous studies, music in/as disputed territory, arts/human rights, and Jerusalem. She believes in coalition across differences, and has long fought against racism, anti-Semitism, Islamophobia, homophobia, and misogyny. Her main research interests are global Indigenous studies, the study of music in disputed territory, contemporary Jerusalem, Arab Jewish popular music and protest music as responsible citizenship. Her activist work complements her academic background that combines training in Jewish studies and ethnomusicology (MA, New York University, 1986) folklore and Israeli studies (Ph.D., University of Pennsylvania, 1994). From 1977-1994, she served as Sweet Honey In The Rock's Artist Representative and was co-incorporator of Roadwork (https://www.roadworkcenter.org/), a multi-racial women's arts coalition with Dr. Bernice Johnson Reagon in 1978. As Acting Director of Smithsonian Folkways Recordings, she received a Grammy as reissue co-producer of Anthology of American Folk Music. Her book, *Mediterranean Israeli Music and the Politics of the Aesthetic* (https://www.amazon.com/kindle-dbs/entity/author/B003BX2IBM) received a Jordan Schnitzer Book Award and is currently being translated into Arabic and Hebrew. Horowitz produced the "Protest Music as Responsible Citizenship" featuring Pete Seeger, Harry Belafonte, Bernice Johnson Reagon and Holly Near. She is a senior fellow at Indiana University Center for the Study of the Middle East and co-director of GALACTIC (Global Arts Language Arts Cultural Traditions in Indigenous Communities) with Navajo Technical University. Her most precious life's blessing was becoming Ariel Horowitz's (https://www.heartbeatmusicproject.org/meet-the-team) mother at the age of 44. Learn more at: http://www.amyhorowitz.org.

CHAPTER 27

# ON THE IMPORTANCE OF REPRESENTATION

## ARIEL ELIZABETH DAVIS

### INTRODUCTION

By Susan J. Erenrich

This chapter features the work of Ariel Elizabeth Davis. When Ariel originally penned this piece for the *Grassroots Leadership & the Arts for Social Change Corner,* she was a Program Manager for the Performing Arts for Everyone and Community Engagement team at the Kennedy Center in Washington, D.C. As of this writing, she serves as Senior Manager of Impact Communications at the Save The Music Foundation. Much of Ariel's career has been devoted to issues of diversity and inclusion within the creative class. The topic of racial and social inequities in the arts is not new. Within recent years, however, it has been gaining a lot of traction.

Ariel starts her chapter by telling her personal story about playing the French horn in a predominantly White environment as a young girl. As she grew up, her experiences catapulted her into a bottom-up leadership role where she is now on the front lines of change within the arts administration community.

It is no secret that arts organizations representing marginalized demographics are financially struggling. In spite of that ever-present vulnerability, these groups still manage to produce meaningful work that debunks racial stereotypes and provides access, educational opportunities, and training.

A special thanks to Ariel for shining the light on this important and timely subject. I hope you enjoy Ariel's chapter along with the episode of the *Wasn't That A Time* radio broadcast that aired on February 16, 2018: Remembering Some of the Black Troubadours of Conscience From the 1960s. These folks helped pave the way for generations of performing artists and arts administrators like Ariel.

## Listen

*Wasn't That A Time - Episode 57: Remembering Black Troubadours Of Conscience from the 1960s*

This show pays tribute to some of the Black troubadours of conscience from the 1960s. Their voices, genres, and perspectives are diverse. Many of them are not household names. Nevertheless, they were extraordinary foot soldiers in a movement for freedom, justice, and racial equality. We are honoring and celebrating them here for the important socio-political and musical footprints that they left behind for generations to come. Listeners will hear songs performed by Julius Lester, Bill McAdoo, Cordell Reagon, Bertha Gober, Odetta, Reverend Frederick Douglass Kirkpatrick & Jimmy Collier, Nina Simone, and Richie Havens.

https://www.mixcloud.com/WasntThatATime/wasnt-that-a-time-episode-57-remembering-black-troubadours-of-conscience-from-the-1960s/

## ON THE IMPORTANCE OF REPRESENTATION

By Ariel Elizabeth Davis

*"From the outside, dominant Western discourse looks much like a Crystal Palace inside which legions of residents, having accepted the inheritance of the subject position from which knowledge is universally contemplated, narcissistically discuss 'the world'. The Palace's many buildings rise in splendor from plains made barren by its levies of exorbitant tribute. Some of the tallest and most decorated structures are the towers of High Culture where the world's great art is housed, fetishized by guardians and hirelings who fabricate theories of aesthetics to lend credibility to the preservation and exaltation of these hieratic objects. Huge batteries of light play across the facade of the Palace blinding those who approach it with unshielded eyes. At other moments the gigantic structures block out the sun. The surrounding plains have seen of late many bold and colorful structures rising from the marshes and weeds, only to be disassembled and erected elsewhere. These edifices are said to pose a nuisance to the Palace residents, who claim that the noises rising from them disturb the classic air and damage property values. Whether because of arrogant missiles hurled by the envious or because of the mounting cost of repairs, the Palace's pink magnificence has shown signs of recent decrepitude. At odd hours one can hear the shrill tinkle of crashing crystal."* - Clyde Taylor, *The Mask of Art*

### My Introduction to the Arts

I'll never forget the day I was first introduced to the French horn. I was anxious, excited, and eleven years old, sitting in Mr. Scott's class. The room was filled with sixth graders. We were practically jumping off the walls, chatting loudly and happily about the new year, at a new school. I was nervous, and elated, to finally get my hands on an instrument. For some time, I'd felt a barrier to full creative expression, and I was ready to involve myself in something, anything, that could help me express that creativity in an ongoing manner.

I was really lucky to start a school program with such a robust music curriculum, and with a director who was really smart about the way he got kids interested in picking up instruments that were a bit under the radar, instruments that had not quite reached the musical lexicon known by the general public. He walked into my sixth-grade class and firmly asked us to sit quietly and attentively as instruments were performed by some of the students in the seventh and eighth grade. He explained that the instruments we were going to see performed were not well known, and that he really needed students to pick them up in order for us to have as complete a band ensemble as possible, with a full range of nuanced sounds and textures.

The first instrument he showed us was the one that would go on to change my life forever. I remember seeing it for the first time, and although it sounds a bit over the top to say, I distinctly recall that feeling of shock and excitement wave through me. The big bell, the glimmering brass, the circular, complicated tubes. It looked like a sculpture, like a trumpet on steroids. Mr. Scott let the class know that this was one of the most challenging instruments out there, and internally I said, "challenge accepted."

What I didn't realize was important then, but deeply recognize now, was that the girl who demonstrated it was someone I could relate to. Although the instrument looked complicated, it was less intimidating to grab because I saw someone playing it that could have been a member of my family. For years, I truly didn't realize how much of an anomaly it was for me to pick it up, nor did I realize how big a deal it was to not take traditional lessons outside of that band class, which took place three days a week. In a world in which Black girls and women were (and continue to be) portrayed in media doing so many things that rarely included brass instruments, my teacher's smart attempt at getting more horn players was a simple, yet revolutionary step in the direction of imbuing representation, and one that I took (and continue to take) in contextualizing the work I do today.

Let's fast forward to now, twenty years later. Today, there are no Black women playing the French horn in major symphony orchestras. There are about 20+ that play regularly/semi regularly as freelancers. This is just one snapshot example among a few too many in the classical music industry. Why is there such a lack of inclusion in major orchestras? Where does this come from? And how can we collectively work, on a grassroots level (like Mr. Scott and so many others), to gain equity in the performing arts, a field in which the representation of musicians holds such a direct correlation to how women are represented in the world at large?

### Journey to Howard University

In 2005, I wasn't sure where I wanted to go to college, but I knew it had to be as close to free as possible. My mother is a woman from St. Elizabeth, Jamaica, and had been in the country for about 20 years at that point. After divorcing from my father, she'd become the primary caretaker and financial provider for me and my two younger brothers. I'd watched her work her way from fast food chains to a career as a full-time nurse, and she'd done it in order to ensure that her family was well taken care of. She was (and continues to be) a clear example of what it means to work hard in support of others.

She also takes impeccable care of herself. To this day, my friends talk about how "Ms. Joy" is "#goals" — the fashion, the style, the grace. She kept a new book in the house regularly and devoted time to read every night (before digging into a juicy reality TV show). She's a proud atheist and has been a staunch supporter of the LGBTQ+ community since I can remember. She took me and my brothers to pride parades long before the White House adapted the flag and splashed it across its white walls.

I wanted to make sure my mother could continue in her own journey. I wanted to make sure she could take care of my brothers (and other extended family). I practiced like crazy, and I took myself to the local library regularly to study for my ACT and SAT. By the time my senior year had come around, I'd been a part of half a dozen youth orchestras (most of which I proudly sat in the first chair, one of a small handful of Black children and usually the only girl). I'd served as my high school's band president my senior year, and as its vice president for two years before that.

My grades, however, just weren't there. I was the student who hated homework but who pulled off decent grades because she'd ace the test. Instead of going home to get my school work done responsibly, I spent a LOT of time in the "G Wing," the section of the school where the "Fine Arts" classes resided. That was home away from home. I was lucky to have Damien Crutcher as a band teacher. He cared deeply for his students and, as luck had it, was also a French horn player. If I needed someone to listen to an excerpt or concerto I was working on, he'd volunteer after school to take a listen to me and the dozen or so students like me who were deeply invested in being better musicians. He also made sure I knew about opportunities to join youth orchestras, and he helped connect me with members of the Detroit Symphony Orchestra for free and reduced cost lessons.

These connections inadvertently led to one of my first tastes of racism in the classical music field. I ended up studying with a highly regarded horn professor who had taught at the University of Michigan. He was a retired horn player who typically charged students up to $75 for lessons (which was quite expensive at that time) and only took top students into his studio. He reduced my rate to $20, out of kindness. It took 45 minutes to drive out to his house, a drive I convinced my mother to do by sharing that there were people who drove up to three hours to study with him — he was that renowned.

But I remember during one lesson he said, "You play too emotionally. I know you people can be highly emotional, but you've gotta turn it down some when you're playing the horn." Another time, he encouraged me to play more loudly by saying: "I know women can't put as much air behind the horn as men, but you need to push it out."

On the day I decided to no longer take lessons with him — because: A. I didn't feel as though the drive and strange interactions were worth it, and B. I needed to concentrate on getting my grades rock solid as I prepared to apply for college — he yelled at me, getting red in the face.

He said that I was ungrateful, and he told me to never tell anyone that I had studied with him.

That experience has never — will never — leave me. Every time I hear from other Black musicians about the discrimination they've faced in the field, those memories from my 17th year come right back.

At the time, I didn't realize those memories would stick with me as long as they have. However, my focus was clear, and my attention was pivoted towards one goal — to obtain as much scholarship funding as possible to get to college without negatively impacting my family.

A month or so after I'd left that private lessons' teacher, I scheduled a lesson and informational session with the horn professor at Michigan State University. I played relatively well during my time with her, and during our conversation, she shared that I might be able to receive $3,000 in scholarship funding, if I ultimately decided to go there. All of my closest friends were planning on attending Michigan State University, and I was over the top excited to learn that I could receive a scholarship to join them. What I wasn't entirely excited about were the course offerings. There were two choices at that time. I could either study music education or music performance. In some ways, I was already in the process of exploring what it meant to pursue those professional areas — I'd begun teaching some of my fellow classmates how to play horn, and, besides playing in every youth orchestra I could get into, I'd also gotten the opportunity to perform concertos as a soloist in local competitions. I loved doing both of these things, but I was unsure if I wanted to devote my life and career entirely to education or performance.

Directly after my audition and lesson with the horn professor at Michigan State, I decided to head back to my high school to finish out my last couple of classes for the day. My final class that afternoon was band, and after it wrapped, Mr. Crutcher called me to the front of the room to introduce me to the guest of the day, Kelvin Washington. Mr. Crutcher let me know that Professor Washington was there from Howard University and was interested in recruiting students. "Would you be interested in playing something for him?" Fresh off the high of another audition, I eagerly accepted. At that time, I hadn't heard of Howard University, but I figured it was worth a shot to play in front of another set of listening ears.

After playing Richard Strauss' Concerto #1 (my go-to piece for audition season that year), Professor Kelvin asked me what my ACT score was. I told him. He asked me if I owned the horn I was playing on. I let him know I did not.

"If you decide to go to Howard University, I can get you in for free. Not only that, I can get you enough money to get a refund check and purchase a horn of your own," he responded. Needless to say, I left this impromptu lesson high with excitement, but nervous. I'd never heard of Howard University, and all of my friends were going to Michigan State University. What would it be like to go to a school out of state? Was this a good decision?

The next day, in my second favorite class (AP English), we were reading the work of Toni Morrison. I was obsessed. *The Bluest Eye* took my breath away. After class, I went over to the teacher to have a fangirl moment about the work we were reading, and I was hoping for any insight she might provide about college choices. She'd made it abundantly clear to students that she was there to help provide one-on-one support to us, if ever needed, and to help lend an ear, if we were torn about making a decision on the best college to go to. I told her I'd gotten an opportunity to attend Howard University but had not heard of the school before. "Well, Toni Morrison did graduate from there, so I imagine it's a pretty good school," she said. Knowing this was all I needed.

Within three days, I'd let my friends know I was no longer going to attend Michigan State alongside them and that I'd made the decision to attend Howard University in Washington, D.C. It was one of the toughest choices I'd ever made, and I often wonder what my "alternative" life would look like had I decided not to attend Howard. But to say I'm grateful I made the decision I did is an understatement.

My horn got me to the doorstep of Howard University. The work of Toni Morrison pushed me in.

### At Howard (and My Brief Journey "AWAY" From the Arts)

My mother, brothers, aunts, and cousins all loaded up a van with the basic necessities, and I drove down to Howard University during the summer of 2005, right before marching band classes began. I was anxious, and I was sad. That summer, I was leaving friends I considered family, many of whom I remain close to. Growing up in Southfield, Michigan, had been one of the best cocoons to grow into adulthood in the early 2000s. It was a period in which the cultural identity of the city had shifted dramatically, but that shift had cultivated a unique and important cultural bed of opportunity for residents. In the mid-90s, when my family and I had first moved there, the town was about 50% White, with some Jewish and Chaldean populations scattered throughout. Between the 90s and the time I left, the city had become predominantly Black — White flight was experienced right before our eyes. The adults in the neighborhood would "joke" about how similar it was to the flight that took place in Detroit, the city next to Southfield, 40 years earlier. The population that stayed in Southfield was deeply interconnected — everyone knew each other. It was an enclave of mixed income households, a suburban city with neighborhoods where people kept their doors unlocked. To this day, my friends and I are quick to reminisce on how distinctly lucky we were to have experienced growing up in a space that was so Black, so diverse economically, and so *culturally* safe — where lugging my French horn around was deeply and readily accepted. Although I had my clique of friends in the band, my deepest and dearest clique of friends were the folks that lived in my neighborhood, folks that weren't musicians. They grew up to be social workers, teachers, doctors, airline employees — they've kept me down-to-earth and grounded.

When I got to Howard, I didn't get that feeling. I got a different one. In retrospect, it was important for me to have had this difference of experience. But at the time, it was hard.

Once my family unpacked my belongings and dropped me off at The Quad on Howard's campus, I began to create a nest for myself. I buried myself in that nest. I went to this new school with new people, and I didn't feel as though I belonged. Living in the city of Washington, D.C., was just SO different than living in Southfield. I didn't know the community, and I became deeply introverted. In the College of Fine Arts, I was quickly recognized within the marching band, jazz band, and concert band circles as one of the best mellophone and horn players around. But that didn't quite matter as much as it did to pledge a band fraternity or sorority, and I just wasn't interested in going through that process. For one, it typically cost money to go through it (money I didn't have). Also, none of my close family or friends had pledged a sorority, so, at the time, I didn't quite understand the reason to go through it (though I fully respect and appreciate the function of these organized bodies today).

To say the least, I was lonely. And that loneliness started practically on day one. Nothing could change it either. I tried having a boyfriend my freshman year. That didn't fill the loneliness. I shut myself up in the practice rooms, hoping to cross paths with other instrumentalists that enjoyed playing like I did. That didn't fill the loneliness. I began looking into ways to transfer, but I felt like there were no concrete options that were financially viable for me at that point.

I doubt many people realized I felt the way I did. I don't even think I realized I felt the way I did. My time was filled with activity — I maintained an active presence in the music program and collected scholarship funding because of it. I signed up for jazz band, orchestra, and concert band, and I even helped implement a quintet that would tour around town and play from time to time. My horn instructor, a guy by the name of Joseph Lovinsky, was incredible. He was principal horn in the United States Army Band, "Pershing's Own," and was the first Black horn player in that position. He was a Julliard grad who grew up in Miami with his Haitian parents. He did everything he could to provide gateways into the gig scene in the city, oftentimes calling on me to substitute for him on days when his Army Band contract had him tied up. He is a force of a musician, and the third reason I'd chosen Howard University (the number one reason being Toni Morrison and the second being the scholarship funding). He also let me know how incredibly difficult it was to make it into major symphony orchestras due to the competition in the field, and he shared that there were classmates of his from Julliard, many of whom were top of the class, that had gone on to study law and other fields of practice due to the scarcity of professional music opportunities.

Being fully equipped with the knowledge of how difficult it was to perform full time was a good piece of knowledge to have. It further cemented my resolve to NOT play professionally, and I was grateful to have signed up for a Music Business degree. That sense of relief was strained, however, by professors and other students who raised their eyebrows when I told them it was what I had signed up for. Time and time again, I was urged to take my playing more seriously and to try to get a gig as a professional player. I felt the pressure of being "one of the only ones," (a Black woman horn player) and I considered (unhappily) what life might look like as a full-time player. Or maybe a teacher? I didn't want either pathway, but I also didn't quite know or understand where a degree in Music Business could take me. I had achieved my goal of getting into college with a full-ride scholarship, but I hadn't figured out what to do next. I was lost.

I continued on through my time at Howard University, and after four years, I got to a point where I found it difficult to get out of bed and go to class. I ended up dropping out of school with only one full-time semester left. My friends all graduated around me, and while they were celebrating stepping into their next stage of adulthood, I was buried in a basement apartment in Columbia Heights trying to dredge up excitement for them and watching their lives play out on Facebook (a platform that, in 2010, was quickly becoming a vitally important part of social life). I was anxious about my future in ways that I didn't expect I'd ever be, and in ways I doubt those around me ever expected me to be.

In the summer of 2010, a friend of mine encouraged me to apply to join the staff of a restaurant that was opening up in 2011 called Cuba Libre. It was opening in the (quickly gentrifying) downtown area of D.C. I was familiar with the area and with working in restaurants. I'd begun doing some work at a couple of restaurants part time and temporarily in my senior year of college after my scholarship funding had run out.

I went ahead and applied for this new spot, and I joined a crew of about 30 people that built the restaurant from the walls up. Our first orientation was in a building that was all colorful plaster and concrete walls. It had a DJ booth and a huge dance floor. It was fun, it was festive, and as it opened, there was a heavy and ongoing mix of music playing from bachata to merengue.

That work experience helped deliver me out of my undiagnosed depression. Nobody there cared that I hadn't finished my degree. Some of my coworkers were a little curious about the strangely shaped horn case I'd store sometimes at the hostess stand with me before I took off to a gig to perform, but it was never the focus of the conversation. There, I was no longer "Ariel the horn player." I was simply Ariel. I was just a little closer to the Ariel I'd been right before I'd begun my studies at Howard University, and I felt more fully myself.

When I wasn't gigging or taking a shift at Cuba Libre, I'd spend time getting to know the world outside of academia. I'd gotten pretty good, during that time, at sitting with myself and exploring the world around me. Thanks to my newfound hospitality chops, I'd also gotten out of my shell and could strike up a relatively decent conversation with strangers nearby.

One of my favorite hangs was a spot called Busboys and Poets. There was a location that wasn't far from Cuba Libre where they had poetry nights on Tuesdays. The vibe was amazing. Here, people got up and expressed themselves in every manner of expression you could imagine. There were nights folks would come up and perform in a band, play a rap track, recite Shakespeare, write something on a napkin and bring it up to the stage — it was creative. It was fun. It was incense filled; it was energy filled. The food was good. I felt like I was home in D.C. when I went there.

Over time, I began to wonder what it might feel like to work there instead of Cuba Libre. Here, another point of transition. I worked at Busboys as a hostess, then worked my way up to bartender. In this creatively driven, arts-filled space, people were a little more intrigued when I mentioned that I was a horn player. I even picked up a chance to "shed" with a well-known artist. He encouraged me to improvise (I failed, terribly), and he tried to catch me by beatboxing on top of my discombobulated scales.

During this time, I was invigorated by the creativity that surrounded me. I was getting fed the opportunity to be around artists and creative folks pretty regularly at this point — not only was I bartending at one of the coolest and most creative spots in the city, but I was realizing that the horn was something I just couldn't untie myself from. Inadvertently, I'd established myself within a network of musicians in D.C. and throughout the United States, and I'd even begun to travel as a horn player. One of my first big gigs was out in Los Angeles (LA) at a gospel music competition as a part of the pit orchestra. That first time in LA, paid in full, with some of my favorite musicians around me, I fully accepted my calling as a part of the music ecosystem.

## From Onstage to Backstage

There was a lot that took place during the time that I decided to freelance as an artist. As time continued to go on, and as galvanizing forces began to coalesce around the Black Lives Matter Movement, I felt the push and the need to *do* something. Knowing that media and culture continued to perpetuate stereotypes in abundance was something I'd been uncomfortable with for some time, but by 2013 the questions I'd been asking about the lack of representation in the arts came at me with greater urgency: What does the world look like when people don't feel as though they belong? What happens in a world in which people are consistently portrayed as villains, and there's no nuance or depth of storytelling about their journey? What does it mean when the industry that is considered to house the "highest" form of "art" is made up of a monolithic body of people overwhelmingly led by men? How does this affect someone and their actions? What could be done to stop the disempowering portrayals that were taking place throughout media and the arts?

2014 was a pivotal year for me. In that year, I began to shift the way I'd been using social media. It was no longer a social device for me, it was a working device. I was committed to amplifying my work as an artist and as one of the few Black women playing the French horn. I was committed to connecting with other Black horn players. I was committed to bringing musicians together around conversations that questioned the nature of the field, to see where we could push the industry. I was committed to doing whatever I needed to do (including finishing my bachelor's degree in Music Business) in order to make my way from onstage to backstage. I needed to become "Oz" — pushing and pulling the levers of the arts landscape behind red velvet curtains became something I was deeply devoted to figuring out.

I went back to school and in 2015, I finished my degree with a 4.0 average. By the time I finished my degree program, I'd self-produced five different events independently, joined a brass quintet in Baltimore devoted to playing pop and non-traditional repertoire, and interned with two different organizations. Ultimately, I landed a full-time position with an organization providing professional development opportunities to other arts leaders, which helped me learn even more about those making crucial decisions in the nonprofit arts sector. I took what I learned and heard there, and, to this day, I carry that as a guide to what it means to be "Oz" in this industry.

## Spinning Out & Cultivating Networks

In 2016, I sat down with a former classmate of mine, named Quanice Floyd. We'd crossed paths at a networking event for non-profit professionals in D.C., and the atmosphere was light, but strangely ridden with undertones of anxiety. This was the summer before the presidential elections, and tensions were higher than normal. As a nation, we were coming to the collective realization that many people's voices were being left out in the arts and culture sector, and, as Quanice and I talked, we discovered that we were both finding ourselves surrounded by arts professionals who were unhappy with the lack of inclusiveness in arts programming. Countless non-profit arts organizations were being questioned about the homogenous nature of their teams, and many were being (and continue to be) challenged on verifying the impact they have on their constituents and community members. They were being scrutinized for the artists they were neglecting to support and uplift, and many stakeholders were beginning to examine the nature of the narratives that were being provided to community members. Were these institutions reflecting a diaspora of communities? Or were programming decisions being made from a narrowed cultural lens?

The evening wore on, and as Quanice and I continued talking, we were joined in conversation by colleagues from throughout the D.C. region who were also interested in working towards diversifying the work programmed by arts organizations. Repeatedly, we came back to the topic of hiring practices, and we brainstormed on what it would take to aid organizations in onboarding staff members with diverse backgrounds, interests, and experiences. We discussed a shared recognition that all organizations, both inside and outside of the arts sector, benefit greatly from hiring staff members that have backgrounds and interests that reflect the diverse communities being served in nuanced and intuitive ways. Creating an environment filled with diverse voices provides cultural organizations with the opportunity to better reflect the different individuals and interests that lie in our shared communities, both in this country and globally.

We took this macro vision on the arts and culture non-profit sector, and we began to narrow it to recognize the actionable steps that could be taken. As emerging administrators, what resources could we provide in order to build a platform and support the voices of people that come from communities that are traditionally not represented in the staff of arts organizations? What were our options in addressing these issues?

The very next day, Quanice began a Facebook group titled the Arts Administrators of Color Network and invited me to join as the first person. I immediately began inviting in the people I'd begun to know. As the group grew, and we pushed forward in panel discussions, social events, and other opportunities to deepen our networks, I accepted the role of Board Chair as Quanice established the group as a non-profit organization. This work continues to teach me, from first-hand accounts among those that take part in the services the group provides, how deeply important it is to organize bodies of people together to push for change.

## Cultivating Greater Representation

These moments in my journey have woven themselves together and have manifested in my adherence to a grassroots approach towards leadership and the arts. If the sector is to continue to cultivate positive social change, it must be harnessed in a way that provides platforms for people of all backgrounds, and the creative world must pay attention to people doing this work at all levels. I do believe there is a collective goal within the United States, home of the "mixing bowl" metaphor, to ensure that people feel welcome and can see their own lives represented on stage. We cannot begin to realize that goal until we embrace and welcome more people of various backgrounds, both onstage and off, and work with them at all levels in an inclusive manner. I often think back to the 11-year-old me, picking up the horn for the very first time. I wouldn't be able to write this today, if I hadn't been surrounded by people that ensured my voice was encouraged, welcomed, embraced, and nurtured. How do we scale this? How do we make it the norm?

I see the sector moving in the right direction. To be frank, I don't think we have a choice at this point. But to make it stick, we've got to open our doors even wider. We've got to push forward and embrace the transformative changes necessary in these times to lead to a more creative, nuanced, and colorful space. The work begins with representation — let it not end there.

## About the Author

Dedicated to supporting cultural organizers and leaders as they design processes and programs that align with their vision and values, Ariel Elizabeth Davis is an arts administrator based in the Washington, DC metropolitan region. She is the Senior Manager of Impact Communications at The Save the Music Foundation, volunteers her time supporting The HBCU Jazz Education Initiative as a founding member and Consulting Director, and is the co-founder of The Arts Administrators of Color Network, an organization she helped establish in 2016. There, she has stewarded programs that provide professional development and networking opportunities for arts leaders internationally.

Previously, Ariel has worked with The Lewis Prize for Music, The John F. Kennedy Center for the Performing Arts, the Los Angeles Fellowship Program with the Inner City Youth Orchestra of LA, National Arts Strategies, Washington Performing Arts, The MusicianShip, The Washington Women in Jazz Festival, and The String Queens.

Ariel has served as a guest speaker and lecturer at Georgetown University, American University, University of Michigan, and her alma mater, Howard University. She has also contributed as a grants panelist for the Department of Education, the DC Commission on the Arts and Humanities, the Maryland State Arts Council, the Arts and Humanities Council of Montgomery County, and the Association of Performing Arts Professionals. She is a proud member of the Recording Academy.

Ariel's passion for the arts began onstage, as a French Horn player. She has had the opportunity to perform with ensembles across the world, from the Grammy's stage with Lizzo to an international festival in Guadeloupe celebrating the work of composer Chevalier de Saint George. She takes as many opportunities to visit her hometown of Detroit, Michigan as she can and currently resides in Mount Rainier, Maryland.

# CHAPTER 28
# CONSENSUS IN THE ARTS: REFLECTIONS
## JILL STRACHAN

## INTRODUCTION

By Susan J. Erenrich

Jill Strachan was the general manager for The Lesbian & Gay Chorus of Washington, D.C. (LGCW) for most of the group's history (1984-2010). She also sang with the ensemble. Moreover, from 2007-2017, Jill served as the Executive Director of the Capital Hill Arts Workshop (CHAW).

During her time with both organizations, she utilized a consensus and participatory decision-making model. While LGCW drew explicitly from the Quaker tradition, group-centered leadership was also employed during the U.S. Civil Rights Movement, perhaps most famously by Ella Baker, who often repeated, "Strong people don't need [a] strong leader" (Ransby, 2015).

One of the unsung sheroes of the Civil Rights Movement, Ella Baker is credited with creating a prototype of the group-centered leadership paradigm. Baker was a seasoned organizer and, in 1944, as the director of branches of the NAACP, she coordinated and facilitated a series of leadership training programs around the motif "Give Light and People Will Find the Way" (Grant, 1998). Regular subjects covered during the sessions included: "Techniques and Strategies of Minority Group Action," "Developing a Program of Action through Branch Committees," and "Postwar Problems and NAACP Branches" (Grant, 1998, p. 73). The preparation of people to engage in decentralized, bottom-up, group-centered leadership was always the overlying, unifying theme. During Baker's tenure at the NAACP, an estimated 10 "Give Light" seminars were conducted between 1944 and 1946 (Grant, 1998). Baker continued to promote the bottom-up leadership archetype throughout her life, which included her tenure as Executive Director of the Southern Christian Leadership Conference (SCLC) and as an advisor to the Student Nonviolent Coordinating Committee (SNCC).

Jill's implementation of a group-centered leadership process was an experimental way of leading for the LGCW and CHAW. I hope readers enjoy Jill's personal, thoughtful, and honest appraisal of implementing consensus decision-making into arts organizations. In spite of the challenges, participatory democracy is a way to "let the disenfranchised vote, let the silenced be heard, let the oppressed be empowered, and let the marginalized move to the center" (Ransby, 2003, p. 368).

## References

Grant, J. (1998). *Ella Baker: Freedom Bound*. John Wiley & Sons.

Ransby, B. (2003). *Ella Baker & The Black Freedom Movement: A Radical Democratic Vision*. The University Of North Carolina Press.

Ransby, B. (2015, June 12). Ella Taught Me: Shattering the Myth of the Leaderless Movement. *Colorlines*. https://www.colorlines.com/articles/ella-taught-me-shattering-myth-leaderless-movement

# CONSENSUS IN THE ARTS: REFLECTIONS

By Jill Strachan

Every Voice Matters was the mission statement of the non-auditioned Lesbian & Gay Chorus of Washington, D.C._(LGCW) during the latter half of its twenty-six-year existence from 1984-2010. I was a singer and the general manager for most of that period. Our principle administrative tool was a consensus-based process that we developed and honed. This chapter explores the use of consensus in the LGCW and offers examples from my career in arts administration of how consensus can function as a successful management tool for arts organizations.

Making administrative decisions by consensus was unusual, but it was groundbreaking that the LGCW applied the same process to its selection of music and programs. The traditional role of a music director prevailed in rehearsal and performance, but LGCW members actively shaped the organization's program by choosing the type of music they wanted to sing.

Examples of consensus decisions included: changing the name of the Chorus from Gay & Lesbian Chorus to Lesbian & Gay Chorus, hiring four music directors over two decades, joining a 2002 nationwide boycott of Cincinnati in support of Black concerns about racial discrimination and violence in the city, and commissioning and attending four international gay and lesbian choral festivals. Commissions and festivals required a substantial fundraising effort from individual members to cover expenses. For festivals, the Chorus helped support individual singers who could not cover the full expense of attending.

In 1999, while planning its 15th anniversary year, LGCW members discussed shifting its programming perspective beyond the stories of gay, lesbian, bisexual, transgendered, and questioning people to sing for other people whose voices were unheard and who society ignored. The choice to perform Robert Convery's *Songs of Children* reflected the concept of unheard voices and the intention to improve its musicianship. Convery's cantata was a musical stretch, but it built the ensemble's musicianship.

The context of the piece was astoundingly suited to the concept of "unheard voices." Composed in memory of all children who perished in the Holocaust, *Songs of Children* for choir, violin, viola, cello, and piano is a cantata of nine poems written by children who were interned at Terezin Concentration Camp.

———

In the earliest days of the LGCW, taking the stage as a lesbian or as a gay man was a courageous act of activism, and we depended on each other for support in this choice. In its first two years, the group strongly resisted formalizing itself, deciding to put off adoption of by-laws — the first step to incorporating and filing for non-profit, tax-exempt status under the U.S. tax code. All business was carried out in a half-hour pre-rehearsal meeting once a month. The group saw itself in understated terms, and because of that foundation, it attracted a music director who envisioned the group in a non-traditional way.

The group possessed a compelling spirit of commitment and purpose, qualities Mark Bowman admired the first time he heard the group at an informal celebration. Bowman had studied piano and organ. He was forced to give up his dream of becoming a Methodist minister when he revealed that he was gay. Before becoming involved with the LGCW, Bowman had been the choir director at a Methodist Church in southwest Washington, D.C. and was active in Affirmation: United Methodists for Gay and Lesbian Concerns.

Bowman brought a strong sense of personal pride, a seemingly unlimited capacity for grassroots organizing, a deep commitment to social justice, and a vision of what the group could become. He agreed to conduct one rehearsal as a favor to one of the charter members, and he stayed for six years. Of particular interest to Bowman, was the promise offered of gay men and lesbians working together. His political thinking encompassed feminist principles and alternative concepts of organizing power. His values were a perfect match for the group and helped the LGCW to build more inclusively on its inherent diversity and make thoughtful choices about its music and organization.

Bowman's concept of the role of the music director was non-traditional. Although he possessed powerful leadership qualities and the competence to create the organization himself, he used a collegial approach with the singers. Bowman encouraged LGCW members to stake their dreams for the organization on its mission rather than around the personality of the music director.

In an interview I conducted with Mark Bowman in August 2000, he discussed his relationship with the LGCW and his first observations of how the group operated. "My recollection is when I came the Chorus was already making decisions as a whole … . I don't have a clear recollection of exactly when we decided we were going to continue the consensus decision-making. It was always there." Shortly after Bowman's arrival, LGCW members articulated the following mission statement:

The purpose of the LGCW is to:

Make quality music

Foster gender cooperation

Demonstrate lesbian and gay pride

Develop talent, and

Have fun.

To create the statement, the group used a consensus process rooted in the Quaker tradition, as explained by our two Quaker members. A facilitator managed the process and agreed to reflect the views and concerns of all present. For their part, all participants agreed to listen and to work together to craft a statement that was acceptable to all. The elements of the mission statement were reaffirmed through subsequent visioning and long-range processes.

Based on this successful and exciting experience, the group made a formal commitment to a consensus process for its governance. This choice reflected the members' vision of an egalitarian and just approach to all issues that the Chorus might face —— allowing for each voice to be expressed and eliminating volatile situations of winners and losers. Of note, this decision was feminist in intention; members believed that an alternative structure would be more likely to engender sharing of power within the organization. The choice reflected a high degree of active trust within the organization. The trust was based on a common purpose: to sing. There was a group consciousness of what lay behind that purpose: to change the world. Chorus members were immediately, passionately, and actively invested in the group.

An essential concept in practicing consensus is the members' understanding that *unanimity is not the same as unity*. The group can decide to act with the knowledge that there is not 100% agreement. What the group relies on is each member's assistance in implementing the action to which the group agreed.

In our interview, Bowman reflected on the Chorus' decision to use consensus. "Consensus is not only helpful because it's a more equitable and fair way of making decisions, but it gives people greater investment within the Chorus, and I think that's really important. In so many choruses you sort of show up and do what you're told. You don't always understand why things are done or the difficult decisions that go into deciding to do something. The gift of the Chorus was it built people's investment to the Chorus."

Within the LGCW's understanding of consensus, the role of facilitator was special but not more powerful than anyone else's role. Facilitators first alternated between male and female members. Eventually, as the business of the chorus became more complicated, co-facilitators served together for one or two years. They organized internal affairs and represented the LGCW to the outside world as well as functioning as internal ears for the LGCW members. About 1990, the LGCW created a second, paid, contractual position of general manager. The music director was the first. The functions of the co-facilitators remained essentially the same, but the general manager was empowered by the

Chorus to conduct general operations, a responsibility once shared by the co-facilitators and other volunteers.

The concept of empowering and trusting certain individuals to perform specific tasks was extended to the roles of the music director and general manager. It became expedient for many decisions to be made in a monthly "Meeting for Business" that everyone was encouraged to attend. In reality, however, the meeting was attended by only a small group of singers despite encouragement in places like the *LCGW Handbook* where, in the 2005-2006 edition, it stated: "Remember that Co-Facilitators cannot represent your point of view for you! If you want to express your opinion and give suggestions that can become a part of our decision-making process, we highly encourage you to attend the Meeting for Business." But, as we passed the two-decade mark, attendance grew even smaller. Larger decisions, however, were still brought to the chorus-at-large.

In June 2000, LGCW members accepted revised by-laws based on the practice of consensus. This decision aligned the consensual practice of the organization with its legal documents, providing a legal grounding for the LGCW's belief that every voice should be equally empowered within its structure.

———

The story of the LGCW remains invigorating and thought-provoking. As someone who was there from the beginning to the end, I must ask myself why it dissolved.

Since the LGCW was formed in 1984, LGBTQ people have made many strides in creating full, proud lives. It is no longer as remarkable to be standing on a stage singing about our lives. The urgency to protest diminished as LGBTQ people became more comfortable in their surroundings and as AIDS cases dropped off in the mid-1990s. There was reduced appetite for LGCW's social justice programming from potential singers and audience members.

In Washington, D.C., a LGBTQ person had innumerable choices for spending leisure time. Competition for people's attention increased. Time itself was more precious. The growth in the region's population translated into longer commuting times. A singer might have been willing to drive a one-hour roundtrip to rehearsal, but over time, that one-hour trip became two hours. The LGCW began to struggle with recruiting and retaining singers.

As the organization focused on recruitment, its own members began to have diminished pride and faith in its success.

I believe that our serious embrace of consensus was, in the end, counterproductive. Our distinctive process tied us down, and we lost its vital organic character. Once named and claimed, there were rules, guidelines, and structures that we dutifully generated and periodically reviewed. A handbook emerged. LGCW members presented workshops at conferences and festivals. We related history, educated in the use of consensus, and the few who were interested became fewer, including a fair number of our members.

Combine uncontrollable factors with expediency and I have my answer. It was easier to give up on our consensus process than to find our way back. Some of us had too much ownership while others had too little or none. Once the consensus icon was attached to a few individuals, the idea and practice grew more abstract, and despite the many, well-intentioned efforts to educate, consensus faded. In one memorable conclusion to a discussion with an outside facilitator, we were asked to stand on one side of the room if we were willing to help with administrative tasks and to stand on the other side if this was not possible. When the dust cleared, it was revealed that the same people stood on the same side of the room where they had stood metaphorically for many years.

In that moment, the run of the LGCW came to an end, although it would take a few more years to disband. That happened after reaching consensus at a Meeting for Business in 2010.

———

Consensus is best learned by doing. It is learned through trust and experience, which makes it organic and sometimes difficult but well worth the effort expended. There are successes, failures, and learning experiences along the way.

Consensus requires a listening gene, but it is a gene that can be developed. If one commits to the idea that every voice is important, *i.e.*, matters, then one must listen. By participating in consensus-based decisions, it becomes easier to listen. It is joyful. It is exhilarating when a group of people acknowledge ownership for a decision, and it is impossible to tell who suggested what and which ideas belonged to whom. The maxim that the whole is bigger than the sum of its parts holds true. We all are responsible, and our whole is stronger.

When I became the executive director of Washington, D.C.'s Capitol Hill Arts Workshop (CHAW) in 2007, I brought along my commitment to consensus as my primary management tool. (At almost fifty years, CHAW is an arts education facility offering classes, performances, and exhibitions across all the arts disciplines to children and adults.) It proved to be an excellent perspective for an organization with varied moving parts. The staff was composed of eight to ten people. A faculty of forty teaching artists were essential to CHAW's service to the community. A 15-member board of directors had oversight for the organization.

One of CHAW's oldest, most successful programs was its Youth Arts Program (YAP). YAP was, and remains, an essential component of CHAW's mission to build community through the arts. It originated in the early 1980s when more women entered the work force and families started to have two working adults. CHAW offered van pickup at Capitol Hill schools for an additional fee. By 2007, YAP needed serious renovation — what had been appealing had become rigid, such as the requirement that YAP students register for all classes over a semester. YAP provided tuition assistance for students who did not have the ability to pay.

We started responding with tweaks, but these did not solve our issues. Instead, the dependable flow of registrations — YAP had for many years brought in 80% of CHAW's revenue — began to falter and wane. Parents were asking for more flexibility. Could they register for some classes instead of all? Could their child take one class per day and wait at CHAW for pickup? The program was too expensive.

If I were an autocratic manager, I would have instructed the director of education and programs to fix the problem immediately. Instead, following a period of gathering data from parents, the director (a former LGCW member) called together a group that drew from staff and faculty to create a new curriculum. The process culled the wisdom of many individuals and resulted in a newly rewired and coalesced program that launched in time for the next semester. The new YAP responded to parents' requests, upgraded classes, offered flexibility, and improved financial return.

In our small organization, the principles of consensus were transformative. With the participation of staff and faculty members in making big decisions, such as the YAP example, top down, rigid hierarchy became unnecessary. The executive director remained "in charge," but individual voices were enhanced. At the same time, the burden of the executive director was lightened as most decisions became easier because of the input of many voices. This process is useful in mentoring junior staff members as it provides an opportunity for them to participate equally in the organization's business. They can also witness the fruits of their labor. In creating a safe space for discussion, untapped strengths and previously hidden perspectives arise to shape an outcome.

Approaching matters that are within the purview of the board of directors can be daunting, particularly if there is division of opinion. Even if board action is bound by *Robert's Rules of Order*, facilitated consensus discussions can achieve thoughtful, practical solutions that easily become approved motions of the board.

A practice of consensus is only one path, but I believe that arts organizations should not settle for traditional administrative management. It is incumbent that we spice up the foundation. We should capture the creative spirits of the artistic endeavor and put them to work improving our organizations. I promise it is infinitely more exhilarating and beneficial to work this way and worth the hard work.

———

I know that consensus honors the individual voice and the resulting collective voice. *For myself, I want to make the choice to work in consensus,* regardless of surrounding circumstances. Leaning into consensus made me a better manager and worked against my engrained training to make decisions forcefully and without sufficient consultation with colleagues.

The LGCW's work with consensus had a substantial influence on me. My academic and prior work experience had taught and encouraged me to prove my opinions against the opinions of others. I thought this was a path to career success. Learning about and tentatively practicing consensus created a gradual, gentle change in how I moved through the world.

I noticed that the benefits of consensus were extending to my personal, work, and group relationships. Being willing to accept that the opinions of others were not something to be overcome or smashed to the ground in empty victory engendered an openness that I had not known or ever envisioned. I found a safe space to become at ease with myself. I found empowering communities in the LGCW and CHAW. I became an intentional listener. I began to enjoy differences instead of fearing them. I got along better with others and together we made change happen.

———

From LGCW Handbook (2005-2006)

Guidelines for Participation in Meetings for Business:

Enter with an open mind

Listen for understanding

Make personal statement (I, me) when talking

Take risks: say or do something that may make others, or you feel uncomfortable

Pay attention to assumptions

Take responsibility for yourself

Consider the result of what you are saying

Be conscious of time

Care for yourself

Celebrate

*"Consensus is. . . Well, I can think of what consensus is not. Consensus is not unanimity. Consensus is not all being of the same mind. Consensus is not about the loudest voices outspeaking the quieter voices and winning. In order for consensus to work, it really takes a commitment by the whole group to be part of a process."* - Mark Bowman

**About the Author**

Jill Strachan, Ph.D., served as the Executive Director of the Capitol Hill Arts Workshop (CHAW) from 2007 until her retirement in 2017. Previously, Jill free-lanced in arts administration from 1987-2007 after having left the corporate-leaning world of a food industry trade association. She received a Ph.D. in the history of religion from Syracuse University in 1981. Doubles tennis is a never-ending challenge, and she sings in the a cappella group Not What You Think. She is the author of *Waterfalls, The Moon and Sensible Shoes-One Lesbian Life.* A long-time resident of Capitol Hill, she loves walking with her partner Jane and their dog Freddy.

# ABOUT THE INTERNATIONAL LEADERSHIP ASSOCIATION

The ILA was created in 1999 to bring together professionals with a keen interest in the study, practice, and development of leadership. Today, ILA is the largest worldwide community committed to leadership scholarship, development, and practice. We accomplish our mission of "**Advancing leadership knowledge and practice for a better world,**" through the synergy that occurs by bringing together our members and partners; collectively having a multiplier impact on leadership and change.

Learn more at ILAGlobalNetwork.org

www.ingramcontent.com/pod-product-compliance
Lightning Source LLC
Chambersburg PA
CBHW050327270326
41926CB00016B/3347